Zabbix 6 IT Infrastructure Monitoring Cookbook

Second Edition

Explore the new features of Zabbix 6 for designing, building, and maintaining your Zabbix setup

Nathan Liefting

Brian van Baekel

BIRMINGHAM—MUMBAI

Zabbix 6 IT Infrastructure Monitoring Cookbook

Second Edition

Group Product Manager: Vijin Boricha
Publishing Product Manager: Vijin Boricha
Senior Editor: Arun Nadar
Content Development Editor: Romy Dias
Technical Editor: Shruthi Shetty
Copy Editor: Safis Editing
Project Coordinator: Shagun Saini
Proofreader: Safis Editing
Indexer: Manju Arasan
Production Designer: Sinhayna Bias
Marketing Coordinator: Nimisha Dua

First published: January 2021
Second edition: March 2022

Production reference: 1180322

Published by Packt Publishing Ltd.
Livery Place
35 Livery Street
Birmingham
B3 2PB, UK.

ISBN 978-1-80324-691-8

www.packt.com

To my grandparents, for supporting my education, my brother, for always being at the ready, and my mom and stepdad, for cheering me on. To my girlfriend, for always supporting whatever new idea I get into my head. To my colleagues throughout the years, my first mentor, Sander F., for inspiring me, and Brian, for making it all possible.

– Nathan Liefting

Foreword

Despite all the challenges brought to us in recent years, IT technology progress inevitably continues with increasing speed. No matter how far in the past we look, we can understand that IT nowadays is not like it was a year or two ago. For monitoring solutions, there is always an ongoing rush after new technology trends just to be able to support new solutions and comply with growing requirements from businesses that expect more and more from their monitoring solutions.

As an area that is covered in product growth, monitoring also becomes more saturated and flexible, which can also make it more complicated, especially for beginners that are just starting their journey in the world of monitoring. And thus, here comes the beauty of open source, where the community bands together and makes a huge effort to help each other with different ideas, approaches, and best practices. This collaboration with the community is what I try to take part in myself, by creating various videos about Zabbix functionality, monitoring ideas, and different use cases. It is important to understand that nobody will be able to provide a solution to any request, but our goal is to give insights into how to use tools that you should use to build solutions adopted precisely as per your needs.

Community drive and a feeling of one team who shares the same goals cannot be missed by anyone who works with the Zabbix monitoring solution. I'm sure that it is only because of the active community that I have had the chance to meet Brian and Nathan. Many years ago, when Brian was participating in a Zabbix certified specialist course, on day 1, he made it clear that his skills are far beyond an average specialist and even back then, he did his best to share his experience and help students who were on their first days with Zabbix. It is great to see that after all these years, the passion is still there. Now, with the tremendous help of Nathan and the huge experience gained by working with different Zabbix installations and different requirements, these guys have not only acquired a huge baggage of experience to share with you but have also learned the best ways to deliver this information to someone who may be far from an expert in Zabbix and monitoring.

I'm sure that for all of us, the main goal is to make Zabbix accessible to anyone in any place with any skill level. That is the purpose of my videos and that is the purpose of this book: to put all-out experience and lessons learned in one place for our community.

Dmitry Lambert

Creator of the Zabbix YouTube channel
https://www.youtube.com/c/ZabbixCookBook

Contributors

About the authors

Nathan Liefting, also known as Larcorba, is an IT consultant, trainer, and content creator (artist). He has more than 6 years of professional experience in IT. His experience ranges from managing networks running EVPN/VXLAN to Linux environments and programming. Nathan started working with Zabbix in 2016 when it was still at Zabbix 2 and Zabbix 3 was just released.

He now works for Opensource ICT Solutions BV in the Netherlands as a Zabbix trainer and consultant, designing and building professional Zabbix environments and Zabbix components for some of the biggest companies around the world.

Brian van Baekel quickly discovered how powerful Zabbix is during his career as a network engineer. Ever since, he has been working with Zabbix in various (large) environments, leading to his official Zabbix Certified Trainer certification in early 2017.

In 2018, Brian founded Opensource ICT Solutions BV in the Netherlands and Opensource ICT Solutions LLC in the US. Both companies primarily focus on building Zabbix environments all over the world. In 2021, further expansion of the business was established by opening a subsidiary in the United Kingdom with a full focus on the Zabbix product. All companies provide support, training, and consultancy services, which means Brian works with the Zabbix product 24/7.

Fun fact: Even his cat is named Zabbix.

About the reviewers

Patrik Uytterhoeven has about 20 years of experience in IT, mostly with HP UNIX and Red Hat Linux. In late 2012, he joined Open-Future, a leading open source integrator and the first Zabbix reseller and training partner in Belgium. When Patrik joined Open-Future, he also became a Zabbix-certified trainer. Since then, he has provided onsite training and public demonstrations around the world in Europe, America, and Asia.

His next step was to author a book, so the first *Zabbix Cookbook* was born. Because Patrik also has a deep interest in configuration management, he wrote some Ansible roles. Patrik was also a technical reviewer of *Learning Ansible* and *Ansible Configuration Management*. Later, Patrik rewrote the popular Zabbix network monitoring book by Richard Olups and *Zabbix 4 Network Monitoring* was born.

Roy van Baekel is an experienced network architect and Linux system administrator with more than 10 years of experience building internet service provider networks (MPLS, QoS, BGP, EVPN, and so on) and highly available Linux platforms (Apache, MySQL, Leepalived, KVM, and OpenStack). All these systems are as good as their monitoring capabilities, and as such, Roy has in-depth experience with common monitoring tools such as PRTG, Icinga, and Zabbix. Roy loves to automate repeating tasks – using tools such as Ansible or Puppet. With experience in multiple programming languages, everything is tied together to provide the best solution to customers.

Julio Daniel Zanette is a Christian and technology enthusiast with over 10 years of experience in information technology. Born in Brazil and moving to the UK in 2018, he graduated in information technology management. Having worked for many years as a Sysadmin and always looking for new knowledge and challenges, in recent years, he has moved to the DevOps role. Having been introduced to Zabbix in 2015, he soon began to call himself a Zabbix enthusiast. In 2017, he passed the certification exams for Zabbix Specialist and Zabbix Professional, and in 2019, he went to Zabbix SIA in Latvia for Zabbix Certified Expert training, returning home with the title of Zabbix Certified Expert.

> *I'd like to thank God first, for His almighty guidance on whatever decisions I make. I would like to thank my wife, Fernanda, and my three daughters, Tata, Nana, and Duda, for their daily support and patience. And to the awesome Zabbix team, for making this incredible software.*

Table of Contents

4

Working with Triggers and Alerts

5

Building Your Own Structured Templates

6
Visualizing Data, Inventory, and Reporting

7
Using Discovery for Automatic Creation

8
Setting Up
Zabbix Proxies

9
Integrating Zabbix with External Services

10
Extending Zabbix Functionality with Custom Scripts and the Zabbix API

11
Maintaining Your Zabbix Setup

12
Advanced Zabbix Database Management

13

Bringing Zabbix to the Cloud with Zabbix Cloud Integration

Preface

Welcome to *Zabbix 6 IT Infrastructure Monitoring Cookbook*. IT infrastructure ranges from Windows and Linux to networking and development, and basically anything that runs on computer hardware. In this book, we will go over various topics useful to anyone in IT that wants to use Zabbix to monitor their IT infrastructure.

Who this book is for

Monitoring systems are often overlooked within IT organizations, but they can provide an overview that will save you time, money, and headaches. This book is for IT engineers that want to learn about Zabbix 6 and how to use it to bring their IT environments to the next level.

What this book covers

Chapter 1, Installing Zabbix and Getting Started Using the Frontend, covers how to set up Zabbix, optionally with HA. We will also work our way through the Zabbix frontend.

Chapter 2, Getting Things Ready with Zabbix User Management, covers how to set up your first users, user groups, and user roles.

Chapter 3, Setting Up Zabbix Monitoring, covers how to set up almost any type of monitoring within Zabbix.

Chapter 4, Working with Triggers and Alerts, covers how to set up triggers and get alerts from them.

Chapter 5, Building Your Own Structured Templates, covers how to build templates that are structured, which will work wonders for keeping your Zabbix setup organized.

Chapter 6, Visualizing Data, Inventory, and Reporting, covers how to visualize data in graphs, maps, and dashboards. It also covers how to use the Zabbix inventory, reporting, and business service monitoring functionality.

Chapter 7, Using Discovery for Automatic Creation, covers how to use Zabbix discovery for automatic host creation as well as items, triggers, and more with agents, SNMP, WMI, and JMX.

Chapter 8, Setting Up Zabbix Proxies, teaches you how to set up Zabbix proxies correctly for use in a production environment.

Chapter 9, Integrating Zabbix with External Services, teaches you how to integrate Zabbix with external services for alerting.

Chapter 10, Extending Zabbix Functionality with Custom Scripts and the Zabbix API, covers how to extend Zabbix functionality by using custom scripts and the Zabbix API.

Chapter 11, Maintaining Your Zabbix Setup, covers how to maintain a Zabbix setup and keep its performance up over time.

Chapter 12, Advanced Zabbix Database Management, teaches you how to manage Zabbix databases for an advanced setup.

Chapter 13, Bringing Zabbix to the Cloud with Zabbix Cloud Integration, covers how to use Zabbix in the cloud with services such as AWS, Azure, and Docker.

To get the most out of this book

You should have a good basis in IT to understand the terminology used in this book. This book is best for people with at least a starting knowledge of monitoring systems, Linux, and network engineering.

Software/hardware covered in the book	Operating system requirements
Zabbix 6	Linux (any)
Python 3	Linux (any)
MariaDB (MySQL)	Linux (any)
PostgreSQL	Linux (any)
Apache	Linux (any)
VIM	Linux (any)

Make sure you have a virtualization environment ready to create virtual machines for use with the recipes. VirtualBox, VMware, or any type of client/hypervisor will do.

Throughout the book, we will make use of VIM to edit files, so make sure to install it. If you do not feel comfortable using VIM, you can substitute the command for NANO or anything else you prefer.

If you are using the digital version of this book, we advise you to type the code yourself or access the code from the book's GitHub repository (a link is available in the next section). Doing so will help you avoid any potential errors related to the copying and pasting of code.

Download the example code files

You can download the example code files for this book from GitHub at:

```
https://github.com/PacktPublishing/Zabbix-6-IT-Infrastructure-
Monitoring-Cookbook
```

If there's an update to the code, it will be updated in the GitHub repository.

We also have other code bundles from our rich catalog of books and videos available at:

```
https://github.com/PacktPublishing/
```

Check them out!

Download the color images

We also provide a PDF file that has color images of the screenshots and diagrams used in this book. You can download it here:

```
https://static.packt-cdn.com/downloads/9781803246918_
ColorImages.pdf
```

Conventions used

There are a number of text conventions used throughout this book.

`Code in text`: Indicates code words in text, database table names, folder names, filenames, file extensions, pathnames, dummy URLs, user input, and Twitter handles. Here is an example: "It's important to back up all of our Zabbix configuration data, which is located in the `/etc/zabbix/` folder."

A block of code is set as follows:

```
# MariaDB Server
# To use a different major version of the server, or to pin to
a specific minor version, change URI below.
deb [arch=amd64] http://downloads.mariadb.com/MariaDB/
mariadb-10.5/repo/ubuntu xenial main
```

Any command-line input or output is written as follows:

```
systemctl start mariadb
```

Bold: Indicates a new term, an important word, or words that you see onscreen. For instance, words in menus or dialog boxes appear in **bold**. Here is an example: "Then we navigate to **Monitoring | Hosts** and click on **Latest data** for the Zabbix server host."

> **Tips or Important Notes**
> Appear like this.

Get in touch

Feedback from our readers is always welcome.

General feedback: If you have questions about any aspect of this book, email us at customercare@packtpub.com and mention the book title in the subject of your message.

Errata: Although we have taken every care to ensure the accuracy of our content, mistakes do happen. If you have found a mistake in this book, we would be grateful if you would report this to us. Please visit www.packtpub.com/support/errata and fill in the form.

Piracy: If you come across any illegal copies of our works in any form on the internet, we would be grateful if you would provide us with the location address or website name. Please contact us at copyright@packt.com with a link to the material.

If you are interested in becoming an author: If there is a topic that you have expertise in and you are interested in either writing or contributing to a book, please visit authors.packtpub.com.

Share Your Thoughts

Once you've read *Zabbix 6 IT Infrastructure Monitoring Cookbook - Second Edition*, we'd love to hear your thoughts! Scan the QR code below to go straight to the Amazon review page for this book and share your feedback.

https://packt.link/r/180324691X

Your review is important to us and the tech community and will help us make sure we're delivering excellent quality content.

1
Installing Zabbix and Getting Started Using the Frontend

Zabbix 6 is like a continuation of Zabbix 5, as this time around we aren't looking at big UI changes. However, in Zabbix 6, you will still find a lot of improvements, both to the UI and core components. For example, the introduction of high availability for the Zabbix server. We will detail all of the important changes throughout the book.

In this chapter, we will install the Zabbix server and explore the Zabbix UI to get you familiar with it. We will go over finding your hosts, triggers, dashboards, and more to make sure you feel confident diving into the deeper material later on in this book. The Zabbix UI has a lot of options to explore, so if you are just getting started, don't get overwhelmed. It's quite structurally built and once you get the hang of it, I am confident you will find your way without issues. You will learn all about these subjects in the following recipes:

- Installing the Zabbix server
- Setting up the Zabbix frontend
- Enabling Zabbix server high availability

- Using the Zabbix frontend
- Navigating the Zabbix frontend

Technical requirements

We'll be starting this chapter with an empty Linux (virtual) machine. Feel free to choose a RHEL- or Debian-based Linux distribution. We will then set up a Zabbix server from scratch on this host.

So before jumping in, make sure you have your Linux host at the ready.

Installing the Zabbix server

Before doing anything within Zabbix, we need to install it and get ready to start working with it. In this recipe, we are going to discover how to install Zabbix server 6.

Getting ready

Before we actually install the Zabbix server, we are going to need to fulfill some prerequisite requirements. We will be using **MariaDB** mostly throughout this book. MariaDB is popular and a lot of information is available on the use of it with Zabbix.

At this point, you should have a prepared Linux server in front of you running either a RHEL- or Debian-based distribution. I'll be installing CentOS and Ubuntu 20.04 on my server; let's call them `lar-book-centos` and `lar-book-ubuntu`.

When you have your server ready, we can start the installation process.

How to do it...

1. Let's start by adding the Zabbix 6.0 repository to our system.

    For RHEL-based systems:

    ```
    rpm -Uvh https://repo.zabbix.com/zabbix/6.0/rhel/8/
    x86_64/zabbix-release-6.0-1.el8.noarch.rpm
    ```
    ```
    dnf clean all
    ```

    For Ubuntu systems:

    ```
    wget https://repo.zabbix.com/zabbix/6.0/ubuntu/pool/
    main/z/zabbix-release/zabbix-release_6.0-1+ubuntu20.04_
    all.deb
    ```

```
dpkg -i zabbix-release_6.0-1+ubuntu20.04_all.deb
apt update
```

2. Now that the repository is added, let's add the MariaDB repository on our server:

```
wget https://downloads.mariadb.com/MariaDB/mariadb_repo_
setup
chmod +x mariadb_repo_setup
./mariadb_repo_setup
```

3. Then install and enable it using the following commands:

    For RHEL-based systems:

```
dnf install mariadb-server
systemctl enable mariadb
systemctl start mariadb
```

    For Ubuntu systems:

```
apt install mariadb-server
systemctl enable mariadb
systemctl start mariadb
```

4. After installing MariaDB, make sure to secure your installation with the following command:

```
/usr/bin/mariadb-secure-installation
```

5. Make sure to answer the questions with yes (Y) and configure a root password that's secure.

6. Run through the secure installation setup and make sure to save your password somewhere. It's highly recommended to use a password vault.

7. Now, let's install our Zabbix server with MySQL support.

    For RHEL-based systems:

```
dnf install zabbix-server-mysql zabbix-sql-scripts
```

    For Ubuntu systems:

```
apt install zabbix-server-mysql zabbix-sql-scripts
```

8. With the Zabbix server installed, we are ready to create our Zabbix database. Log in to MariaDB with the following:

    ```
    mysql -u root -p
    ```

9. Enter the password you set up during the secure installation and create the Zabbix database with the following commands. Do not forget to change `password` in the second command:

    ```
    create database zabbix character set utf8mb4 collate
    utf8mb4_bin;
    create user zabbix@localhost identified by 'password';
    grant all privileges on zabbix.* to zabbix@localhost
    identified by 'password';
    flush privileges;
    quit
    ```

    > **Tip**
    >
    > For those who might require it, Zabbix does also support `utf8mb4` now. We've changed `utf8` to `utf8mb4` in the command above and everything will work. For a reference, check the Zabbix support ticket here: `https://support.zabbix.com/browse/ZBXNEXT-3706`.

10. Now we need to import our Zabbix database scheme to our newly created Zabbix database:

    ```
    zcat /usr/share/doc/zabbix-sql-scripts/mysql/server.sql.
    gz | mysql -u zabbix -p zabbix
    ```

    > **Important Note**
    >
    > At this point, it might look like you are stuck and the system is not responding. Do not worry though as it will just take a while to import the SQL scheme.

We are now done with the preparations for our MariaDB side and are ready to move on to the next step, which will be configuring the Zabbix server:

1. The Zabbix server is configured using the Zabbix server config file. This file is located in `/etc/zabbix/`. Let's open this file with our favorite editor; I'll be using Vim throughout the book:

    ```
    vim /etc/zabbix/zabbix_server.conf
    ```

2. Now, make sure the following lines in the file match your database name, database user username, and database user password:

```
DBName=zabbix
DBUser=zabbix
DBPassword=password
```

> **Tip**
> Before starting the Zabbix server, you should configure SELinux or AppArmor to allow the use of the Zabbix server. If this is a test machine, you can use a permissive stance for SELinux or disable AppArmor, but it is recommended to not do this in production.

3. All done; we are now ready to start our Zabbix server:

```
systemctl enable zabbix-server
systemctl start zabbix-server
```

4. Check whether everything is starting up as expected with the following:

```
systemctl status zabbix-server
```

5. Alternatively, monitor the log file, which provides a detailed description of the Zabbix startup process:

```
tail -f /var/log/zabbix/zabbix_server.log
```

6. Most of the messages in this file are fine and can be ignored safely, but make sure to read well and see if there are any issues with your Zabbix server starting.

How it works...

The Zabbix server is the main process for our Zabbix setup. It is responsible for our monitoring, problem alerting, and a lot of the other tasks described in this book. A complete Zabbix stack consists of at least the following:

- A database (MySQL, PostgreSQL, or Oracle)
- A Zabbix server
- Apache or NGINX running the Zabbix frontend with PHP 7.2+, but PHP 8 is currently not supported

We can see the components and how they communicate with each other in the following figure:

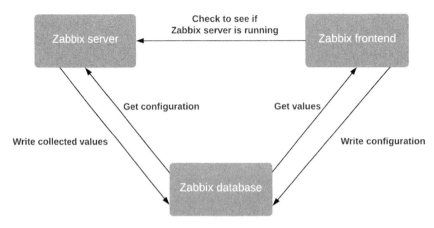

Figure 1.1 – Zabbix setup communications diagram

We've just set up the Zabbix server and database; by running these two, we are basically ready to start monitoring. The Zabbix server communicates with the Zabbix database to write collected values to it.

There is still one problem though: we cannot configure our Zabbix server to do anything. For this, we are going to need our Zabbix frontend, which we'll set up in the next recipe.

Setting up the Zabbix frontend

The Zabbix frontend is the face of our server. It's where we will configure all of our hosts, templates, dashboards, maps, and everything else. Without it, we would be blind to what's going on, on the server side. So, let's set up our Zabbix frontend in this recipe.

Getting ready

We are going to set up the Zabbix frontend using Apache. Before starting with this recipe, make sure you are running the Zabbix server on a Linux distribution of your choice. I'll be using the `lar-book-centos` and `lar-book-ubuntu` hosts in these recipes to show the setup process on CentOS 8 and Ubuntu 20.

How to do it...

1. Let's jump right in and install the frontend. Issue the following command to get started.

    For RHEL-based systems:

    ```
    dnf install zabbix-web-mysql zabbix-apache-conf
    ```

    For Ubuntu systems:

    ```
    apt install zabbix-frontend-php zabbix-apache-conf
    ```

    > **Tip**
    >
    > Don't forget to allow ports 80 and 443 in your firewall if you are using one. Without this, you won't be able to connect to the frontend.

2. Restart the Zabbix components and make sure they start up when the server is booted with the following.

    For RHEL-based systems:

    ```
    systemctl enable httpd php-fpm
    systemctl restart zabbix-server httpd php-fpm
    ```

    For Ubuntu systems:

    ```
    systemctl enable apache2
    systemctl restart zabbix-server apache2
    ```

3. We should now be able to navigate to our Zabbix frontend without any issues and start the final steps to set up the Zabbix frontend.

4. Let's go to our browser and navigate to our server's IP. It should look like this:

    ```
    http://<your_server_ip>/zabbix
    ```

5.   We should now see the following web page:

Figure 1.2 – The Zabbix welcome screen

If you don't see this web page, it's possible you have missed some steps in the setup process. Retrace your steps and double-check your configuration files; even the smallest typo could prevent the web page from serving.

6.   Let's continue by clicking **Next step** on this page, which will serve you with the next page:

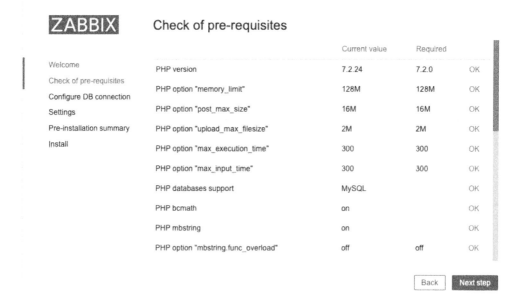

Figure 1.3 – The Zabbix installation pre-requisites page

7. Every single option here should be showing **OK** now; if not, fix the mistake it's showing you. If everything is **OK**, you may proceed by clicking **Next step** again, which will take you to the next page:

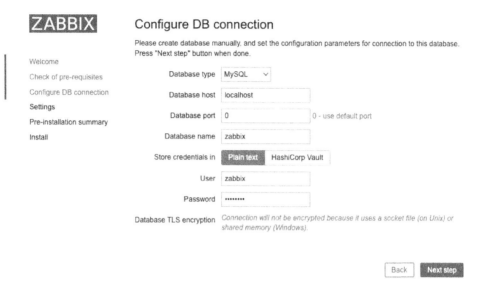

Figure 1.4 – The Zabbix installation DB connection page

8. Here, we need to tell our Zabbix frontend where our MySQL database is located. Since we installed it on **localhost**, we just need to make sure we issue the right database name, database user username, and database user password.

9. This should make the Zabbix frontend able to communicate with the database. Let's proceed by clicking **Next step** again:

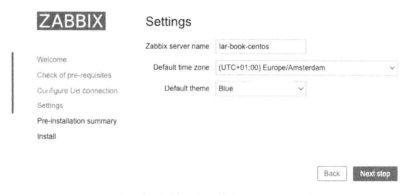

Figure 1.5 – The Zabbix installation server details page

Next up is the Zabbix server configuration. Make sure to name your server something useful or something cool. For example, I've set up a production server called Meeseeks because every time we got an alert, we could make Zabbix say *"I'm Mr. Meeseeks look at me."* But something like zabbix.example.com also works.

10. Let's name our server, set up the time zone to match our own time zone and proceed to the next step:

Figure 1.6 – The Zabbix installation summary page

11. Verify your settings and proceed to click **Next step** one more time.

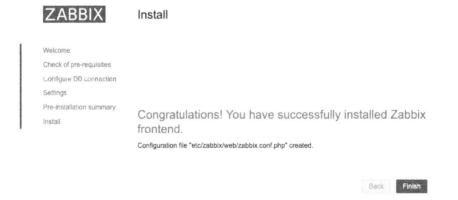

Figure 1.7 – The Zabbix installation finish page

12. You have successfully installed the Zabbix frontend. You may now click the **Finish** button and we can start using the frontend. You'll be served with a login page where you can use the following default credentials:

```
Username: Admin
Password: zabbix
```

How it works...

Now that we've installed our Zabbix frontend, our Zabbix setup is complete and we are ready to start working with it. Our Zabbix frontend will connect to our database to edit the configuration values of our setup, as we can see in the following figure:

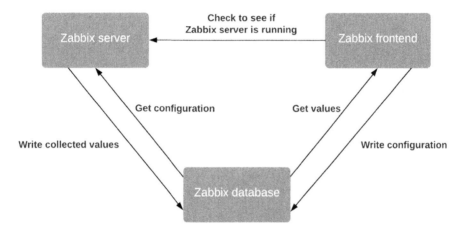

Figure 1.8 – Zabbix setup communications diagram

The Zabbix frontend will also talk to our Zabbix server, but this is just to make sure the Zabbix server is up and running. Now that we know how to set up the Zabbix frontend, we can start using it. Let's check this out after the next recipe.

There's more...

Zabbix provides a very convenient setup guide, which contains a lot of detail regarding the installation of Zabbix. I would always recommend keeping this page open during a Zabbix installation, as it contains information like the link to the latest repository. Check it out here:

```
https://www.zabbix.com/download
```

Enabling Zabbix server high availability

Zabbix 6 is here, with one of the most anticipated features of all time. High availability will bring your Zabbix setup to the next level by making sure that if one of your Zabbix servers is having issues, another one will take over.

A great thing about this implementation is that it supports an easy proprietary way to put one to many Zabbix servers in a cluster. A great way of making sure your monitoring stays in the air at all times (or at least as much as possible).

Now I do have to be honest, we cannot do anything like load balancing yet. But that is included on the Zabbix roadmap using the Zabbix proxies in a later version. Keep an eye out for any updates regarding that here:

```
https://www.zabbix.com/roadmap
```

Getting ready

Before getting started, please note that creating a high availability setup is considered an advanced topic. It might be more difficult than other recipes in this chapter.

For this setup, we will need three new virtual machines, as we are going to create a split Zabbix setup, unlike the setup that we created in the first recipe of this chapter. Let's take a look at how I have named our three new virtual machines and what their IP addresses will be:

- `lar-book-ha1` (192.168.0.1)
- `lar-book-ha2` (192.168.0.2)
- `lar-book-ha-db` (192.168.0.10)

Two of these servers will run our Zabbix server cluster and a Zabbix frontend. The other server is just for our MySQL database. Please take note that the IP addresses used in the example may be different for you. Use the correct ones for your environment.

We will also need a virtual IP address for our cluster nodes. We will use `192.168.0.5` in the example.

> **Tip**
> In our setup, we are using only one MySQL Zabbix database. For making sure all parts of Zabbix are set up as highly available, it might be worth looking into setting up MySQL in a master/master setup. This would be a great combination with the Zabbix server's high availability.

This cookbook will NOT use SELinux or AppArmor, so make sure to disable those or add the correct policies before using this guide. Additionally, this guide also does not detail how to set up your firewall, so make sure to do this beforehand as well.

How to do it...

For your convenience, we've split this *How to do it...* section into three parts. One is setting up the database, the other is setting up the Zabbix server cluster, and the last is how to set up the Zabbix frontend redundantly. The *How it works...* section will then provide an explanation about the entire setup.

Setting up the database

Let's start with setting up our Zabbix database, ready to be used in a highly available Zabbix server setup:

1. Log in to `lar-book-ha-db` and install the MariaDB repository with the following command on RedHat based systems:

    ```
    wget https://downloads.mariadb.com/MariaDB/mariadb_repo_
    setup
    chmod +x mariadb_repo_setup
    ./mariadb_repo_setup
    ```

2. Then, let's install the MariaDB server application with the following command.

    For RHEL-based systems:

    ```
    dnf install mariadb-server
    systemctl enable mariadb
    systemctl start mariadb
    ```

    For Ubuntu systems:

    ```
    apt install mariadb-server
    systemctl enable mariadb
    systemctl start mariadb
    ```

3. After installing MariaDB, make sure to secure your installation with the following command:

    ```
    /usr/bin/mariadb_secure_installation
    ```

4. Make sure to answer the questions with yes (Y) and configure a root password that's secure. It's highly recommended to use a password vault for storing it.

5. Now let's create our Zabbix database for our Zabbix servers to connect to. Log in to MariaDB with the following command:

    ```
    mysql -u root -p
    ```

6. Enter the password you set up during the secure installation and create the Zabbix database with the following commands. Do not forget to change the password in the second, third, and fourth commands:

    ```
    create database zabbix character set utf8mb4 collate
    utf8mb4_bin;
    create user zabbix@'192.168.0.1' identified by
    'password';
    create user zabbix@'192.168.0.2' identified by
    'password';
    create user zabbix@'192.168.0.5' identified by
    'password';
    grant all privileges on zabbix.* to
    'zabbix'@'192.168.0.1' identified by 'password';
    grant all privileges on zabbix.* to
    'zabbix'@'192.168.0.2' identified by 'password';
    grant all privileges on zabbix.* to
    'zabbix'@'192.168.0.5' identified by 'password';
    flush privileges;
    quit
    ```

7. Lastly, we need to import the initial Zabbix database configuration, but for that, we need to install the Zabbix repository.

    For RHEL based systems:

    ```
    rpm -Uvh https://repo.zabbix.com/zabbix/6.0/rhel/8/
    x86_64/zabbix-release-6.0-1.el8.noarch.rpm
    dnf clean all
    ```

    For Ubuntu systems:

    ```
    wget https://repo.zabbix.com/zabbix/6.0/ubuntu/pool/
    main/z/zabbix-release/zabbix-release_6.0-1+ubuntu20.04_
    all.deb
    ```

```
dpkg -i zabbix-release_6.0-1+ubuntu20.04_all.deb
apt update
```

8. Then, we need to install the SQL scripts Zabbix module.

    For RHEL-based systems:

    ```
    dnf install zabbix-sql-scripts
    ```

    For Ubuntu systems:

    ```
    apt install zabbix-sql-scripts
    ```

9. Then, we issue the following command, which might take a while so be patient until it is done:

    ```
    zcat /usr/share/doc/zabbix-sql-scripts/mysql/server.sql.
    gz | mysql -uroot -p zabbix
    ```

Setting up the Zabbix server cluster nodes

Setting up the cluster nodes works in the same way as setting up any new Zabbix server. The only difference is that we will need to specify some new configuration parameters.

1. Let's start by adding the Zabbix 6.0 repository to our systems lar-book-ha1 and lar-book-ha2:

    ```
    rpm -Uvh https://repo.zabbix.com/zabbix/6.0/rhel/8/
    x86_64/zabbix-release-6.0-1.el8.noarch.rpm
    dnf clean all
    ```

    For Ubuntu systems, use the following command:

    ```
    wget https://repo.zabbix.com/zabbix/6.0/ubuntu/pool/
    main/z/zabbix-release/zabbix-release_6.0-1+ubuntu20.04_
    all.deb
    dpkg -i zabbix-release_6.0-1+ubuntu20.04_all.deb
    apt update
    ```

2. Now let's install the Zabbix server application with the following command.

    For RHEL-based systems:

    ```
    dnf install zabbix-server-mysql
    ```

    For Ubuntu systems:

    ```
    apt install zabbix-server-mysql
    ```

3. We will now edit the Zabbix server configuration files, starting with
    `lar-book-ha1`. Issue the following command:

    ```
    vim /etc/zabbix/zabbix_server.conf
    ```

4. Then, add the following lines to allow a database connection:

    ```
    DBHost=192.168.0.10
    DBPassword=password
    ```

5. To enable high availability on this host, add the following lines in the same file:

    ```
    HANodeName=lar-book-ha1
    ```

6. To make sure our Zabbix frontend knows where to connect to if there is a node fail
    over, fill in the following:

    ```
    NodeAddress=192.168.0.1
    ```

7. Save the file and let's do the same for our `lar-book-ha2` host by editing its file:

    ```
    vim /etc/zabbix/zabbix_server.conf
    ```

8. Then, add the following lines to allow a database connection:

    ```
    DBHost=192.168.0.10
    DBPassword=password
    ```

9. To enable high availability on this host, add the following lines in the same file:

    ```
    HANodeName=lar-book-ha2
    ```

10. To make sure our Zabbix frontend knows where to connect to if there is a node fail
    over, fill in the following:

    ```
    NodeAddress=192.168.0.2
    ```

11. Save the file and let's start our Zabbix server:

    ```
    systemctl enable zabbix-server
    systemctl start zabbix-server
    ```

Setting up Apache with high availability

To make sure our frontend is also set up in such a way that if one Zabbix server has issues it fails over, we will set them up with keepalived. Let's see how we can do this.

1. Let's start by logging in to both `lar-book-ha1` and `lar-book-ha2` and installing keepalived.

    For RHEL-based systems:

    ```
    dnf install -y keepalived
    ```

    For Ubuntu systems:

    ```
    apt install keepalived
    ```

2. Then, on `lar-book-ha1`, edit the keepalived configuration with the following command:

    ```
    vim /etc/keepalived/keepalived.conf
    ```

3. Delete everything from this file and add the following text to the file:

    ```
    vrrp_track_process chk_apache_httpd {
            process httpd
            weight 10
    }
    vrrp_instance ZBX_1 {
            state MASTER
            interface ens192
            virtual_router_id 51
            priority 244
            advert_int 1
            authentication {
                    auth_type PASS
                    auth_pass password
            }
            track_process {
                    chk_apache_httpd
            }
            virtual_ipaddress {
    ```

```
                        192.168.0.5/24
            }
    }
```

4. Do not forget to update `password` to something secure and edit the interface `ens192` to your own interface name/number. For Ubuntu, change `httpd` to `apache2`.

> **Important Note**
>
> In the previous file, we specified `virtual_router_id 51`. make sure the virtual router ID 51 isn't used anywhere in the network yet. If it is, simply change the virtual router ID throughout this recipe.

5. On `lar-book-ha2`, edit the same file with the following command:

```
vim /etc/keepalived/keepalived.conf
```

6. Delete everything from the file with `dG` and this time we will add the following information:

```
vrrp_track_process chk_apache_httpd {
        process httpd
        weight 10
}
vrrp_instance ZBX_1 {
        state BACKUP
        interface ens192
        virtual_router_id 51
        priority 243
        advert_int 1
        authentication {
                auth_type PASS
                auth_pass password
        }
        track_process {
                chk_apache_httpd
        }
        virtual_ipaddress {
```

```
                          192.168.0.5/24
              }
      }
```

7. Once again, do not forget to update `password` to something secure and edit the interface `ens192` to your own interface name/number. For Ubuntu, change `httpd` to `apache2`.

8. Now let's install the Zabbix frontend with the following command.

   For RHEL-based systems:

   ```
   dnf install httpd zabbix-web-mysql zabbix-apache-conf
   ```

   For Ubuntu systems:

   ```
   apt install apache2 zabbix-frontend-php zabbix-apache-conf
   ```

9. Start the web server and keepalived to make your Zabbix frontend available with the following command:

   ```
   systemctl enable httpd keepalived
   systemctl start httpd keepalived
   ```

10. Then, we are ready to configure our Zabbix frontend. Navigate to your virtual IP address (in the example IP case, `http://192.168.0.5/zabbix`) and you will see the following page:

Figure 1.9 – The Zabbix initial configuration window

11. Click on **Next step** twice until you see the following page:

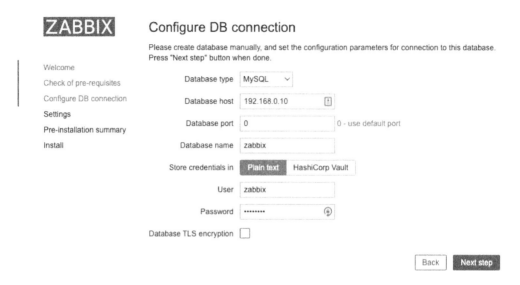

Figure 1.10 – The Zabbix database configuration window for lar-book-ha1

12. Make sure to fill in **Database host** with the IP address of our Zabbix MariaDB database (192.168.0.10). Then, fill in the database password for our **zabbix** database user.

13. Then, for the last step, for our first node, set up the **Zabbix server name** as lar-book-ha1 and select your time zone as seen in the following screenshot.

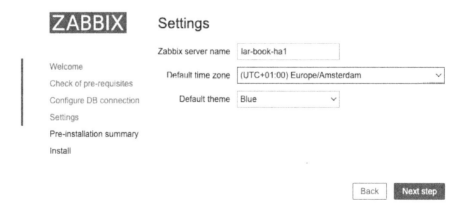

Figure 1.11 – The Zabbix server settings window for lar-book-ha1

14. Then click **Next step** and **Finish**.

15. Now we need to do the same thing to our second frontend. Log in to
    `lar-book-ha1` and issue the following.

    On RHEL-based systems:

    ```
    systemctl stop httpd
    ```

    For Ubuntu systems:

    ```
    systemctl stop apache2
    ```

16. When navigating to your virtual IP (in the example IP case,
    `http://192.168.0.5/zabbix`), you will see the same configuration wizard
    again.

17. Fill out the database details again:

Figure 1.12 – The Zabbix database configuration window for lar-book-ha2

18. Then make sure to set up the **Zabbix server name** as `lar-book-ha2` as seen in the screenshot.

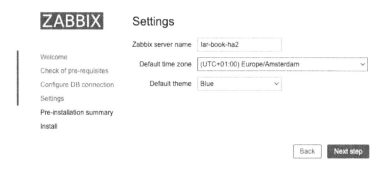

Figure 1.13 – The Zabbix server settings window for lar-book-ha2

19. Now we need to reenable the `lar-book-ha1` frontend by issuing the following.

On RHEL-based systems:

```
systemctl start httpd
```

For Ubuntu systems:

```
systemctl start apache2
```

That should be our last step. Everything should now be working as expected. Make sure to check your Zabbix server log file to see if the HA nodes are running as expected.

How it works...

Now that we have done it, how does the Zabbix server actually work in a high availability mode? Let's start by checking out the **Reports | System information** page in our Zabbix frontend.

Parameter	Value	Details
Zabbix server is running	Yes	localhost:10051
Number of hosts (enabled/disabled)	1	1 / 0
Number of templates	288	
Number of items (enabled/disabled/not supported)	97	88 / 0 / 9
Number of triggers (enabled/disabled [problem/ok])	55	55 / 0 [1 / 54]
Number of users (online)	2	1
Required server performance, new values per second	1.42	
High availability cluster	Enabled	Fail-over delay: 1 minute

Name	Address	Last access	Status
lar-book-ha1	localhost:10051	0	Active
lar-book-ha2	localhost:10051	3s	Standby

Figure 1.14 – The Zabbix server system information with HA information

We can now see that we have some new information available. For example, the **High availability cluster** parameter. This parameter is now telling us if high availability is enabled or not and what the fail over delay is. In our case, this is 1 minute, meaning that it could take up to 1 minute before fail over is initiated.

Furthermore, we can see every single node in our cluster. As Zabbix now supports one to many nodes in a cluster, we can see every single one taking part in our cluster right here. Let's take a look at the setup we have built:

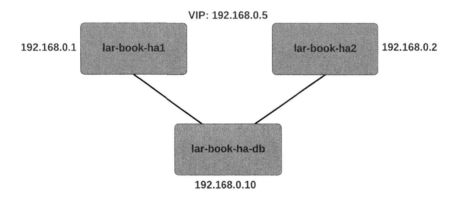

Figure 1.15 – The Zabbix server HA setup

As you can see in the setup, we have connected our two Zabbix server nodes **lar-book-ha1** and **lar-book-ha2** to our single Zabbix database **lar-book-ha-db**. Because our Zabbix database is our single source of truth, it can be used to keep our cluster configuration as well. In the end, everything Zabbix does is always kept in the database, from host configuration to history data to the high availability information. That's why building a Zabbix cluster is as simple as putting the `HANodeName` in the Zabbix server configuration file.

We also included the `NodeAddress` parameter in the configuration file. This parameter is used by the Zabbix frontend to make sure that our system information (widget) and Zabbix server are not running frontend notification work. The `NodeAddress` parameter will tell the frontend what IP address to connect to for each respective server once it becomes the active Zabbix server.

To take things a bit further, I have added a simple keepalived setup to this installation as well. Keepalived is a way to build simple VRRP fail over setups between Linux servers. In our case, we have entered the VIP as `192.168.0.5` and added the `chk_apache_httpd` process monitoring to determine when to fail over. Our fail over works as follows:

```
lar-book-ha1 has priority 244
lar-book-ha2 has priority 243
```

If HTTPd or Apache 2 is running on our node, that adds a weight of 10 to our priority, leading to the total priority of `254` and `253`, respectively. Now let's imagine that `lar-book-ha1` no longer has the web server process running. That means its priority drops to `244`, which is lower than `253` on `lar-book-ha2`, which does have the web server process running.

Whichever host has the highest priority is the host that will have the VIP `192.168.0.5`, meaning that host is running the Zabbix frontend which will be served.

Combining these two ways of setting up high availability, we have just created redundancy for two of the parts that make up our Zabbix setup, making sure we can keep outages to a minimum.

There's more...

Now you may wonder, what if I wanted to go further in terms of setting up high availability. First, the Zabbix high availability feature is built to be simple and understandable to the entire Zabbix user base. Meaning that as of now, you might not see the same amount of features you would get with a third-party implementation.

Nevertheless, the new Zabbix server high availability feature has proved itself to be a long-awaited feature that really adds something to the table. If you want to run a high availability setup like this, the best way to add one more level of complexity to high availability is a MySQL master/master setup. Setting up the Zabbix database with high availability, which is the main source of truth, will make sure that your Zabbix setup really is reliable in as many ways as possible. For more information regarding MariaDB replication, check out the documentation here: `https://mariadb.com/kb/en/ standard-replication/`.

Using the Zabbix frontend

If this is your first time using Zabbix, congratulations on getting to the UI. If you are a returning Zabbix user, there have been some changes to the Zabbix 6 UI that you might notice. We'll be going over some of the different elements that we can find in the Zabbix frontend so that during this book, you'll feel confident in finding everything you need.

Getting ready

To get started with the Zabbix UI, all we need to do is log in to the frontend. You will be served with the following page at the IP on which your server is running the Zabbix frontend:

Figure 1.16 – The Zabbix login screen

Make sure you log in to the Zabbix frontend with the default credentials:

- **Username**: Admin
- **Password**: zabbix

> **Tip**
> Just like in Linux, Zabbix is case-sensitive in most places. When entering your username, make sure to include the right cases; otherwise, you won't be able to log in!

How to do it...

After you log in, you'll be served with the default page, which is the default dashboard. This is what Zabbix has called **Global view** and it provides us with a nice overview of what's going on. We can completely customize this and all the other dashboards that Zabbix supplies, but it's a good idea to familiarize yourself with the default setup before building something new:

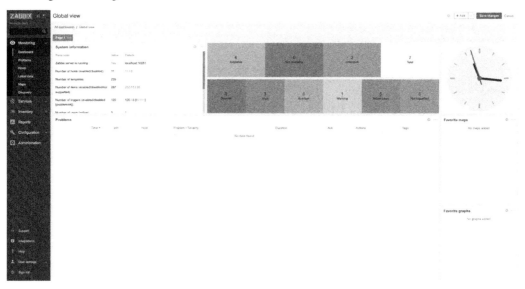

Figure 1.17 – The Global view dashboard

So, let's get started on getting to know this Zabbix 6 frontend by looking at the default dashboard. Please follow along in the frontend by clicking and checking out the content mentioned.

Zabbix uses dashboards and they are filled with widgets to show you the information. Let's go over the different widgets in the default dashboard and detail their information.

From left to right, let's start with the **System information** widget:

System information

Parameter	Value	Details
Zabbix server is running	Yes	localhost:10051
Number of hosts (enabled/disabled)	11	11 / 0
Number of templates	235	
Number of items (enabled/disabled/not supported)	287	252 / 0 / 35
Number of triggers (enabled/disabled [problem/ok])	120	120 / 0 [8 / 112]
Number of users (online)	3	1
Required server performance, new values per second	3.71	
High availability cluster	Disabled	

Figure 1.18 – The System information widget

This is the **System information** widget, which as you might have guessed details all the system information for you. This way, we can keep an eye on what's going on with our Zabbix server and see whether our Zabbix is even running. Let's go over the parameters:

- **Zabbix server is running**: Informs us whether the Zabbix server backend is actually running and where it is running. In this case, it's running, and it's running on `localhost:10051`.

- **Number of hosts**: This will detail the number of hosts **enabled** (11), the number of hosts **disabled** (0), and the number of **templates** we have (235). It gives us a quick overview of our Zabbix server host information.

- **Number of items**: Here, we can see details of our Zabbix server's items—in this case, **enabled** (287), **disabled** (0), and **not supported** (35).

- **Number of triggers**: This details the number of triggers. We can see how many are **enabled** (120) and **disabled** (0), but also how many are in a **problem** state (8) and how many are in an **ok** state (112).

- **Number of users (online)**: The first value details the total number of users. The second value details the numbers of users currently logged in to the Zabbix frontend.

- **Required server performance, new values per second**: Perhaps I'm introducing you to a completely new concept here, which is **New Values Per Second**, or **NVPS**. A server receives or requests values through items and writes these to our MariaDB database (or another database). The NVPS information detailed here shows the estimated number of NVPS received by the Zabbix server. Keep a close eye on this as your Zabbix server grows, as it's a good indicator to see how quickly you should scale up.

- **High availability cluster**: If you are running a Zabbix server high availability cluster, you will see if it is enabled here and what the fail over delay is. Additionally, the **System information** page will display additional high availability information.

You might also see three additional values here depending on your setup:

- **Database history tables upgraded**: If you see this, it's indicating that one of your database history tables hasn't been upgraded yet. Numeric (float) tables have been expanded to allow for more characters to be saved per data point. This table isn't upgraded automatically coming from Zabbix 4 to 5 or higher, as not everyone needs it and it might take a long time to upgrade.

- **Database name**: If you see the name of your database with the value of your version it might indicate you are running a non-supported database version. You could see a message like: `Warning! Unsupported <DATABASE NAME> database server version. Should be at least <DATABASE VERSION>`.

   Now, that's one of the most important widgets when it comes to your Zabbix server and it's a great one to keep on your main dashboard if you ask me.

Let's move on to the next widget, **Host availability**:

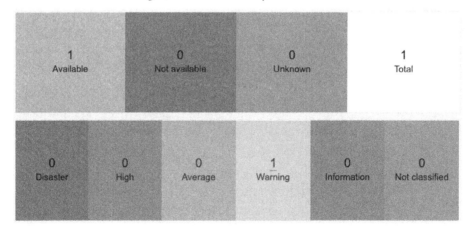

Figure 1.19 – The Host availability widget

The **Host availability** widget is a quick overview widget showing you everything you want to know about your monitored host's availability status. In this widget, it shows whether the host is **Available**, **Not Available**, or **Unknown**. This way, you get a good overview of the availability of all the hosts you could be monitoring with your Zabbix server in a single widget.

On top of that, it also shows you how many hosts currently have a trigger in a certain state. There are several default severities in Zabbix:

- **Disaster**
- **High**
- **Average**
- **Warning**
- **Information**
- **Not classified**

We can fully customize the severity levels and colors; for example, what severity levels we want to put on which triggers. So, if you are worried about the severities right now, don't be; we'll get to that later.

> Tip
> Customizing the severity levels and colors can be very useful to your organization. We can customize the severity levels to match levels used throughout our company or even to match some of our other monitoring systems used.

The next widget is **Local**:

Figure 1.20 – The Local widget, indicating a time

It's a clock with the local Linux system time. Need I say more? Let's move on to the **Problems** widget:

Problems

Time ▼	Info	Host	Problem • Severity	Duration	Ack	Actions	Tags
10:49:37	•	Zabbix server	Zabbix agent is not available (for 3m)	37s	No		

Figure 1.21 – One of the Problems widgets available

Now, this is an interesting widget that I use a lot. We see our current problems on this screen, so if we have our triggers set up correctly, we get valuable information here. A quick overview of how many hosts are having problems is one thing, but the **Problems** page also gives us more details about the problem:

- **Time**: At what time this problem was first noticed by the Zabbix server
- **Info**: Information about the event, with Manual close and Suppressed statuses being represented here.
- **Host**: What host this problem occurred on.
- **Problem/Severity**: What the problem is and how severe it is. The severity is shown in a color, in this case, orange meaning **Average**.
- **Duration**: How long this has been a problem.
- **Ack**: Whether this problem has been acknowledged or not by yourself or another Zabbix user.
- **Actions**: What actions have been taken after this problem occurred, for example, a custom script that executes on problem creation. If you hover over any action, it will show you detailed information about all actions that have been taken for this problem.
- **Tags**: What tags are assigned to this problem.

The **Problems** widget is very useful. We have different types of this widget available and as mentioned before, it is completely customizable, based on how this widget shows our problems to us. Take a quick look at some of the options, which we'll detail further in a later chapter:

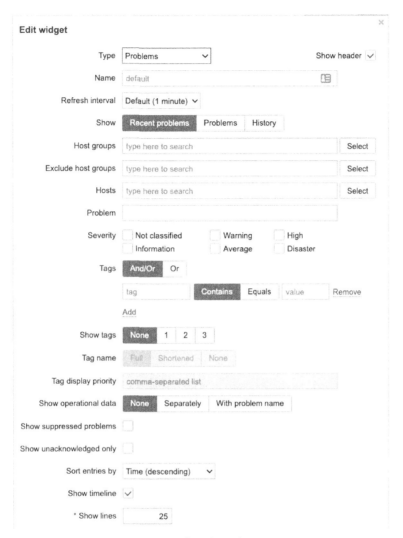

Figure 1.22 – The Edit widget screen

Tip

We can hide severity levels from these widgets to make sure we only see important ones. Sometimes, we don't want to see informational severity problems on our dashboards; it can distract you from a more important problem. Keep your dashboards clean by customizing the widget to its full extent.

Now, there are two more widgets that are completely empty on our default dashboard. These are the **Favourite maps** and **Favourite graphs** widgets. These widgets can be filled with a quick link to your favorite maps and graphs, respectively, giving you a fast way to access them without clicking through the menus:

Figure 1.23 – The Favourite widgets

Now we know how to work with the Zabbix frontend and we can continue further on with how to navigate our instance.

Navigating the frontend

Navigating the Zabbix frontend is easier than it looks at first glance, especially with some of the amazing changes made to the UI starting from Zabbix 5.0. Let's explore the Zabbix navigational UI some more in this recipe by looking at the navigation bar and what it has to offer.

Getting ready

Now that we've seen the first page after logging in with the default dashboard, it is time to start navigating through the Zabbix UI and see some of the other pages available. We'll move through the sidebar and explore the pages available in our Zabbix installation so that when we start monitoring our networks and applications, we know where we can find everything.

So, before continuing, make sure you have the Zabbix server ready as set up in the previous recipes.

How to do it...

The Zabbix navigation bar is the gateway to all of our powerful tools and configuration settings. Zabbix uses a left-side navigation bar to keep our UI as clean as possible. On top of that, they have made the sidebar disappear so that we can keep a close look at all of our content, without the sidebar blocking our vision.

> **Tip**
>
> We cannot change the Zabbix navigation menu location, but it is possible to hide it to a smaller form or completely hide it. If you want the navigation bar to hide (or not), click the first icon on the right side of the Zabbix logo. If you want to fully hide the navigation bar, click the second icon on the right side of the Zabbix logo.

Let's take a look at the Zabbix sidebar as we see it from our default page and get to know it. Please follow along in the frontend by clicking and checking out the content mentioned:

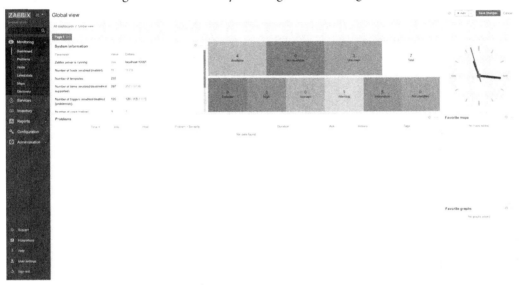

Figure 1.24 – The default Zabbix page as seen in your own web browser

We've got some categories here to choose from, and one level below the categories, we've got our different pages. First, let's start by detailing the categories:

- **Monitoring**: The **Monitoring** category is where we can find all of our information about our collected data. It's basically the category you want to use when you're working with Zabbix to read any collected information you've worked hard to acquire.

- **Services**: The **Services** category is new to Zabbix 6 and comes as part of the improved Business Service Monitoring features. We can find all of the information regarding service and SLA monitoring here.

- **Inventory**: The **Inventory** category is a cool extra feature in Zabbix that we can use to look at our host-related inventory information. You can add stuff such as software versions or serial numbers to hosts and look at them here.

- **Reports**: The **Reports** category contains a variety of predefined and user-customizable reports focused on displaying an overview of parameters such as system information, triggers, and gathered data.

- **Configuration**: The **Configuration** category is where we build everything we want to see in **Monitoring**, **Inventory**, and **Reporting**. We can edit our settings to suit our every need so that Zabbix can show us that data in a useful way.

- **Administration**: The **Administration** category is where we administer the Zabbix server. You'll find all your settings from the server here to enable you and your colleagues to have a good working Zabbix experience.

You'll go over all of these quite a lot while using this book, so remember them well. Let's dive a little deeper into the categories by looking at them one by one. Let's start with the **Monitoring** category:

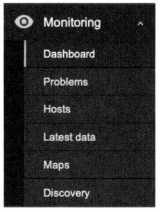

Figure 1.25 – The Monitoring section of the sidebar

The **Monitoring** tab contains the following pages:

- **Dashboard**: This is where you will find the default dashboard we showed in *Figure 1.24*. It is also where we can add many more dashboards for everything we can think of.

- **Problems**: We can look at our current problem in detail here. We are provided with a bunch of filter options to narrow down our problem search if needed.

- **Hosts**: **Hosts** will provide a quick overview of what's going on with hosts. It also provides links to navigate to pages showing the data for our hosts.

- **Latest data**: Here is a page we're going to use quite a lot throughout our professional Zabbix lifetime. The **Latest data** page is where we can find collected values for every single host, which we can of course filter on.

- **Maps**: Maps are a very helpful tool in Zabbix to get an overview of your infrastructure. We can use them for network overviews and such.

- **Discovery**: This page provides us with an overview of discovered devices. We'll work more on this later.

Next, we have the **Services** category:

Figure 1.26 – The Services section of the sidebar

This part of the sidebar contains the following pages:

- **Services**: This is where we configure all of our services that we want to monitor.

- **Service actions**: The section where we can set up any actions for our configured services. You'll find options like sending our notifications for SLAs and more.

- **SLA**: We can configure any SLAs here that we can then use in our services.

- **SLA report**: A detailed overview of configured services with their SLAs and if they are being met or not.

Then, we have the **Inventory** category:

Figure 1.27 – The Inventory section of the sidebar

The **Inventory** tab contains the following pages:

- **Overview**: A quick overview page for your inventory information.

- **Hosts**: A more detailed look into inventory values on a per-host basis.

Next, we have the **Reports** category:

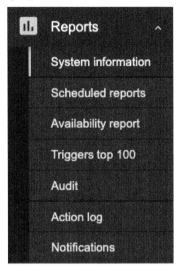

Figure 1.28 – The Reports section of the sidebar

The **Reports** tab contains the following pages:

- **System information**: You can look at the system information here; it contains the same information as the **System information** widget.

- **Scheduled reports**: This is where we configure any automatic PDF reporting that we might want to send out.

- **Availability report**: On this page, we can see the percentage of time a trigger has been in a **problem** state compared to the **ok** state. This is a helpful way of seeing for how long certain items are actually healthy.

- **Triggers top 100**: The top 100 triggers that have changed their state most often within a period of time.

- **Audit**: We can see who changed what on our Zabbix server here. This is a great way to see which colleague locked you out by accident or whether it was on purpose.

- **Action log**: We can see a list of actions that have been taken, for example, due to triggers going to a **problem** or **ok** state.

- **Notifications**: On this page, we can see the number of notifications sent to our users.

Next, we have the **Configuration** category:

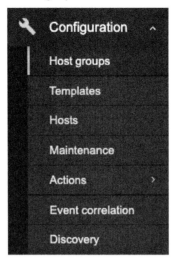

Figure 1.29 – The Configuration section of the sidebar

The **Configuration** tab contains the following pages:

- **Host groups**: We configure our host groups here; for instance, a group for all *Linux servers*.

- **Templates**: This is where we configure our templates that we can use to monitor hosts from the Zabbix server.

- **Hosts**: Another hosts tab, but this time it is not for checking the data. This is where we add and configure host settings.

- **Maintenance**: In Zabbix, we have the availability to set maintenance periods; this way, triggers or notifications won't disturb you while you take something offline for maintenance, for example.

- **Actions**: Remember how I mentioned we can configure actions for when a trigger changes state? This is where we configure those actions.

- **Event correlation**: We can correlate problems here to reduce noise or prevent event storms. This is achieved by closing new or old problems when they correlate to other problems.

- **Discovery**: This is where we configure Zabbix discovery for automatic host creation.

Finally, we have the **Administration** category:

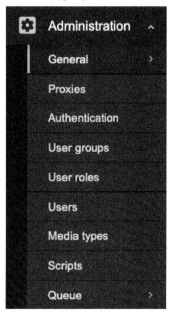

Figure 1.30 – The Administration section of the sidebar

The **Administration** tab contains the following pages:

- **General**: The general page contains our Zabbix server configuration. Settings ranging from housekeeper to frontend theme are found here.

- **Proxies**: This is where we configure proxies that should be connected to this Zabbix server.

- **Authentication**: We can find our authentication settings here, such as LDAP, SAML, and HTTP.

- **User groups**: This is where we configure user groups and the permissions for these user groups.

- **User roles**: It's possible to configure different users' roles here, to limit or extend certain frontend functionality to certain users.

- **Users**: Add users to this page.

- **Media types**: There are several media types pre-configured in Zabbix, which you'll find here already. We can also add custom media types.

- **Scripts**: This is where we can add custom scripts, for extending Zabbix functionality in the frontend.

- **Queue**: View your Zabbix server queue here. Items might be stuck in a queue due to data collection or performance issues.

> **Tip**
>
> When using Zabbix authentication such as HTTP, LDAP, or SAML, we still need to create our users internally with the right permissions. Configure your users to match your authentication method's username in Zabbix and use the authentication method for password management. Keep an eye on the following Zabbix case to see updates on the implementation or leave a vote:
>
> `https://support.zabbix.com/browse/ZBXNEXT-276`

2
Getting Things Ready with Zabbix User Management

In this chapter, we will work on creating our first user groups, users, and user roles. It's very important to set these up in the correct manner, as they will give people access to your Zabbix environment with the correct permissions. By going over these things step by step, we will make sure we have a structured Zabbix setup before continuing on with this book.

As a bonus, we will also set up some advanced user authentication using SAML to make things easier for your Zabbix users and provide them with a way to use the login credentials they might already be using throughout your company. We will go over all these steps in order of the following recipes:

- Creating user groups
- Using the new Zabbix user roles
- Creating your first users
- Advanced user authentication with SAML

Technical requirements

We can do all of the work in this chapter with any installed Zabbix setup. If you haven't installed Zabbix yet, check out the previous chapter to learn how to do so. We will go through our Zabbix setup to get everything ready for our users to start logging in and using the Zabbix frontend.

Creating user groups

To log in to the Zabbix frontend, we are going to need users. Right now, we are logged in with the default user, which is logical because we need a user to create users. This isn't a safe setup though, because we don't want to keep using `zabbix` as a password. So, we are going to learn how to create new users and group them accordingly.

It's important to choose how you want to manage users in Zabbix before setting up user accounts. If you want to use something such as LDAP or SAML, it's a smart idea to make the choice to use one of those authentication methods right away, so you won't have any migration trouble.

Getting ready

Now that we know how the Zabbix UI is structured and we know how to navigate it, we can start doing some actual configuration. We'll start out by creating some user groups to get familiar with the process and start using them. This way, our Zabbix setup gets not only more structured but also more secure.

To get started with this, we'll need a Zabbix server like the one we used in the previous recipes and the knowledge we've acquired there to navigate to the correct frontend sections.

Looking at the following figure, we can see how our example company, **Cloud Hoster**, is set up. We will create the users seen in the diagram to create a structured and solid user setup:

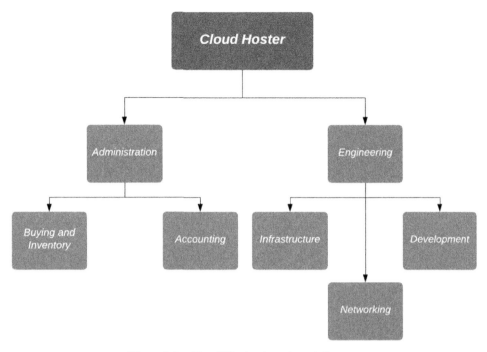

Figure 2.1 – Cloud Hoster department diagram

So, **Cloud Hoster** has some departments that need access to the Zabbix frontend and others who don't need it at all. Let's say we want to give the following departments access to the Zabbix frontend:

- **Networking**: To configure and monitor their network devices
- **Infrastructure**: To configure and monitor their Linux servers
- **Buying and Inventory**: To look at inventory information and compare it to other internal tools

How to do it...

Let's get started with creating these three groups in our Zabbix UI:

1. To do this, navigate to **Administration | User groups**, which will show you the following page:

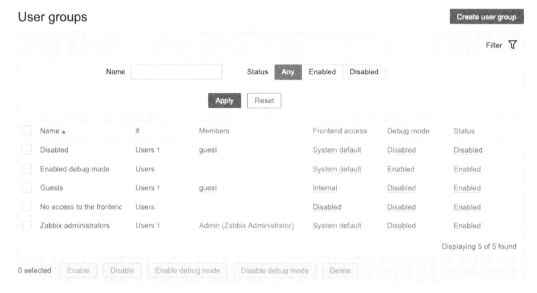

Figure 2.2 – The Zabbix User groups window

2. Now, let's start by creating the **Networking** group by clicking **Create user group** in the top-right corner. This will bring you to the following screen:

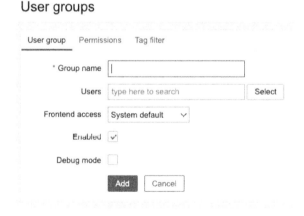

Figure 2.3 – The Zabbix User groups configuration window

We will need to fill in the information, starting with **Group name**, which of course will be Networking. There are no users for this group yet, so we'll skip that one. **Frontend access** is the option to provide us with authentication; if you select **LDAP** here, LDAP authentication will be used for authenticating. We will keep it as **System default**, which is the internal Zabbix authentication.

3. Now, let's navigate to the next tab on this page, which is **Permissions**:

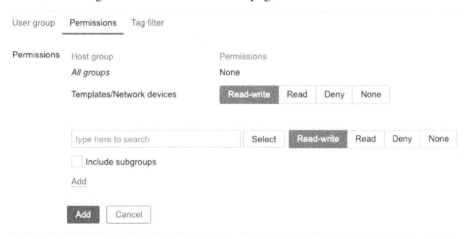

Figure 2.4 – The Zabbix User groups Permissions configuration window

Here, we can specify what host groups our group will have access to. There's a default host group for **Networking** already, which we will use in this example.

4. Click **Select** to take you to a pop-up window with host groups available. Select **Templates/Network devices** here and it'll take you back to the previous window, with the group filled in.

5. Select **Read-write** and click the smaller-text **Add** button to add these permissions.

6. We won't be adding anything else, so click the bigger blue **Add** button to finish creating this host group.

> **Tip**
> When using Zabbix authentication such as HTTP, LDAP, or SAML, we still need to create our users internally with the right permissions. Configure your users to match your authentication method's username in Zabbix and use the authentication method for password management.

Now we will have a new host group called **Networking** that is only allowed to read and write to the **Templates/Network devices** host group:

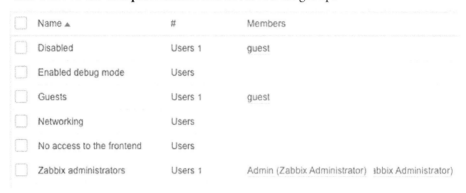

Figure 2.5 – The Zabbix User groups window

7. Let's repeat this process for the **Infrastructure** host group, except instead of adding the **Templates/Network devices** host group, we'll add the **Linux servers** host group, like this:

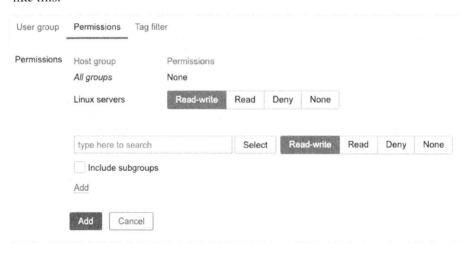

Figure 2.6 – The Zabbix User groups Permissions configuration window with one host group

8. Click **Add** to save this host group.

9. Repeat the steps again and to add **Buying and Inventory**, we'll do something differently. We'll repeat the process we've just done except for the part with the permissions. We want **Buying and Inventory** to be able to read our inventory data, but we don't want them to actually change our host configuration. Add both **Templates/Network devices** and **Linux servers** to the group, but with only **Read** permissions like this:

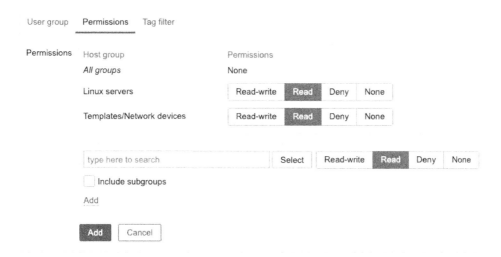

Figure 2.7 – The Zabbix User groups Permissions configuration window with two host groups

Congratulations! Finishing this means you've ended up with three different host groups and we can continue to create our first new users! Let's get to it.

There's more...

Zabbix user groups are quite extensive and there is a lot more to it than there seems at first. As the entire permission system is based on what user group(s) and user role(s) you are part of, it is always a good idea to read the Zabbix documentation first: `https://www.zabbix.com/documentation/current/en/manual/config/users_and_usergroups/usergroup`.

Using the new Zabbix user roles

New functionality has been introduced to this Zabbix 6.0 LTS release. It is now possible to create your own user roles in Zabbix. In older Zabbix versions, we had the ability to assign one of three user types:

- **User**
- **Admin**
- **Super admin**

What these user types did in earlier releases was restrict what Zabbix users could see in the frontend. This was always pre-defined though. Now with the addition of user roles that we can create ourselves, we can set up our own frontend-related restrictions, making it possible to only show certain parts of the UI to certain Zabbix users, while still respecting the permissions set up using user groups.

Getting ready

For this recipe, we will need a Zabbix server, preferably the one set up in the previous recipe. In the previous recipe, we set up different user groups, to provide for different permissions on host groups. Completely separate from the user group, we will apply certain user roles to our users to determine what they can see in the UI. Let's check out how to set up our user roles.

How to do it...

1. First, navigate to the Zabbix frontend and go to **Administration | User roles**. This will show us the default user roles as you know them from older Zabbix versions.

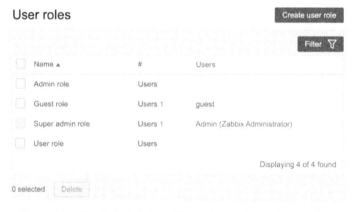

Figure 2.8   The default Zabbix User roles configuration window

2. Here, we can click on the blue **Create user role** button in the top-right corner.

3. We'll set up a new user role called User+ role. This role will be for Zabbix users that will only have read permissions, but who need more access than just the **Monitoring**, **Inventory**, and **Reports** navigational elements.

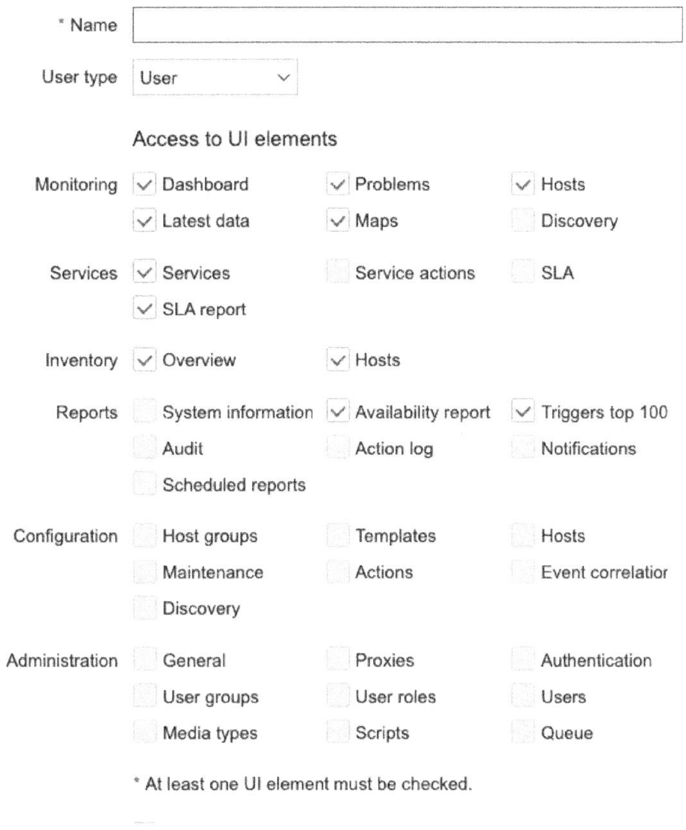

* Name			
User type	User ⌄		

Access to UI elements

Monitoring	✓ Dashboard	✓ Problems	✓ Hosts
	✓ Latest data	✓ Maps	Discovery
Services	✓ Services	Service actions	SLA
	✓ SLA report		
Inventory	✓ Overview	✓ Hosts	
Reports	System information	✓ Availability report	✓ Triggers top 100
	Audit	Action log	Notifications
	Scheduled reports		
Configuration	Host groups	Templates	Hosts
	Maintenance	Actions	Event correlatior
	Discovery		
Administration	General	Proxies	Authentication
	User groups	User roles	Users
	Media types	Scripts	Queue

* At least one UI element must be checked.

Figure 2.9 – The top part of a new Zabbix User role configuration window

4. First things first, make sure to fill out **Name** as User+ role.

5. Let's focus on the part where it states **Access to UI elements** first. When **User** is selected for **User type**, we are not able to add some access to the user role. So let's change the **User type** by selecting **Admin** in the dropdown.

6. I specifically want this user role named `User+ role` to have the ability to access the maintenance page. Setting this up will look like this:

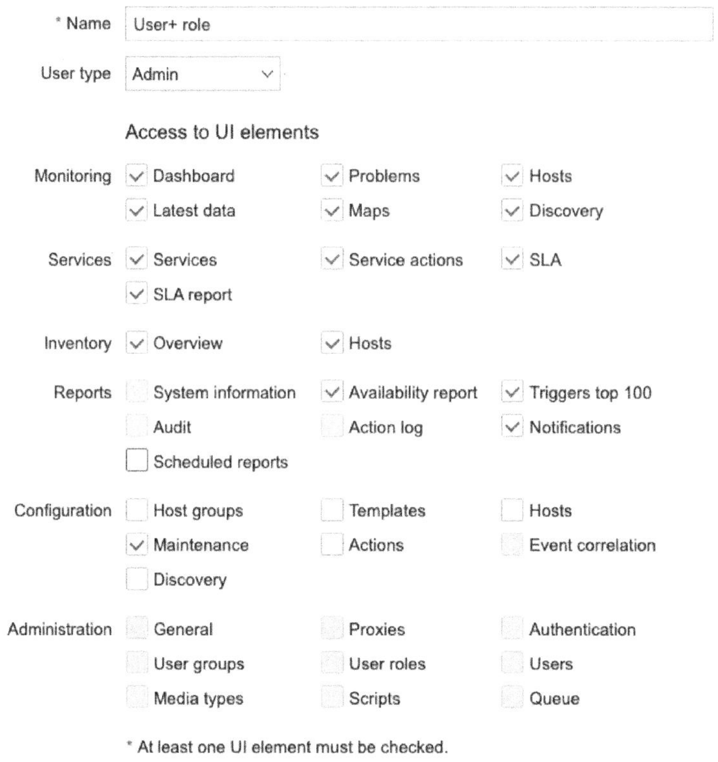

* Name	User+ role		
User type	Admin ∨		

Access to UI elements

Monitoring	✓ Dashboard	✓ Problems	✓ Hosts
	✓ Latest data	✓ Maps	✓ Discovery
Services	✓ Services	✓ Service actions	✓ SLA
	✓ SLA report		
Inventory	✓ Overview	✓ Hosts	
Reports	System information	✓ Availability report	✓ Triggers top 100
	Audit	Action log	✓ Notifications
	Scheduled reports		
Configuration	Host groups	Templates	Hosts
	✓ Maintenance	Actions	Event correlation
	Discovery		
Administration	General	Proxies	Authentication
	User groups	User roles	Users
	Media types	Scripts	Queue

* At least one UI element must be checked.

Figure 2.10 – A new Zabbix User+ role with access to Maintenance

7. Make sure to also change the **Access to actions** section of the form by deselecting **Manage scheduled reports** as follows:

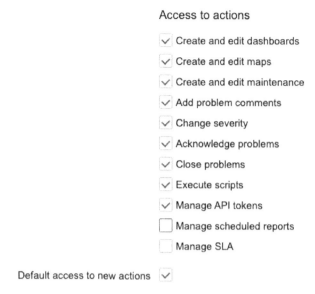

Figure 2.11 – A new Zabbix User+ role with correct Access to actions settings

8. Last but not least, click on the blue **Add** button at the bottom of the form to add this new user role.

How it works...

First, let's break down the options we have when creating user roles in Zabbix:

- **Name**: We can set a custom name for our user role here.

- **User type**: User types still exist in Zabbix 6, although now they are a part of user roles. There's still a limit to what can be seen by a certain user type and the Super admin type is still unrestricted when it comes to permissions.

- **Access to UI elements**: Here, we can restrict what a user can see on the Zabbix UI when they are assigned to this user role.

- **Access to services**: Service or SLA monitoring can be restricted here, as we might not want all users to have access to it.

- **Access to modules**: Custom Zabbix frontend modules are fully integrated into the user role system, meaning we can select what frontend modules a Zabbix user can see.

- **Access to API**: The Zabbix API can be restricted to certain user roles. For example, you might only want a specific API user role, limiting the rest of the users' access to the Zabbix API.

- **Access to actions**: In Zabbix user roles, certain actions can be limited, like the ability to edit dashboards, maintenance API tokens, and more.

Now, let's look at what we've changed between the user role called User role and the user role called User+ role. The default user role called User role has the following access to UI elements:

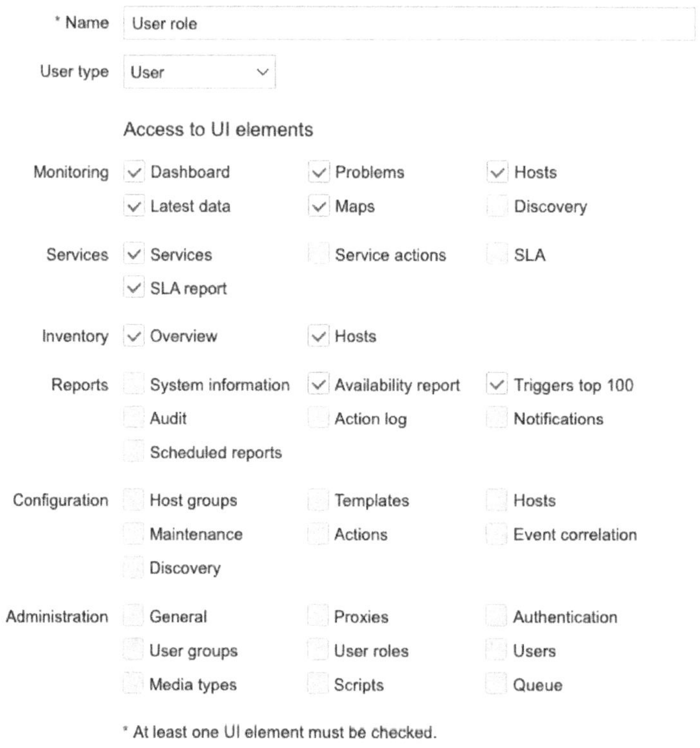

Figure 2.12 – Default Zabbix user role called User role Access to UI elements

By default, we have three user roles in Zabbix 6, which mirror the user types that are available. The user role we see here in **Name** mirrors the user type we have called User. It gives us access to the UI elements seen above, restricting the user role called User role to only be able to see certain things and make no configuration changes.

For example, it's considered an impactful permission to be able to set **Maintenance**. Because of course, you could restrict important notifications by setting **Maintenance**. But here comes the catch, what if you explicitly want a Zabbix user to only be able to read information but still not have access to configuration pages? In Zabbix 5.0, this wasn't possible because you could only select the **User**, **Admin**, or **Super admin** type, immediately giving access to the entire configuration section when using the **Admin** and **Super admin** user types.

Now, let's see what we did by creating a new user role called `User+ role`:

Figure 2.13 – New Zabbix user role called User+ role Access to UI elements

Here, we can see what happens if we change the user type to **Admin** but do not select all the available **Access to UI elements**. We now have a user role with no access to important configuration pages, but with access to **Maintenance**.

Combining that with the settings for **Access to actions**, where we added the **Create and edit maintenance** setting as seen in *Figure 2.11*, we would have full access to maintenance settings.

When we assign this role to a user in the next recipe and log in to that user, we will be able to see the following in our Zabbix sidebar.

Figure 2.14 – Custom User role Zabbix sidebar

This, of course, is just one of the many types of configurations you can use. You have the ability to allow Zabbix users access to menus and options through a number of parameters under a bunch of custom user roles. You are free to set this up however you feel like, adding a lot of user flexibility within Zabbix.

There's more...

Zabbix is currently in the process of working out user roles further, meaning that some parts might still be missing or you might see issues with them. As it is a new feature, it is constantly being improved and extended. Check out the Zabbix documentation for more information regarding this feature: `https://www.zabbix.com/documentation/current/en/manual/web_interface/frontend_sections/administration/user_roles`.

Creating your first users

With our newly created user groups, we've taken our first step toward a more structured and secure Zabbix setup. The next step is to actually assign some users to the newly created user groups to make sure they are assigned our new user permissions from the group.

Getting ready

To get started, we'll need the server and the newly created user groups from the last recipe. So, let's start the configuration.

Now we know there are three departments in the company called **Cloud Hoster** that are going to use our Zabbix installation. We've created host groups for them but there are also users in those departments that actually want to use our installation. Let's meet them:

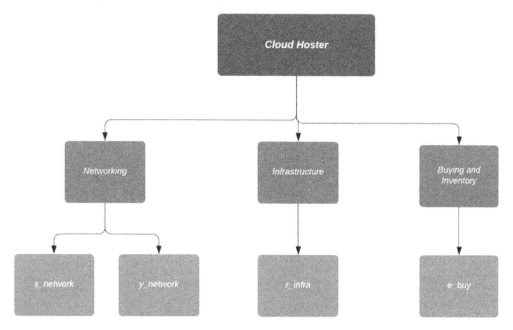

Figure 2.15 – Cloud Hoster users diagram

These are the users we need to configure for **Cloud Hoster** to use.

How to do it...

Let's start creating the users. We will start with our **Networking** department:

1. Navigate to **Administration | Users**, which will bring you to this page:

Figure 2.16 – The Zabbix Users window

2. This is where all the user creation magic is happening, as we will be managing all of our users from this page. To create our first **Networking** department user named s_network, click the **Create user** button in the top-right corner, bringing us to the following screen:

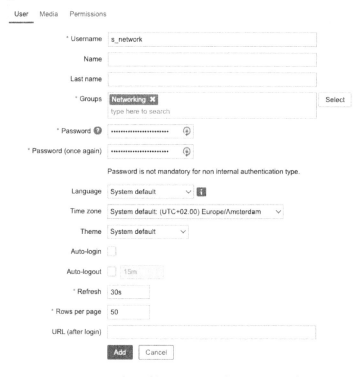

Figure 2.17 – The Zabbix Users configuration window

3. Fill out **Username** to provide us with the username this user will be using, which will be s_network.

4. Also, it's important to add this user to the group we have just created to give our user the right permissions. Click **Select** and pick our group called **Networking**.

5. Last but not least, set a secure password in the **Password** fields; don't forget it because we will be using it later.

6. After this, move on to the **Permissions** tab as we won't be configuring **Media** just yet:

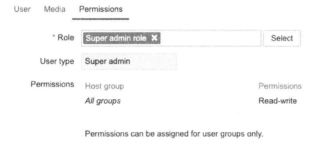

Figure 2.18 – The Zabbix user Permissions configuration window

7. Select the **Role** option named **Super admin role** here. This will enable our user to access all UI elements and see and edit information about all host groups in the Zabbix server.

The following user roles are available in Zabbix by default:

Default User Roles	Description
User role	The Zabbix User role has access to the Monitoring, Services, Inventory, and Reporting menus. The user has no access to any resources by default and any permissions to host groups must be explicitly assigned.
Admin role	The Zabbix Admin role has access to the Monitoring, Services, Inventory, Reporting and Configuration menus. The user has no access to any resources by default and any permissions to host groups must be explicitly assigned.
Super admin role	The Zabbix Super admin role has access to the Monitoring, Services, Inventory, Reporting, Configuration, and Administration menus. The user has read-write access to all host groups by default and permissions to any host groups cannot be revoked by denying access.

Figure 2.19 – A table detailing the different Zabbix user roles

8. Let's repeat the previous steps for the user named `y_network` but in the
    Permissions tab, select the **Admin role** option like this:

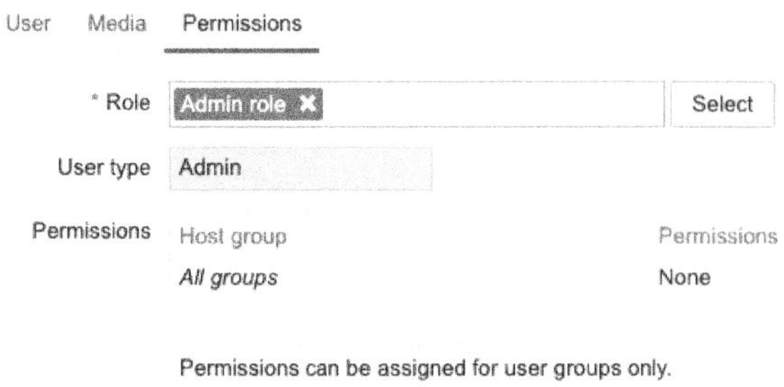

User	Media	Permissions

* Role   [Admin role **X**]   [Select]

User type   Admin

Permissions   Host group   Permissions
               All groups   None

Permissions can be assigned for user groups only.

Figure 2.20 – The Zabbix user Permissions configuration window

After creating these two users, let's move on to create the infrastructure user,
`r_ infra`. Repeat the steps we took for `s_network`, changing the **Username**,
of course. Then, add this user to the group and give our user the right permissions.
Click **Select** and pick our group called **Infrastructure**. It will look like this:

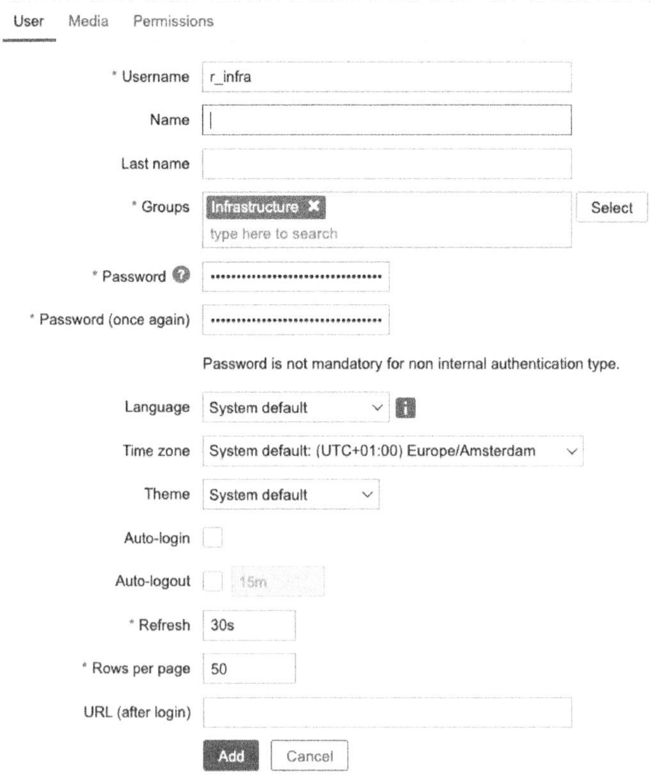

User	Media	Permissions

* Username   [r_infra]

Name   [|]

Last name   [ ]

* Groups   [Infrastructure **X**]   [Select]
            [type here to search]

* Password **?**   [...............................]

* Password (once again)   [...............................]

Password is not mandatory for non internal authentication type.

Language   [System default   ∨] **i**

Time zone   [System default: (UTC+01:00) Europe/Amsterdam   ∨]

Theme   [System default   ∨]

Auto-login   [ ]

Auto-logout   [ ] [15m]

* Refresh   [30s]

* Rows per page   [50]

URL (after login)   [ ]

[Add]   [Cancel]

Figure 2.21 – The Zabbix user configuration window for r_infra

Lastly, make this user another **Super admin**.

9. Now, for our last user, let's repeat our steps again, changing the **Username** and the group in the **User** tab like this:

Figure 2.22 – The Zabbix User configuration window for e_buy

10. If you didn't follow the previous recipe, you can change this user's **Role** to User role at the **Permissions** tab. But if you did follow the previous recipe, we can use the User+ role we created like this:

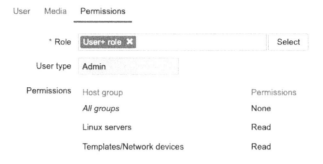

Figure 2.23 – The Zabbix user configuration window for e_buy

Setting the user up with the User+ role will also let the user e_buy create maintenance periods.

When you're done, you'll end up with the following:

- s_network: A user with access to the **Networking** user group permissions and that has the **Super admin** role.

- y_network: A user with access to the **Networking** user group permissions and that has the **Admin** role.

- r_infra: A user with access to the **Infrastructure** user group permissions and that has the **Super admin** role.

- e_buy: A user with access to the **Buying and Inventory** user group permissions and that has the User role or the User+ role.

Advanced user authentication with SAML

In this recipe, we will use SAML authentication, a widely used form of authentication in the IT world. We'll be using this as a form of managing passwords for our Zabbix users. Please note that if you've worked with Zabbix before and you've configured LDAP, SAML, like LDAP, allows user authentication with passwords. You still have to create users with their permissions.

Getting ready

To get started with SAML authentication, we will need our configured Zabbix server from the previous recipe. It's important that we have all the configured users from the previous recipe. We will also need something to authenticate with SAML. We will be using Azure **Active Directory** (**AD**) SAML.

Make sure to set up users in your (Azure) AD before continuing with this recipe. You can use your existing AD users for authentication, so you can use this recipe with your existing AD setup.

We will be using the `s_network` user as an example:

Figure 2.24 – The Azure Users and groups window

These are our user details:

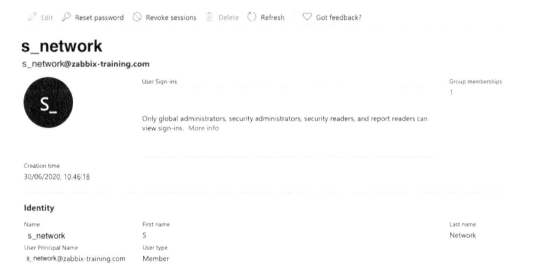

Figure 2.25 – The Azure user details window

To set up SAML, retrieve your SAML settings from your AD or another SAML provider. To work with Zabbix, we will need the following:

- IdP entity ID

- SSO service URL

- SLO service URL

- Username attribute

- SP entity ID

- SP name ID format

How to do it...

Now that we have our Azure AD ready, let's see how we can configure SAML using our setup:

1. Let's navigate to the following URL: `portal.azure.com`.

2. After logging in, navigate to Azure AD and click on **Enterprise Applications**.

3. Now click on **+ New Application** to create our new application. At the next window, click on **Create your own application**:

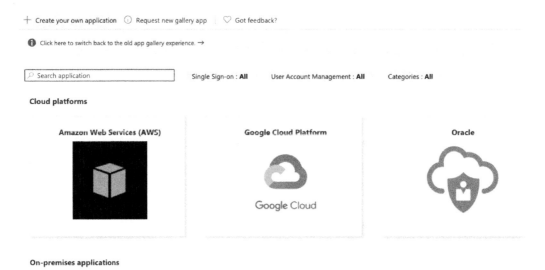

Figure 2.26 – The Azure enterprise application creation page

4. In the next window, name your new application `Zabbix` and click on the blue **Create** button:

Create your own application
What's the name of your app?
Zabbix
What are you looking to do with your application?
Configure Application Proxy for secure remote access to an on-premises application
Register an application you're working on to integrate with Azure AD
Integrate any other application you don't find in the gallery
Create

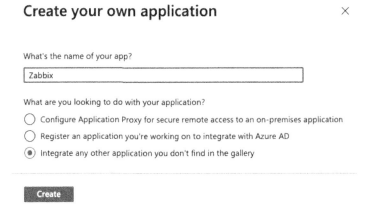

Figure 2.27 – The Azure enterprise new application page

5. Select your new application from the list and click on **Assign Users and Groups** to add the correct users. In our case, this will be `s_network`:

Selected items
S_
S_network
S_network@zabbix-training.com
Remove
Select

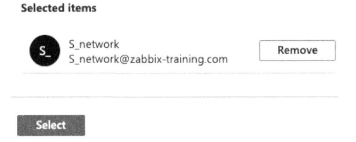

Figure 2.28 – The Azure enterprise application Users and Groups page

6. Click on **Select** and then **Assign**.
7. Now let's move on to the SAML settings by clicking on **Single sign-on** in the sidebar.
8. Now click on **SAML** on the page shown in the following screenshot and continue:

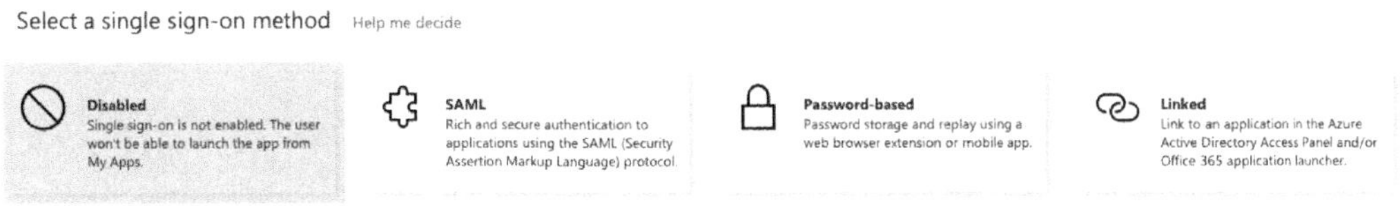

Select a single sign-on method
Help me decide
Disabled
Single sign-on is not enabled. The user won't be able to launch the app from My Apps.
SAML
Rich and secure authentication to applications using the SAML (Security Assertion Markup Language) protocol.
Password-based
Password storage and replay using a web browser extension or mobile app.
Linked
Link to an application in the Azure Active Directory Access Panel and/or Office 365 application launcher.

Figure 2.29 – The Azure enterprise application SAML option

9. Now at **1**, we can add the following information, where the black marks are our Zabbix server URL:

Figure 2.30 – The Azure SAML setting 1

10. At **2**, fill out the following:

Figure 2.31 – The Azure SAML setting 2

11. Number **3** will be automatically filled. Click on **Download** for **Certificate (Base64)**:

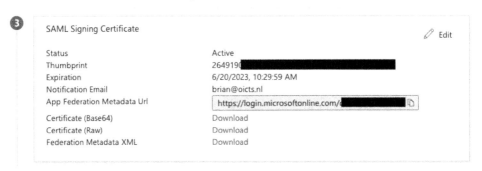

Figure 2.32 – The Azure SAML setting 3

12. Log in to the Zabbix server CLI and create a new file with the following command:

```
vim /usr/share/zabbix/conf/certs/idp.cert
```

13. Paste the contents from the downloaded file in *Step 11* here and save the file.

14. Now back at Azure for **4**, we will get the following information:

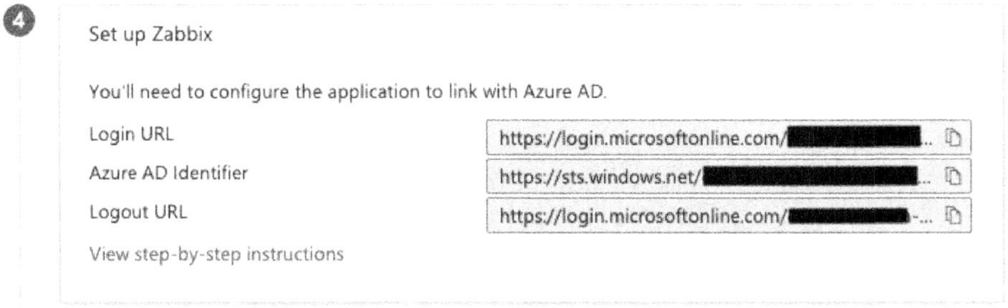

Figure 2.33 – The Azure SAML setting 4

15. At the Zabbix frontend, go to the **Administration | Authentication | SAML settings** page and fill in the following information and click on **Update**:

Figure 2.34 – The Zabbix SAML settings

16. Navigate to **Administration | Users** and change the s_network user to include the used Azure domain, for example:

Figure 2.35 – The Zabbix edit user screen for our SAML setup

17. After following these steps, it should now be possible to log in with your user configured in Zabbix and use the password set in Azure AD for this:

Figure 2.36 – The Zabbix login window

How it works...

Zabbix advanced user authentication is used to centralize password management. While we are not able to actually assign user groups and permissions to users via this setup, we can use it for password management.

This way, we can make sure it is easier for users to keep their passwords centralized in medium to big office environments:

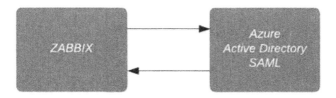

Figure 2.37 – Zabbix SAML authentication diagram

Zabbix communicates with our Azure AD SAML component when we click the **Sign in** button. The user is then authenticated against your Azure AD user and a confirmation is sent back to the Zabbix server. Congratulations, you are now logged in to your Zabbix server!

There's more...

We can do this kind of authentication not only with SAML but also with HTTP and LDAP. This way, you can choose the right form of advanced authentication for your organization.

Check out the Zabbix documentation for more information on the different forms of authentication:

```
https://www.zabbix.com/documentation/current/en/manual/web_
interface/frontend_sections/administration/authentication
```

It's also possible to work with an identity provider such as Okta, OneLogin, or any other. Meaning your options aren't limited to Azure AD, as long as it supports SAML you can use it to authenticate against your Zabbix server.

3
Setting Up Zabbix Monitoring

Zabbix is built to be flexible and should be able to monitor just about anything you could ever require. In this chapter, we will learn more about working with Zabbix to build a lot of different options for monitoring. We'll go over them recipe by recipe, so you'll end up with a solid understanding of how they work. We'll cover the following recipes on the different monitoring types:

- Setting up Zabbix agent monitoring
- Working with SNMP monitoring
- Creating Zabbix simple checks and Zabbix trapper
- Working with calculated and dependent items
- Creating external checks
- Setting up JMX monitoring
- Setting up database monitoring
- Setting up HTTP agent monitoring
- Using Zabbix preprocessing to alter item values

Technical requirements

We will need a Zabbix server capable of performing monitoring, with the following requirements:

- A server with Zabbix server installed on a Linux distribution of your choice, such as CentOS or Ubuntu, but a distribution such as Debian, Rocky Linux, or anything else will suit you just as well

- A MariaDB server to monitor

I'll be using the same server as we used in the previous chapter, but any Zabbix server should do.

Setting up Zabbix agent 2 monitoring

Starting from the release of Zabbix 5, Zabbix also officially started support for the new Zabbix agent 2. Zabbix agent 2 brings some major improvements and is even written in another coding language, which is Golang instead of C. In this recipe, we will be exploring how to work with Zabbix agent 2 and explore some of the new features introduced by it.

Getting ready

To get started with Zabbix agent 2, all we need to do is install it on a host that we want to monitor. Make sure you have an empty Red Hat Enterprise Linux (RHEL)-based or Ubuntu Linux host ready to monitor.

How to do it...

Let's see how to install Zabbix agent 2 and then move on to actually working with it.

Installing Zabbix agent 2

Let's start by installing Zabbix agent 2 on the Linux host we want to monitor. I'll be showing you how to do the steps on both RHEL and Ubuntu systems:

1. Issue the following command to add the repository:

    For RHEL-based systems:

    ```
    rpm -Uvh https://repo.zabbix.com/zabbix/6.0/rhel/8/
    x86_64/zabbix-release-6.0-1.el8.noarch.rpm
    ```

For Ubuntu systems:

```
wget https://repo.zabbix.com/zabbix/6.0/ubuntu/pool/
main/z/zabbix-release/zabbix-release_6.0-1+ubuntu20.04_
all.deb
```

```
dpkg -i zabbix-release_6.0-1+ubuntu20.04_all.deb
```

2. Then issue the following command to install Zabbix agent 2:

For RHEL-based systems:

```
dnf -y install zabbix-agent2
```

For Ubuntu systems:

```
apt install zabbix-agent2
```

Congratulations, Zabbix agent 2 is now installed and ready to use.

> **Important note**
>
> When adding new repositories to your system, always check out the Zabbix download page. We can find the right up-to-date repository for our system here:
>
> https://www.zabbix.com/download

Using a Zabbix agent in passive mode

Let's start by building a Zabbix agent with passive checks:

1. After installing Zabbix agent 2, let's open the Zabbix agent configuration file for editing:

```
vim /etc/zabbix/zabbix_agent2.conf
```

In this file, we edit all the Zabbix agent configuration values we could need from the server side.

2. Let's start by editing the following parameters:

```
Server=127.0.0.1
Hostname=Zabbix server
```

3. Change the value of `Server` to the IP of the Zabbix server that will monitor this passive agent. Change the value for `Hostname` to the hostname of the monitored server. We can get the IP address of our server with the following command:

```
ip addr
```

4. Now restart the Zabbix agent 2 process:

```
systemctl enable zabbix-agent2
systemctl restart zabbix-agent2
```

5. Next, move to the frontend of your Zabbix server and add this host for monitoring.

6. Go to **Configuration | Hosts** in your Zabbix frontend and click **Create host** in the top-right corner.

7. To create this host in our Zabbix server, we need to fill in the values as seen in the following screenshot:

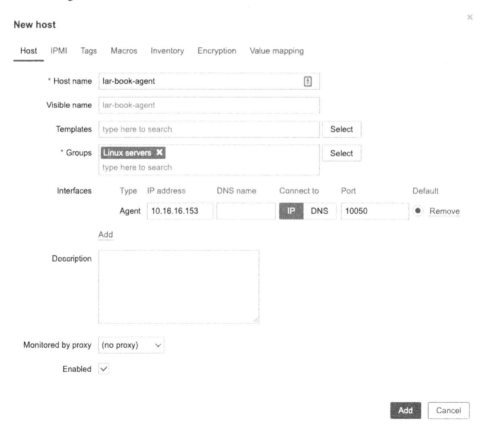

Figure 3.1 – The Zabbix host creation page for host lar-book-agent

It's important to add the following:

- **Host name**: To identify this host.

- **Groups**: To logically group hosts.

- **Interfaces**: To monitor this host on a specific interface. No interface means no communication. It's possible to have a host without an interface in Zabbix 6, if we don't need it. In the case of a Zabbix agent monitored host, we need an agent interface.

8. Make sure to add the correct IP address to the **Agent** interface configuration.

9. It is also important to add a template to this host, which with Zabbix 6 must be done on the same tab. As this is a Linux server monitored by a Zabbix agent, let's add the correct out-of-the-box template, as shown in the following screenshot:

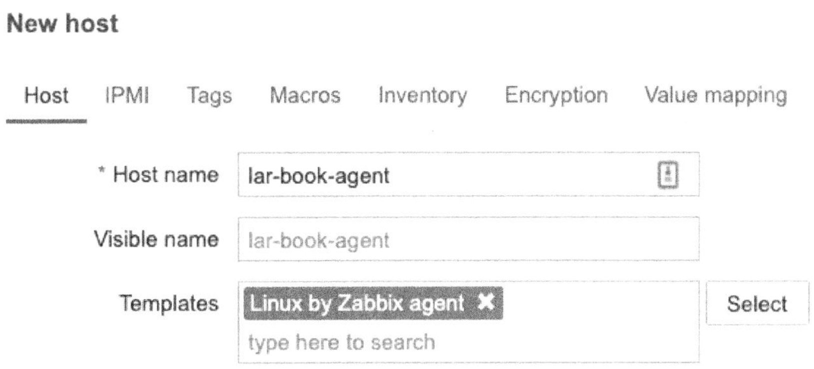

New host

| Host | IPMI | Tags | Macros | Inventory | Encryption | Value mapping |

* Host name   `lar-book-agent`

Visible name   `lar-book-agent`

Templates   `Linux by Zabbix agent ✕`
`type here to search`   `Select`

Figure 3.2 – The Zabbix host template page for host lar-book-agent

10. Click the blue **Add** button and you're done creating this agent host. Now that you've got this host, make sure the **ZBX** icon turns green, indicating that this host is up and being monitored by the passive Zabbix agent:

Status   Availability   Agent encryption

Enabled   ZBX   None

Figure 3.3 – The Zabbix configuration hosts page, host lar-book-agent

11. Because we configured our host and added a template with items, we can now see the values received on items for this host by going to **Monitoring | Hosts** and checking the **Latest data** button. Please note that the values could take a while to show up:

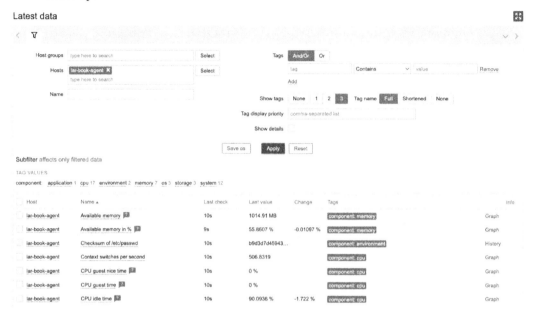

Figure 3.4 – The Zabbix Latest data page for host lar-book-agent

Using a Zabbix agent in active mode

Now let's check out how to configure the Zabbix agent with active checks. We need to change some values on the monitored Linux server host side:

1. Start by executing the following command:

```
vim /etc/zabbix/zabbix_agent2.conf
```

2. Now let's edit the following value to change this host to an active agent:

```
ServerActive=127.0.0.1
```

3. Change the value for ServerActive to the IP of the Zabbix server that will monitor this passive agent and also change the value of Hostname to lar-book-agent:

```
Hostname=lar-book-agent
```

> **Important note**
>
> Keep in mind that if you are working with multiple Zabbix servers or Zabbix proxies, for example when you are running Zabbix server in high availability, that you need to fill in all the Zabbix servers' or Zabbix proxies' their IP addresses at the **ServerActive** parameter. **High Availability** (**HA**) nodes are delimited by a semicolon (;) and different Zabbix environment IPs by a comma (,).

4. Now restart the Zabbix agent 2 process:

```
systemctl restart zabbix-agent2
```

5. Then move to the frontend of your Zabbix server and let's add another host with a template to do active checks instead of passive ones.

6. First, let's rename our passive host. To do that, go to **Configuration | Hosts** in your Zabbix frontend and click the host we just created. Change **Host name** as follows:

Figure 3.5 – The Zabbix host configuration page for host lar-book-agent_passive

We are doing this because for an active Zabbix agent, the hostname in the Zabbix agent configuration file needs to match the configuration of our host as seen on the Zabbix frontend.

7. Click on the blue **Update** button to save the changes.

8. Go to **Configuration | Hosts** in your Zabbix frontend and click **Create host** in the top-right corner.

9. Now let's create the host as follows:

New host   ✕

Host   IPMI   Tags   Macros   Inventory   Encryption   Value mapping

* Host name	lar-book-agent 🔃
Visible name	lar-book-agent
Templates	type here to search **Select**
* Groups	Linux servers ✖ **Select**
	type here to search

Interfaces	Type	IP address	DNS name	Connect to	Port	Default
	Agent	10.16.16.153		IP DNS	10050	● Remove

Add

Description
[   ]

Monitored by proxy   (no proxy) ⌄

Enabled   ✓

Add   Cancel

Figure 3.6 – The Zabbix host configuration page for host lar-book-agent

10. Also, make sure to add the correct template, named `Linux by Zabbix agent active`:

Figure 3.7 – The Zabbix host template page for host lar-book-agent

Please note that the **ZBX** icon won't turn green for an active agent. But when we navigate to **Monitoring | Hosts** and check **Latest data**, we can see our active data coming in.

> Tip
>
> As you might have noticed just now, a Zabbix agent can run in both passive and active mode at the same time. Keep this in mind when creating your own Zabbix agent templates, as sometimes you might want to combine the check types.

How it works...

Now that we have configured our Zabbix agents and know how they should be set up, let's see how the different modes work.

Passive agent

The **passive agent** works by collecting data from our host with the Zabbix agent. Every time an item on our host reaches its *update interval*, the Zabbix server asks the Zabbix agent what the value is now:

Figure 3.8 – Communication diagram between server and passive agent

Passive agents are great when working in environments where you want to keep communication initiated from the Zabbix server or Zabbix proxy side, for example, when there is a firewall that is only allowing outgoing traffic, as seen from the Zabbix server or proxy side.

Active agent

The **active agent** works by sending data from the Zabbix agent to a Zabbix server or Zabbix proxy. Every time an item on our agent reaches its update interval, the agent will send the value to our server.

Figure 3.9 – Communication diagram between server and active agent

The active agent is great when working with an environment where there is a firewall that is only accepting outgoing connections, as seen from the Zabbix agent side. This is the case in a lot of environments, and it can mitigate one of the main security concerns that is mostly associated with monitoring hosts.

On the other hand, the Zabbix agent working in active mode can also be a lot more efficient. Most of the load that comes from getting data to your Zabbix server is now on the Zabbix agent side. Because there are more Zabbix agents out there than you have Zabbix servers or proxies, offloading load like this is a great idea.

As mentioned, we can use both types of checks at the same time, giving us the freedom to configure every type of check we could possibly need. Our setup would then look like this:

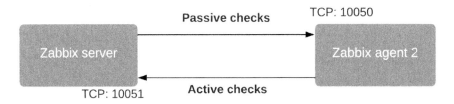

Figure 3.10 – Communication diagram between server and both agent types

This might be the case in situations where we want to mainly monitor passively, but, for example, log file monitoring with the Zabbix agent must be done with an active Zabbix agent. We can then combine our modes and make sure to use the full scale of our features provided in the Zabbix agent.

See also

There's a lot of stuff going on under the hood of Zabbix agent 2; if you're interested in learning more about the core of Zabbix agent 2, check out this cool blog post by Alexey Petrov: `https://blog.zabbix.com/magic-of-new-zabbix-agent/8460/`.

Working with SNMP monitoring

Now let's do something I enjoy most when working with Zabbix: build SNMP monitoring. My professional roots lie in network engineering, and I have worked a lot with SNMP monitoring to monitor all these different network devices.

Getting ready

To get started, we need the two Linux hosts we used in the previous recipes:

- Our Zabbix server host
- The host we used in the previous recipe to monitor via the Zabbix active agent

How to do it...

Monitoring via SNMP polling is easy and very powerful. We will start by configuring SNMPv3 on our monitored Linux host:

1. Let's start by issuing the following commands to install SNMP on our host.

   For RHEL-based systems:

   ```
   dnf install net-snmp net-snmp-utils
   ```

   For Ubuntu systems:

   ```
   apt install snmp snmpd libsnmp-dev
   ```

2. Now, let's create the new SNMPv3 user that we will use to monitor our host. Please note that we'll be using insecure passwords, but make sure to use secure passwords for your production environments. Issue the following command:

   ```
   net-snmp-create-v3-user -ro -a my_authpass -x my_privpass
   -A SHA -X AES snmpv3user
   ```

   This will create an SNMPv3 user with the username snmpv3user, the authentication password my_authpass, and the privilege password my_privpass.

3. Make sure to edit the SNMP configuration file to allow us to read all SNMP objects:

```
vim /etc/snmp/snmpd.conf
```

4. Add the following line at the rest of the `view systemview` lines:

```
view    systemview    included    .1
```

5. Now start and enable the `snmpd` daemon to allow us to start monitoring this server:

```
systemctl enable snmpd
```
```
systemctl start snmpd
```

This is all we need to do on the Linux host side; we can now go to the Zabbix frontend to configure our host. Go to **Configuration | Hosts** in your Zabbix frontend and click **Create host** in the top-right corner.

6. Now fill in the host configuration page:

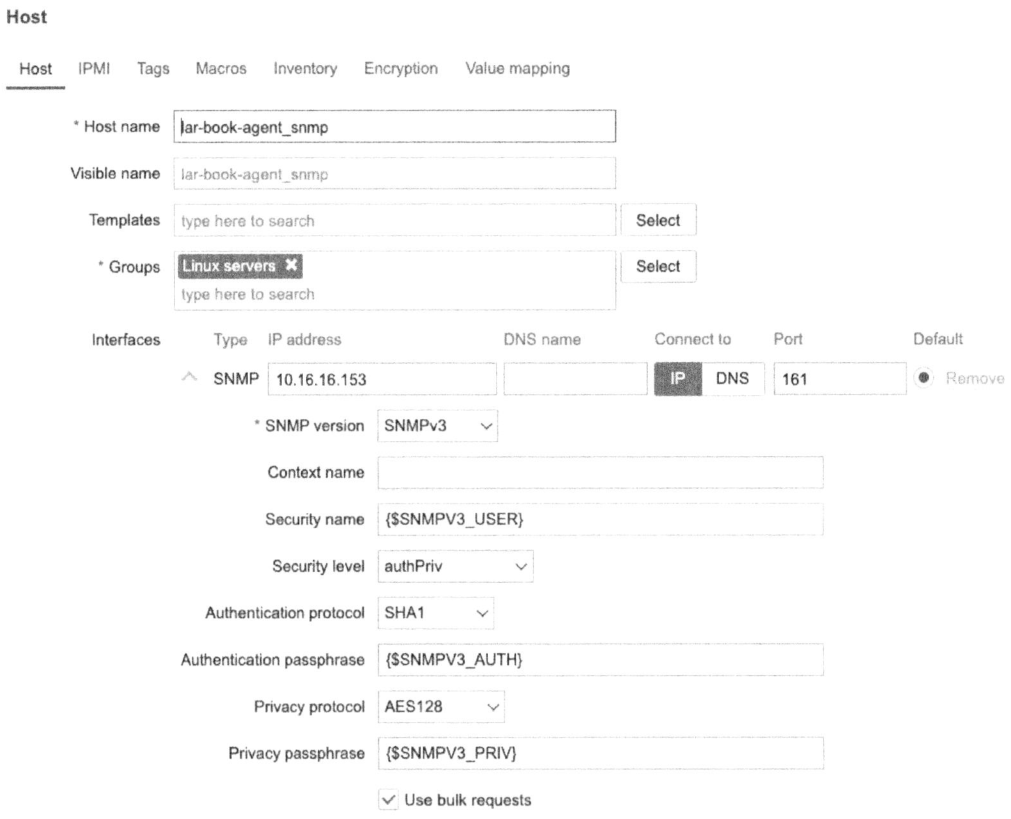

Figure 3.11 – Zabbix host configuration page for host lar-book-agent_snmp

7. Don't forget to change the IP address of the SNMP interface to your own value.

8. Make sure to add the right out-of-the-box template as shown in the following screenshot:

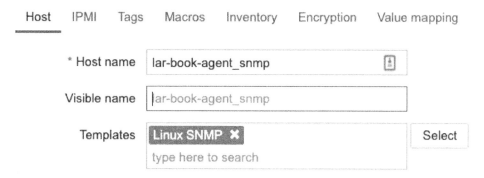

Figure 3.12 – Adding the template Linux SNMP to the host

> **Tip**
> While upgrading from an earlier Zabbix version to Zabbix 6, you won't get all the new out-of-the-box templates. If you feel like you are missing some templates, you can download them at the Zabbix Git repository: `https://git.zabbix.com/projects/ZBX/repos/zabbix/browse/templates`.

9. We are using some macros in our configuration here for the username and password. We can use these macros to actually add a bunch of hosts with the same credentials. This is very useful, for instance, if you have a bunch of switches with the same SNMPv3 credentials.

Let's fill in the macros under **Administration | General** and use the dropdown to select **Macros**. Fill in the macros like this:

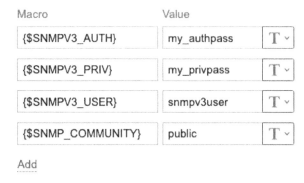

Figure 3.13 – Zabbix global macro page with SNMP macros

> **Tip**
>
> A cool feature in Zabbix 6 is the ability to hide macros in the frontend by using the macro type **Secret text**. Do keep in mind that macros of the type **Secret text** are still unencrypted in the Zabbix database, and for fully encrypted macros we would need something like HashiCorp Vault. Check out the documentation for more information: `https://www.zabbix.com/documentation/current/en/manual/config/secrets`.

10. Use the dropdown to change **{$SNMPV3_AUTH}** and **{$SNMPV3_PRIV}** to **Secret text**:

Figure 3.14 – Zabbix Secret text used for hiding sensitive (authentication) data

11. Now, after applying these changes by clicking **Update**, we should be able to monitor our Linux server via SNMPv3. Let's go to **Monitoring | Hosts** and check the **Latest data** page for our new host:

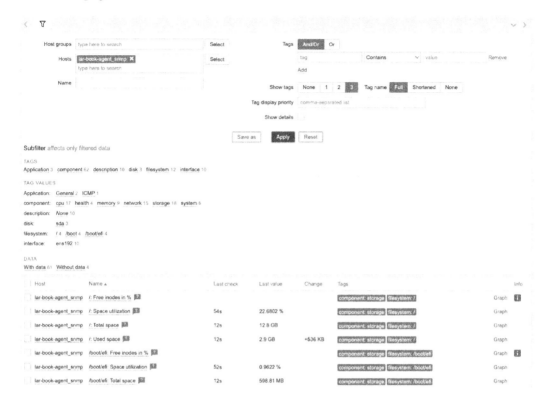

Figure 3.15 – SNMP Latest data for host lar-book-agent_snmp

Do note that it might take some time for your data to show up here.

> **Tip**
> When working with macros, there are three levels in cascading order: Global-, Template-, and Host-level macros. When working with Global level macros, keep in mind that they are not exported with templates or hosts. You want to use Template level and Host level for most cases, to keep your exports independent of Zabbix global settings.

How it works...

When we create a host as we did in *step 4*, Zabbix polls the host using SNMP. Polling SNMP like this works with SNMP OIDs. For instance, when we poll the item called **Free memory**, we ask the SNMP agent running on our Linux host to provide us the value for **1.3.6.1.4.1.2021.4.6.0**. That value is then returned to us on the Zabbix server:

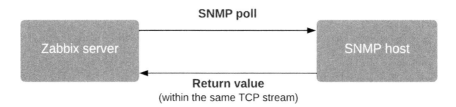

Figure 3.16 – Diagram showing communication between Zabbix server and SNMP host

SNMPv3 adds authentication and encryption to this process, making sure that when our Zabbix server requests information, that request is first encrypted and the data is sent back encrypted as well.

We also included the option to use **Bulk requests** when configuring our host. Bulk requests request several OIDs in the same stream, making this the preferred method of doing SNMP requests as it is more efficient. Only disable it for hosts that do not support bulk requests.

Lastly, let's take a look at SNMP OIDs, the most important part of our SNMP request. OIDs work in a tree-like structure, meaning that every number behind the dot can contain another value. For example, let's look at this OID for our host:

```
1.3.6.1.4.1.2021.4 = UCD-SNMP-MIB::memory
```

If we poll that OID with either the SnmpWalk CLI tool or our Zabbix server, we will get several OIDs back:

```
.1.3.6.1.4.1.2021.4.1.0 = INTEGER: 0
.1.3.6.1.4.1.2021.4.2.0 = STRING: swap
.1.3.6.1.4.1.2021.4.3.0 = INTEGER: 1679356 kB
.1.3.6.1.4.1.2021.4.4.0 = INTEGER: 1674464 kB
.1.3.6.1.4.1.2021.4.5.0 = INTEGER: 1872872 kB
.1.3.6.1.4.1.2021.4.6.0 = INTEGER: 184068 kB
```

That includes our `1.3.6.1.4.1.2021.4.6.0` OID with the value that contains our free memory. This is how SNMP is built, like a tree.

Creating Zabbix simple checks and the Zabbix trapper

In this recipe, we will go over two checks that can help you build some more customized setups. The Zabbix simple checks provide you with an easy way to monitor some specific data. The Zabbix trapper combines with Zabbix sender to get data from your hosts into the server, allowing for some scripting options. Let's get started.

Getting ready

To create these checks, we will need a Zabbix server and a Linux host to monitor. We can use the host with a Zabbix agent and SNMP monitoring from the previous recipes.

Do note for these checks that we do not actually need the Zabbix agent.

How to do it...

Working with simple checks is quite simple, as the name suggests, so let's start.

Creating simple checks

We will create a simple check to monitor whether a service is running and accepting TCP connections on a certain port:

1. To get this done, we will need to create a new host in the Zabbix frontend. Go to **Configuration | Hosts** in your Zabbix frontend and click **Create host** in the top-right corner.

2. Create a host with the following settings:

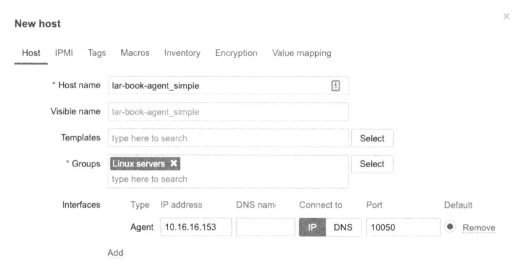

Figure 3.17 – Zabbix host configuration page for host lar-book-agent_simple

3. Now go to **Configuration | Hosts**, click the newly created host, and go to **Items**. We want to create a new item here by clicking the **Create item** button.

   We will create a new item with the following values, and after doing so, we will click the **Add** button at the bottom of the page:

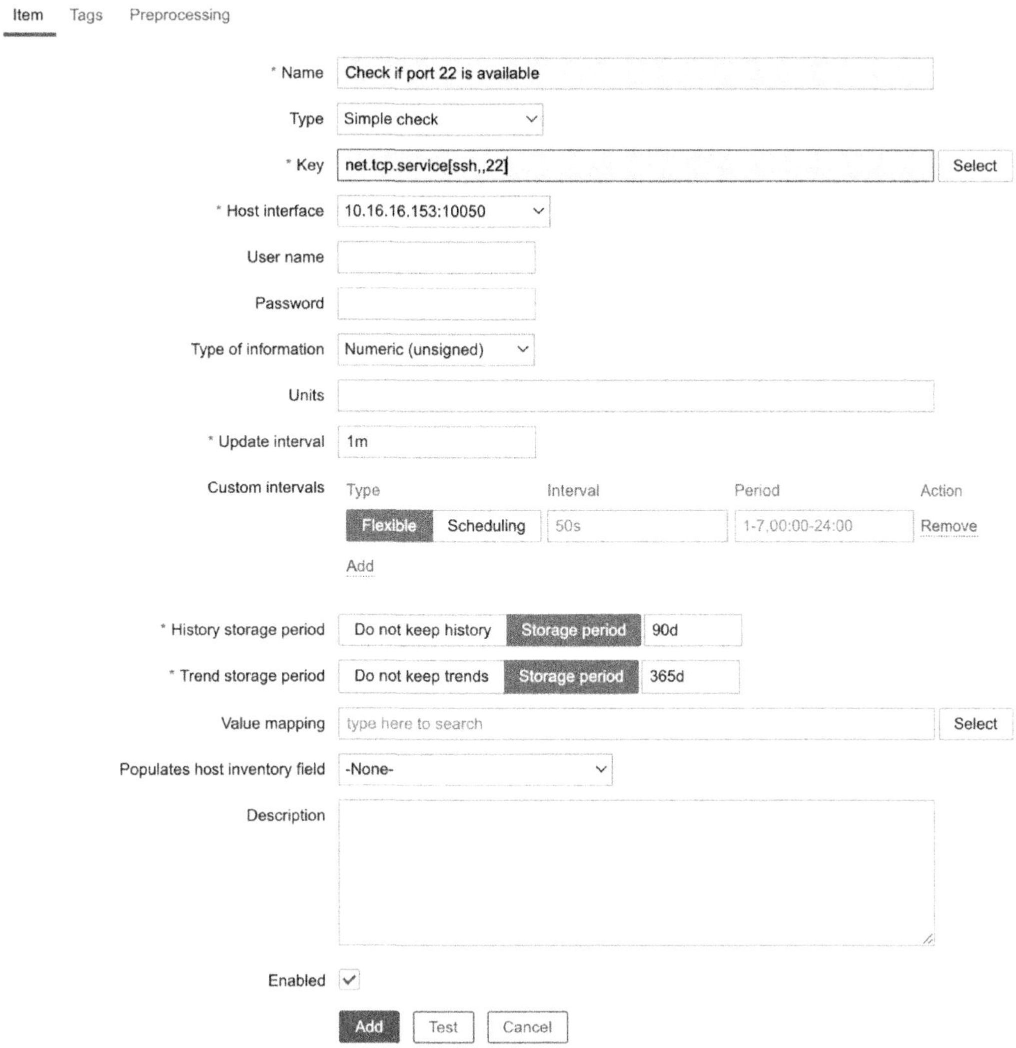

Item   Tags   Preprocessing

* Name	Check if port 22 is available
Type	Simple check ⌄
* Key	net.tcp.service[ssh,,22] Select
* Host interface	10.16.16.153:10050 ⌄
User name	
Password	
Type of information	Numeric (unsigned) ⌄
Units	
* Update interval	1m

Custom intervals

Type	Interval	Period	Action
Flexible Scheduling	50s	1-7,00:00-24:00	Remove

Add

* History storage period	Do not keep history Storage period 90d
* Trend storage period	Do not keep trends Storage period 365d
Value mapping	type here to search Select
Populates host inventory field	-None- ⌄
Description	

Enabled ✓

Add   Test   Cancel

Figure 3.18 – The Zabbix item configuration page for the port 22 check on the lar-book-agent_simple host

4. Make sure to add a tag to the item as well, as we need this in several places to filter and find our item when working with Zabbix. Set it up like this:

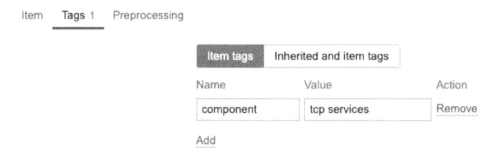

Figure 3.19 – Zabbix SSH port item, Tag tab

> **Important note**
> We are adding the item key net.tcp.services[ssh,,22] here. The port in this case is optional, as we can specify the service SSH with a different port if we want to.

5. Now we should be able to see whether our server is accepting SSH connections on port 22 on our **Latest data** screen. Navigate to **Monitoring | Hosts** and check the **Latest data** screen for our new value:

Figure 3.20 – Zabbix Latest data page for host lar-book-agent_simple, item port 22 check

6. There is one more thing wrong here. As you can see, we do not currently have a value mapping setup. The **Last value** is just displaying a 1 or 0. To change this, navigate back to **Configuration | Hosts** and edit the **lar-book-agent_simple** host.

7. Click on the **Value mapping** tab and click the small **Add** button to add a value mapping. Create the following:

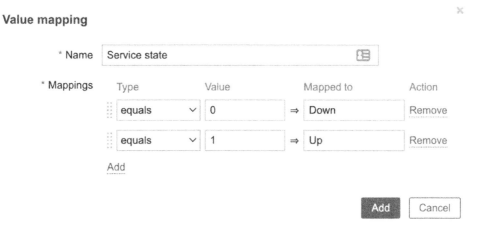

Figure 3.21 – Host lar-book-agent_simple, value mapping window

8. Click on the blue **Add** button and click on the blue **Update** button.

9. Then, back at the full **Configuration | Hosts** list, navigate to our `lar-book-agent_simple` host and click on **Items** for this host.

10. Edit the **Check if port 22 is available** item and add the value mapping as follows:

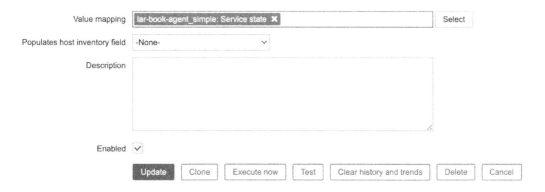

Figure 3.22 – Host lar-book-agent_simple, edit item window

That's all there is to creating your simple checks in Zabbix. The latest data page will now look like this:

Figure 3.23 – Latest data page for our port 22 check item

As you can see, there is a human-readable value now displaying either **Up** or **Down**, giving us a human-readable entry, which is easier to understand. Now let's move on to the Zabbix trapper item.

Creating a trapper

We can do some cool stuff with Zabbix trapper items once we get more advanced setups. But for now, let's create an item on our `lar-book-agent_simple` host:

1.   Go to **Configuration | Hosts** and click the host, then go to **Items**. We want to create a new item here again by clicking the **Create item** button.

Now let's create the following item and click the **Add** button:

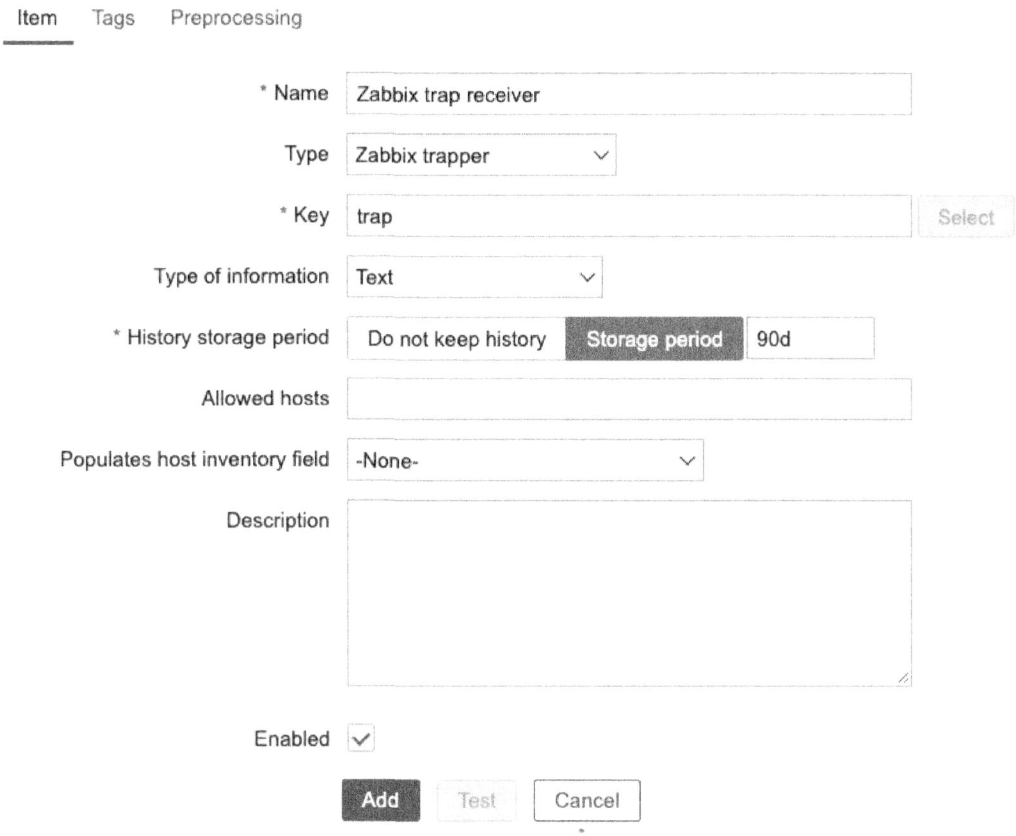

Item   Tags   Preprocessing

* Name	Zabbix trap receiver
Type	Zabbix trapper ▾
* Key	trap `Select`
Type of information	Text ▾
* History storage period	Do not keep history Storage period 90d
Allowed hosts	
Populates host inventory field	-None- ▾
Description	
Enabled	✓

Add   Test   Cancel

Figure 3.24 – Zabbix item trap receiver configuration screen for host lar-book-agent_simple

2. Make sure to also navigate to the **Tags** tab and add a tag that we will use later for filtering:

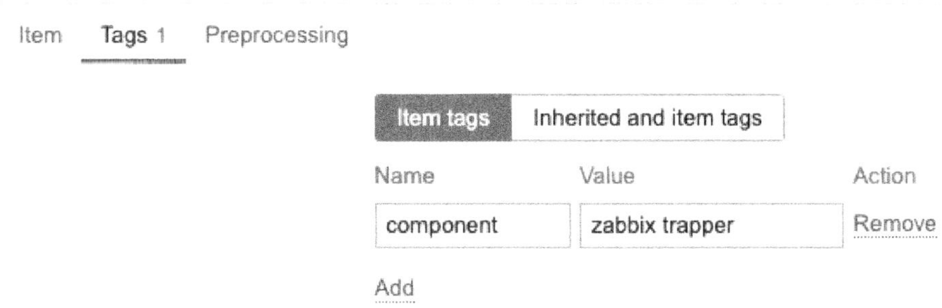

Item   **Tags** 1   Preprocessing

Item tags   Inherited and item tags

Name	Value	Action
component	zabbix trapper	Remove

Add

Figure 3.25 – Zabbix item trap receiver tag configuration screen for host lar-book-agent_simple

3. If we go to the CLI of our monitored server, we can now execute the following to install Zabbix sender:

```
RHEL-based systems:
dnf -y install zabbix-sender
Ubuntu systems:
apt install zabbix-sender
```

4. After installation, we can use Zabbix sender to send some information to our server:

```
zabbix_sender -z 10.16.16.152 -s "lar-book-agent_simple"
-k trap -o "Let's test this book trapper"
```

Now we should be able to see whether our monitored host has sent out the Zabbix trap and the Zabbix server has received this trap for processing.

5. Navigate to **Monitoring | Hosts** and check the **Latest data** screen for our new value:

Host	Name ▲	Last check	Last value
lar-book-agent_simple	Zabbix trap receiver	18s	Let's test this boo…

Figure 3.26 – Zabbix Latest data page for host lar-book-agent_simple, item trap receiver

There it is, our Zabbix trap in our Zabbix frontend.

How it works…

Now that we have built our new items, let's see how they work by diving into the theoretical side of Zabbix simple checks and trappers.

Simple checks

Zabbix simple checks are basically a list of built-in checks made for monitoring certain values. There is a list and description available on the Zabbix documentation for all the simple checks that are available here: `https://www.zabbix.com/documentation/current/manual/config/items/itemtypes/simple_checks`.

All of these checks are performed by the Zabbix server to collect data from a monitored host. For example, when we do the Zabbix simple check to check whether a port is open, our Zabbix server requests whether it can reach that port and turns that into a status we can then see in our Zabbix frontend.

This means that if your monitored host's firewall is blocking port 22 from Zabbix server, we'll get a service is *down* value. However, this does not necessarily mean that SSH isn't running on the server; it simply means SSH is down as seen from the side of the Zabbix server or proxy.

Figure 3.27 – Zabbix server-to-host communication diagram

> **Tip**
> Keep in mind that working with simple checks is dependent on external factors such as the firewall settings on the monitored host. When you build your own simple checks, make sure to check these factors as well.

Trappers

When working with Zabbix sender, we are doing exactly the opposite of most checks. We are building an item on our Zabbix server, which allows us to capture trap items. This allows us to build some custom checks to send data to our Zabbix server from a monitored host:

Figure 3.28 – Zabbix server trap receiver diagram

Let's say, for instance, that you want to build a custom Python script that, at the end of running the scripts, sends output to the Zabbix server. We could ask Python to send this data using the Zabbix sender utility, and then you'd have this data available for processing on the Zabbix server.

For example, it is used by some companies who write their own software to completely integrate their software into Zabbix. As you can see, we can greatly extend our options with Zabbix trapper and customize our Zabbix server even further.

Working with calculated and dependent items

Calculated and dependent items are used in Zabbix to produce additional values from existing values. Sometimes, we have already collected a value and we need to do more with the values created by that item. We can do exactly that by using calculated and dependent items.

Getting ready

To work with calculated items and dependent items, we are going to need the Zabbix server and monitored hosts from the previous recipes. We will add the items on the `lar-book-agent_passive` host and our Zabbix server (or any MySQL server) host, so we already have some items available to calculate and make dependent.

How to do it...

Let's see how we can extend our items by getting started with the calculated items.

Working with calculated items

1. Let's navigate to our host configuration by going to **Configuration | Hosts** and clicking on our `lar-book-agent_passive` host's **items**. In the filter field named **Name**, enter `memory` and you will get the following output:

Name ▲	Triggers	Key	Interval	History	Trends	Type	Status	Tags	Info
Linux by Zabbix agent: Available memory	Triggers 1	vm.memory.size[available]	1m	7d	365d	Zabbix agent	Enabled	component: memory	
Linux by Zabbix agent: Available memory in %	Triggers 1	vm.memory.size[pavailable]	1m	7d	365d	Zabbix agent	Enabled	component: memory	
Linux by Zabbix agent: Available memory in %: Memory utilization	Triggers 1	vm.memory.utilization		7d	365d	Dependent item	Enabled	component: memory	
Linux by Zabbix agent: Total memory	Triggers 1	vm.memory.size[total]	1m	7d	365d	Zabbix agent	Enabled	component: memory	

Displaying 4 of 4 found

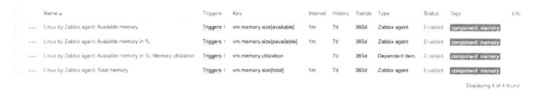

Figure 3.29 – Zabbix item page for host lar-book-agent_passive

2. What we are going to do now is create a calculated item that is going to show us the average memory utilization over a period of 15 minutes. We can use this value to determine how busy our host was during that period, without having to look at the graphs.

3. Let's click the **Create item** button and start creating our new calculated item. We want our item to have the following values:

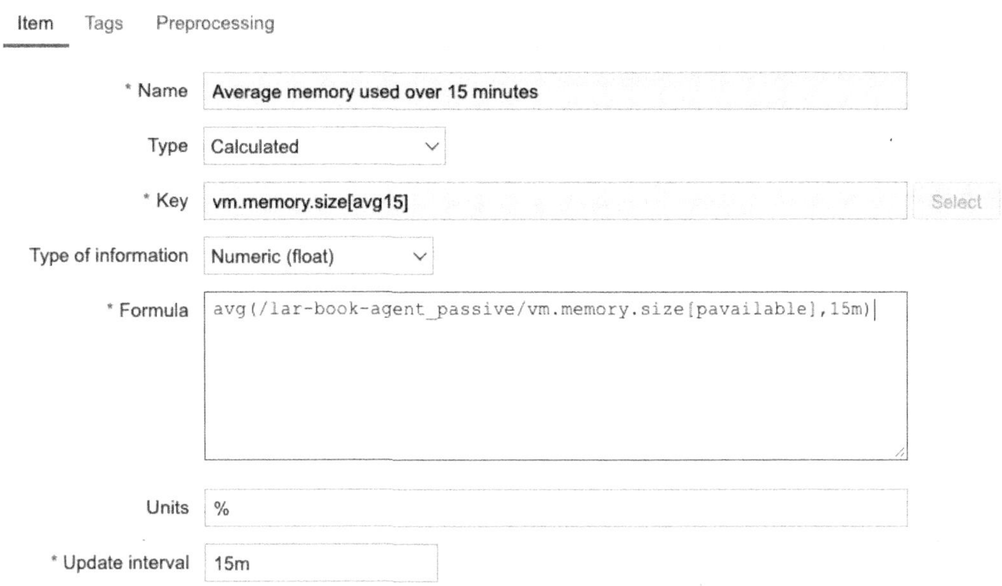

Item   Tags   Preprocessing

* Name	Average memory used over 15 minutes
Type	Calculated
* Key	vm.memory.size[avg15]
Type of information	Numeric (float)
* Formula	avg(/lar-book-agent_passive/vm.memory.size[pavailable],15m)
Units	%
* Update interval	15m

Figure 3.30 – Zabbix item configuration page, average memory used

4. Make sure to also navigate to the **Tags** tab and add a tag that we will use later for filtering:

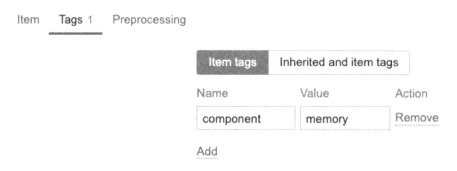

Figure 3.31 – Calculated item Tags tab

5. Now if we go to check our **Monitoring | Hosts** page and select **Latest data**, we can check out our value. Make sure to filter in the **Name** field for memory, so we see the correct values:

Host	Name ▲	Last check	Last value	Change
lar-book-agent_passive	Average memory used over 15 minutes	12m 35s	47.6076 %	+2.0391 %

Figure 3.32 – Zabbix Latest data page for host lar-book-agent_passive, memory items

Now we can clearly see that we are calculating the 15-minute average of the memory utilization on our newly created item.

Working with dependent items

Time to make our first dependent item. I'll use the lar-book-agent_centos host or our (as it's called by default) **Zabbix server**, but any MySQL database server should work. Let's say we want to request some variables from our MySQL database in one big batch. We can then create dependent items on top of the first item to further process the data:

1. Let's start by creating the main check. Navigate to **Configuration | Hosts**, select our host, and then let's click the **Create item** button to start creating our first new item. We want an item with the following variables:

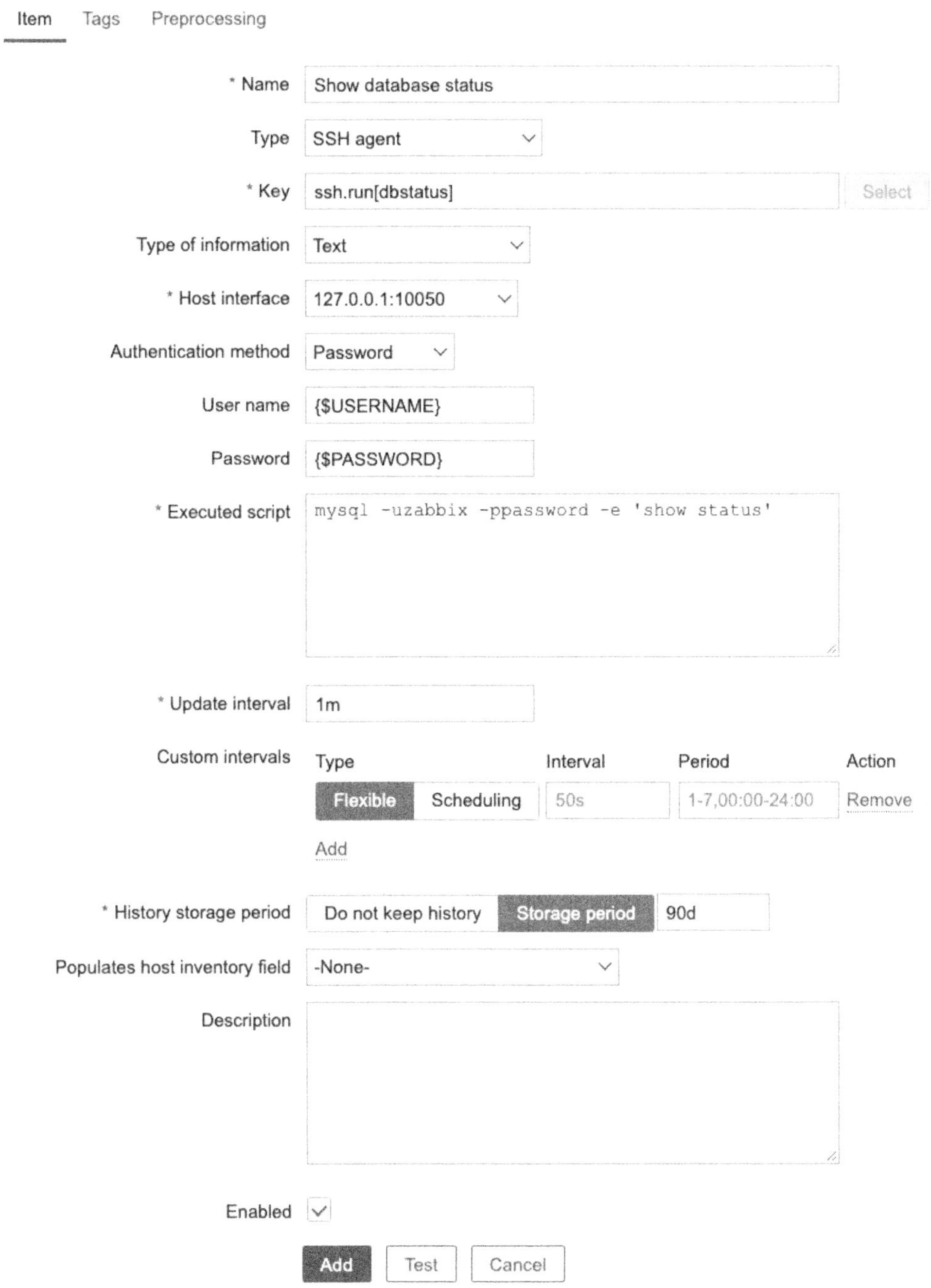

Item   Tags   Preprocessing

* Name	Show database status
Type	SSH agent ∨
* Key	ssh.run[dbstatus] Select
Type of information	Text ∨
* Host interface	127.0.0.1:10050 ∨
Authentication method	Password ∨
User name	{$USERNAME}
Password	{$PASSWORD}
* Executed script	mysql -uzabbix -ppassword -e 'show status'
* Update interval	1m

Custom intervals

Type		Interval	Period	Action
Flexible	Scheduling	50s	1-7,00:00-24:00	Remove

Add

* History storage period	Do not keep history Storage period 90d
Populates host inventory field	-None- ∨
Description	
Enabled	✓

Add   Test   Cancel

Figure 3.33 – Zabbix item configuration page, database status

Now, this item is an SSH check that logs in to our Zabbix server host using SSH and then executes the code as entered in the **Executed script** field. This code will then log in to our MariaDB database and it will print the status. Make sure to enter your credentials correctly.

> **Tip**
> Instead of using plain text credentials in the MySQL command, which is not recommended. Use macros in your **Executed script** field. This way, you can use the macro type **Secret text** to make sure no one can read your password from the frontend.

2. Before saving this new item, make sure to also add a tag like this:

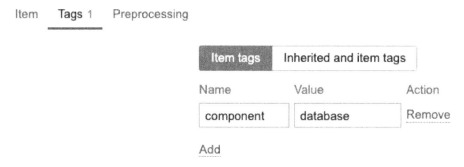

Figure 3.34 – Zabbix master item configuration page, Tags tab

3. Now click the blue **Add** button to save this new item.

4. Back at the list of items, let's click on this host's hostname and then **Macros**. Create a new {$USERNAME} and {$PASSWORD} macro with your SSH username and password as the **Value**.

5. Next, go to **Monitoring | Latest data** and check out the data for our new check. There should be a long list of MariaDB values. If so, we can continue with our next step of creating the dependent item.

6. To create the dependent item, navigate to **Configuration | Hosts**, select our host, and let's click the **Create item** button. We want this item to get the following variables:

Item   Tags   Preprocessing

* Name | MariaDB database aborted clients |

Type | Dependent item ⌄ |

* Key | mysql.aborted.clients | Select

Type of information | Numeric (unsigned) ⌄ |

* Master item | lar-book-centos: Show database status ✖ | Select

Units | |

* History storage period | Do not keep history | **Storage period** | 90d |

* Trend storage period | Do not keep trends | **Storage period** | 365d |

Value mapping | type here to search | Select

Populates host inventory field | -None- ⌄ |

Description | |

Enabled   ☑

Add   Test   Cancel

Figure 3.35 – Zabbix item configuration page, MariaDB aborted clients

7.   Make sure to add the tag, as follows:

Item   **Tags** 1   Preprocessing

Item tags	Inherited and item tags
Name	Value	Action
component	database	Remove

Add

Figure 3.36 – Zabbix dependent item configuration page, Tags tab

8. It's very important to add preprocessing to this item as well, otherwise, we will simply get the same data as our master item. So, let's add the following:

Figure 3.37 – Zabbix item Preprocessing page, MariaDB aborted clients

With the preprocessing added, the result will be the number of aborted clients for our MariaDB instance:

Host	Name ▲	Last check	Last value
lar-book-centos	MariaDB database aborted clients	18s	9

Figure 3.38 – Zabbix Latest data page, MariaDB aborted clients

As you can see, using a dependent item, we can use already available information from other Zabbix items and split them up into dependent items.

How it works...

The types we've discussed in this *How to do it…* section can be quite complicated; let's go over how the items actually work.

Calculated items

Working with calculated items can be a great way to get even more statistics out of your existing data. Sometimes you just need to combine multiple items into one specific value.

What we did just now works by taking several values of 1 item in a period of 15 minutes and calculating the average, as follows:

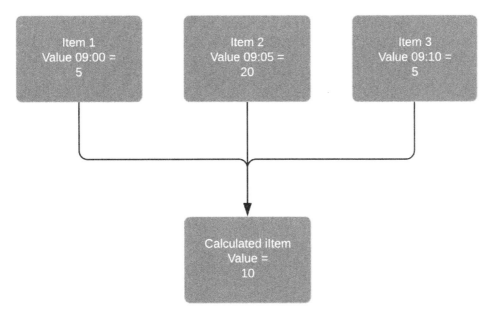

Figure 3.39 – Zabbix dependent item diagram

We're taking those values and calculating the average every 15 minutes. It gives us a nice indication of what we are doing over a set period of time.

Dependent items

Dependent items work simply by taking the data from a master item and processing that data into other data. This way, we can structure our data and keep our check interval for all these items the same:

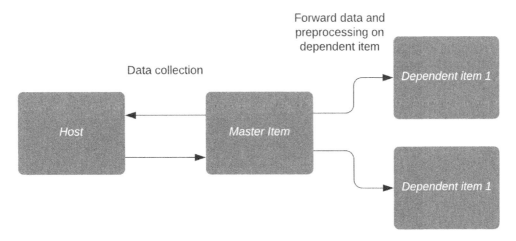

Figure 3.40 – Dependent item diagram

As seen here, dependent items basically work as duplicators, with additional preprocessing options. Do note that preprocessing must be used to extract data from the master item. Without preprocessing, our data will be exactly the same as the master item.

> **Tip**
>
> Sometimes we do not require our master item to be saved in our database; we already have the information in our dependent items. When we don't want the master item to be saved, we simply select the **Do not keep history** option on that master item.

Creating external checks

To further extend Zabbix functionality, we can use our own custom scripts, which are used by Zabbix external checks. Not everything that we want to monitor will always be standard in Zabbix, although a lot is. There's always something that could be missing, and external checks are just a way to bypass some of these.

Getting ready

For this recipe, we are going to need just our Zabbix server. We can create an item on our lar-book-centos host, which is our Zabbix server monitored host.

How to do it...

1. First, let's make sure our Zabbix server configuration is set up correctly. Execute the following on the Zabbix server CLI:

    ```
    cat /etc/zabbix/zabbix_server.conf | grep ExternalScripts=
    ```

2. This should show us the path where we will place the script that is used by the Zabbix external check. By default, this is /usr/lib/zabbix/externalscripts/, and we will create a new script called test_external in this folder with the following command:

    ```
    vim /usr/lib/zabbix/externalscripts/test_external
    ```

    Add the following code to this file and save:

    ```
    #!/bin/bash
    echo $1
    ```

3. Make sure our Zabbix server can execute the script by adding the right permissions to the file. The `zabbix` user on your Linux server needs to be able to access and execute the file:

```
chmod +x /usr/lib/zabbix/externalscripts/test_external
```

```
chown zabbix:zabbix /usr/lib/zabbix/externalscripts/test_external
```

4. Now we are ready to go to our host to create a new item. Navigate to **Configuration | Hosts**, select our host, **lar-book-centos**, and click the **Create item** button. We want this item to get the following variables:

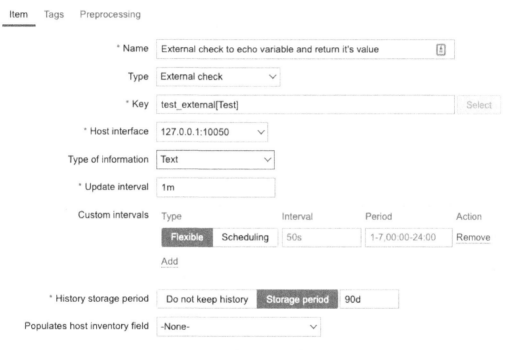

Figure 3.41 – Zabbix item configuration page

5. After adding this new item, let's navigate to **Monitoring | Hosts** and check the **Latest data** page for our host. We should get our **Test** variable returned by our script as the **Last value** in Zabbix, as shown in the following screenshot:

Figure 3.42 – Zabbix Latest data page

> **Tip**
>
> Use the macros in the frontend as variables to send data from your frontend to your scripts. You can further automate your checks with this to enhance your external checks.

How it works...

External checks seem like they have a steep learning curve, but they are actually quite simple from the Zabbix side. All we do is send a command to an external script and expect a result output:

Figure 3.43 – Zabbix server external script communication diagram

Like in our example, we sent the value `Test` to our script, which the script then, in turn, echoed back to us as `$1`.

When you have good knowledge of a programming language such as Python, you can use this function to build a lot more expansions on top of the current existing Zabbix feature set – a simple yet powerful tool to work with.

Setting up JMX monitoring

Built into Zabbix is JMX monitoring, so we can monitor our Java applications. In this recipe, we'll check out how to monitor Apache Tomcat with Zabbix JMX so we can get a feel for what this monitoring option is all about.

Getting ready

To get ready for this recipe, we are going to need our Zabbix server to monitor our JMX application.

I used a CentOS 7 machine for the example in this recipe, with Tomcat installed. It can be quite tricky to use Tomcat on later CentOS versions due to package dependencies, so I recommend sticking with CentOS 7 for the example. You can add the following to your Tomcat configuration after installation to get it working in our recipe:

```
JAVA_OPTS="-Djava.rmi.server.hostname=10.16.16.155
dcom.sun.management.jmxremote
```

```
dcom.sun.management.jmxremote.port=12345
dcom.sun.management.jmxremote.authenticate=false
dcom.sun.management.jmxremote.ssl=false"
```

If you want to set up JMX monitoring in your production environment, you can use the settings you have probably already set up there. Simply change the port and IP address accordingly.

How to do it...

To set up JMX monitoring, we are going to add a host to our Zabbix server that will monitor our Apache Tomcat installation. But first, we will need to add some settings to our /etc/zabbix/zabbix_server.conf file:

1. Let's edit the zabbix_server.conf file by logging in to our Zabbix server and executing the following command:

    ```
    vim /etc/zabbix/zabbix_server.conf
    ```

2. We will then need to add the following lines to this file:

    ```
    JavaGateway=127.0.0.1
    StartJavaPollers=5
    ```

    > **Tip**
    >
    > It's possible to install your Java gateway to a separate host from your Zabbix. This way we can spread the load and scale more easily. Simply install it to a separate host and add the IP address of that host to the **JavaGateway** parameter. We won't be doing this in the example, but keep the Java gateway setup on the Zabbix server host itself.

3. We will also need to install the zabbix-java-gateway application on our Zabbix server with the following command.

    RHEL-based systems:

    ```
    dnf install zabbix-java-gateway
    systemctl enable zabbix-java-gateway
    systemctl start zabbix-java-gateway
    systemctl restart zabbix-server
    ```

Ubuntu systems:

```
apt install zabbix-java-gateway
systemctl enable zabbix-java-gateway
systemctl start zabbix-java-gateway
systemctl restart zabbix-server
```

That is all we need to do on the server side of things to get JMX monitoring to work. Zabbix doesn't include these settings by default, so therefore we need to add the text to our file and install the application.

4. To get started with monitoring our JMX host, go to **Configuration | Hosts** in your Zabbix frontend and click **Create host** in the top-right corner.

    We will then add a host with the following settings:

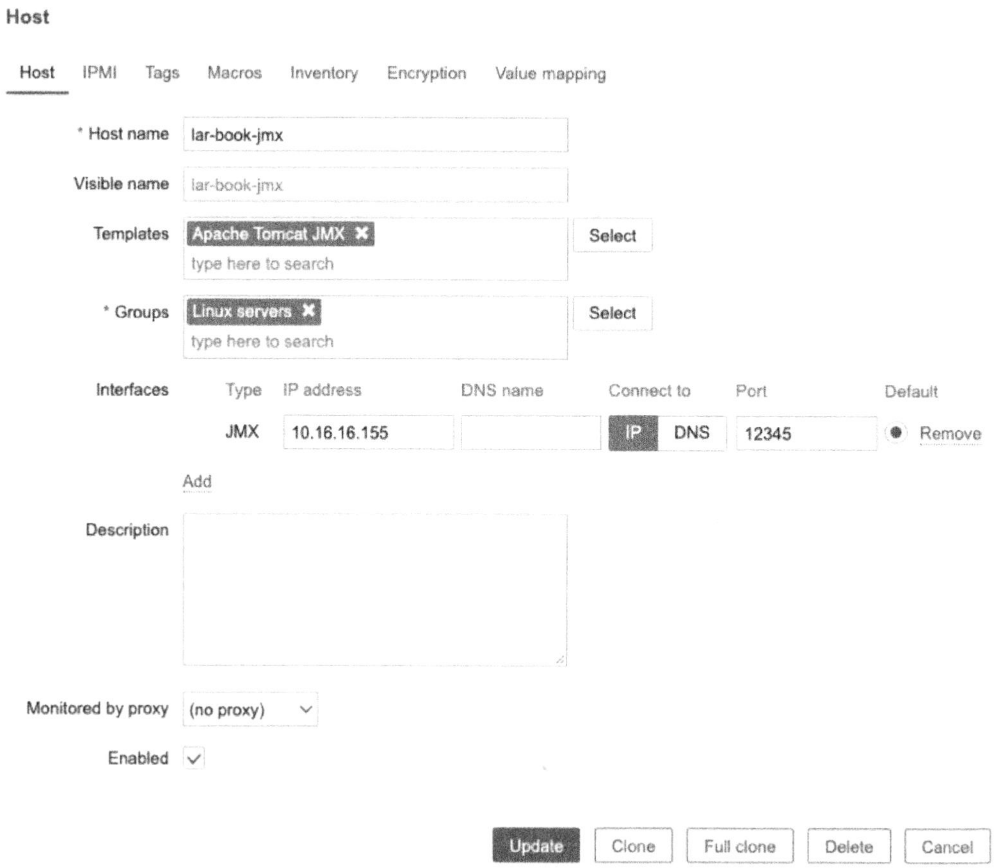

Figure 3.44 – Zabbix item configuration page

5. After this, our JMX icon should turn green; let's check this under **Monitoring |
    Hosts**. It should look like this:

Figure 3.45 – Zabbix Monitoring | Hosts page

6. If we click on **Latest data** for our new JMX monitored host, we should also see our
    incoming data. Check it out; it should return stats like these:

Figure 3.46 – Zabbix Latest data page

How it works...

Zabbix utilizes a Java gateway either hosted on the Zabbix server itself or hosted on
another server (proxy) to monitor JMX applications:

Figure 3.47 – Communication diagram between Zabbix server and Java

Zabbix polls the Java gateway and the Java gateway, in turn, communicates with our JMX
application, as it does with Tomcat in our example. The data in turn is then returned
through the same path and we can see our data in our Zabbix server.

See also

There are loads of applications that can be monitored through Zabbix JMX. Check out
the Zabbix monitoring and integrations page for more uses of Zabbix JMX monitoring:
`https://www.zabbix.com/integrations/jmx`.

Setting up database monitoring

Databases are a black hole to a lot of engineers; there's data being written to them and there's something being done with this data. But what if you want to know more about the health of your database? That's where Zabbix database monitoring comes in – we can use it to monitor the health of our database.

Getting ready

We'll be monitoring our Zabbix database, for convenience. This means that all we are going to need is our installed Zabbix server with our database on it. We'll be using MariaDB in this example, so if you have a PostgreSQL setup, make sure to install a MariaDB instance on a Linux host.

How to do it...

Before getting started with the item configuration, we'll have to do some stuff on the CLI side of the server:

1. Let's start by installing the required modules on our server.

   RHEL-based systems:

   ```
   dnf install unixODBC mariadb-connector-odbc
   ```

   Ubuntu systems:

   ```
   apt install odbc-mariadb unixodbc unixodbc-dev odbcinst
   ```

2. Now let's verify whether our **Open Database Connectivity** (**ODBC**) configuration files exist:

   ```
   odbcinst -j
   ```

   Your output should look as follows:

   ```
   unixODBC 2.3.7
   DRIVERS............: /etc/odbcinst.ini
   SYSTEM DATA SOURCES: /etc/odbc.ini
   FILE DATA SOURCES..: /etc/ODBCDataSources
   USER DATA SOURCES..: /root/.odbc.ini
   SQLULEN Size.......: 8
   SQLLEN Size........: 8
   SQLSETPOSIROW Size.: 8
   ```

3. If the output is correct, we can go to the Linux CLI and continue by editing `odbc.ini` to connect to our database:

```
vim /etc/odbc.ini
```

Now fill in your Zabbix database information. It will look like this:

```
[book]
Description = MySQL book test database
Driver      = mariadb
Server      = 127.0.0.1
Port        = 3306
Database    = zabbix
```

4. Now let's test whether our connection is working as expected by executing this:

```
isql -v book
```

You should get a message saying **Connected**; if you don't, then check your configuration files and try again.

5. Now let's move to the Zabbix frontend to configure our first database check. Navigate to **Configuration | Hosts** and click the host called `lar-book-centos`, or it might still be called **Zabbix server**. Now go to **Items**; we want to create a new item here by clicking the **Create item** button.

> **Tip**
>
> If you haven't already, a great way to keep your Zabbix structured is to keep all hostnames in Zabbix equal to the real server hostname. Rename your default **Zabbix server** host in the frontend to what you've actually called your server.

We want to add an item with the following parameters:

Item   Tags   Preprocessing

* Name	Numer of items configured in Zabbix database
Type	Database monitor ⌄
* Key	db.odbc.select[mariadb-simple-check,book] Select
Type of information	Numeric (unsigned) ⌄
User name	{$ODBC.USERNAME}
Password	{$ODBC.PASSWORD}
* SQL query	select count(*) from items
Units	
* Update interval	1m

Figure 3.48 – Zabbix item configuration page, items in Zabbix database

6.   Make sure to also add a tag to the item:

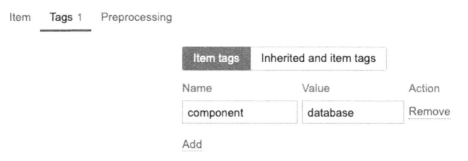

Item   **Tags** 1   Preprocessing

Item tags	Inherited and item tags	
Name	Value	Action
component	database	Remove
Add		

Figure 3.49 – Zabbix item configuration page, items in Zabbix database, Tags tab

7. Now click the **Add** button and click on the name of the host to add the macros, as follows:

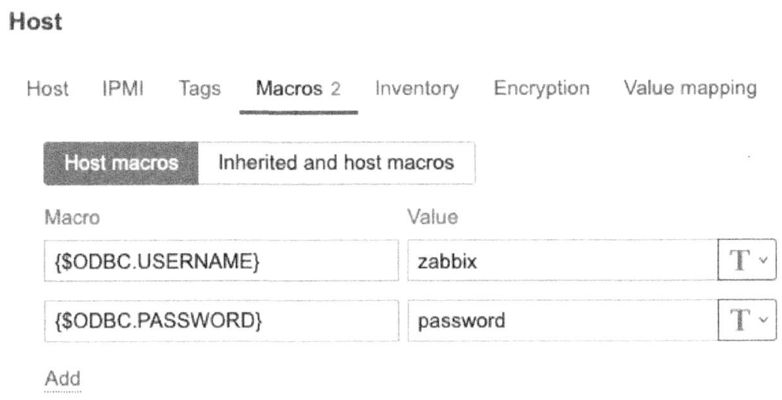

Host

| Host | IPMI | Tags | **Macros** 2 | Inventory | Encryption | Value mapping |

| **Host macros** | Inherited and host macros |

Macro	Value	
{$ODBC.USERNAME}	zabbix	T ˅
{$ODBC.PASSWORD}	password	T ˅

Add

Figure 3.50 – Zabbix host macro configuration page

8. Now if you go to **Monitoring | Hosts** and click on **Latest data** for our host, you'll get to see this:

| Host ▾ | Name | Last check | Last value | Change | Tags |
| lar-book-centos | Number of items configured in Zabbix database | 1m 5s | 3899 | | Application: Database |

Figure 3.51 – Zabbix Latest data page for host lar-book-centos, items in Zabbix database

We can now see directly from the database how many items are written to it.

How it works...

The Zabbix database monitoring works by connecting to your database with the ODBC middleware API. Any database supported by ODBC can be queried with Zabbix database monitoring:

Figure 3.52 – A diagram showing communication between the Zabbix server and ODBC

Basically, your Zabbix server sends a command with, for instance, your MySQL query to the ODBC connector. Your ODBC connecter sends this query to the database through the ODBC API, which in turn returns a value to ODBC. ODBC then forwards the value to the Zabbix server and hey presto: we have a value under our item.

There's more...

You can do loads of queries to your databases with Zabbix database monitoring, but keep in mind that you are working with actual queries. Querying a database takes time and processing power, so keep your database monitoring structured and define the right execution times.

Alternatively, we can use Zabbix agent 2 to monitor most databases natively. This can improve security and performance and keep complexity lower.

Setting up HTTP agent monitoring

With the Zabbix HTTP agent, we can monitor a web page or API by retrieving data from it. For instance, if there's a counter on a web page and we want to keep an eye on that counter value, we can do so with the Zabbix HTTP monitor.

Getting ready

We are going to need a web page to monitor and we will need our Zabbix server. For your convenience, we've added a page to our own website to retrieve a value from. Here's the page: `https://oicts.com/book-page/`.

Please also note that your Zabbix server will need an active internet connection for this recipe.

How to do it...

Let's poll the special web page we've created for you showing a visitor count that's currently configured on it. This is a real counter for the number of times (unique) visitors have opened the URL:

1.   Navigate to your Zabbix frontend and navigate to **Configuration | Hosts**, then click the host called **lar-book-agent_simple**.

2. Now go to **Items**; we want to create a new item here by clicking the **Create item** button. We are going to need to create an **HTTP agent** item as shown in the following screenshot:

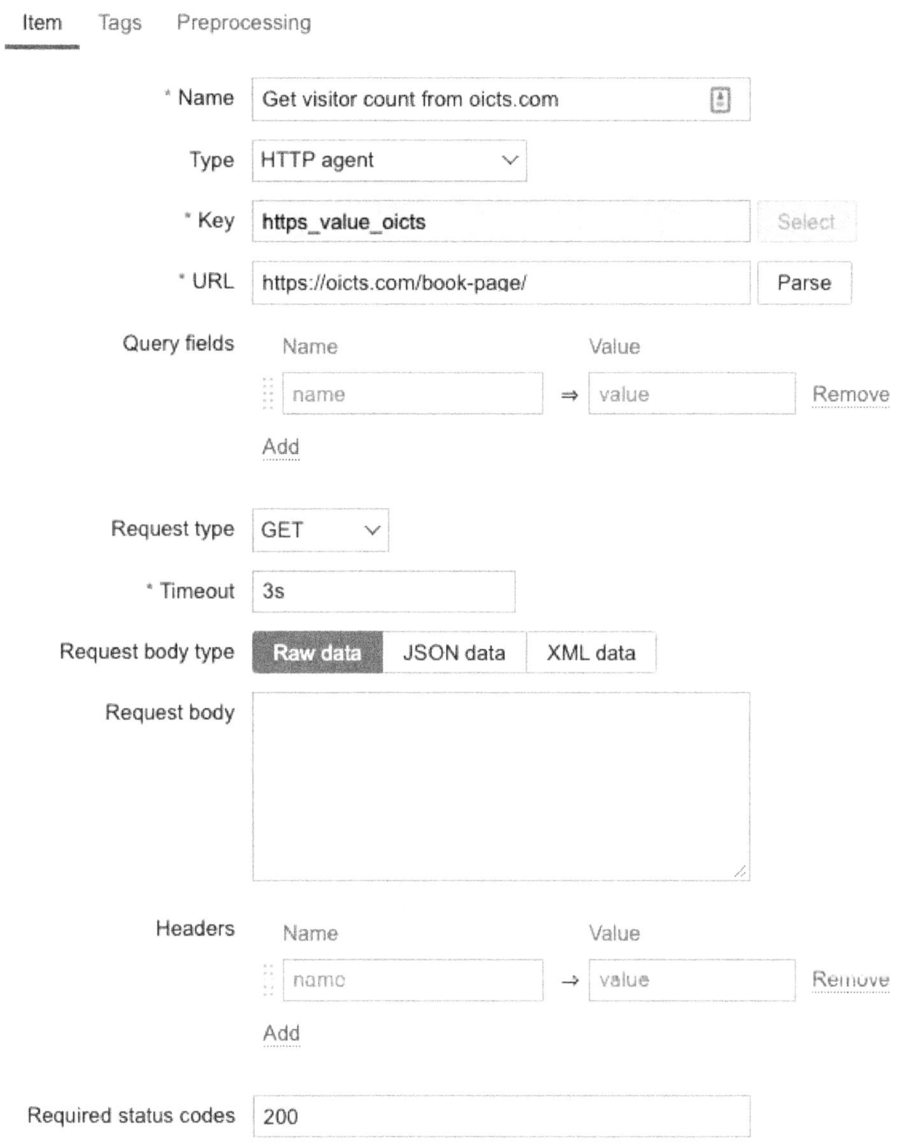

Item   Tags   Preprocessing

* Name	Get visitor count from oicts.com
Type	HTTP agent
* Key	https_value_oicts Select
* URL	https://oicts.com/book-page/ Parse
Query fields	Name Value
	name ⇒ value Remove
	Add
Request type	GET
* Timeout	3s
Request body type	Raw data JSON data XML data
Request body	
Headers	Name Value
	name → value Remove
	Add
Required status codes	200

Figure 3.53 – Zabbix Item configuration page, visitor count on the oicts.com page

3.   Do not forget to edit **Type of information**.

Figure 3.54 – Zabbix Item configuration page, visitor count on oicts.com page, lower part of the page

4.   We'll also need to add a tag to this item.

Figure 3.55 – Zabbix Item configuration page, visitor count on oicts.com page, Tags tab

5.   Use the following preprocessing steps:

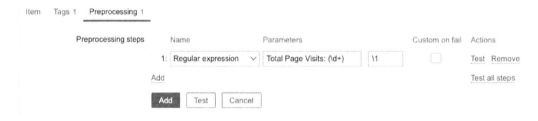

Figure 3.56 – Zabbix Item configuration page, visitor count on oicts.com page, Preprocessing tab

6.   Now navigate to **Monitoring | Hosts** and open the **Latest data** page for our `lar-book-agent_simple` host. If everything is working as it should, we should now be requesting this page's visitor count every 15 minutes as follows:

Figure 3.57 – Zabbix Latest data page

How it works...

What we do here is request the complete web page from Zabbix by navigating to the page with the HTTP agent and downloading it. When we have the complete content of the page, in this case, an HTML/PHP page, we can process the data:

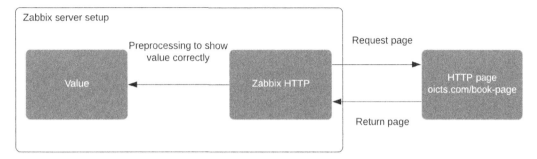

Figure 3.58 – Diagram showing Zabbix HTTP agent communication

We ask our preprocessor via a regex to go through the requested code and only show the number behind where it says **Total Page Visits:**.

All that's left is the number, ready for us to use in graphs and other types of data visualization.

Using Zabbix preprocessing to alter item values

Preprocessing item values is an important functionality in Zabbix; we can use it to create all kinds of checks. We've already done some preprocessing in this chapter, but let's take a deeper dive into it and what it does.

Getting started

We are going to need a Zabbix server to create our check for. We will also need a passive Zabbix agent on a Linux host to get our values from and preprocess them. We can use the agent that is running on our Zabbix server for this; in my case, this is `lar-book-centos`.

How to do it...

1. Let's start by logging in to our Zabbix frontend and going to **Configuration | Hosts**.

2. Click on your Zabbix server host; in my case, it's called `lar-book-centos`.

3. Now go to **Items** and click on the blue **Create item** button in the top-right corner. Let's create a new item with the following information:

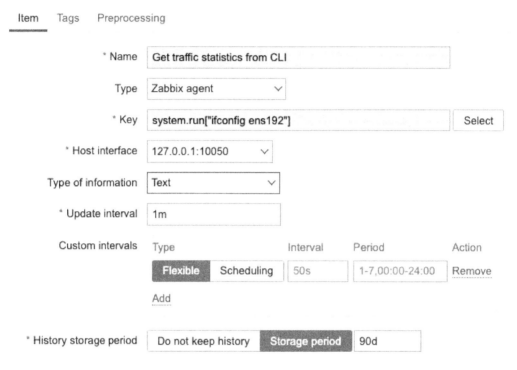

Figure 3.59 – New item creation screen, Get traffic statistics from CLI

4. Do not forget to add your tag:

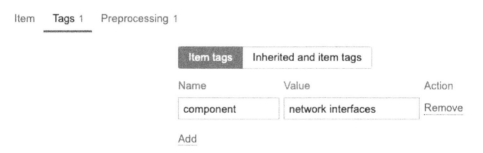

Figure 3.60 – New item creation screen, Get traffic statistics from CLI, Tags tab

5. Make sure to change `ens192` to your own primary network interface. You can find your primary network interface by logging in to the Linux CLI and executing the following:

```
Ifconfig
```

6. Back at the create item screen, click on the blue **Add** button. This item will use the Zabbix agent to execute a remote command on the Linux CLI.

7. When we navigate to this new item, we can see that the item becomes unsupported. This is because when we use the `system.run` key, we need to allow it in the Zabbix agent configuration:

Figure 3.61 – Unsupported item information, Unknown metric system.run

8. Log in to the Linux CLI of the monitored host and edit the Zabbix agent configuration with this:

```
vim /etc/zabbix/zabbix_agent2.conf
```

9. Go to the **Option: AllowKey** line and add **AllowKey=system.run[*]** as shown here:

```
### Option: AllowKey
#       Allow execution of item keys matching pattern.
#       Multiple keys matching rules may be defined in combination with DenyKey.
#       Key pattern is wildcard expression, which support "*" character to match any
  number of any characters in certain position. It might be used in both key name and
  key arguments.
#       Parameters are processed one by one according their appearance order.
#       If no AllowKey or DenyKey rules defined, all keys are allowed.
#
# Mandatory: no
AllowKey=system.run[*]
```

Figure 3.62 – Zabbix agent configuration file, AllowKey=system.run[*]

10. Save the file and restart the Zabbix agent with this:

```
systemctl restart zabbix-agent2
```

11. Back at the Zabbix frontend, the error we noticed in *step 7* should be gone after a few minutes.

12. Navigate to **Monitoring | Latest data** and filter on your Zabbix server host **lar-book-centos** and the name of the new **Get traffic statistics from CLI** item.

13. The value should now be pulled from the host. If we click on **History**, we can see the full value; it should look as follows:

```
Timestamp          Value

2020-12-08 11:47:24  ens192: flags=4163<UP,BROADCAST,RUNNING,MULTICAST>  mtu 1500
                        inet 10.16.16.152  netmask 255.255.255.0  broadcast 10.16.16.255
                        inet6 fe80::c462:d30e:b24a:b31d  prefixlen 64  scopeid 0x20<link>
                        ether 00:0c:29:5e:c8:2c  txqueuelen 1000  (Ethernet)
                        RX packets 128297172  bytes 24030338556 (22.3 GiB)
                        RX errors 0  dropped 783  overruns 0  frame 0
                        TX packets 134639844  bytes 42556882891 (39.6 GiB)
                        TX errors 0  dropped 0 overruns 0  carrier 0  collisions 0
```

Figure 3.63 – Zabbix agent system.run command executing ifconfig ens192 results

14. The information seen in the image is way too much for just one item. We need to split this up. Let's use preprocessing to get the number of RX bytes from the information.

15. Go back to **Configuration | Hosts** and click on your Zabbix server host. Go to **Items** on this host.

16. Click on the **Get traffic statistics from CLI** item to edit it. Change the name to `Total RX traffic in bytes for ens192` and add B to **Units**, where B stands for bytes. It will look like this:

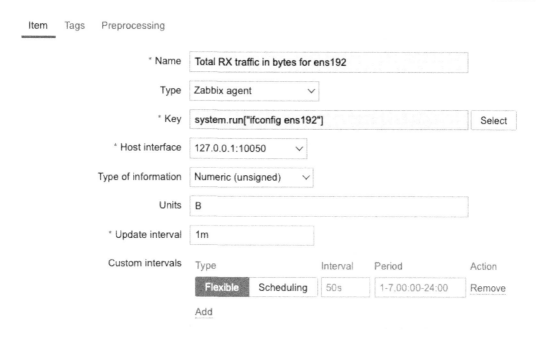

Figure 3.64 – Zabbix agent system.run item

17. Add your tag:

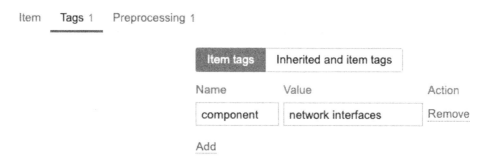

Figure 3.65 – New item creation screen, Get traffic statistics from CLI, Tags tab

18. Now click on **Preprocessing** and click on the underlined **Add** button.

19. A **Regular expression** (regex) field will be added, which we are going to fill to match the total number of bytes for your interface. Fill in the following:

Figure 3.66 – Zabbix agent system.run item preprocessing

20. Make sure to also select the box under **Custom on fail**.

21. Let's click on the underlined **Add** button again and use the drop-down menu for this new step to select **Discard unchanged**. The end result will look like this:

Figure 3.67 – Zabbix agent system.run item preprocessing

22. We can now click the blue **Update** button to finish editing this item.

23. Navigate back to **Monitoring | Latest data** and filter on your host and the new item name, **Total RX traffic in bytes for ens192**. Make sure to use your own interface name.

24. We can now see our value coming in, and we have an item displaying our total RX traffic for our main interface:

Figure 3.68 – Zabbix Total RX traffic item latest data

How it works...

We've already done some preprocessing in the *Working with calculated and dependent items* recipe to get data from a master item. We also used preprocessing in the *Setting up HTTP agent monitoring* recipe to get a specific value from a web page. We didn't go over the preprocessing concepts used in those recipes, though, so let's go over them.

When working with preprocessing, it's important to know the basic setup. Let's take a look at the incoming data before we used preprocessing:

Timestamp	Value
2020-12-08 11:47:24	ens192: flags=4163<UP,BROADCAST,RUNNING,MULTICAST> mtu 1500
	inet 10.16.16.152 netmask 255.255.255.0 broadcast 10.16.16.255
	inet6 fe80::c462:d30e:b24a:b31d prefixlen 64 scopeid 0x20<link>
	ether 00:0c:29:5e:c8:2c txqueuelen 1000 (Ethernet)
	RX packets 128297172 bytes 24030338556 (22.3 GiB)
	RX errors 0 dropped 783 overruns 0 frame 0
	TX packets 134639844 bytes 42556882891 (39.6 GiB)
	TX errors 0 dropped 0 overruns 0 carrier 0 collisions 0

Figure 3.69 – Zabbix agent system.run command executing ifconfig ens192 results

This is a lot of information. When we look at how Zabbix items are used, we try to put graspable information in a single item. Luckily, we can preprocess this item before we store the value in Zabbix. In the following figure, we can see the preprocessing steps we added to our item:

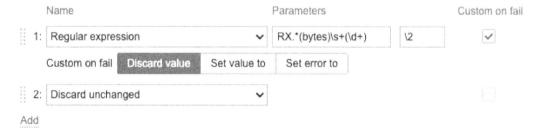

Figure 3.70 – Zabbix agent system.run item preprocessing with two steps

Our first step is a regex. This step will make sure to only use the numbers we need. We match on the word **RX**, then the word **bytes**, and a sequence of numbers after them. This way, we end up with the total number of RX bytes in capture group 2. This is why we fill in \2 in the **output** field. We also specify **Custom on fail**, which will discard any value if the regex doesn't match.

Our second step is to discard any values that are the same as the value received before. Instead of storing duplicate values, we simply discard them and save some space in our Zabbix database.

> **Tip**
>
> It's a lot easier to build a regex when using an online tool such as `https://regex101.com/`. You can see what number your capture groups will get, and there's a lot of valuable information in the tools as well.

It's important to note here that steps are executed in the sequence they are defined in the frontend. If the first step fails, the item becomes unsupported unless **Custom on fail** is set to do something else.

By adding preprocessing to Zabbix, we open up a whole range of options for our items, and we are able to alter our data in almost any way required. These two steps are just the beginning of the options opened up when diving into the world of Zabbix preprocessing.

See also

Preprocessing in Zabbix is an important subject, and it's impossible to cover every aspect of it in a single recipe. The two preprocessing steps in this recipe's example are just two of the many options we can use. Check out the official Zabbix documentation to see the other options we can use:

`https://www.zabbix.com/documentation/current/en/manual/config/items/preprocessing`

4
Working with Triggers and Alerts

Now, what use would all of that collected data in Zabbix be without actually doing some alerting with it? Of course, we can use Zabbix to collect our data and just go over it manually, but Zabbix gets a lot more useful when we actually start sending out notifications to users. This way, we don't have to always keep an eye on our Zabbix frontend, but we can just let our triggers and alerts do the work for us, redirecting us to the frontend only when we need it.

In Zabbix 6, you will find a new trigger expressions syntax compared to Zabbix 5. This syntax has been available since Zabbix 5.4, so this is the first time we'll be working with it in an LTS release. If you've worked with Zabbix before version 6, keep in mind that you might need to get used to this new syntax.

We will learn all about setting up effective triggers with the new expression format and about alerts in the following recipes:

- Setting up triggers
- Setting up advanced triggers
- Setting up alerts
- Keeping alerts effective
- Customizing alerts

Technical requirements

For this chapter, we will need a Zabbix server—for instance, the one used in the previous chapter, which would be the following:

- A server with Zabbix server installed on a Linux distribution of your choice, such as CentOS or Ubuntu, but a distribution such as Debian or any other will suit you just as well

- MariaDB set up to work with your Zabbix server

- NGINX or Apache set up to serve the Zabbix frontend

We will also need a Linux host to monitor so that we can actually build some cool triggers to use.

Setting up triggers

Triggers are important in Zabbix because they notify you as to what's going on with your data. We want to get a trigger when our data reaches a certain threshold.

So, let's get started with setting up some cool triggers. There are loads of different options for defining triggers, but after reading this recipe you should be able to set up some of the most prominent triggers. Let's take your trigger experience to the next level.

Getting ready

For this recipe, we will need our Zabbix server ready and we will need a Linux host. I will use the `lar-book-agent_simple` host from the previous chapter because we already have some items on that.

We'll also need one more host that is monitored by the Zabbix agent with the Zabbix agent template. We'll use one of the items on this host to create a trigger. This will be the `lar-book-agent_passive` host from the previous chapter.

On this host, we will already have some triggers available, but we will extend these triggers further to inform us even better.

How to do it...

In this section, we are going to create three triggers to monitor state changes. Let's get started by creating our first trigger.

Trigger 1 – SSH service monitoring

Let's create a simple trigger on the `lar-book-agent_simple` host. We made a simple check on this host called `Check if port 22 is available`, but we haven't created anything to notify us on this yet:

1. First, let's get started by going to **Configuration | Hosts**, then clicking the host and going to **Triggers**. This is where we will find our triggers and where we can create them. We want to create a new trigger here by clicking the blue **Create trigger** button in the top-right corner.

2. Let's create a new trigger with the following information:

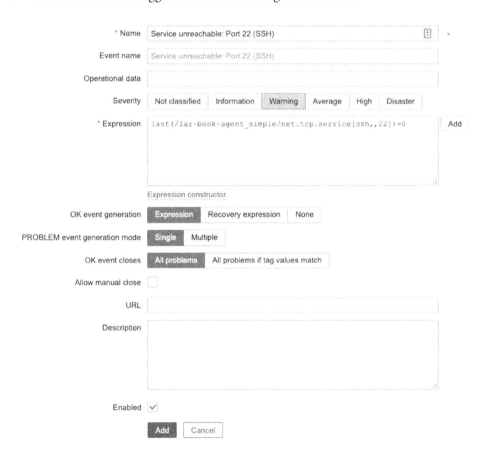

Figure 4.1 – The Zabbix trigger creation page, Service unreachable

3. Click on **Add** and finish creating the trigger. This will create a trigger for us that will fire when our **Secure Shell (SSH)** port goes down.

4. Let's test this by navigating to our host **command-line interface (CLI)** and executing some commands to shut our Zabbix server off from port 22. We will add an `iptables` rule to block off all incoming traffic on port 22 (SSH):

```
iptables -A INPUT -p tcp -i ens192 -s 10.16.16.152
--destination-port 22 -j DROP
```

5. Make sure to change the network card `ens192` and the IP address `10.16.16.152` to your own values respectively. You can use the following command to get that information:

```
ip addr
```

6. Now, if we check out **Monitoring | Dashboard**, after a while we should see the following:

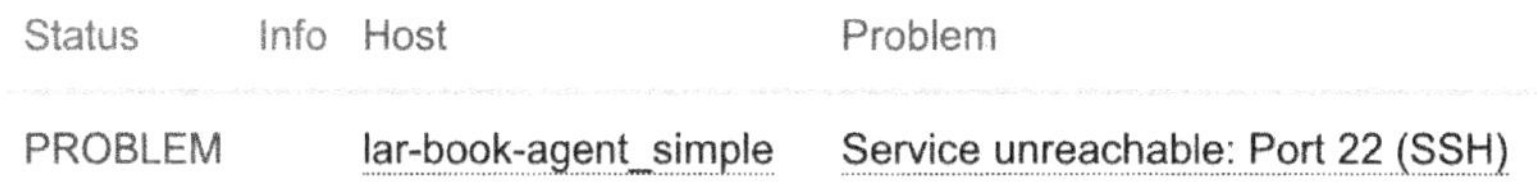

Status	Info	Host	Problem
PROBLEM		lar-book-agent_simple	Service unreachable: Port 22 (SSH)

Figure 4.2 – The Zabbix problem page, port 22 down

Trigger 2 – Triggering on-page visitor count

Now, to create our second trigger, let's ramp it up a bit. If you followed *Chapter 3*, *Setting Up Zabbix Monitoring*, in the recipe titled *Setting up HTTP agent monitoring*, we created an item that polls one of our website pages for its visitor count. Now, what we probably want to do ourselves is keep an eye out for how well all of our readers are doing reaching the web page part of the book and building an item for it:

1. Let's navigate to **Configuration | Hosts** and click the `lar-book-agent_simple` host.

2. Now, go to **Triggers** and click the **Create trigger** button. We will build our trigger with the following settings:

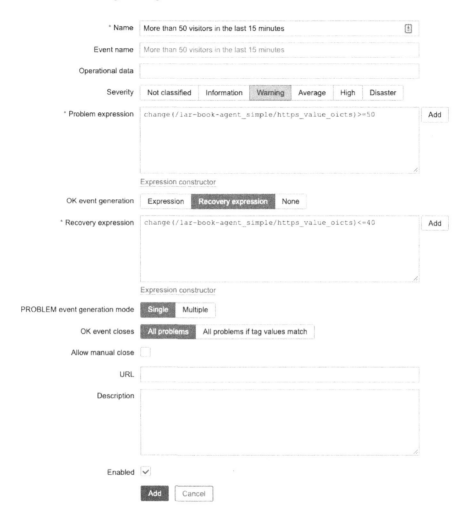

Figure 4.3   The Zabbix trigger creation page, More than 50 visitors trigger

3. Click on **Add** and finish creating the trigger.

4. Now, this might not actually trigger for you in the frontend, but I'll explain to you just how this trigger works in the *How it works...* section of this recipe.

Trigger 3 – Using multiple items in a trigger

We have seen triggers that use one item, but we can also use multiple items in a single trigger. Let's build a new trigger by using multiple items in the same expression:

1. Let's navigate to **Configuration | Hosts** and click the `lar-book-agent_ passive` host. Now, go to **Triggers** and click the **Create trigger** button.

2. We are going to create a trigger with the following settings:

Figure 4.4 – The Zabbix trigger creation page, inbound or outbound packets trigger

3. Please note that your item keys might actually need different interface names. In my case, the interface is called `ens192`, so use the correct name for your interface in its place. Use the following Linux command to get the interface on your host:

    ```
    ip addr
    ```

4. Click on **Add** and finish creating the trigger.

    Tip: On the trigger creation page, use the **Add** button next to the **Expression** field to add a condition and build your expression easily. For example, we can use the **Select** button to pick an item from a list. Also very useful, when using the **Function** drop-down menu, there's a short explanation for every trigger function included:

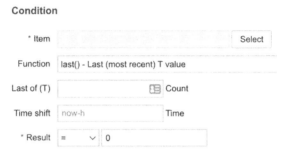

Figure 4.5 – Trigger creation page

5. That's all we need to do to build a trigger that will function on two items.

How it works...

We need a good understanding of how to build triggers and how they work, so we can create a well-set-up monitoring system. Especially important here is that we make sure that our triggers are set up correctly and we test them well. Triggers are a very important part of Zabbix as they will be informing you of things actively. Configure your triggers too loosely and you will be missing things. Configure them too strictly and you will be overloaded with information.

In all of these triggers, we have also included a trigger severity, as we can see in the screenshot below.

Figure 4.6 – A Zabbix trigger severity selector

These severities are important to make sure your alerts will be correctly defined by importance. We can also filter on these severities in several places in the Zabbix frontend and even in things like actions.

Now, let's discover why we built our triggers as we did.

Trigger 1 – SSH service monitoring

This is a very simple but effective trigger to set up in Zabbix. When our value returns us either a 1 for UP or a 0 for DOWN, we can easily create triggers such as these—not just for monitoring logical ports that are up or down, but for everything that returns us a simple value change from, for example, 1 to 0 and vice versa.

Now, if we break down our expression, we will see the following:

Figure 4.7 – A Zabbix trigger expression, port 22 (SSH)

When building an expression, we have four parts:

- **Trigger function**: The trigger function is the part of the expression that determines what we expect of the value, such as whether we want just the value or an average value over a period of time.

- **Host**: The host part of the expression is where we define which host we are using to trigger on. Most of the time, it's simply just the host (or template) we are working on.

- **Item key**: The item key is the part of the expression where we define which item key we'll be using to retrieve a value on a host.

- **Operator**: The operator determines what our function will use to calculate the trigger expression against the constant or another item. The operator can be anything like the following:

=	Equal to
<>	Not equal to
>	Bigger than
<	Smaller than
>=	Bigger than or equal to
<=	Smaller than or equal to
+	Add
-	Subtract
/	Divide by
*	Multiply by

Table 4.1 – Operators and their functions

- **Constant**: The constant is the actual constant (often a value) that our trigger function uses to determine whether the trigger should be in an OK or a PROBLEM state.

Now, for our first trigger, we defined our host and the item that gives us the SSH status. What we are asking in the trigger function is that we want the last value to be 0 before triggering it.

For this item, that would mean it would trigger within a minute because in our item we specified the following:

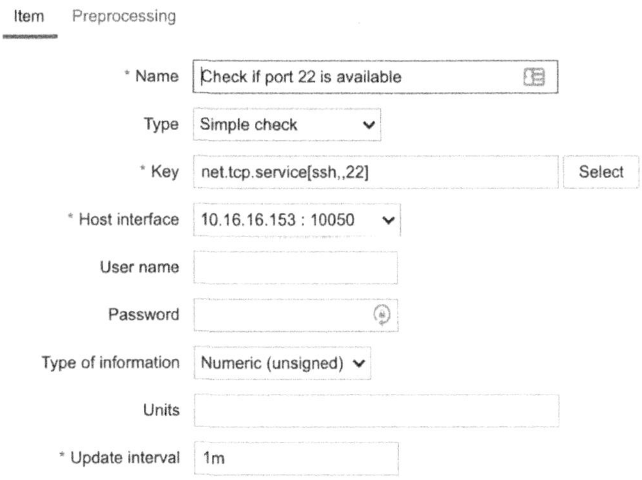

Figure 4.8 – The Zabbix item configuration page, port 22 availability item

Looking at the **Update interval** field on the **Item** configuration page, we can determine that when building this trigger, we are expecting our value to be 0 and that it will take a maximum of 1 minute of SSH port 22 downtime due to the 1-minute interval.

Trigger 2 – Triggering on-page visitor count

Now, for our second trigger, we did something different. We not only made an expression for triggering this problem, but also one for recovering from the trigger. What we do in the **Problem expression** option is define a trigger function, telling our host to compare the last value with the latest value and calculate the difference between the values. We then state this trigger function has to be >=50, meaning equal to or higher than 50.

Figure 4.9 – A Zabbix trigger expression, HTTPS check

So, our trigger will only be activated when we have more than or equal to 50 visitors between the last and previous value for this specific page. Now, we could do the same with the previous trigger and let it recover once it hits the same value again, but the other way around. This means that, for this trigger, it would recover once our visitor count between the last and previous value drops below 50 again. But I want to keep this trigger in the PROBLEM state just a little longer.

Therefore, I defined a recovery expression as well. I'm telling it that this problem can only recover if the visitor count between the last and previous value has dropped below or was equal to 40. Check out the recovery expression up close:

Figure 4.10 – Another Zabbix trigger expression, HTTPS check with different value

Recovery expressions are powerful when you want to extend your trigger functionality with just a bit more control over when it comes back into the OK state.

> **Tip**
>
> You can use the recovery expression for extending the trigger's PROBLEM state beyond what you defined in the **Problem expression** option. This way, we know we are still close to the PROBLEM state. We define that we only want the trigger to go back to the OK state after we've reached another threshold as defined in the recovery expression.

Trigger 3 – Using multiple items in a trigger

Now, trigger 3 might seem complicated because we've used more than one item, but it's basically the same setup:

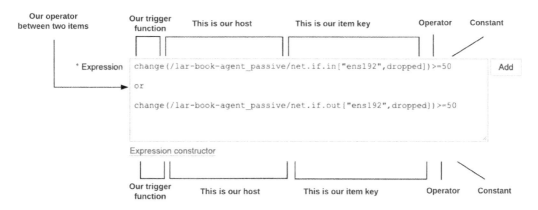

Figure 4.11 – A Zabbix trigger expression using several items

We have the same setup for the expression, with function/host/item key/value. Yet when we are working with multiple items, we can add an or statement between the items. This way, we can say we need to match one of the items before triggering the PROBLEM state. In this case, we trigger when either item reaches above the threshold.

> **Important Note**
>
> In this trigger expression, we have some empty lines between the different item expressions. Empty lines between item expressions are totally fine and actually make for good readability. Use this wisely when building triggers.

Old versus new trigger expression syntax

Now if you've worked with Zabbix before, the next part might be interesting to you. As mentioned in our introduction, there is a big update to expressions within Zabbix. Trigger expressions now work in a new way, which is the same way as you will see in calculated items and other places for a unified experience.

Let's take a look at the old expression syntax as seen in Zabbix 5.2 and older versions:

Figure 4.12 – A Zabbix trigger expression using the old syntax

In the old syntax, we always started with a *curly bracket* and then the hostname or template name. Between the hostname or template name and the item key, we had a colon. Marking the end of the item key we had a *dot*, but item keys can also include dots themselves. Then after the *dot*, we have the trigger function followed by the ending *curly bracket*. Then all we have left is the operator and constant we want to hold the expression against.

As you might see, this could become confusing at times, especially when using dots in item keys. Now let's check out the new trigger syntax:

Figure 4.13 – A Zabbix trigger expression using the new syntax

Our new trigger syntax starts off right away with our trigger function; no hassle, just immediately showing you what we're doing with this line. This is followed by a *bracket* and a *forward slash* before entering the host or template name. We then use another *forward slash* to divide the hostname or template name and the item key. We end with a *bracket* and then all we have left is the operator and value we want to hold the expression against.

Starting with the trigger function makes for a clear indicator of what your line is doing. Putting the hostname or template name into brackets and then dividing it with forward slashes from the item key make for a more cohesive experience when writing expressions. We also don't have confusing extra dots any longer. Altogether a very nice change to the trigger syntax, which in all honesty might take a bit of time to get used to.

It's the small stuff that makes the entire software feel more professional and thought out. Zabbix including changes like these really helps that along.

There's more...

Not only can we match one of the items in a trigger expression—but we can also do an `and` statement. This way, you can make sure our trigger only goes into a `PROBLEM` state when multiple items are reaching a certain value. Triggers are very powerful like this, allowing us to define our own criteria in great detail. There's no predefinition—we can add as many `and/not/or` statements and different functions as we like in the trigger expressions. Customize your triggers to exactly what you need, and suddenly you are going to have a lot more peace of mind because you know your triggers will notify you when something is up.

See also

To know more about trigger expressions, check out the Zabbix documentation. There's a lot of information on which functions you can use to build the perfect trigger. For more details, go to `https://www.zabbix.com/documentation/current/en/manual/config/triggers/expression`.

Setting up advanced triggers

Triggers in Zabbix keep getting more advanced and it might be hard to keep up. For people working with Zabbix 5.2 or older and upgrading to Zabbix 6, not only is there a new Zabbix trigger syntax but there's also a whole new array of functions.

Let's dive into setting up some more advanced triggers in Zabbix 6.

Getting ready

For this recipe, we will need our Zabbix server ready and we'll need one host that is monitored by a Zabbix agent with the Zabbix agent template. We'll use the items on this host to create triggers. Let's use the `lar-book-agent_passive` host from the previous chapter.

If you don't have this host from the previous chapters, simply hook up a new host with the default passive Linux monitoring template called `Linux by Zabbix agent`.

We'll also be touching on some more advanced topics that are discussed later in the book. If you don't know how to use **Low-Level Discovery** (**LLD**) for example, it might be smart to dive into *Chapter 7, Using Discovery for Automatic Creation*, first.

How to do it...

Let's take a look at three *more advanced* triggers, compared to the three we've seen in the previous recipe: `trendavg` for going through trend data, `timeleft` to predict values in the future, and **time shifting** to compare to the past.

Advanced trigger 1 – Trend average function

First, we'll take a look at one of the newer trigger functionalities, the trend average function:

1. Let's start off by creating a new trigger in our frontend. Navigate to **Configuration | Hosts** and select `lar-book-agent_passive`.

2. Navigate to **Triggers** and click on the blue **Create trigger** button in the top-right corner.

3. Next to the **Expression** field, click on the white **Add** button. Fill out the trigger using the expression builder:

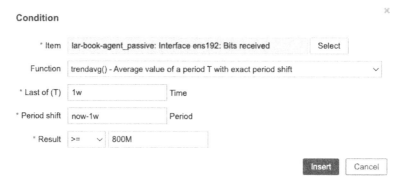

Figure 4.14 – trendavg trigger expression builder

4.   Click on **Insert** and add a name. It will look like this if done correctly.

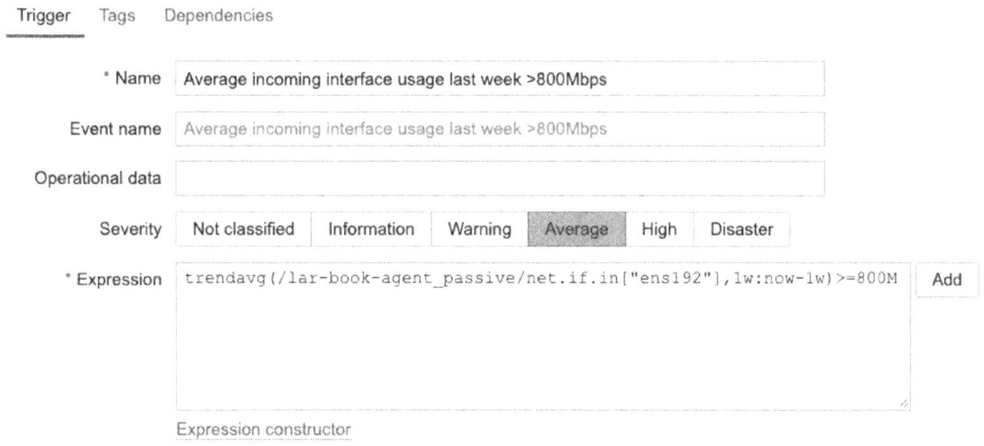

Trigger	Tags	Dependencies

* Name	Average incoming interface usage last week >800Mbps
Event name	Average incoming interface usage last week >800Mbps
Operational data	
Severity	Not classified Information Warning **Average** High Disaster
* Expression	trendavg(/lar-book-agent_passive/net.if.in["ens192"],1w:now-1w)>=800M Add

Expression constructor

Figure 4.15 – trendavg trigger form filled out

5.   Now let's click the blue **Add** button at the bottom of the page to finish creating this trigger.

That's all for creating this trigger. Check out the *How it works…* section of this recipe to get more information about the trigger.

Advanced trigger 2 – Time left function

Next up is our `timeleft` function, which is very useful for things like space utilization. Let's take a look:

1.   We'll create a new trigger in our Zabbix frontend. Navigate to **Configuration | Hosts** and select `lar-book-agent_passive`.

2.   Navigate to **Discovery rules** and click on **Trigger prototype** next to **Mounted filesystem discovery**.

> **Important Note**
> In this case, we are creating the trigger prototype directly on the host, using an existing template discovery rule. If you want to apply a trigger like this to every host using a template, make sure to create the trigger on a template level. Furthermore, discovery rules are explained further in *Chapter 7, Using Discovery for Automatic Creation,* of this book.

3. Click on **Create trigger prototype**.

4. Next to the **Expression** field, click on the white **Add** button. Fill out the trigger using the expression builder:

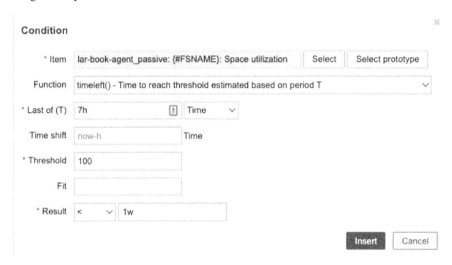

Figure 4.16 – timeleft trigger expression builder

> **Important Note**
> Using short intervals in predictive triggers to predict long time periods is not recommended. Make sure to use the right data set for the time period we want to use in relation to the time we want to predict.

5. Click the blue **Insert** button and the finished trigger will look like this.

Figure 4.17 – timeleft trigger form filled out

6.   Click the blue **Add** button at the bottom of the page to finish setting up the trigger.

We now have a new trigger using the `timeleft` function to tell us when hard disks are filling up within a week. Check out the *How it works...* section of this recipe to get more information about the trigger.

Advanced trigger 3 – Time shifting using mathematical functions

Lastly, we are going to work with time shifting and in this case, we'll do so in combination with a mathematical function. Time shifting is a little bit of a difficult example, so bear with me.

1.   Let's navigate to **Configuration | Hosts** and select our host `lar-book-agent_passive`.

2.   Go to **Triggers** and click the blue **Create trigger** button.

3.   Add the following trigger, as seen in the screenshot.

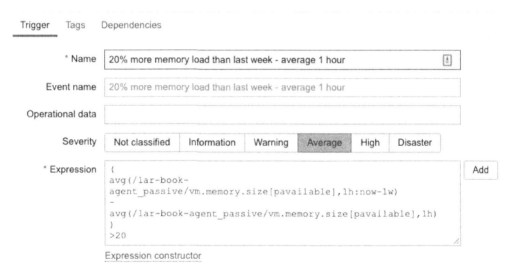

Figure 4.18 – Time shifting average trigger form filled out

This is a very complex trigger to set up, so let's dive right into how it's set up in the *How it works...* section.

How it works...

Advanced triggers can get very complex. The triggers we have just set up are just the tip of the iceberg. Do not worry if these triggers seem intimidating, as there is plentiful documentation out there to help you set them up, which we can find here: `https://www.zabbix.com/documentation/current/en/manual/config/triggers`.

It's near impossible to cover every single use case in this book, so the triggers we set up will show you what's possible. Use what you have learned in the examples in your own scenarios, but make sure to apply your own thinking to it.

Advanced trigger 1 – Trend average function

Let's start off the *How it works...* section with the trend average. Trend average is one of the few trigger functions that use trend data instead of history data. Let's do a short crash course on the history and trend data in Zabbix. History data is the exact value every time an item reaches its configured update interval. Trend data is the average, minimum, and maximum value over one hour (1h) created from the history data and a count of the number of values.

Now, let's look at the available functions for creating triggers using trend data:

- `trendavg`: For getting the average value from trend values within a time period.
- `trendmax`: For getting the maximum value from trend values within a time period.
- `trendmin`: For getting the minimum value from trend values within a time period.
- `trendcount`: For getting the number of retrieved trend values within a time period.
- `trendsum`: For getting a sum of trend values within a time period.

As I said, all of these will use our trend values. The values used are stored in a special Zabbix trend cache, for use in our trigger. We've used the `trendavg` function. Let's check out how we used it in our trigger expression again.

Figure 4.19 – trendavg trigger expression

We start off our trigger with the function `trendavg` and then the *host/template* and *item key* as we've seen earlier in our last recipe. What's new here is the part where we state `1w:now-1w`. This is the time period where we state to use a value from one week ago.

What this means is that, if the average value from our trends 1 week ago is above 800 Mbps, then this trigger will go into a problem state.

Advanced trigger 2 – Time left function

`timeleft` is another very interesting trigger function. We can use `timeleft` to create triggers that only fire when it expects something to reach a certain threshold in the future. This is called a predictive trigger, as it makes a prediction based on older data.

Let's check out our trigger expression again.

| * Expression | `timeleft(/lar-book-agent_passive/vfs.fs.size[{#FSNAME},pused],7h,100)<1w` | Add |

Figure 4.20 – timeleft trigger expression

As we can see, we start our expression as usual: the *trigger function, host/template*, and our *item key*. In this case, we combine that with a time period we want to use for our predictive trigger to define its prediction. We use `7h`, to tell this expression to use 7 hours of historic data. Combine that with a threshold of `100`, to make sure this will trigger if we expect to reach 100% disk space usage. Now we only need one more element to complete this, the expected result, which in this case is `<1w`.

To sum it all up, this trigger expression looks at *7 hours* of historic data and if it expects to reach *100%* disk space in *less than 1 week*, it will go into a problem state, alerting you that you will need to make sure your disks don't run out of space.

Tip: Combine the `timeleft` trigger function with other functions to limit how many times you get alerted. For example, with disk space, we might expect a disk to fill up in a week, but you might not want to see that unless the used space is at least less than 50 Gigabytes. Add another expression and you are golden:

```
last(/Linux filesystems by Zabbix agent/vfs.fs.size[{#FSNAME},pused])>90%
and
timeleft(/Linux filesystems by Zabbix agent/vfs.fs.size[{#FSNAME},pused],1h,100)<1d)
```

Figure 4.21 – timeleft trigger function expression

Advanced trigger 3 – Time shifting using mathematical functions

As a Zabbix trainer, time shifting trigger expressions is where I and my students always need to spend some additional time on what they are all doing exactly. This makes sense, as it is one of the more complex expressions, and in this example, we even combined it with some mathematical functions.

So let's take another look at our expression and break it down.

```
1  (
2  avg(/lar-book-agent_passive/vm.memory.size[pavailable],1h:now-1w)
3  -
4  avg(/lar-book-agent_passive/vm.memory.size[pavailable],1h)
5  )
6  >20
```

Figure 4.22 – Time shifting trigger expression

I've added line numbers for our convenience. Now we can go over each line and explain what they mean.

1. This is the opening bracket for our mathematical statement, using the operator between two items.

2. Our first item, using the time shift function. This item will get our memory availability as a percentage from 1 week ago starting from this moment exactly. If the current date and time is Monday the 24th of November at 14:00, it will get the 1-hour average value for Monday the 17th of November between 13:00 and 14:00.

3. Our mathematical operator, stating a minus. Meaning, we'll subtract the first item from the second item.

4. This is our second item, not using a time shift. This item will be filled with a 1-hour average value of the last hour.

5. The closing bracket ends our mathematical statement.

6. Finally, an operator and constant. Stating that this trigger will only trigger if the mathematical result is higher than 20.

That's it for looking at the lines. Now that we know what they do, let's take a look at how it performs in a real-life scenario. We're going to fill out the values manually and see if the expression is **TRUE** or **FALSE**. **TRUE** means that there is a problem and **FALSE** means everything is fine. So the math is as follows:

```
(Last week - This week) = Result
If the Result is higher than 20 then the expression is True
This expression is: TRUE/FALSE
```

Filling it out with 80% memory available last week and only 50% available this week, we can see the following happening:

```
(80 - 50) = 30
If 30 is higher than 20 the expression is TRUE
This expression is TRUE
```

Let's do it one more time but with 80% memory available last week and 70% this week:

```
(80 - 70) = 10
If 10 is higher than 20 the expression is TRUE
This expression is FALSE
```

This is how you should go about setting up your time shifting expressions. Simply use a notebook or whatever you like, write down your expression in simple text for yourself, and do the calculations.

There's more...

Trigger expressions can also be tested within Zabbix itself. If we go to **Configuration | Hosts**, then **Triggers** and we select any of our three advanced triggers, we can do a little test. For example, using the time shifting trigger, we can click **Expression constructor**.

Figure 4.23 – Time shifting trigger expression constructor

Over here, we can select **Test** and then fill out our values. Let's use the same 80% and 50% we did in the earlier example.

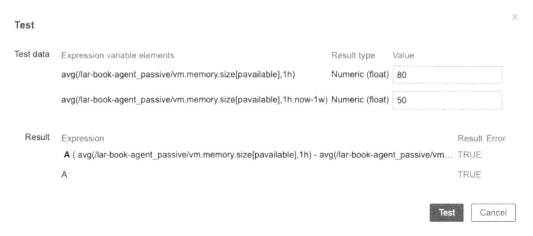

Figure 4.24 – Time shifting trigger expression constructor, Test

As you can see, this will tell us whether our expression ends up being **TRUE** or **FALSE**, using any values we want to fill. In short, if you want to be sure your math on paper is doing the same thing directly in Zabbix, use the **Expression constructor** to test it.

Setting up alerts

Alerting can be a very important part of your Zabbix setup. When we set up alerts, we want the person on the other end to be informed of just what is going on. It's also important to not spam someone with alerts; we want it to be effective.

So, in this recipe, we will go over the basics of setting up alerts, so we know just how to get it right from the start.

Getting ready

For this recipe, we will only need two things. We will have to use our Zabbix server to create our alerts and we will need some triggers, like the triggers from the previous recipe. The triggers will be used to initiate the alerting process to see just how the Zabbix server will convey this information.

How to do it...

1. Let's start by setting up our action in the Zabbix frontend. To do this, we will navigate to **Configuration | Actions** and we will be served with this screen:

Figure 4.25 – The Zabbix Trigger actions page with 1 trigger action

There already is one action set up to notify **Zabbix administrators** of problem events. In Zabbix 6, a lot of features such as **Actions** and **Media** are predefined. Most of the time, all we need to do is enable them and fill out some information.

2. We will set up our own action, so let's create a new action to notify a user in the **Zabbix administrators** group of our new triggers. Click the blue **Create action** button to be taken to the next page:

Actions

| Action | Operations |

| | * Name | Action to notify our book reader of a problem |

| Conditions | Label | Name | Action |
| | Add | | |

Enabled ✓

* At least one operation must exist

Add   Cancel

Figure 4.26 – The Zabbix Action creation page, notify book reader

3. On this page, we are going to want to check the **Enabled** checkmark to make sure that this action will actually do something. Make sure to name your action clearly so that you won't have any issues differentiating between actions.

4. Now, move on to our **Operations** tab:

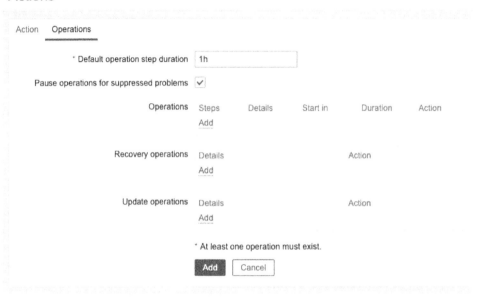

Figure 4.27 – The Zabbix Action creation page at the Operations tab, notify book reader

5. The **Operations** tab is empty by default, so we are going to want to create some operations here. There are three forms of operation that we are going to create here—let's start with the **Operations** operation by clicking **Add**:

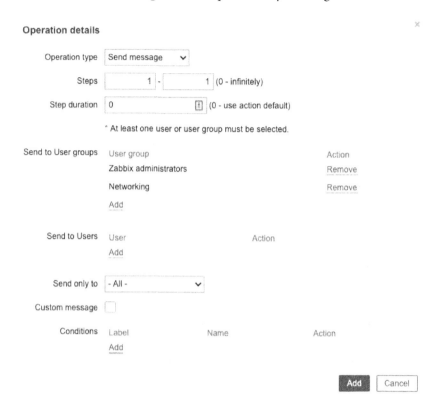

Figure 4.28 – Zabbix Operation details page, notify book reader

6. We have the option to add **Users** and **User groups** here that we want to alert. If you've followed along with *Chapter 1, Installing Zabbix and Getting Started Using the Frontend*, we can just select the **Networking** user group here. If not, selecting just your **Zabbix administrators** group is fine.

7. After clicking the blue **Add** button at the bottom of the form, we will be taken back to the **Actions** screen.

8. Now, we will create the next operation, named **Recovery operations**. What we do here is create an operation, as follows:

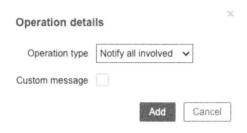

Figure 4.29 – Zabbix Recovery operations details, notify book reader

9. This option will notify all users involved in the initial operation defined earlier. All users that got a PROBLEM generation notification will also receive the recovery this way. Click **Add**, and let's continue.

    Now, if you're like me and you want to stay on top of things, you are able to create an update notification. This way, we know that—for instance—someone acknowledged a problem and is working on it. Normally, I would select different channels for stuff such as this—for instance, using **SMS** for high-priority alerts and a Slack or Teams channel for everything else.

10. Let's click **Add** under **Update operations** to add the following to our setup:

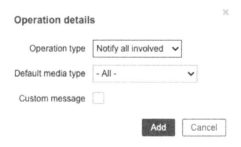

Figure 4.30 – Zabbix Update operation details, notify book reader

11. We will do the same thing here as we did for the **Recovery operations** option. Notify all users involved of any update to this problem. After clicking **Add** here, click the blue **Add** button again on our **Actions** screen to finish creating the action.

12. Now, the next thing we want to do is create a media type for actually notifying our users of the issue. Go to **Administration | Media types**, and you will be presented with the following screen:

Name ▲	Type	Status
Discord	Webhook	Enabled
Email	Email	Enabled
Email (HTML)	Email	Enabled
Jira	Webhook	Enabled
Jira ServiceDesk	Webhook	Enabled
Jira with CustomFields	Webhook	Enabled
Mattermost	Webhook	Enabled
MS Teams	Webhook	Enabled
Opsgenie	Webhook	Enabled
PagerDuty	Webhook	Enabled
Pushover	Webhook	Enabled
Redmine	Webhook	Enabled
ServiceNow	Webhook	Enabled
SIGNL4	Webhook	Enabled
Slack	Webhook	Enabled
SMS	SMS	Enabled
Telegram	Webhook	Enabled
Zammad	Webhook	Enabled
Zendesk	Webhook	Enabled

Figure 4.31 – The Zabbix Media types page with predefined media options

As you can see, there are quite a lot of predefined media types in Zabbix 6. We have them for Slack, Opsgenie, and even Telegram. Let's start with something almost everyone has, though: email.

13. Click the **Email** media type and let's edit this one to suit our needs:

Figure 4.32 – The Zabbix Media type creation page for email

14. I set it up to reflect my Office 365 settings, but any **Simple Mail Transfer Protocol (SMTP)** server should work. Fill in your SMTP settings, and we should be able to receive notifications.

15. Be sure to also check the next tab, **Message templates**. For example, the message template for a `Problem` generation event looks like this:

Message template   ✕

Message type | Problem   ⌄ |

Subject | Problem: {EVENT.NAME} |

Message | Problem started at {EVENT.TIME} on {EVENT.DATE}
           | Problem name: {EVENT.NAME}
           | Host: {HOST.NAME}
           | Severity: {EVENT.SEVERITY}
           | Operational data: {EVENT.OPDATA}
           | Original problem ID: {EVENT.ID}
           | {TRIGGER.URL} |

                        Update   Cancel

Figure 4.33 – The default Zabbix Message template page for problems

We set this up like this so that we get a message telling us just what's going on. This is fully customizable as well, to reflect just what we want to know.

16. Let's keep the default settings for now. Last, but not least, go to **Administration | Users** and edit a user in the **Zabbix administrators** or **Networking** group. I will use the **Admin** user as an example:

Users

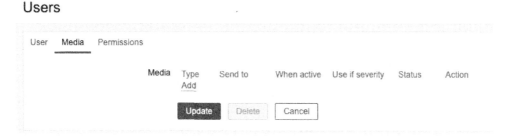

Figure 4.34 – The Zabbix User Media page for the Admin user

17. At this **Users** edit window, go to **Media** and click the **Add** button. We want to add the following to notify us of all trigger severities at our email address:

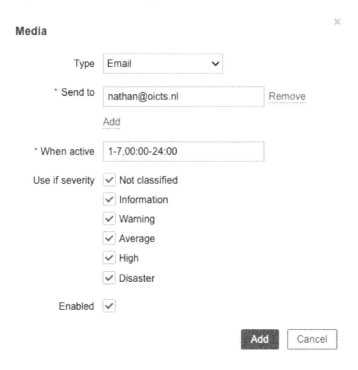

Figure 4.35 – The Zabbix User Media creation page for the Admin user

18. Now, click on the blue **Add** button and finish creating this user media.

How it works...

Now, that's how we set up alerts in Zabbix. You will now receive alerts on your email address, as shown in the following flowchart:

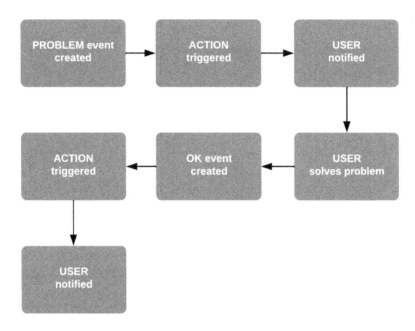

Figure 4.36 – Diagram showing Zabbix problem flow

When something breaks, a **PROBLEM** in Zabbix is triggered by our trigger configuration. Our **ACTION** will then be triggered by our **PROBLEM** event and it will use the **Media Type** and **User Media** configuration to notify our user. Our user then fixes the issue (for instance, rebooting a stuck server), and then an **OK** event will be generated. We will then trigger the **ACTION** again and get an **OK** message.

> **Tip**
> Before building alerts such as this, make a workflow (as shown in *Figure 4.36*) for yourself, specifying just which user groups and users should be notified. This way, you keep it clear for yourself just how you will use Zabbix for alerting.

There's more...

There are loads of media types and integrations, and we've just touched the tip of the iceberg by seeing a list of predefined ones. Make sure to check out the Zabbix integration list (`https://www.zabbix.com/integrations`) for more options or build your own using the Zabbix webhooks and other extensions available.

Keeping alerts effective

It's important to keep our alerts effective to make sure we are neither overwhelmed nor underwhelmed by notifications. To do this, we will change our trigger and the **Email** media type to reflect just what we want to see.

Getting ready

We will be using *Trigger 1* from the first recipe and the default email media type in Zabbix.

Furthermore, of course, we'll also be using our Zabbix server.

How to do it...

To create effective alerts, let's follow these steps:

1. Let's get started on *Trigger 1*, which we created in this chapter's *Setting up triggers* recipe. Navigate to our `lar-agent-simple` host by going to **Configuration | Hosts** and clicking **Trigger** for the host.

2. Here, sometimes people use a different trigger name like the one we see below:

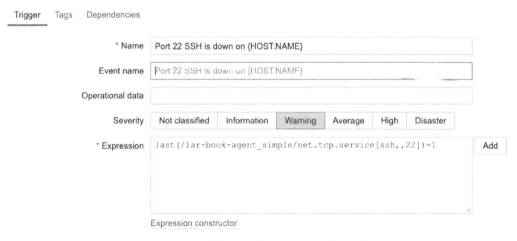

Figure 4.37 – Trigger 1 from the previous recipe

Even when you've used the macro {HOST.NAME} in the trigger, it's quite simple, so fortunately there isn't a lot to change here. If you've used the hostname in the trigger name, we can change the name to reflect a message that is clearer.

3. Make sure to use a short and descriptive trigger name, like the following:

Figure 4.38 – New trigger 1 name

4. Next, navigate to the **Tags** page to add a tag for keeping the triggers organized. Let's add the following:

Trigger   **Tags** 1   Dependencies

Trigger tags	Inherited and trigger tags	
Name	Value	Action
scope	availability	Remove

Add

Figure 4.39 – Trigger 1 tags

5. Another great way of keeping everything organized is changing media type messages. Let's change a media type to reflect our own structured needs. Navigate to **Administrations | Media types** and select our media type named **Email**.

6. Select **Message** templates and click **Edit** next to our first problem. This will bring us to the following window:

Message template

Message type	Problem ∨
Subject	Problem: {EVENT.NAME}
Message	Problem started at {EVENT.TIME} on {EVENT.DATE} Problem name: {EVENT.NAME} Host: {HOST.NAME} Severity: {EVENT.SEVERITY} Operational data: {EVENT.OPDATA} Original problem ID: {EVENT.ID} {TRIGGER.URL}

Update   Cancel

Figure 4.40 – Standard email media type message

Now, Zabbix uses the default configured message under the media type when we do not use a custom message. But if we want to change that message, we can do that here by creating a custom message. Our default under the **Email** media type looks like the previous screenshot.

7. We can change the message on the media type. For instance, if we don't want to see the **Original problem ID** or when we want a more customized message, simply remove that line, as shown in the following screenshot:

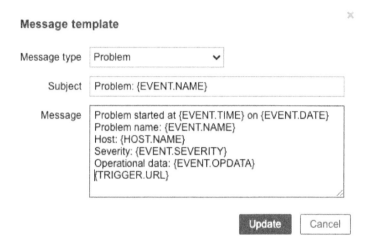

Figure 4.41 – Custom email media type message

How it works...

We've done two things in this recipe. We've changed our trigger name and we've added a tag to our trigger.

Keeping trigger names clear and defined in a structured way is important to keeping our Zabbix environment structured. Instead of just naming our trigger Port 22 SSH down on {HOST.NAME}, we've added standardization to our setup and can now do cool structuration such as this with our future triggers:

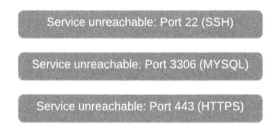

Figure 4.42 – Trigger structure diagram

Our triggers are all clear and we can immediately see which host, port, and service are down.

On top of that, we've added a tag for the service that is down, which will now immediately display our service in a clear way, alerting us to exactly what is going on:

Host	Problem	Duration	Ack	Actions	Tags
lar-book-agent_simple	Service unreachable: Port 22 (SSH)	1s	No		component: tcp services scope: availability

Figure 4.43 – Trigger down, structured

In Zabbix 6.0 there is a new tag policy. As we created the item used in the trigger with a **component** tag and we just added a trigger tag for **scope**, we followed the new standard. In the problem view in the screenshot above, it becomes immediately apparent that we have a problem affecting the availability of the TCP service SSH. The **scope** tag generally contains either one of 5 options: `availability`, `performance`, `notification`, `security`, and `capacity`.

For more information about the new Zabbix 6.0 tag policy, check out the link below:

`https://blog.zabbix.com/tags-in-zabbix-6-0-lts-usage-subfilters-and-guidelines/19565/`

Another thing we've done is remove the macro {HOST.NAME} if you've used it before. As we can already see which host this trigger is on by checking the **Host** field, we do not need to add the {HOST.NAME} macro. We need to keep trigger names short and effective and use the hostname macros in **Media** or simply use the field already available in the frontend.

We've also changed our action in this recipe. Changing a message on **Media types** is a powerful way to keep our problem channels structured. Sometimes, we want to see less or more information on certain channels and changing media type messages is one way to do this.

We can also create custom messages on an **Action** level, changing all the messages sent to the selected channels.

There's more...

What I'm trying to show you in this recipe is that although it might be simple to set up Zabbix, it is not simple to set up a good monitoring solution with Zabbix—or any monitoring tool, for that matter—if you don't plan. Carefully plan out how you want your triggers to be structured before you build everything in your Zabbix installation.

An engineer that works in a structured way and that takes time to build a good monitoring solution will save a lot of hours in the future because they will understand the problem before anyone else.

Customizing alerts

Alerting is very useful, especially in combination with some of the tricks we've learned in this book so far to keep everything structured. But sometimes, we need a little more from our alerts than what we are already getting from Zabbix out of the box.

In this recipe, we'll do a small bit of customization to make the alerts more our own.

Getting ready

For this chapter, all we are going to need is our current Zabbix server installation.

How to do it...

To customize alerts, follow these steps:

1. Let's create some custom severities in our Zabbix server to reflect our organization's needs. Navigate to **Administration | General** and select **Trigger displaying options** from the side menu:

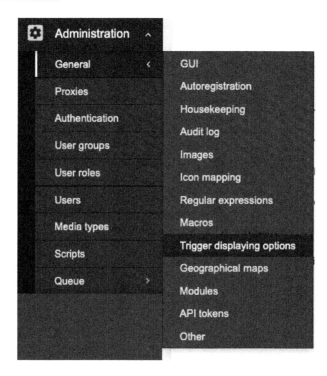

Figure 4.44 – Side menu at Administration | General

After selecting this, we'll be taken to our next page. This window contains the default Zabbix **Trigger severities**, as shown in the following screenshot:

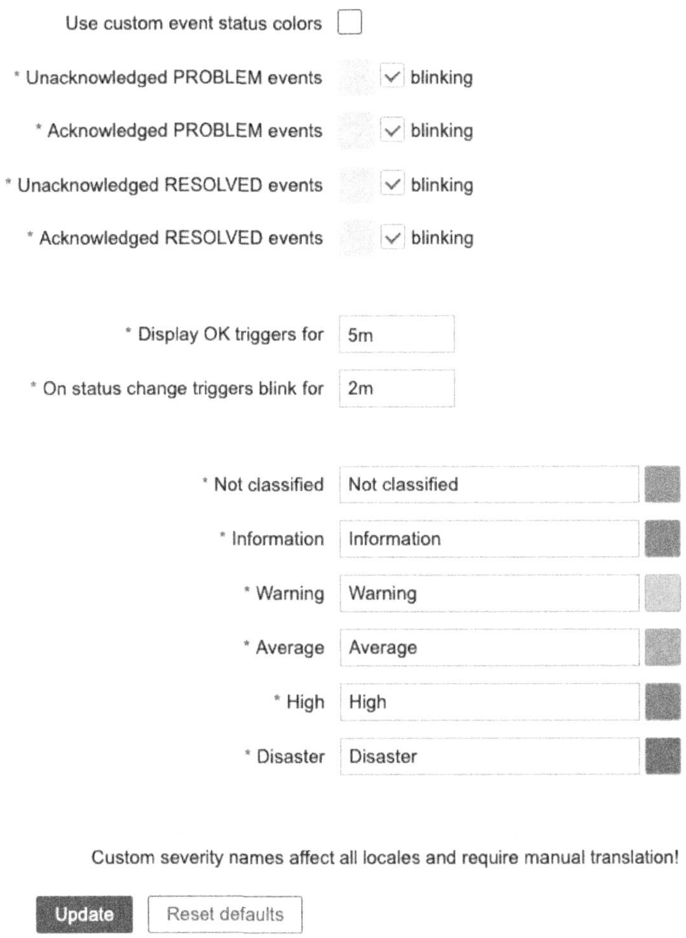

Use custom event status colors ☐

* Unacknowledged PROBLEM events   ☑ blinking

* Acknowledged PROBLEM events   ☑ blinking

* Unacknowledged RESOLVED events   ☑ blinking

* Acknowledged RESOLVED events   ☑ blinking

* Display OK triggers for   5m

* On status change triggers blink for   2m

* Not classified   Not classified

* Information   Information

* Warning   Warning

* Average   Average

* High   High

* Disaster   Disaster

Custom severity names affect all locales and require manual translation!

Update   Reset defaults

Figure 4.45 – Default Trigger severities window page

2. Next up, we could customize the default **Trigger severities**, as follows:

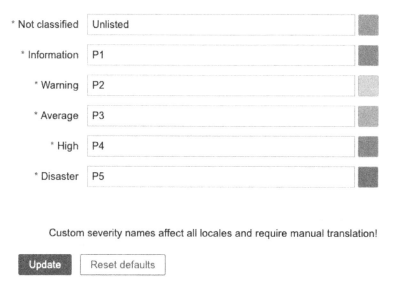

Figure 4.46 – Custom Trigger severities window page

3. Do not forget to click the blue **Update** button at the bottom of the page to save the changes.

How it works...

Not all companies like using terms such as **High** and **Disaster**, but prefer using different severities such as **P1** and **P2**. Using custom severities, we can customize Zabbix to make it more our own and thus reflect what we've already been using in different tools, for example.

Changing custom severities is not a necessity by any means, but it can be a good way to adopt Zabbix more easily if you are used to something different.

5

Building Your Own Structured Templates

It's time to start with one of the most important tasks in Zabbix: building structured templates. A good Zabbix setup relies heavily on templating, and there is a huge difference between a good and a bad template. So, if you're new to Zabbix or you haven't started building your own templates yet, then pay close attention to this chapter.

In this chapter, we will go over how to set up your templates, and how to fill them with the right items and triggers. Also, it is important to make use of macros and **Low-Level Discovery (LLD)** in the right way. After following these recipes, you will be more than ready to build solid Zabbix templates with the right format, and even LLD.

In this chapter, we'll cover the following recipes:

- Creating your Zabbix template
- Setting up template-level tags
- Creating template items
- Creating template triggers

- Setting up different kinds of macros
- Using LLD on templates
- Nesting Zabbix templates

Technical requirements

We will need our Zabbix server from *Chapter 4, Working with Triggers and Alerts*, to monitor our **Simple Network Management Protocol** (**SNMP**) host. For the SNMP host, we can use the host we set up in the *Working with SNMP monitoring* recipe in *Chapter 3, Setting Up Zabbix Monitoring*.

Creating your Zabbix template

In this recipe, we will start with the basics of creating a Zabbix template. We will go over the structure of Zabbix templating and why we need to pay attention to certain aspects of templating.

Getting ready

All you will need in this recipe is your Zabbix server.

How to do it...

Now, let's get started with building our structured Zabbix template:

1. Open your Zabbix frontend and navigate to **Configuration | Templates**.
2. On this page, click the **Create template** button in the top-right corner. This will lead you to the following page:

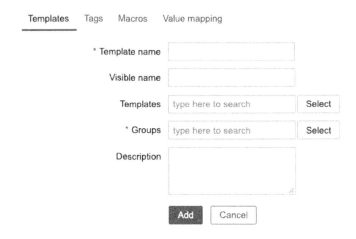

Figure 5.1 – The create template page, empty

At this point, we are going to need to name our template and assign a group to it. We will be creating an SNMP template to monitor a Linux host. I'll be using SNMP in the example to show how the templates are structured.

> **Important Note**
>
> Use SNMP to monitor network equipment, custom equipment supporting SNMP, and more. SNMP is very versatile and easy to understand, and is implemented by a lot of hardware manufacturers. For Linux hosts, I'd still recommend the very powerful Zabbix agent, which we covered in the *Setting up Zabbix agent monitoring* recipe in *Chapter 3, Setting Up Zabbix Monitoring*.

3.   Create your template with the following information:

| Templates | Tags | Macros | Value mapping |

* Template name: Custom Linux by SNMP

Visible name: Custom Linux by SNMP

Templates: type here to search   [Select]

* Groups: Templates/Operating systems ✕
type here to search   [Select]

Description:

Figure 5.2 – The create template page filled with information for the SNMP template

We will not link any **Templates**, **Tags**, and **Macros** yet, but we'll address some of these functionalities later. That's all there is to creating our template, but there's nothing in it besides a name, group, and description so far.

How it works...

There's not a lot of work involved in creating our first template—it's quite straightforward. What we need to keep in mind is the right naming convention here.

Now, you might think to yourself: *Why is naming a template so important?* Well, we are going to create a lot of templates when working with Zabbix. For example, this is a small part of the list of out-of-the-box templates:

Figure 5.3 – Some out-of-the-box templates

As you can see, this is already a large list, and all of these templates are following a singular straightforward naming convention. Looking at the name of the template we have just built ourselves and, for example, the built-in Apache template, they follow the same convention. Breaking down the convention, it looks like this:

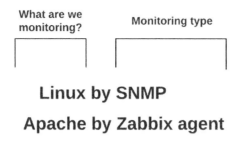

Figure 5.4 – Template naming convention explanation

Looking at the list and comparing it to the naming convention we went over in *Figure 5.4*, we can see the following pattern:

- **What are we monitoring?**: (Linux) We name the template—in this case, we'll call it Linux because the OS we monitor will be Linux.

- **Monitoring type**: (by SNMP) We will add our data collection method at the end of the template as we might monitor the Linux OS in other ways besides SNMP, like the Zabbix agent.

Adhering to the guidelines in this naming convention and thus using the correct template names is our first step in creating the correct structure for our template. This makes it easy to find out which templates we want to use on which hosts.

In our case, we've also added a short custom prefix to make sure we can distinguish our template from others already created in the Zabbix setup. Normally we can omit this prefix, but for the book it's useful. Alternatively, you could prefix or suffix your template names with a company name to not overwrite the default templates.

There's more...

When building templates, adhere to the Zabbix guidelines. That's what we will do in this book as well, combined with our experience in creating templates. If you want to learn more about Zabbix templating guidelines, check the following URL: `https://www.zabbix.com/documentation/guidelines/en/thosts`.

Setting up template-level tags

Our next step in setting up our Zabbix template is setting up template-level tags. Tags on a template level are used to give every single event (problem) created on a host by this template a tag. The tag is then used to filter events in things like dashboards, actions, and the **Monitoring | Problems** view.

Getting ready

To get started with this recipe, you will need a Zabbix server and a template on that server, preferably our template created in the previous recipe.

How to do it...

Creating template-level tags is a way to make sure that only events created by a certain template will get a configured tag. To get started, the first thing you will need to do is navigate to the template and follow these steps:

1. Go to **Configuration | Templates** and click on our template, called **Custom Linux by SNMP**.

2. Here, you will click the **Tags** tab at the top of the form and you'll be taken to this tab:

Figure 5.5 – Zabbix Tags tab for the SNMP template

Now, the first thing we can do is create a tag, **OS:Linux**, to make sure we know all events from this template will be Linux-related.

3. Start creating tags by clicking the dotted-underlined **Add** button and filling out **Name** as class. Then, in the **Value** field, we fill in os.

4. Click the small **Add** button and fill in the **Name** for the second tag as target. Then, in the **Value** field, we fill in linux. It will look like this.

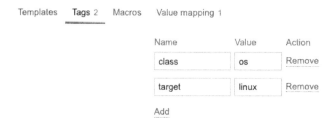

Figure 5.6 – Zabbix Tags tab filled out for the SNMP template

5. Do not forget to click the blue **Update** button to save your tag to this template.

How it works...

Now, there's a lot more to creating tags than it might seem at first through following this recipe. Tags play a key part in keeping your Zabbix environment structured. You will use the template-level tags to filter in a lot of places like the **Monitoring | Problems** window, and with a lot of events created by one host, they will create readability by making problems easy to filter.

For example, once we have configured some triggers later in this recipe when checking the **Monitoring | Problems** page for our host, we could see something like the following:

Figure 5.7 – Example Monitoring | Problems page for host lar-book-agent_snmp

As you can see the problem we are looking at here is displaying the tags **target:linux** and **class:os** at the end of the page. The event was tagged with the template-level tag and we can now see that it will always carry that tag, allowing us to filter.

This gives us loads of opportunities, because we aren't limited to template-level tags. We also have host-level tags, item-level tags, and trigger-level tags. We could tag everything from a template with **target:linux** and **class:os** or even tag a specific trigger with something like `department:architecture`.

We could then, for example, create an action that sends out everything Linux-related to a certain Linux engineering email address or Teams/Slack channel based on the **class:linux** tag, but only send specific problems with a trigger-level tag like `department:architecture` to a more specific email address or Teams/Slack channel.

For more information regarding the tag policy starting from Zabbix 6, check out the following link:

```
https://blog.zabbix.com/tags-in-zabbix-6-0-lts-usage-
subfilters-and-guidelines/19565/
```

See also

In this chapter, the recipe titled *Using LLD on templates* will also explain **tag prototypes**, where we will create tags automatically based on the LLD settings. Tag prototypes are the recommended way of working with tags when creating discovery and are amazing for keeping templates structured. More about that later.

Creating template items

Let's get started with finally creating some real template items because, in the end, items are what it is all about in Zabbix. Without items, we don't have data, and without data, we do not have anything to work with in our monitoring system.

Getting ready

Now, moving along, we are going to need our Zabbix server and a host that we can monitor with SNMP. In *Chapter 3, Setting Up Zabbix Monitoring*, we monitored a host with SNMP, so we can use this host again. We'll also use the Zabbix template from the previous recipes.

How to do it...

1. First of all, let's log in to our Zabbix server **command-line interface** (**CLI**) and enter `snmpwalk`, with the following command:

   ```
   snmpwalk -v3 -l authPriv -u snmpv3user -a SHA -A "my_
   authpass" -x AES -X "my_privpass" 10.16.16.153 .1
   ```

   Make sure to change the IP address `10.16.16.153` to your own correct value. We will receive an answer such as this:

```
[larcorba@lar-book-centos ~]$ snmpwalk -On -v2c -c public 10.16.16.153
.1.3.6.1.2.1.1.1.0 = STRING: Linux lar-book-agent 4.18.0-193.6.3.el8_2.x86_64 #1 SMP Wed Jun 10 11:09:32 UTC 2020 x86_64
.1.3.6.1.2.1.1.2.0 = OID: .1.3.6.1.4.1.8072.3.2.10
.1.3.6.1.2.1.1.3.0 = Timeticks: (568102251) 65 days, 18:03:42.51
.1.3.6.1.2.1.1.4.0 = STRING: Root <root@localhost> (configure /etc/snmp/snmp.local.conf)
.1.3.6.1.2.1.1.5.0 = STRING: lar-book-agent
.1.3.6.1.2.1.1.6.0 = STRING: Unknown (edit /etc/snmp/snmpd.conf)
.1.3.6.1.2.1.1.8.0 = Timeticks: (1) 0:00:00.01
.1.3.6.1.2.1.1.9.1.2.1 = OID: .1.3.6.1.6.3.10.3.1.1
.1.3.6.1.2.1.1.9.1.2.2 = OID: .1.3.6.1.6.3.11.3.1.1
.1.3.6.1.2.1.1.9.1.2.3 = OID: .1.3.6.1.6.3.15.2.1.1
.1.3.6.1.2.1.1.9.1.2.4 = OID: .1.3.6.1.6.3.1
.1.3.6.1.2.1.1.9.1.2.5 = OID: .1.3.6.1.6.3.16.2.2.1
.1.3.6.1.2.1.1.9.1.2.6 = OID: .1.3.6.1.2.1.49
.1.3.6.1.2.1.1.9.1.2.7 = OID: .1.3.6.1.2.1.4
.1.3.6.1.2.1.1.9.1.2.8 = OID: .1.3.6.1.2.1.50
.1.3.6.1.2.1.1.9.1.2.9 = OID: .1.3.6.1.6.3.13.3.1.3
.1.3.6.1.2.1.1.9.1.2.10 = OID: .1.3.6.1.2.1.92
.1.3.6.1.2.1.1.9.1.3.1 = STRING: The SNMP Management Architecture MIB.
.1.3.6.1.2.1.1.9.1.3.2 = STRING: The MIB for Message Processing and Dispatching.
.1.3.6.1.2.1.1.9.1.3.3 = STRING: The management information definitions for the SNMP User-based Security Model.
.1.3.6.1.2.1.1.9.1.3.4 = STRING: The MIB module for SNMPv2 entities
.1.3.6.1.2.1.1.9.1.3.5 = STRING: View-based Access Control Model for SNMP.
.1.3.6.1.2.1.1.9.1.3.6 = STRING: The MIB module for managing TCP implementations
.1.3.6.1.2.1.1.9.1.3.7 = STRING: The MIB module for managing IP and ICMP implementations
.1.3.6.1.2.1.1.9.1.3.8 = STRING: The MIB module for managing UDP implementations
.1.3.6.1.2.1.1.9.1.3.9 = STRING: The MIB modules for managing SNMP Notification, plus filtering.
.1.3.6.1.2.1.1.9.1.3.10 = STRING: The MIB module for logging SNMP Notifications.
```

Figure 5.8 – snmpwalk reply

Now, let's capture our hostname in our template first, as it is an important item to have. When working with SNMP, I always like to work with untranslated SNMP **Object Identifiers** (**OIDs**). For our hostname, this is `.1.3.6.1.2.1.1.5.0`.

2. If we have an **Management Information Base** (**MIB**), we can translate this OID to make sure it is actually the system name. Enter the following command at the Zabbix server CLI:

```
snmptranslate .1.3.6.1.2.1.1.5.0
```

Which will return the following reply:

```
[larcorba@lar-book-centos ~]$ snmptranslate .1.3.6.1.2.1.1.5.0
SNMPv2-MIB::sysName.0
```

Figure 5.9 – snmptranslate reply

> **Tip**
>
> Using `-On` in your SNMP command makes sure that we are receiving the OIDs instead of the MIB translation. If we want to work the other way around, we can omit the `-On` in our command and `snmptranslate` the translated OID.

3. Now that we know how to get our hostname, add this to our template. Navigate to **Configuration | Templates** and select our **Custom Linux by SNMP** template.

4. Here, we will go to **Items**. In the upper-right corner, select **Create item** to create the following item:

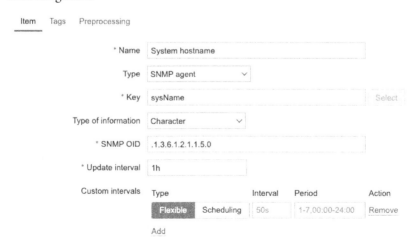

Figure 5.10 – Item for sysName SNMP OID

5. Make sure to also add an item-level tag. These are important for grouping and filtering items. Click the **Tags** tab and add the following:

Figure 5.11 – Item for sysName SNMP OID, Tags tab

Now that we have our first item, let's create a host as well and assign this template to that host.

6. Navigate to **Configuration | Hosts** and click **Create host** in the top-right corner. Create a host with the following settings.

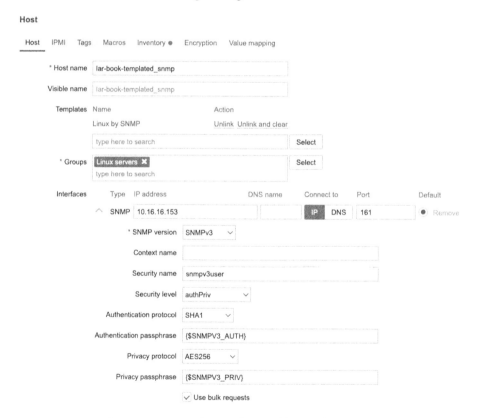

Figure 5.12 – New host with our self-created template

7. Don't forget to add the macros to our new host before clicking the **Add** button. Click on **Macros** and fill in the following information:

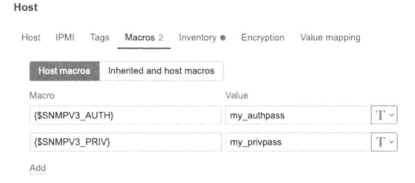

Figure 5.13 – Add macros tab on a host

8. Now, you can click the **Add** button, and our new host will be monitored.

How it works...

When we create items such as this on our template when assigning the template to our hosts, the item will also be created on the host. The great thing about this is that we can assign a template to multiple hosts, meaning we only have to configure the item on the template level once, instead of creating the item on every single host. For instance, our newly created host will show the following latest data:

Figure 5.14 – Monitoring | Latest data for our new host

The value for this item will then be different for all your monitored hosts, depending on the value received by that host.

> **Important Note**
> When creating an SNMP item, keep the following in mind. The **Item** SNMP OID always contains the non-translated OID. This is to make sure that we do not actually need MIB files for our templates to work.

Furthermore, the item key will be based on the translated OID. In our case, the translated OID was sysName, which we then turned into the sysName item key. These are general rules that we should all abide by when creating our templates, to make sure they are structured the same for everyone.

See also

To learn more about Zabbix and SNMP OIDs/MIBs, check out this awesome blog post by Zabbix's head of customer support, Dmitry Lambert:

```
https://blog.zabbix.com/zabbix-snmp-what-you-need-to-know-and-
how-to-configure-it/10345/#snmp-oid
```

Creating template triggers

Now, creating templated triggers works in about the same way as creating templated items or normal triggers. Let's go over the process, to see how we do it and how to keep it structured.

Getting ready

We will need the Zabbix server and the host from the previous recipe for this recipe.

How to do it...

We have configured one item on our template so far, so let's create a trigger for this item.

1. Navigate to **Configuration | Templates** in our Zabbix frontend and select our **Custom Linux by SNMP** template.
2. Now, click **Triggers** and then **Create Trigger** in the top-right corner. This will take us to the next page, where we will enter the following information:

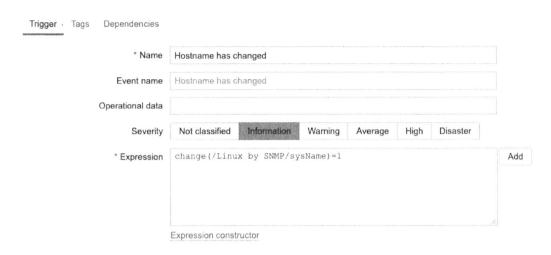

Figure 5.15 – Create trigger window for the SNMP template

3. As discussed in the previous chapter, for triggers there's also the `scope` tag that we need to add:

Figure 5.16 – Create trigger window for the SNMP template – tag

4. Last, but not least, let's edit the hostname on our host to see if the trigger is working correctly. Change the hostname entry by executing the following command on the Linux host CLI:

```
hostnamectl set-hostname lar-book-agent-t
```

5. Then, make sure the changes take effect by executing the following command:

```
exec bash
systemctl restart snmpd
```

How it works...

When editing the template, the created trigger will immediately be added to our host named `lar-book-templated_snmp`. This is because when we edited the template, the host was already configured with this template. When we have changed the hostname, the trigger can immediately be triggered after the item is polled again:

Time ▼	Info	Host	Problem • Severity
11:13:21	•	lar-book-templated_snmp	Hostname has changed

Figure 5.17 – Hostname has changed trigger for host lar-book-templated_snmp

Because we used the `change` function in our trigger, the second time we poll this item the problem will automatically go away again. In our case, this will happen after 30 minutes.

> **Important Note**
> Like a lot of other Zabbix users, I always liked to use the `{HOST.NAME}` macro in trigger names, but according to Zabbix guidelines, this isn't recommended. If you prefer this you can still use it, but it's a lot more useful to use the `Host` fields throughout the Zabbix frontend and the built-in macros for notifications. This will keep trigger names short and won't show us redundant information.

Setting up different kinds of macros

Now, when we are working with templates, a very efficient way to make your templates more useful is through the use of macros. In this recipe, we'll discover how to use macros to do this.

Getting ready

We are going to need our Zabbix server and our SNMP-monitored host from the previous recipes. We'll also need our Zabbix template, as created in the previous recipe.

How to do it...

Now, let's start with creating some macros on a template level. We'll be making two different types of macros.

Defining a user macro

1. Now, let's start this recipe off by defining a user macro on our template. Navigate to **Configuration | Templates** and click our **Custom Linux by SNMP** template.

2. Here, we will go to **Macros** and fill in the following fields:

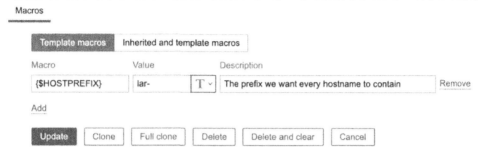

Figure 5.18 – Template-level macros

3. Click on **Update**, and let's move to **Trigger** to define a new trigger:

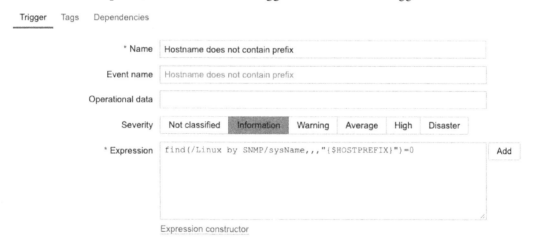

Figure 5.19 – Trigger creation window for the SNMP template

4. Let's also add the trigger tag:

Figure 5.20 – Trigger creation window for the SNMP template – tag

5. Now, change the hostname entry by executing the following command on the host CLI:

```
hostnamectl set-hostname dev-book-agent
```

6. Then, make sure the changes take effect by executing the following command:

```
exec bash
systemctl restart snmpd
```

7. Our trigger should fire, as shown in the following screenshot.

Figure 5.21 – Trigger created problem for hostname prefix on host lar-book-templated_snmp

Defining a built-in macro

1. Now, let's work on defining a built-in macro on our template. Navigate to **Configuration | Templates** and click on our **Custom Linux by SNMP** template.

2. Now, click **Triggers**, and in the top-right corner, click on **Create trigger**. Create a trigger with the following settings:

Figure 5.22 – Trigger creation window for hostname match

3. Let's also add the trigger tag:

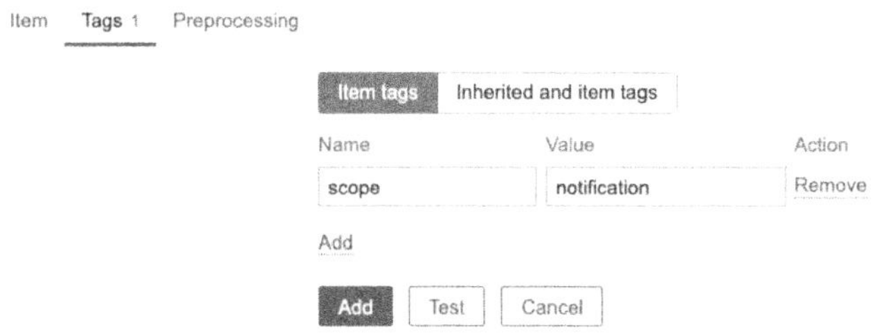

Figure 5.23 – Trigger creation window for the SNMP template – tag

4. This will then trigger a problem, as expected.

Figure 5.24 – Trigger created problem Hostname does not match

How it works...

There are three types of macros: built-in, user, and LLD. All of these macros can be used on templates, but also directly on hosts. Macros are powerful for creating unique values in places that would otherwise contain static information.

Let's discover how they work in this *How it works...* section.

How a user macro works

Now, because we want all of our hosts on this template to contain lar as a prefix, we create a user macro on a template level. This way, the user macro that will be used on every host with this template will be the same.

We then define our user macro in our trigger to use the value, which is lar- in this case. We can reuse this user macro in other triggers, items, and more. The great thing is that defining a user macro on a template level isn't the end of our possibilities. We can override template-level user macros by defining a host-level user macro. So, if we want a single host to contain a different prefix, we simply use that to override the template-level macro, like this:

Figure 5.25 – Host-level macros page

If we then look at the inherited and host-level macros screen on our host, we will see the following:

Figure 5.26 – Inherited and host-level macros page

We see the effective value now would be dev-, not lar-, which is exactly what we would be expecting to happen here.

How a built-in macro works

Now, a built-in macro comes from a predefined list of macros, defined by Zabbix. They are used to get Zabbix elements and put them in items, triggers, and more. This means that our built-in macro used in this case already contains a value.

In this case, we used {HOST.HOST}, which is the hostname we defined on our Zabbix host, like this:

Figure 5.27 – Zabbix host configuration page for host lar-book-templated_snmp

For every single host, this built-in macro would be different as our **Host name** value will be unique. This means that our trigger, although defined on a template level, will always be unique as well. This method is a very powerful way to use built-in macros in triggers, as we'll pull information from Zabbix directly into Zabbix again.

There's more...

A complete list of supported (built-in) macros can be found here:

```
https://www.zabbix.com/documentation/current/en/manual/
appendix/macros/supported_by_location
```

This list will be updated by Zabbix, just as with every good Zabbix documentation page. This way, you can always use this page as a reference for up-to-date (built-in) macros for building your Zabbix elements.

Using LLD on templates

Now, let's get started on my favorite part of template creation: LLD. I think this is one of the most powerful and most used parts of Zabbix.

Getting ready

To get ready for this recipe, you will need your Zabbix server, the SNMP-monitored host from the previous recipes, and our template from the previous recipe.

Working knowledge of the SNMP tree structure is also recommended. So, make sure to read the *Working with SNMP monitoring* recipe in *Chapter 3, Setting Up Zabbix Monitoring*, thoroughly.

How to do it...

1. Let's get started by navigating to **Configuration** | **Templates** and selecting our **Custom Linux by SNMP** template.

    > **Important Note**
    >
    > First, we will add a value mapping, which we'll use for multiple item prototypes. Keep in mind, value mappings in Zabbix 6 are no longer global, but template- or host-specific. This is to make sure that the templates and hosts (once exported) are even more independent from the global Zabbix settings, starting with Zabbix 6.

2. Click on the **Value mapping** tab and the dotted **Add** button. Add the following.

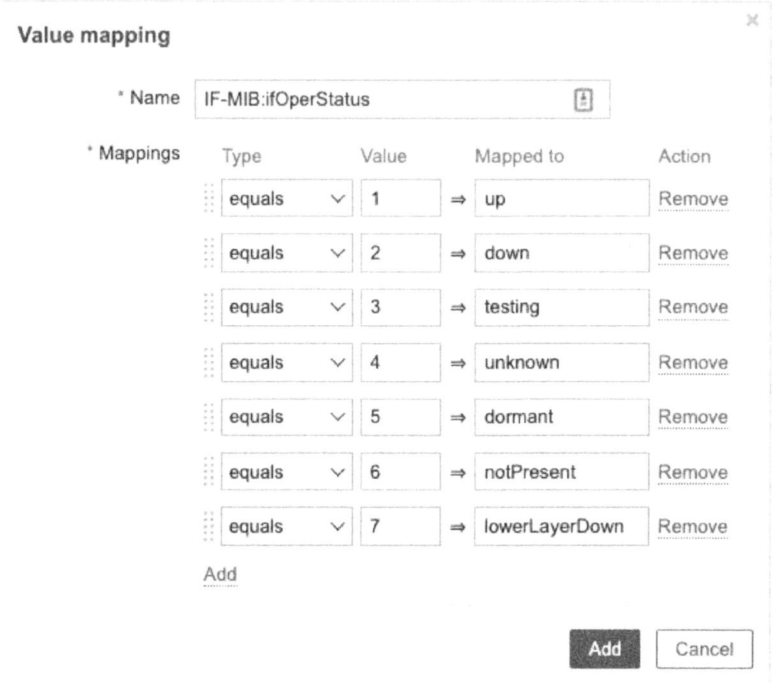

Figure 5.28 – Zabbix add Value mapping page

3. Make sure to save this change by clicking the blue **Add** button and then the blue **Update** button.

4. Now, go back to the template and go to **Discovery rules**, and in the top-right corner, click **Create discovery rule**. This will lead you to the LLD creation page:

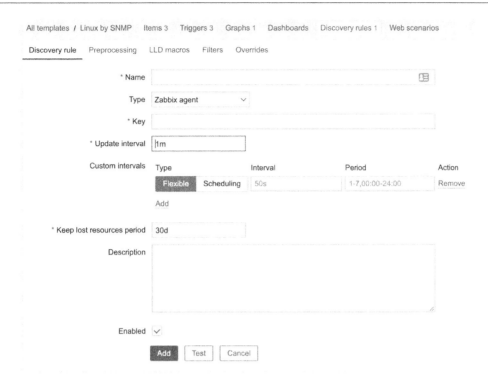

Figure 5.29 – Zabbix LLD creation page, empty

Now, we will be making a discovery rule to discover our interfaces on the Linux host. The Linux SNMP tree for interfaces is at OID `.1.3.6.1.2.1.2.`

> **Important Note**
>
> Make sure that Linux `net-snmp` is configured correctly in the `/etc/snmp/snmpd.conf` file. It's important to change the view in this file to show everything from `.1` and up, like this: `view systemview included .1`

5. Now, let's continue with creating our LLD rule by adding the following to our LLD creation page:

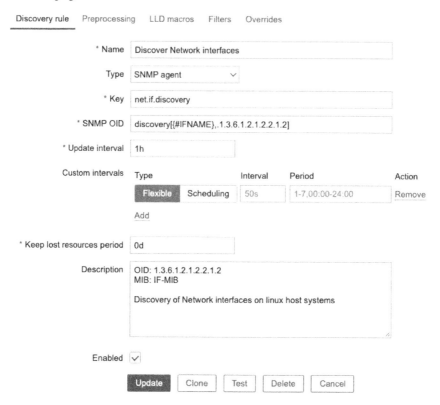

Figure 5.30 – Zabbix LLD creation page filled with our information for network interface discovery

6. After clicking the **Add** button, we can navigate back to our template at **Configuration | Templates** and click **Custom Linux by SNMP**.

> **Important Note**
>
> We define a **Keep lost resources period** of 0 days; we do this because this is a test template. This option is used by LLD to remove created resources (like items and triggers) if they are no longer present on our monitored host. Using 0 days can lead to lost resources because we might get a resource back within a set amount of time, so make sure to adjust this value to your production environment's standard.

7. Go to **Discovery rules** and click our newly created rule, **Discover Network interfaces**.

8. Now, we will go to **Item prototypes** and click **Create item prototype** in the top-right corner. This will take us to the **Item prototype** creation screen, as shown in the following screenshot:

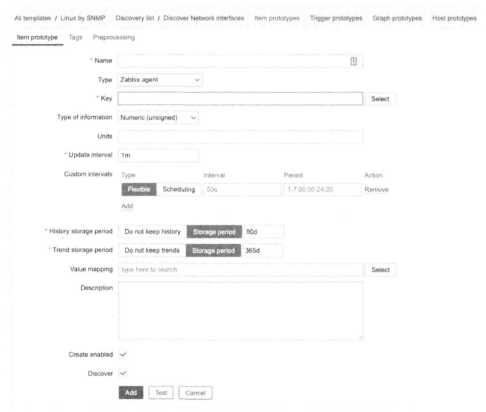

Figure 5.31 – Zabbix LLD Item prototype creation page, empty

Here, we will create our first prototype for creating items from LLD. This means we have to fill it with the information we want our items to contain.

9. Let's start by filling in an item prototype for the interface operational status, like this:

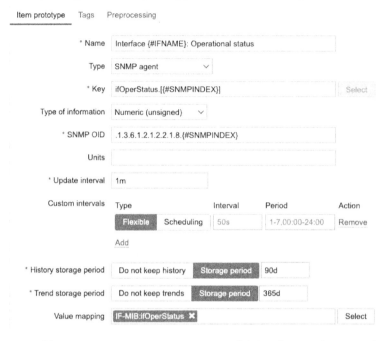

Figure 5.32 – Zabbix LLD item prototype creation page filled with our information for interface operational status

10. At the **Tags** tab, make sure to also add a tag prototype as follows:

Figure 5.33 – Zabbix LLD item prototype tag creation tab

> **Tip**
> In the next step, we'll create an item that is very similar to the item we just created. It's super useful to use the **Clone** button instead of filling in the entire form from scratch again.

11. After clicking the **Add** button, let's repeat the process and also add the following item prototype:

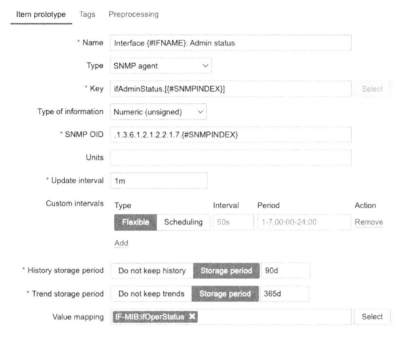

Figure 5.34 – Zabbix LLD item prototype creation page filled with our information for interface admin status

12. Do not forget the **Tags** tab:

Figure 5.35 – Zabbix LLD item 2 prototype tag creation tab

13. Now, move over to the **Trigger prototype** page and click the **Create trigger** prototype button in the top-right corner, and create the following trigger:

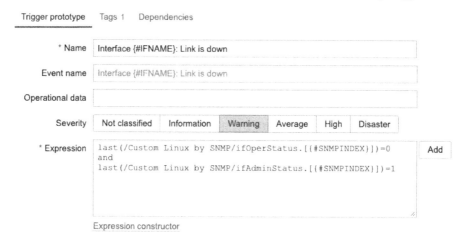

Figure 5.36 – Zabbix LLD trigger prototype creation page filled with our information for interface link status

14. Last, but not least, add the trigger tag:

Figure 5.37 – Zabbix LLD trigger prototype creation page Tags tab

How it works...

Now, LLD is quite an extensive topic in Zabbix, but by following the steps in this recipe you should be able to build almost every form of LLD there is to configure in Zabbix. First of all, let's look at how the discovery works.

In the discovery rule, we just configured the following:

Figure 5.38 – Zabbix LLD discovery key and OID for key net.if.discovery

What we are basically saying here is for every interface after OID
`.1.3.6.1.2.1.2.2.1.2`, fill the `{#IFNAME}` LLD macro. In our case, this would be
the following OIDs:

```
.1.3.6.1.2.1.2.2.1.2.1 = STRING: lo
.1.3.6.1.2.1.2.2.1.2.2 = STRING: ens192
```

So, we are saving these for use in our prototypes. Now, when we look at what we did to
our **Operational status** prototype, this all comes together:

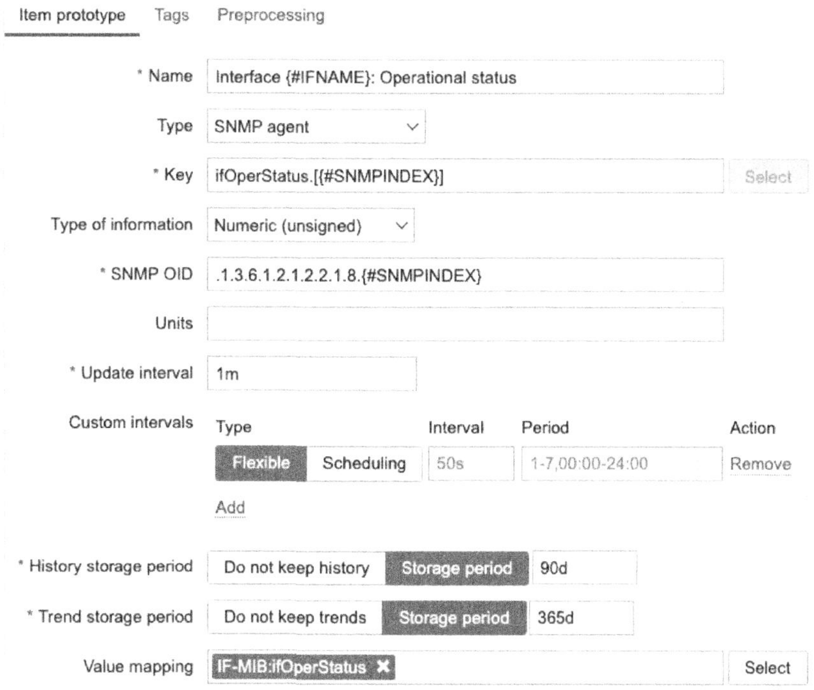

Figure 5.39 – Zabbix LLD item prototype name, type, key, and OID

We are telling our item prototype to create an item for every single `{#IFNAME}` value
using the key defined plus the `{#SNMPINDEX}` LLD macro. The `SNMPINDEX` is the last
number of our SNMP poll. In this case, we would see the following:

```
.1.3.6.1.2.1.2.2.1.8.1 = INTEGER: up(1)
.1.3.6.1.2.1.2.2.1.8.2 = INTEGER: up(1)
```

For all the vendors in the world, there's a set of predefined SNMP rules they need to abide by. Our first interface entry when polling `.1.3.6.1.2.1.2.2.1.2` was the `.1` SNMPINDEX with the value `lo`. This means that when polling `.1.3.6.1.2.1.2.2.1.8`, the `.1` SNMPINDEX here should still contain a value for `lo`.

Zabbix LLD will now create an item with the name `Interface lo: Operational status`, which will poll the SNMP OID:

```
.1.3.6.1.2.1.2.2.1.8.1 = INTEGER: up(1)
```

It will also create an item with the name `Interface ens192: Operational status`, which will poll the SNMP OID:

```
.1.3.6.1.2.1.2.2.1.8.2 = INTEGER: up(1)
```

The created items will then look like this:

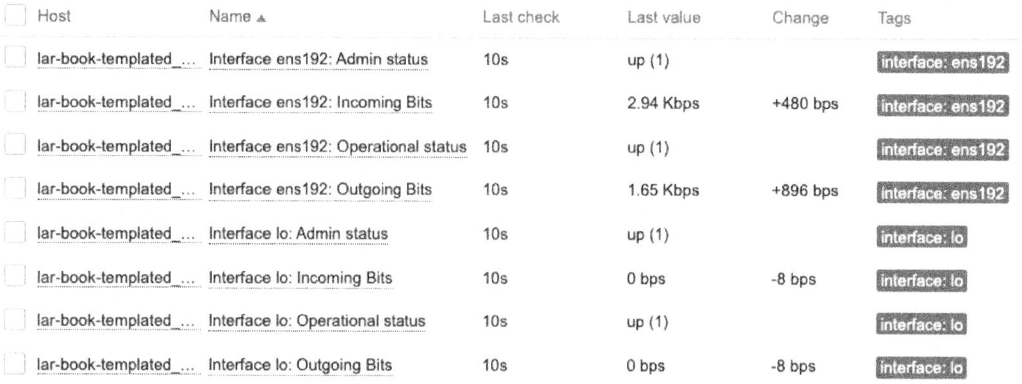

	Host	Name ▲	Last check	Last value	Change	Tags
☐	lar-book-templated_...	Interface ens192: Admin status	10s	up (1)		interface: ens192
☐	lar-book-templated_...	Interface ens192: Incoming Bits	10s	2.94 Kbps	+480 bps	interface: ens192
☐	lar-book-templated_...	Interface ens192: Operational status	10s	up (1)		interface: ens192
☐	lar-book-templated_...	Interface ens192: Outgoing Bits	10s	1.65 Kbps	+896 bps	interface: ens192
☐	lar-book-templated_...	Interface lo: Admin status	10s	up (1)		interface: lo
☐	lar-book-templated_...	Interface lo: Incoming Bits	10s	0 bps	-8 bps	interface: lo
☐	lar-book-templated_...	Interface lo: Operational status	10s	up (1)		interface: lo
☐	lar-book-templated_...	Interface lo: Outgoing Bits	10s	0 bps	-8 bps	interface: lo

Figure 5.40 – Zabbix latest data screen for our SNMP-monitored host

Besides creating these LLD items, we also created an LLD trigger prototype. This works in the same manner as item prototypes. If we check our host triggers, we can see two created triggers:

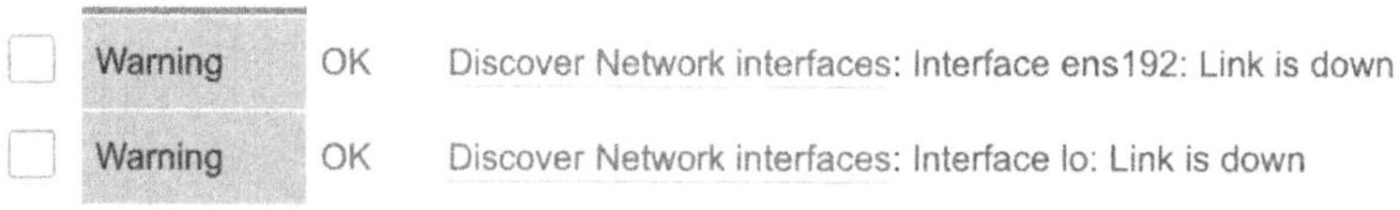

☐	Warning	OK	Discover Network interfaces: Interface ens192: Link is down
☐	Warning	OK	Discover Network interfaces: Interface lo: Link is down

Figure 5.41 – Our SNMP-monitored host triggers

These triggers have been created in the same manner as the items and are then filled with the correct items for triggering on:

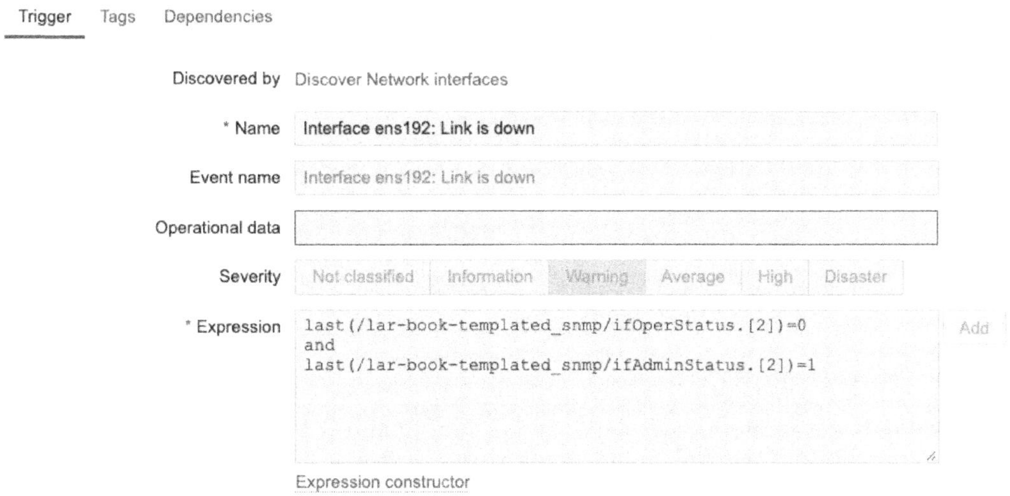

| Trigger | Tags | Dependencies |

Discovered by   Discover Network interfaces

* Name   Interface ens192: Link is down

Event name   Interface ens192: Link is down

Operational data

Severity   Not classified | Information | Warning | Average | High | Disaster

* Expression
```
last(/lar-book-templated_snmp/ifOperStatus.[2])=0
and
last(/lar-book-templated_snmp/ifAdminStatus.[2])=1
```
Add

Expression constructor

Figure 5.42 – Our SNMP-monitored host trigger for ens192

We can see that for the interface operation status we have an SNMPINDEX of 2, and for the `Interface ens192: Admin status` item as well. Our trigger will now trigger when the operation status is 0 (*down*) and our admin status is 1 (*up*).

A neat trigger, to make sure we only have a problem when the admin status is *up*; after all, we want our interface down when we configure it to be admin *down*.

> **Tip**
> It's possible to use discovery filters to only add the interfaces that have admin status *up* to our monitoring. This way, we keep our required Zabbix server performance lower and our data cleaner. Consider using discovery filters for use cases such as this.

See also

Discovery is an extensive subject and takes a while to master. It's something that can be used like we did in this chapter with SNMP, but also with the Zabbix agent, and for a lot of other use cases. Once you start working with Zabbix discovery and you keep it structured, that's when you'll start building the best templates you've seen yet.

Check out the following link for the Zabbix LLD documentation:

`https://www.zabbix.com/documentation/current/en/manual/discovery/low_level_discovery`

Nesting Zabbix templates

Now, using a simple template per device or group of devices is one way to create Zabbix templates, but it isn't the only way. We can also use nested templates to break pieces of them apart and put them back together in the highest template in the nest.

In this recipe, we'll go over how to configure this and why.

Getting ready

We are going to need our Zabbix server, our SNMP-monitored host, and the template we created in the previous recipe.

How to do it...

1. Let's start by navigating to our **Configuration | Templates** page and clicking the **Create template** button in the top-right corner.

2. We are going to create a new template for monitoring the uptime of our SNMP host. Input the following information:

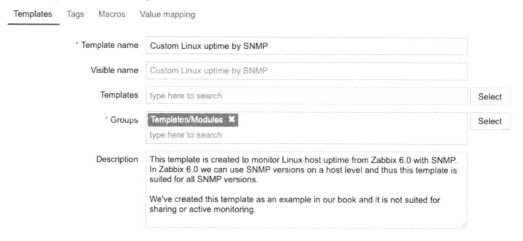

Figure 5.43 – New template creation page for uptime with SNMP

3. Next, we are going to click the **Add** button and click our **Custom Linux uptime by SNMP** template name. This will take us to our template edit screen.

4. Click on **Items** and **Create item** in the top-right corner. We will create an example item here, like this:

Figure 5.44 – New item on the template creation page, System Uptime

5. Do not forget to add a tag as shown in the screenshot by going to the **Tags** tab:

| Item | Tags 1 | Preprocessing |

| | Item tags | Inherited and item tags |

Name	Value	Action
component	system	Remove

Add

Figure 5.45 – New item on the template creation page, System Uptime, Tags tab

6. Make sure to click the blue **Add** button to finish adding this item.

7. Now, let's navigate to our original template by going back to the **Configuration | Templates** page and clicking **Custom Linux by SNMP**.

8. On this page, link a template to the current template by adding it in the **Templates** entry field, like this:

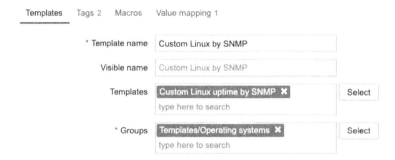

Figure 5.46 – Template link page for master SNMP template

9. Click on the blue **Update** button to finish linking the template.

10. Last, but not least, navigate to **Configuration | Hosts**, click our `lar-book-templated_snmp` SNMP-monitored host, and check out the **Items** page if the item is present:

Figure 5.47 – Our Hosts | Items page for host lar-book-templated_snmp

The item is present, and it shows it's actually from another template. That's all there is to do to actually link a template—easy to work with but harder to keep it structured. Let's see how this works.

How it works...

Now, nesting templates work with a simple tree structure, just like this:

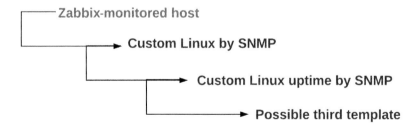

Figure 5.48 – Template nesting tree structure

So, we have our Zabbix-monitored host, which in turn has `Custom Linux by SNMP` linked as the only template. Now, because we have a nested template on `Custom Linux by SNMP` (which is, of course, `Custom Linux uptime by SNMP`), the items on that template will also be linked to our Zabbix-monitored host.

We can use this for a great deal of cases—one of my favorites is for networking equipment. If we have a Juniper EX (or Cisco Catalyst) and a Juniper QFX (or Cisco Nexus) series switch, both series of switches use the same SNMP discovery for interfaces. So, we can create a template for interfaces and nest this in the main template of the EX or QFX series, which do use different SNMP OIDs for other values.

This way, we don't have to write the same discovery rules, items, graphs, and everything else on a template a hundred times. We can simply do it once and nest the template neatly.

6
Visualizing Data, Inventory, and Reporting

When working with Zabbix, it is important that collected data is put to good use. After all, the data is of no use if we do not have a place to easily access it. Zabbix already puts our data to good use with the **Latest data** page and with problems created from triggers, but we can also put our data to good use by building some stuff ourselves, such as graphs, maps, and inventory, and by using reporting.

After working through these recipes, you'll be able to set up the most important parts of Zabbix data visualization. You'll also be able to make good use of your inventory and reporting systems, to get the most out of their useful features.

In this chapter, we'll go over these subjects to show you how to achieve good results in these recipes:

- Creating graphs to access visual data
- Creating maps to keep an eye on infrastructure
- Creating dashboards to get the right overview

- Setting up Zabbix inventory
- Working through Zabbix reporting
- Setting up scheduled PDF reports
- Setting up improved business service monitoring

Technical requirements

For this chapter, we will need our Zabbix server, our **System Network Management Protocol** (**SNMP**)-monitored host from *Chapter 5, Building Your Own Structured Templates*. We'll be doing most of our work in the frontend of Zabbix, so have your mouse at the ready.

The code files can also be accessed from the GitHub repository here:

```
https://github.com/PacktPublishing/Zabbix-6-IT-Infrastructure-
Monitoring-Cookbook/tree/main/chapter06
```

Creating graphs to access visual data

Graphs in Zabbix are a powerful tool to show what's going on with your collected data. You might have already found some graphs by using the **Latest data** page, but we can also create our own predefined graphs. In this recipe, we will go over doing just that.

Getting ready

Make sure to get your Zabbix server ready, along with a Linux host that we can monitor (with SNMP). If you have followed along with the recipes in *Chapter 5, Building Your Own Structured Templates*, you should already have created your own personal template.

Alternatively, download the templates here:

```
https://github.com/PacktPublishing/Zabbix-6-IT-Infrastructure-
Monitoring-Cookbook/tree/main/chapter6
```

If you are using the downloaded templates, download and import **Template OS Linux uptime by SNMP** first, and then **Linux by SNMP**. Importing a template can be done at **Configuration | Templates** by clicking the blue **Import** button in the top-right corner.

Make sure to put the template on a host and monitor it.

How to do it...

1. Let's start by navigating to our templates by going to **Configuration | Templates** and selecting the template. For me, it is still called **Custom Linux by SNMP**.

2. Go to **Items** and create the following item on the template:

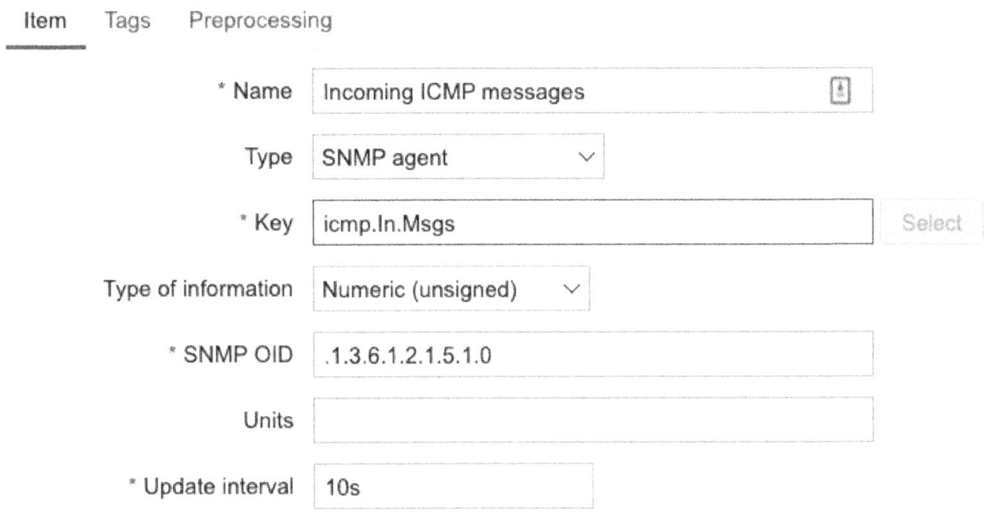

Figure 6.1 – ICMP Item creation page

3. Make sure to go to the **Tags** tab and add a tag as follows:

Figure 6.2 – ICMP Item creation page, Tags tab

4. Click the blue **Add** button to save this item.

5. Now, back at the template configuration page, go to **Graphs**. This is where we can see all of our configured graphs in this template; at the moment, there are none.

6. Click **Create graph** in the top-right corner. This will take you to the graph creation page:

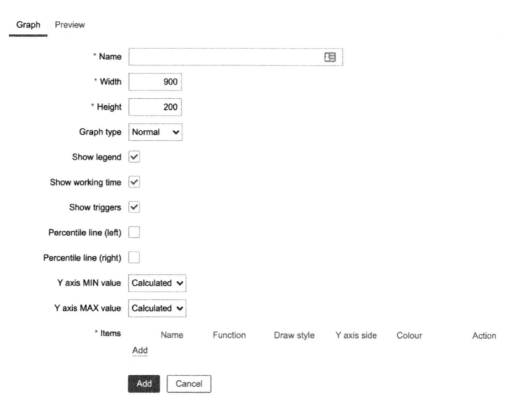

Figure 6.3 – Graph creation page

This is where we can create graphs for standalone items. Let's create a graph to see our uptime.

7. Fill in the graph creation page with the following information:

Figure 6.4 – Graph creation page filled with our information

> **Tip**
>
> When working with graphs, it's a good idea to keep colorblind people in mind. Worldwide, about 8% of all males and 0.5% of all females are affected by this condition. There are great sources online that explain which colors to use for your production environment. You can find one such source here: `https://www.tableau.com/about/blog/2016/4/examining-data-viz-rules-dont-use-red-green-together-53463`

8. Now, ping your SNMP-monitored host for a while. Do this from your Zabbix server **command-line interface (CLI)**:

```
ping 10.16.16.153
```

9. Afterward, navigate to **Monitoring | Hosts** and click the **Graphs** button next to your host. In my case, the host is still called `lar-book-templated_snmp`.

10. Now, this will immediately take us to an overview of graphs for this host, where we can see our new **Incoming ICMP messages** graph:

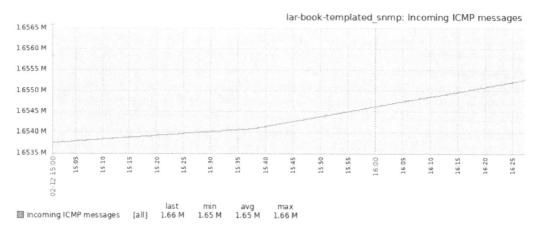

Figure 6.5 – Monitoring | Hosts graph page with our graph

We can also make graphs for discovery items; this is called a graph prototype. They work in about the same way as our item prototypes. Let's create one of these as well:

1. Navigate to **Configuration | Templates** and select our **Linux by SNMP** template.

2. Go to **Discovery rules**, and then, for the **Discover Network Interfaces** discovery rule, click on **Item prototypes**. In the top-right corner, click **Create item prototype** and create the following item prototype:

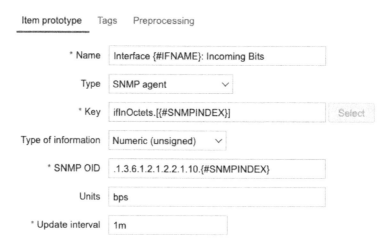

Figure 6.6 – Item prototype Incoming bits page filled with our information

3. Then let's add a tag on the **Tags** tab:

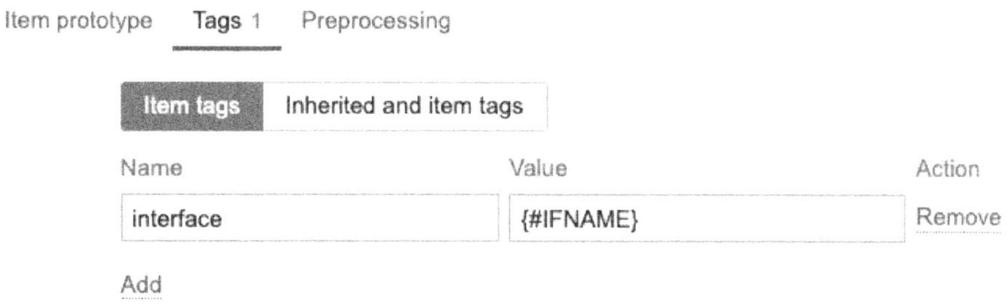

Item prototype   **Tags** 1   Preprocessing

Item tags   Inherited and item tags

Name	Value	Action
interface	{#IFNAME}	Remove

Add

Figure 6.7 – Item prototype Incoming bits, Tags tab

4. Lastly, make sure to add the following on the **Preprocessing** page:

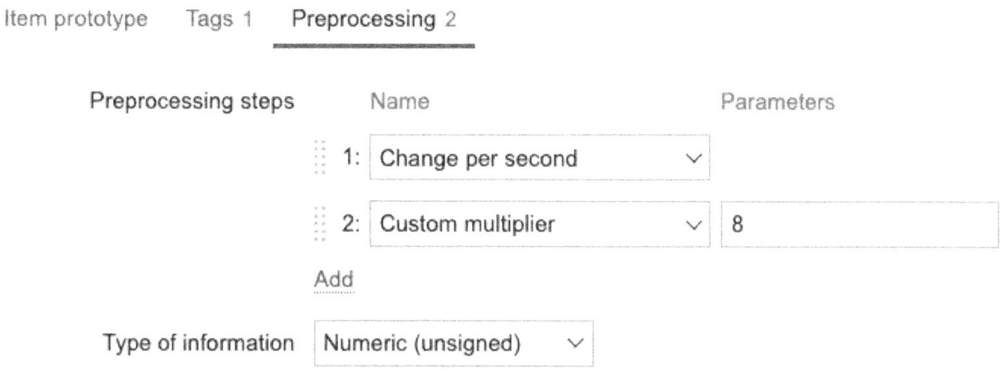

Item prototype   Tags 1   **Preprocessing** 2

Preprocessing steps   Name   Parameters

1: Change per second ⌄

2: Custom multiplier ⌄   8

Add

Type of information   Numeric (unsigned) ⌄

Figure 6.8 – Item prototype Incoming bits Preprocessing tab filled with our information

> **Important note**
> Preprocessing is quite an extensive topic. In short, the preprocessing in this step will make sure that 1: Our data is calculated as change per second, with the mathematical formula **(value-prev_value)/(time-prev_time)**, and 2: Our data is multiplied by 8 to change from bytes to bits.

5. Click the blue **Add** button to finish creating this item prototype.

6. Now, back at our discovery rule **Discover Network interfaces**, click the **Graph prototypes** button.

7. In the top-right corner, click **Create graph prototype** and fill the next page with the following information:

Figure 6.9 – Graph prototype Incoming bits page filled with our information

8. Now, if we go back to **Monitoring | Hosts** and we click the **Graphs** button, we can see two new graphs:

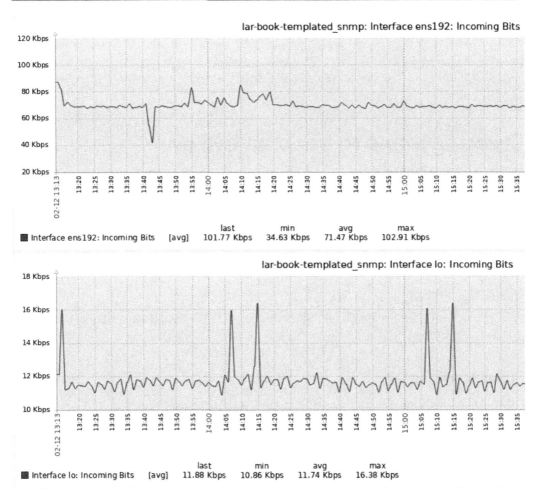

Figure 6.10 – Graphs page for our host

It might take some time for the graph to fill up with data, as we just added the item. Give it some time and you will start to see this graph fill up.

How it works...

Now, graphs work simply by putting your collected values in a visual form. We collect our data from our host—through SNMP, for example—and we put that data in our database. Our graphs in turn collect this data from the database and put it in this visual form. For us, this is a lot better to read, and we can interpret the data easily.

The graph prototype works in almost the same way as our item prototype. For every single discovered interface, we create a graph using a name containing the {#IFNAME} **Low-Level Discovery** (**LLD**) macro. This way, we get a versatile structured environment because when a new interface is created (or deleted), a new graph is also created (or deleted).

Creating maps to keep an eye on infrastructure

Maps in Zabbix are a great way to get an overview of infrastructure—for instance, they're amazing for following traffic flows or seeing where something is going off in your environment. They're not only super-useful for network overviews but also for server management overviews, and even for a lot of cool customization.

Getting ready

We will need our Zabbix server, our SNMP-monitored host, and the templates from the previous recipe.

How to do it...

1. Let's start this recipe off by navigating to **Configuration | Template** and selecting our **Linux by SNMP** template.

2. Go to **Discovery rules** and then **Item prototypes**. Create the following item prototype by filling in the fields in the **Item prototype** creation page:

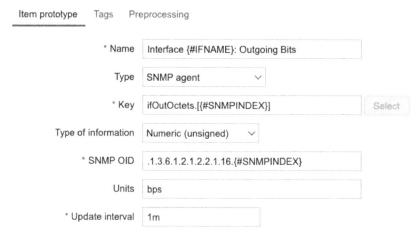

Figure 6.11 – Item prototype creation page

3. We'll also need to go to **Tags** to add a new tag, like the one in the following screenshot:

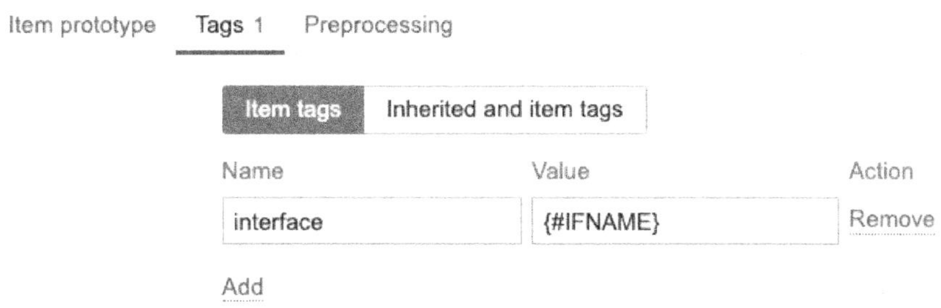

Figure 6.12 – Item prototype creation page, Tags tab

4. Lastly, do not forget to add preprocessing by going to the **Preprocessing** tab.

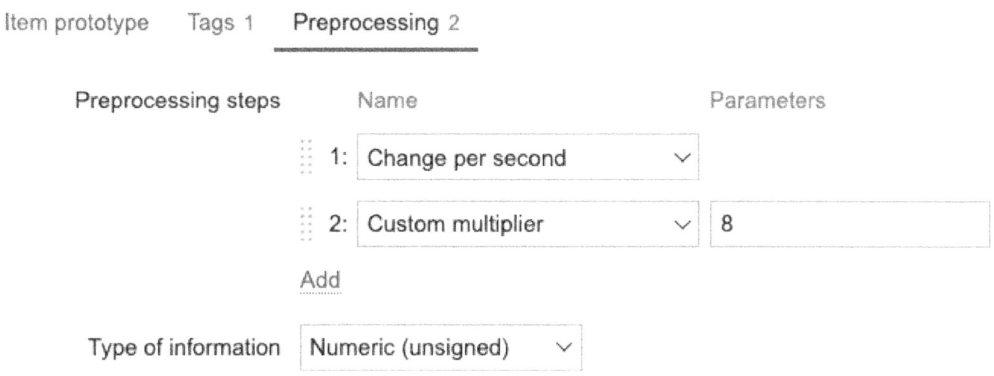

Figure 6.13 – Item prototype Preprocessing creation page

5. Click on the blue **Add** button to finish.

6. Next up, navigate to **Monitoring | Maps**. There's already a default map here included in all Zabbix server installs, titled **Local network**. Feel free to check it out:

Figure 6.14 – The default Local network map

7. There's not much to see here, besides your local Zabbix server host and if it is in a problem state or not. So, let's click on **All maps**.

8. We are going to create our own map, so click the **Create map** button in the top-right corner. Create the map by filling in the following fields:

Figure 6.15 – Map creation page

9. After clicking the blue **Add** button, the frontend will take you back to the **Map** overview page. Click the newly created `Templated SNMP host` map here.

10. Click **Edit map** in the top-right corner to start editing the map.

11. Now, what we want to do here is select the **Add** button next to **Map element**, which is in the horizontal menu at the top of the map. This will add the following element:

New element

Figure 6.16 – The added element

12. Click the newly added element—this will open the following screen:

Map element

Type	Image ▾
Label	New element
Label location	Default ▾
Icons	Default Server_(96) ▾
Coordinates	X 0 Y 0

URLs   Name   URL   Action

                                                                                Remove

Add

Apply   Remove   Close

Figure 6.17 – New Map element edit window

13. Now, here we can fill out our host information. Let's add the following information to the fields:

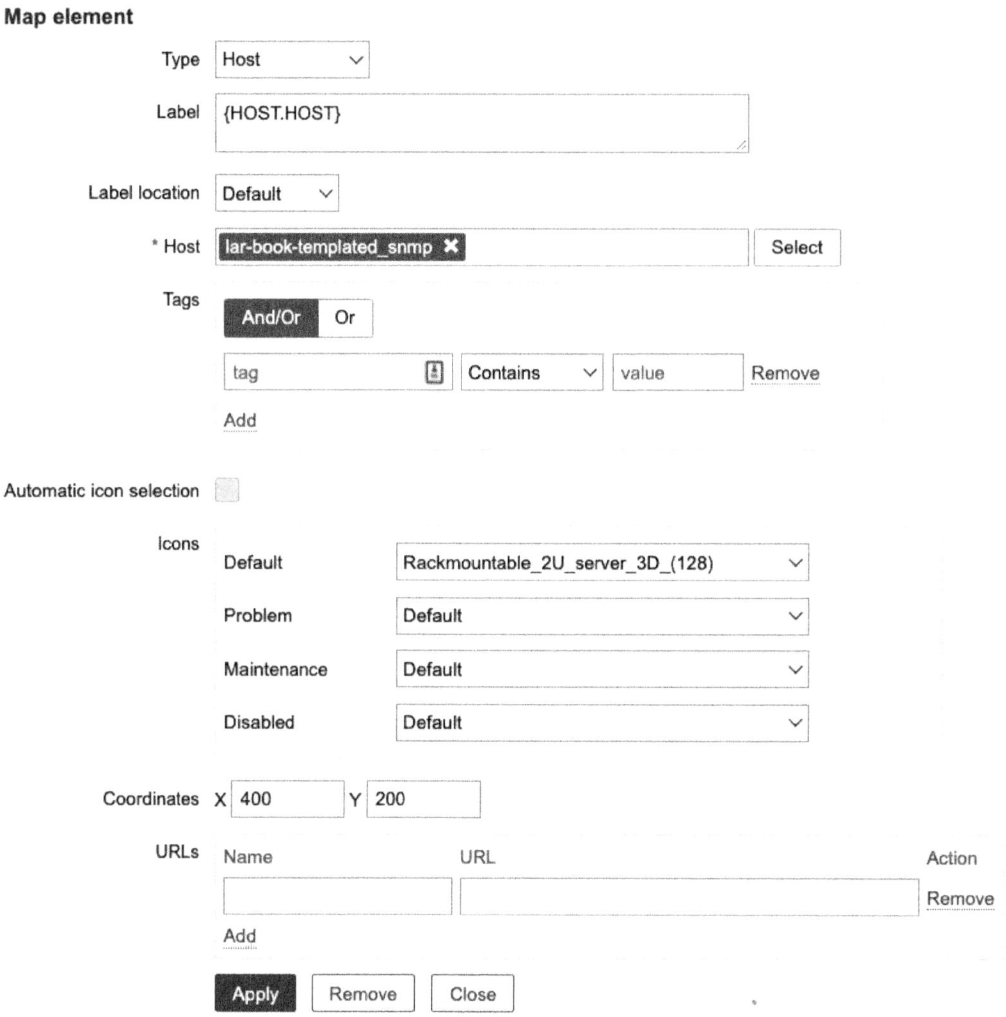

Map element

Type	Host ∨
Label	{HOST.HOST}
Label location	Default ∨
* Host	lar-book-templated_snmp ✖ Select
Tags	And/Or Or
	tag ▣ Contains ∨ value Remove
	Add

Automatic icon selection ☐

Icons

Default	Rackmountable_2U_server_3D_(128) ∨
Problem	Default ∨
Maintenance	Default ∨
Disabled	Default ∨

Coordinates X 400   Y 200

URLs   Name   URL   Action

		Remove

Add

Apply   Remove   Close

Figure 6.18 – Map element lar-book-templated_snmp edit window

Click **Apply** and move the element by dragging it to **X**:400 and **Y**:200 (see *Figure 6.20*).

14. Now, add another element by clicking the **Add** button next to **Map element**. Edit the new element and add the following information.

Map element

Type   Image ▾

Label   Vswitch

Label location   Default ▾

Icons

Default   Switch_(96) ▾

Coordinates   X 150   Y 200

URLs   Name   URL   Action

Remove

Add

Apply   Remove   Close

Figure 6.19 – Map element Vswitch edit window filled with information

After creating both elements, let's move the new switch element to **X**:150 and **Y**:200, as seen in *Figure 6.20.*

15. Now, select both elements by holding the *Ctrl* key (*Command* on a Mac) on your keyboard.

16. Then, click **Add** next to **Link** to add a link between the two elements. It should now look like this:

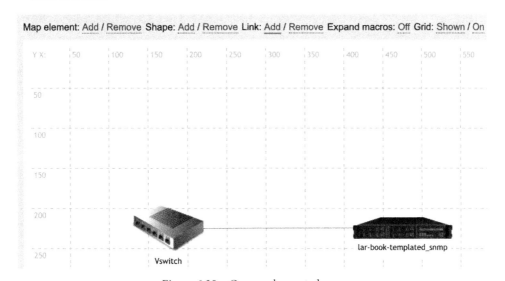

Figure 6.20 – Our newly created map

17. Edit the information for our server again after creating the link by clicking on our icon. Click on **Edit** next to the newly created link, as shown in the following screenshot:

Figure 6.21 – Edit link in the Map element edit window

18. Add the following information to the window:

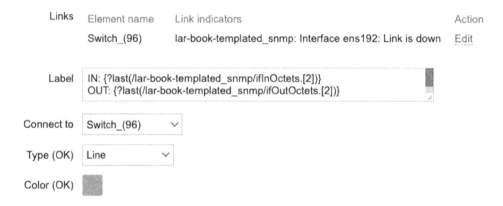

Figure 6.22 – Edit the link in the Map element edit window with our information

19. Let's also click **Add** in the **Link indicators** section and add the following trigger with the color red:

Figure 6.23 – Link indicator filled with a trigger

20. Now, click **Apply** at the bottom of the window and then **Update** in the top-right corner of the page. That's our first map created!

How it works...

Now, after creating and opening our map, we can see the following:

Figure 6.24 – Our newly created map

The map shows our switch (which is not a monitored host at the moment) and our server (which is a monitored host). This means that when something is wrong with our server, the **OK** status will turn into a **PROBLEM** status on the map.

We can also see our configured label (see *Figure 6.24)*, which is showing us real-time information of traffic statistics. Now, when we break down the label, we get the following:

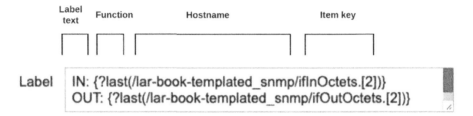

Figure 6.25 – Map label breakdown

We can pull real-time statistics into a label by defining which statistics we want to pull into the label between { }. In this case, we collect our values for interface traffic and put them directly in the label, creating a real-time traffic analysis map.

We also put a trigger on this link. The cool thing about putting triggers such as this on our map is that when our link goes down, we can see the following happen:

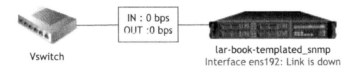

Figure 6.26 – Map showing problems

Traffic stopped flowing because the link is now down, and our line has turned red. Also, our host is now showing a **PROBLEM** state under the hostname.

We can even create orange lines with triggers that state 50% traffic utilization like this and trace **Distributed Denial of Service (DDoS)** traffic through our network.

Creating dashboards to get the right overview

Now that we've created some graphs and a map, let's continue on by not only visualizing our data but also getting the visualization in an overview. We're going to create a dashboard for our Linux-monitored hosts.

Getting ready

Make sure you followed the previous two recipes and that you have your Zabbix server ready. We'll be using our SNMP-monitored host from the previous recipe, as well as our item, triggers, and map.

How to do it...

1. Navigate to **Monitoring | Dashboards** and click **All dashboards** in the left corner of the page.

2. Now, click the **Create dashboard** button in the top-right corner and fill in your dashboard name, like this:

Figure 6.27 – Create dashboard window

> **Tip**
> Keeping Zabbix elements such as maps and dashboards owned by the Zabbix **Admin** user is a great idea. This way, they aren't dependent on a single user who might leave your environment at a later stage. The elements can be owned by a disabled user as well.

3. Now, click **Apply**, and you'll be taken to your dashboard immediately:

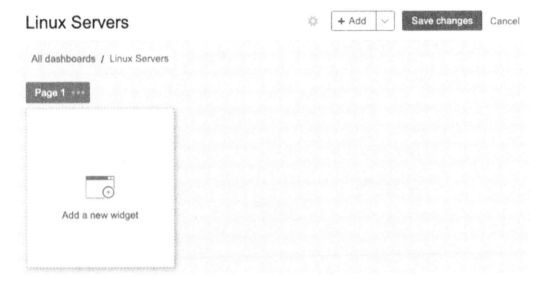

Figure 6.28 – New empty dashboard

After creating our dashboard, we will see that it is empty. We need to fill it with several widgets to create a good overview.

4. Let's start by adding a problem widget. Click **+ Add widget** in the top-right corner. Add the following widget by filling out all the fields:

Figure 6.29 – New problem widget creation window

5. Click **Add**, and we have our first widget on our dashboard, displaying all **Unacknowledged Problems**. It will only show them for the **Severity** warning and higher on all Linux servers:

Figure 6.30 – Our Unacknowledged Problems widget

6. Let's immediately add some more widgets, starting with our **Map** widget. Click **+ Add widget** in the top-right corner, and add the following widget:

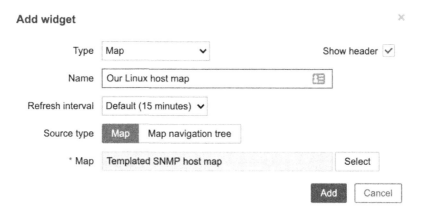

Figure 6.31 – New Map widget creation window

7. Also, add a **Graph** type widget by clicking **+ Add widget** in the top-right corner again. This one is a bit more difficult. Let's add our name first:

Figure 6.32 – New Graph widget creation window

8. Then, we need to add our first **Data set**, like this:

Figure 6.33 – Adding data set in New Graph widget creation window

9. Then, add a second one by clicking **+ Add new data set** and adding the following:

Figure 6.34 – Adding another dataset in the New Graph widget creation window

10. We can then click **Add**, and our graph will be added to our dashboard.

11. Let's also add the **Item value** widget to the page. Click on **+ Add widget** again. Then set up the following widget:

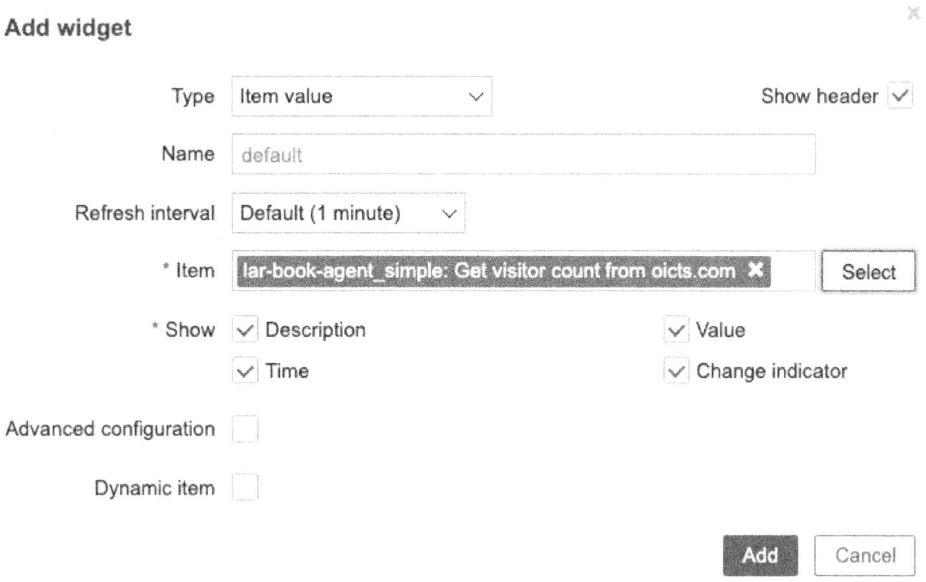

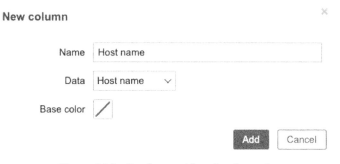

Figure 6.35 – Adding the widget Item value

If you are interested in changing exactly how this widget looks, be sure to use the **Show** and **Advanced configuration** fields in this widget configuration screen.

12. Another we personally love is the very useful new **Top hosts** widget. Let's add it by using the **+ Add widget** button again.

13. On the widget configuration screen, set up the **Host groups** as Linux servers.

14. Next, click on the **Add** button next to **Columns** to add a column with information. Fill out the form like this:

Figure 6.36 – Top hosts widget 1, column 1

15. Click on the **Add** button next to **Columns** again and add the following:

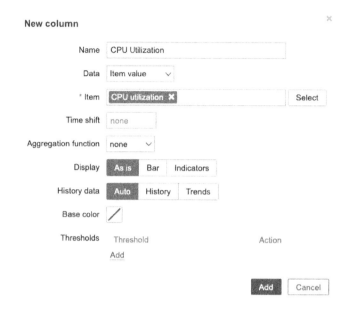

Figure 6.37 – Top hosts widget 1, column 2

16. The end result should look like this:

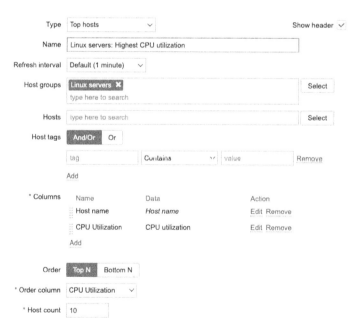

Figure 6.38 – Top hosts widget 1

17. Do not forget to click the blue **Add** button at the bottom of the form to save the changes.

18. Let's create one more **Top hosts** widget by using the **+ Add widget** button again.

19. Set up the **Host groups** as `Linux servers` again. Then click on the **Add** button next to **Columns** again. Add the following:

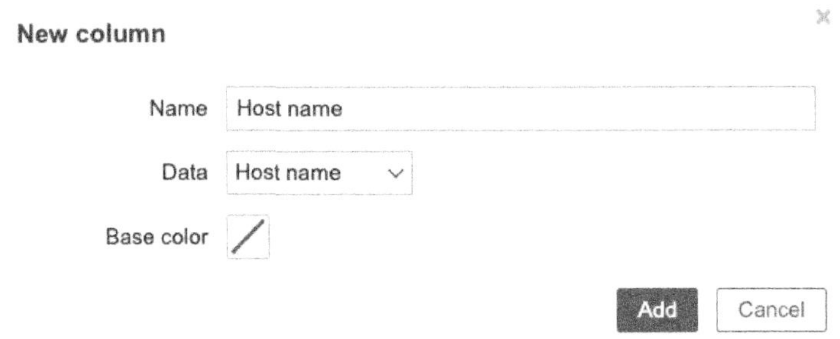

Figure 6.39 – Top hosts widget 2, column 1

20. Click on the **Add** button next to **Columns** again and add the following:

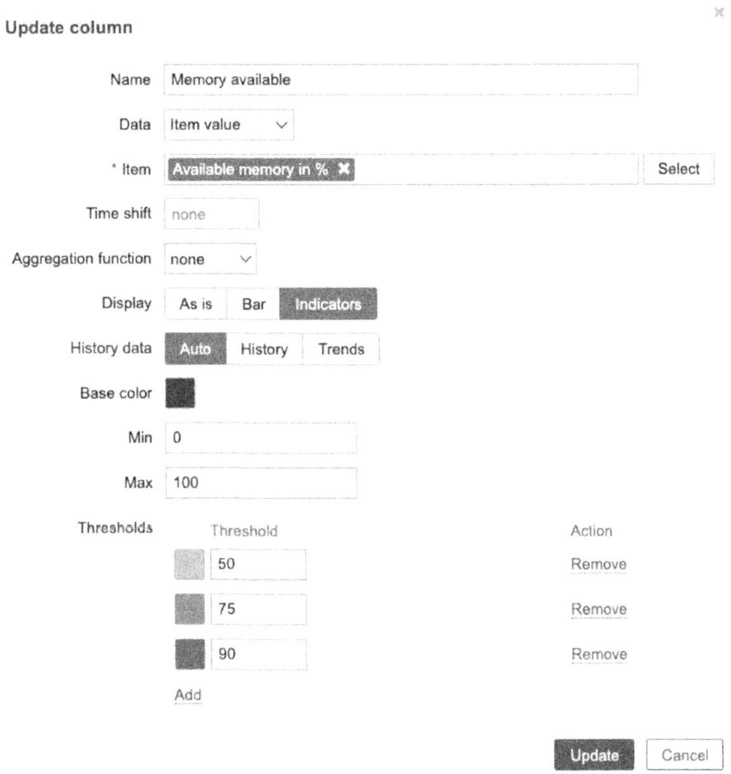

Figure 6.40 – Top hosts widget 2, column 2

21. The end result will look like this:

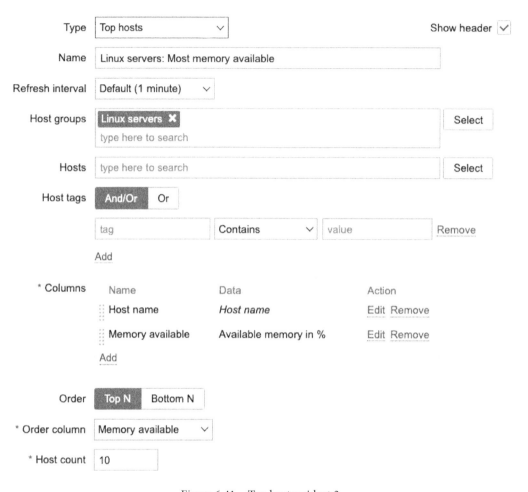

Figure 6.41 – Top hosts widget 2

22. We can then freely move around the widgets until we get this, for example:

Figure 6.42 – Our dashboard with information

23. Click **Save changes** in the top-right corner, and you are done.

How it works...

Creating dashboards is the best way to create overviews for quick access to data during troubleshooting, day-to-day problem monitoring, and—of course—for use with big TV walls. We've probably all seen the big operation centers with TVs displaying data. Zabbix is great for all these purposes and more, as you can see from this recipe.

> **Important note**
>
> Zabbix has removed the **Screens** functionality, which is why you might be confused about where it went. **Screens** is fully replaced by **Dashboards**, and thus we will only be working with building dashboards now. **Dashboards** have the **slideshow** and host-specific functionality now.

Setting up Zabbix inventory

Zabbix inventory is a feature I personally love, but it hasn't had a lot of love from the Zabbix development team lately. Sorry—I still love you, Zabbix developers, but if you're reading this, feel free to put some time into the feature!

The feature makes it possible for us to automatically put collected data in a visual inventory in the Zabbix frontend. Let's get started.

Getting ready

Make sure to log in to the Zabbix frontend and keep your SNMP-monitored host from the previous recipes ready.

How to do it...

1. Let's start by making sure our Zabbix server puts all of our hosts' inventory information into the fields. I like to do this by going to **Administration | General** and then selecting **Other** from the dropdown in the top-left corner.

2. We can then set our **Default host inventory mode** parameter to **Automatic**. Don't forget to click **Update**:

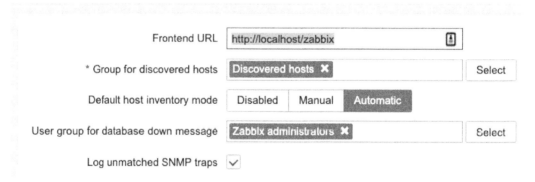

Figure 6.43 – Administration | General | Other configuration parameters page

3. Alternatively, we can do this at a host level. Go to **Configuration | Hosts** and select our `lar-book-templated_snmp` SNMP-monitored host.

4. Select **Inventory** and set it to **Automatic** here as well. As you may have noticed, the default applies only to newly created hosts from now on.

Important note

Changing the global setting does not apply it to all existing hosts but only to newly created hosts. It might be a good idea to run a **Mass update** for all the hosts, or change the inventory mode manually, host by host.

---

5. Now let's go to **Configuration | Templates** and select **Linux by SNMP**.

6. Go to **Items** and edit **System hostname**. We have to change the **Populates host inventory field** setting, like this:

Figure 6.44 – Edit item page

7. Click **Update** and navigate to **Inventory | Hosts**. You will see the following:

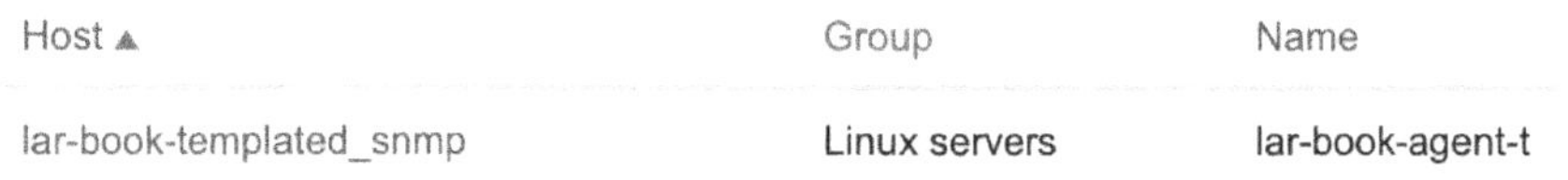

Host ▲	Group	Name
lar-book-templated_snmp	Linux servers	lar-book-agent-t

Figure 6.45 – Inventory | Hosts page

How it works...

Zabbix inventory is simple but underdeveloped at the moment. It's not amazing to filter to a point where it shows exactly what we want to see, but it can be very useful nonetheless.

If you are working with a lot of equipment, such as in a **managed service provider** (MSP) environment, it can become overwhelming to log in to every device and get the serial number by hand. If you poll the serial number and you populate the **inventory** field, suddenly you have an active list of up-to-date serial numbers.

The same of course works with anything from hardware information to software versions. We could get the active operating system versions from devices and generate an extensive list of all our operating system versions: very useful if you ever have to patch something, for example.

Use Zabbix inventory wisely when creating items, and put the population to **Automatic**, like we did in this chapter—you'll then never even have to think too much about the feature. You configure it almost automatically this way, and have nice lists waiting for you when you are in need of them.

Using the new Zabbix Geomap widget

Now that we have seen how to create dashboards in the previous recipe, let's set up another dashboard. We'll use this one to create a full-fledged geographical overview of some of our hosts in Zabbix. We'll do this by using the Zabbix inventory functionality we have just learned how to use.

Getting ready

All we need for this recipe is our Zabbix setup with access to the frontend. It is also smart to follow the previous two recipes about dashboards and inventory. If you have not followed those yet, it is recommended to follow them first.

How to do it...

Using the Zabbix Geomap functionality is quite easy. We simply need to use our Zabbix inventory on our hosts in combination with a dashboard widget:

1. First, let's navigate to our **Configuration | Hosts** page and edit one of our hosts. I'll be using the `lar-book-templated_snmp` host.

2. Go to the **Inventory** tab and make sure that it is set to **Manual** or **Automatic**.

Figure 6.46 – Inventory mode selector on the Zabbix host Inventory tab

3. Now, in the **Location latitude** and **Location longitude** fields, fill in the following:

Figure 6.47 – Inventory tab fields on a Zabbix host

4. Click on the blue **Update** button to save these changes.

5. Back at **Configuration | Hosts**, let's do the same thing for another host. I'll use `lar-book-agent_simple`.

6. Go to the **Inventory** tab and fill in the **Location latitude** and **Location longitude** fields again:

Figure 6.48 – Inventory tab fields on another Zabbix host

7. Click on the blue **Update** button to save these changes.

8. Now let's go to **Monitoring | Dashboards** and, at **All dashboards**, create a new dashboard or use our existing **Linux servers** dashboard, which is what I'll do.

9. Click on the blue **Edit dashboard** button in the top-right corner and use the **Add** button dropdown to click on **Add page**:

Figure 6.49 – Existing dashboard Add page button

10. We'll add the following new page.

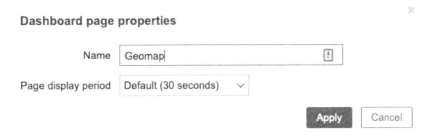

Figure 6.50 – Existing dashboard Add page properties

11. Click on **Apply** to add this new page.

12. We can now add our Geomap widget simply by clicking anywhere on the page. Fill it in as follows.

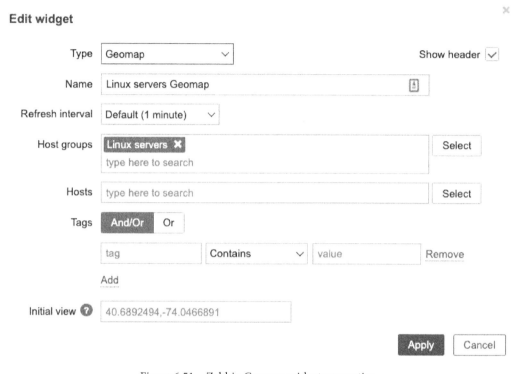

Figure 6.51 – Zabbix Geomap widget properties

13. Click on **Apply** to save the widget configuration.

14. We can now click on the blue **Save changes** button in the top-right corner to save our dashboard changes.

15. This will take us back to our dashboard, where we can click the **Geomap** page of this dashboard.

Figure 6.52 – Zabbix Geomap widget on a dashboard with two hosts

We now have a functioning Geomap in our Zabbix dashboard, using the latitude and longitude that are available in our Zabbix inventory.

How it works...

Instead of creating an entire new **Monitoring | Geomap** page, Zabbix has chosen to include this new feature using a widget, giving us the option to create even more advanced dashboards. It's important to note here that Zabbix also made the choice to use existing inventory data. Because it is possible to automatically fill in inventory data as we have seen in the *Setting up Zabbix inventory* recipe, we can also automate our Geomap widget content.

So, whether you go the manual route or the automatic route, the Geomap widget is a valuable extension of our dashboard. In general, Zabbix is extending the dashboard functionality quite a bit by including a bunch of new widgets in Zabbix 6.

We will also set up our Zabbix automatic reporting in this chapter of the book, which will also use the dashboard functionality. If you'd like you can combine a Geomap widget with your automatic report to send out a geographical report. The key takeaway here is that Zabbix is building interoperability between components and giving us flexibility in the way we want to use a new widget like this.

When working with the initial release of the Geomap widget, some people asked us if it was possible to change the kind of map used by the Geomap widget. If we navigate to **Administration | Geographical maps** we can actually choose a number of built-in map providers:

Figure 6.53 – Zabbix Administration | Geographical maps options

If that is not enough, it is also possible to add our own custom map provider using the **Other** option under **Tile provider**. Simply fill in the form and you are all set:

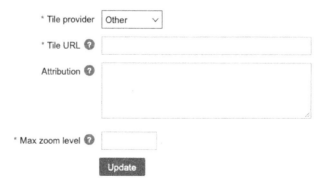

Figure 6.54 – Zabbix Administration | Geographical maps other form

A lot of possibilities have been added through this single widget, as you can see. One of the most requested features from the Zabbix community, we can now set it up and use it in the latest Zabbix releases.

Working through Zabbix reporting

Zabbix reporting got some well-deserved love from Zabbix development, especially with regard to getting reports out of the system and improving the audit log. First, let's take a look at some powerful features to show you exactly what's going on with your statistics right from the Zabbix frontend. Then, in the next recipe, we will take a look at how to create automatic PDF reports, a new and much-anticipated feature.

Getting ready

For this recipe, all you'll need is the Zabbix frontend and a monitored host. I'll be using the SNMP-monitored host from the previous recipes.

How to do it...

There isn't anything to configure really, as reporting is present in Zabbix from the start. So, let's dive into what each page of reporting offers us.

System information

If you navigate to **Reports** | **System information**, you will find the following table:

System information

Parameter	Value	Details
Zabbix server is running	Yes	localhost:10051
Number of hosts (enabled/disabled)	11	11 / 0
Number of templates	235	
Number of items (enabled/disabled/not supported)	287	252 / 0 / 35
Number of triggers (enabled/disabled [problem/ok])	120	120 / 0 [8 / 112]
Number of users (online)	3	1
Required server performance, new values per second	3.71	
High availability cluster	Disabled	

Figure 6.55 – Reports | System information page

You might have seen this table before, as it is also configurable as a dashboard widget. This page gives us all of the quick information we need about our Zabbix server, such as the following:

- **Zabbix server is running**: Informs us whether the Zabbix server backend is actually running and where it is running. In this case, it's running, and it's running on `localhost:10051`.

- **Number of hosts**: This will detail to us the number of hosts **enabled** (7), the number of hosts **disabled** (0), and the number of **templates** we have (146). It gives us a quick overview of our Zabbix server host information.

- **Number of items**: Here, we can see details of our Zabbix server's items—in this case, **enabled** (318), **disabled** (1), and **not supported** (38).

- **Number of triggers**: This details the number of triggers to us. We can see how many are **enabled** (151) and **disabled** (1), but also how many are in a **problem** state (7) and how many are in an **ok** state (144).

- **Number of users (online)**: The first value details the total number of users. The second value details the numbers of users currently logged in to the Zabbix frontend.

- **Required server performance, new values per second**: Perhaps I'm introducing you to a completely new concept here, which is **New Values Per Second**, or **NVPS**. A server receives or requests values through items and writes this to our MariaDB database (or another database). The NVPS information detailed here shows the estimated number of NVPS received by the Zabbix server. Keep a close eye on this as your Zabbix server grows, as it's a good indicator to see how quickly you should scale up.

You might also see three additional values here depending on your setup:

- **Database history tables upgraded**: If you see this, it's indicating that one of your database history tables hasn't been upgraded yet. Numeric (float) tables have been expanded to allow for more characters to be saved per data point. This table isn't upgraded automatically coming from Zabbix 4 to 5 or higher, as not everyone needs it and it might take a long time to upgrade.

- **Database name**: If you see the name of your database with the value of your version it might indicate you are running a non-supported database version. You could see a message like `Warning! Unsupported <DATABASE NAME> database server version. Should be at least <DATABASE VERSION>`.

- **High availability cluster**: If you are running a Zabbix server high availability cluster you will see if it is enabled here and what the failover delay is. Additionally, the **System information** page will display additional high availability information.

Availability report

Navigating to **Reports | Availability report** will give us some useful information about how long a trigger has been in a **Problems** state versus an **Ok** state for a certain time period:

Availability report

Mode | By host

‹ Zoom out › | Last 30 days ⏱ | Filter ▽

Host	Name	Problems	Ok	Graph
lar-book-agent_passive	Zabbix agent is not available (for 3m)	10.6665%	89.3335%	Show
lar-book-agent_simple	lar-book-agent_simple - Port 22 (SSH) down	89.3331%	10.6669%	Show
lar-book-agent_simple	More than 50 visitors on lar-book-agent_simple in the last 10 minutes		100.0000%	Show

Figure 6.56 – Reports | Availability report page

Looking at one of our hosts, we can see that in the last 30 days, the **Zabbix agent is not available (for 3m)** trigger has been in a **Problems** state for **10.6665%** of the time. This might be useful for us to know so that we can define how often a certain problem arises.

Trigger top 100

Navigating to **Reports | Trigger top 100**, we will find the top 100 triggers that have been firing in a certain amount of time:

100 busiest triggers

‹ Zoom out › | Last 30 days ⏱ | Filter ▽

Host	Trigger	Severity	Number of status changes
lar-book-centos	sda: Disk read/write request responses are too high (read > 20 ms for 15m or write > 20 ms for 15m)	Warning	8
lar-book-agent_passive	sda: Disk read/write request responses are too high (read > 20 ms for 15m or write > 20 ms for 15m)	Warning	7
lar-book-agent	sda: Disk read/write request responses are too high (read > 20 ms for 15m or write > 20 ms for 15m)	Warning	7

Figure 6.57 – Reports | Trigger top 100 page

For my Zabbix server, the busiest trigger was a **Disk read/write** trigger on a server. It's a useful page to see what we are putting most of our time into, problem-wise.

Audit

The audit log, which is a small addition to Zabbix, is found at **Reports | Audit**:

Time	User	IP	Resource	ID	Action	Recordset ID	Details
2022-02-12 17:05:12	Admin	192.168.0.254	Trigger	19725	Update	ckzk1598q0000dlzjy70cqqz2	Description: Average incoming interface usage last week >800Mbps
							trigger.expression: trendavg(/lar-book-agent_passive/net.if.in["ens192"], 1w:now/w)=800M => trendavg(/lar-book-agent_passive/net.if.in["ens192"],1w:now-1w)>=800M
2022-02-12 15:53:56	Admin	192.168.1.132	User	1	Login	ckzjylmer0000dlzjm62j8lnp	
2022-02-12 15:53:56	guest	192.168.1.132	User	2	Failed login	ckzjylmer0000dlzjm62j8lnp	
2022-02-12 15:53:50	guest	192.168.1.132	User	2	Failed login	ckzjylhlt0000pbzjwktmgu53	

Figure 6.58 – Reports | Audit log page

We can see which user has done what on our Zabbix server—identifying a culprit for something that shouldn't have been done, for instance.

Action log

When we go to **Reports | Action log**, we land on a page that shows which actions have been fired. If you've configured **Actions**, then you can get a list here, like this:

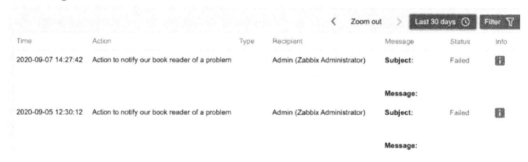

Figure 6.59 – Reports | Action log page

If you're not sure if your action succeeded, then look at this list. It is very useful to troubleshoot your actions to a point where you get them up and running as you want.

When you hover over the **Info** box, you also get to see what went wrong. For example, for the **Failed** items on my Zabbix instance, I should define the appropriate media type for the **Admin** user:

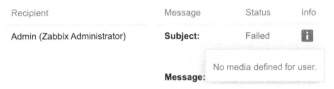

Recipient	Message	Status	Info
Admin (Zabbix Administrator)	**Subject:**	Failed	ℹ
	Message:	No media defined for user.	

Figure 6.60 – Reports | Action log info box

Notifications

Last, but not least, navigating to **Reports | Notifications** will show us the number of notifications sent to a certain user for a period of time:

Notifications

From	Till	MS Teams	brian@oicts.nl (Brian OICTS SAML)	bvbaekel (bvbaekel Administrator)
2021-12-27 00:00	2022-01-03 00:00	10		30
2022-01-03 00:00	2022-01-10 00:00	10		30
2022-01-10 00:00	2022-01-17 00:00	15		45
2022-01-17 00:00	2022-01-24 00:00	17		51
2022-01-24 00:00	2022-01-31 00:00	22		66
2022-01-31 00:00	2022-02-07 00:00	28		96
2022-02-07 00:00	2022-02-14 00:00	85		258
2022-02-14 00:00	2022-02-21 00:00	42		129
2022-02-21 00:00	2022-02-28 00:00	38		123
2022-02-28 00:00	2022-03-07 00:00	34		102

Figure 6.61 – Reports | Notifications page

In my case, 50 notifications have been sent to the **Admin** user this year, and 0 to other users.

Setting up scheduled PDF reports

This much-wanted feature was added in Zabbix 5.4 and is now finally available in an LTS release starting from Zabbix 6.0: sending automatic PDF reports through email. Now, let me start off by stating that this implementation might not fully cover every Zabbix user's situation yet. What this feature does is basically take a screenshot of any Zabbix dashboard and send it through email. It's the first setup from the Zabbix developers and I think we should really appreciate it for what it is.

On top of that, it is a very flexible way of implementing this, as we can choose any kind of widget with filters to send in an automatic report. On top of that it gives the Zabbix development team the flexibility to add new widgets on the fly, which immediately work with your PDF reports.

Getting ready

We will need an existing Zabbix installation with access to the frontend and the CLI. We can use the server we have been using throughout this book for this or you can use your own installation.

In the case of a multi-host setup, the easiest method is to install this where the Zabbix server is also running, but it is possible to run this on any host. In the example, we've used our single-host installation.

You will also need to have set up a user with an email media type.

How to do it...

To get started with Zabbix scheduled reports, we need to install some things to our Zabbix server first:

1. Let's log in to our Zabbix server CLI and execute the following command to install the Google Chrome browser.

    On RHEL-based systems:

    ```
    wget https://dl.google.com/linux/direct/google-chrome-
    stable_current_x86_64.rpm
    ```

    ```
    dnf install google-chrome-stable_current_x86_64.rpm
    ```

    On Ubuntu systems:

    ```
    wget https://dl.google.com/linux/direct/google-chrome-
    stable_current_amd64.deb
    ```

    ```
    apt install google-chrome-stable_current_amd64.deb
    ```

2. Now let's install our required Zabbix web services package with the following commands.

    On RHEL-based systems:

    ```
    yum install zabbix-web-service
    ```

    On Ubuntu systems:

    ```
    apt install install zabbix-web-service
    ```

3. Now let's edit our new Zabbix web service configuration file:

```
vim /etc/zabbix/zabbix_web_service.conf
```

4. We can find a bunch of Zabbix web-service-specific parameters here, including encryption. Make sure the following line is set up to match your Zabbix server(s) IP(s):

```
AllowedIP=127.0.0.1,::1
```

5. Now let's edit our Zabbix server configuration file:

```
vim /etc/zabbix/zabbix_server.conf
```

6. Edit the `WebServiceURL` parameter to match your Zabbix web service IP and `StartReportWriters` to make sure we have a reporting subprocess:

```
WebServiceURL=https://localhost:10053/report
StartReportWriters=3
```

> **Important note**
>
> For scheduled reporting to work you will need to set up SSL encryption for your Zabbix frontend; we recommend using Let's Encrypt. Alternatively, set the `IgnoreURLCertErrors=1` parameter in `/etc/zabbix/zabbix_web_service.conf`.

7. That's it for the CLI part. Let's log in to our frontend and navigate to **Administration | General | Other**.

8. Make sure to fill out the **Frontend URL** parameter on this page with your own frontend URL like this:

Figure 6.62 – Administration | General | Others page with Frontend URL filled in

9. Click the blue **Update** button at the bottom of the page and navigate to **Reports |**
    Scheduled reports.

10. Now we are on the page where we set up and maintain our scheduled reports, so
    let's create a new one using the blue **Create report** button in the top-right corner.

11. This will take us to a new page where we can set up a new report. Let's set up a
    weekly report using our existing dashboard **Global view**. First, we'll name this
    report `Weekly overview of the Global view dashboard`.

12. Select the dashboard's **Global view** by clicking the **Select** button next to
    Dashboard.

13. Put **Cycle** on **Weekly** with a start time of 9 : 00 and set **Repeat on** to **Monday**.

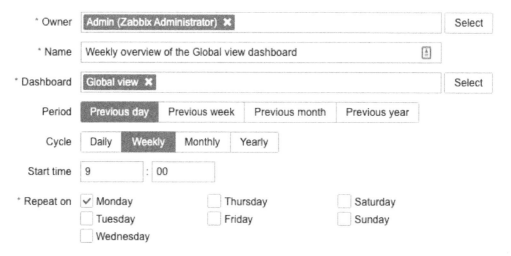

Figure 6.63 – Reports | Scheduled reports, create new report page top part

14. Also, make sure to fill in **Subject** and **Message** and set up the **Subscriptions** to
    match users that have media with the type of email set on their user profile.

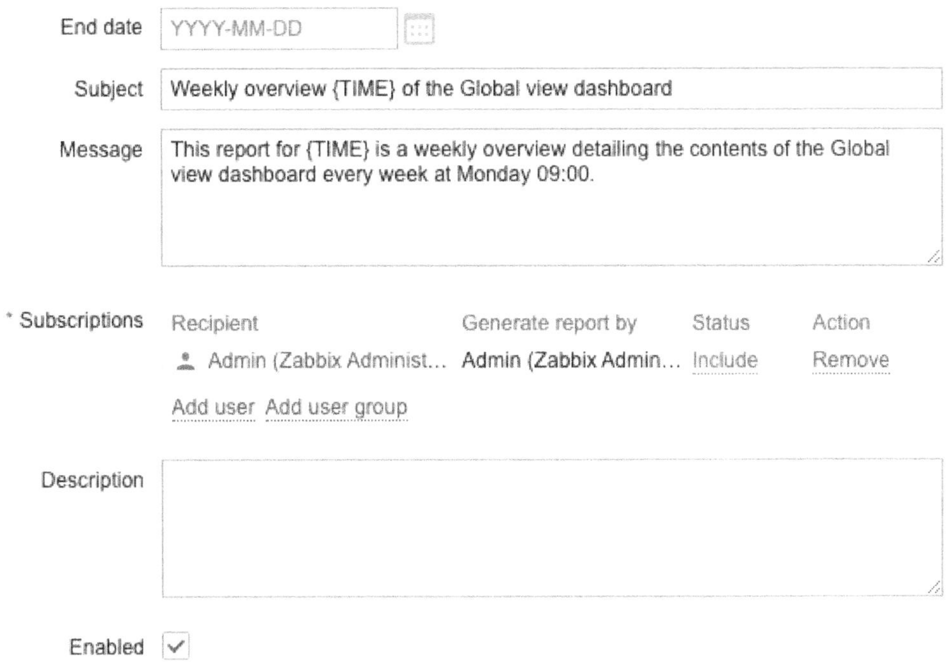

End date   YYYY-MM-DD

Subject   Weekly overview {TIME} of the Global view dashboard

Message   This report for {TIME} is a weekly overview detailing the contents of the Global view dashboard every week at Monday 09:00.

* Subscriptions

Recipient	Generate report by	Status	Action
👤 Admin (Zabbix Administ...	Admin (Zabbix Admin...	Include	Remove

Add user   Add user group

Description

Enabled   ✓

Figure 6.64 – Reports | Scheduled reports, create new report page bottom part

15. You can now click the **Test** button to see if the report is working. Once it is, use the blue **Add** button to finish setting up this scheduled report.

How it works...

This feature is long awaited and finally here, but it's not finished and is simply still a building block for more advanced scheduled reports coming later. There are some key things to keep in mind with this new reporting functionality. I always state that Zabbix development tries to keep everything as customizable as possible by adding features and interconnecting them to make sure we can use existing functionality in new ways.

The Zabbix development team could have decided to create a fully-fledged PDF reporting engine for Zabbix. But by going the way of using Zabbix dashboards as building blocks for all your PDF reports, they have created versatility and customizability. Every single new dashboard widget that is added is now available for you to use in your PDF reports, and my guess is that more and more reporting-focused widgets will be added in the near future.

Zabbix simply grabs the information from your dashboard and sends it to you in a PDF form using the new Zabbix web services module and the Google Chrome browser. Once we get these prerequisites out of the way, we are provided with a way to send PDF reports to any of our Zabbix users, provided they have an email media type set up.

Setting up improved business service monitoring

In Zabbix 6, business service monitoring has had an entire overhaul. If you've set it up in older versions, it might be wise to spend some time rediscovering the basics using this recipe. If you are entirely new to business service monitoring, do not worry as we will go through setting it up step by step in this recipe.

Getting ready

We will need our Zabbix server and access to its frontend. I'll be using my `lar-book-centos` host with the configuration we have done so far. We will also need a monitored host, for which I will use the Zabbix server itself.

How to do it...

I'll be using the Zabbix frontend as an example to set up business service monitoring, for which we will create a new host called `lar-book-zabbix-frontend` with some items and triggers.

Setting up the items and triggers

If you have followed the previous recipes, by now you should have a good understanding of setting up items and triggers. Let's go through it again and set up some for our business service monitoring example:

1. First, let's create a new template by logging in to our Zabbix frontend and navigating to **Configuration | Templates**.

2. Click on the blue **Create template** button in the top-right corner and fill in the page as follows:

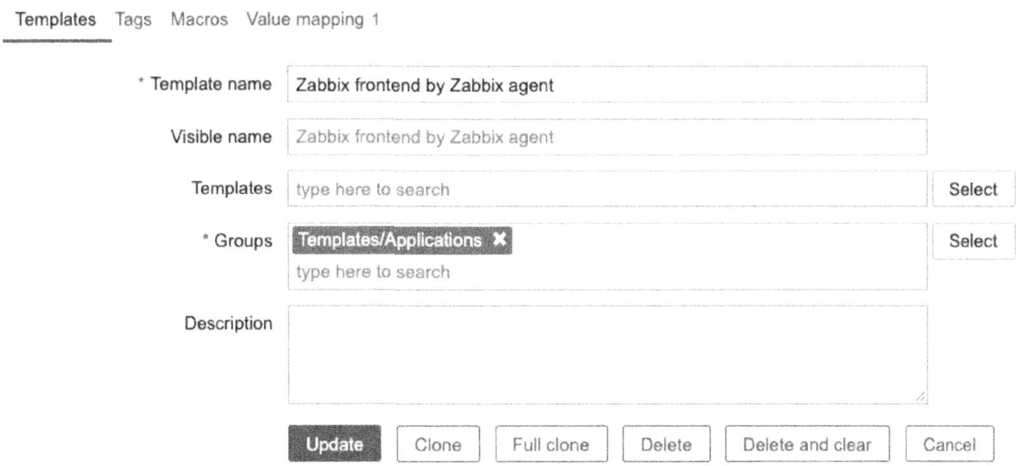

Templates   Tags   Macros   Value mapping 1

* Template name	Zabbix frontend by Zabbix agent
Visible name	Zabbix frontend by Zabbix agent
Templates	type here to search Select
* Groups	Templates/Applications ✖ Select type here to search
Description	

Update   Clone   Full clone   Delete   Delete and clear   Cancel

Figure 6.65 – New Zabbix frontend template configuration page

3. Make sure to save this new template by clicking the blue **Add** button.

4. Then let's set up our new host navigating to **Configuration | Hosts**.

5. Click on the blue **Create host** button in the top-right corner and fill in the page as follows:

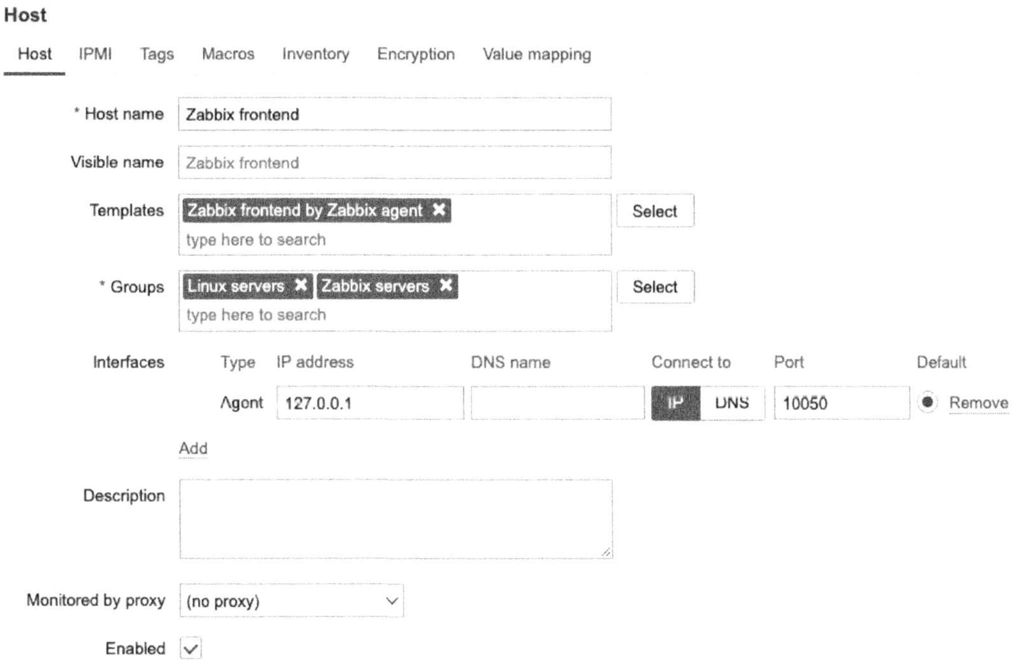

Host

Host   IPMI   Tags   Macros   Inventory   Encryption   Value mapping

* Host name	Zabbix frontend
Visible name	Zabbix frontend
Templates	Zabbix frontend by Zabbix agent ✖ Select type here to search
* Groups	Linux servers ✖ Zabbix servers ✖ Select type here to search

Interfaces	Type	IP address	DNS name	Connect to	Port	Default
	Agent	127.0.0.1		IP DNS	10050	● Remove

Add

Description	

Monitored by proxy   (no proxy) ⌄

Enabled   ✓

Figure 6.66 – New Zabbix frontend host configuration page

6. Then, add the following tag by navigating to the **Tags** page:

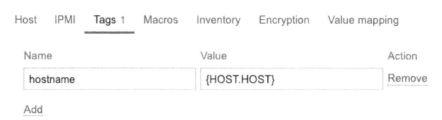

Figure 6.67 – New Zabbix frontend host configuration page, Tags tab

7. Click the blue **Add** button to save this new host configuration and navigate to **Configuration | Templates**.

8. Edit the **Zabbix frontend by Zabbix agent** template and go to **Value mapping**.

9. Click on the small **Add** button with the blue dotted line under it and add the following value mapping:

Figure 6.68 – Template Zabbix frontend by Zabbix agent, Service state value mapping

10. Make sure to click the blue **Update** button. Then, back on the template, go to **Items**.

11. Click on the blue **Create item** button and add the following:

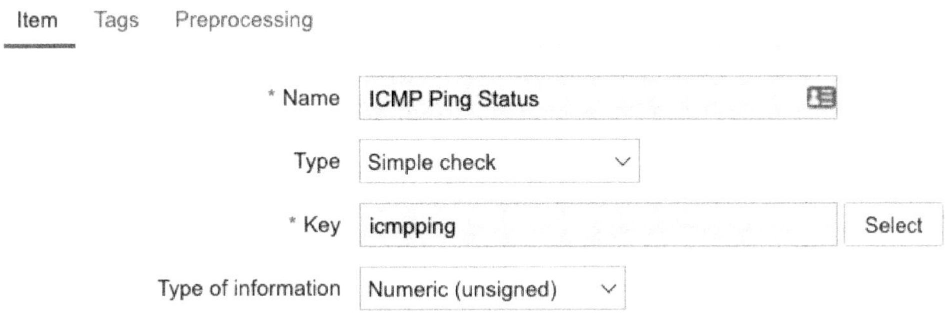

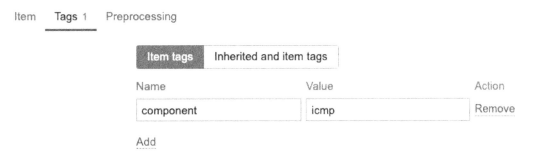

Figure 6.69 – ICMP ping item

12. Before adding the item, make sure to also add the **Value mapping** as follows:

Figure 6.70 – ICMP ping item value mapping

13. Then we will also go to the **Tags** page to add some tags to this item:

Figure 6.71 – ICMP ping item Tags tab

14. Now click the blue **Add** button at the bottom of the page.

15. Back at **Items**, click on the blue **Create item** button to create another item. Fill in the following:

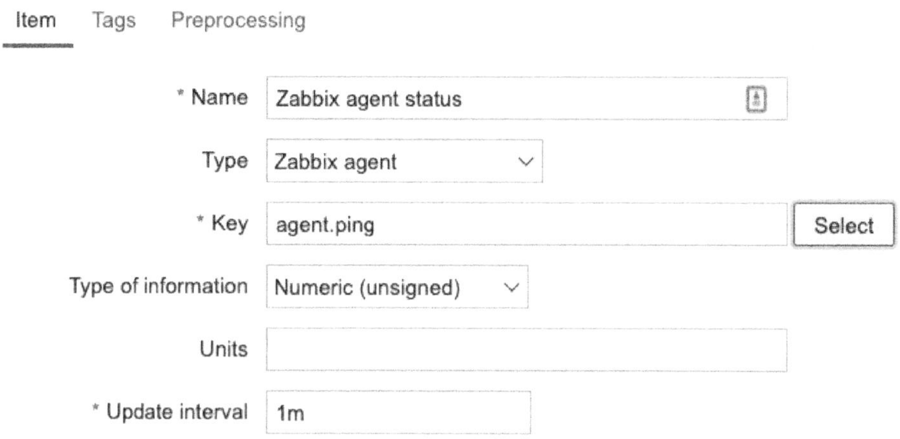

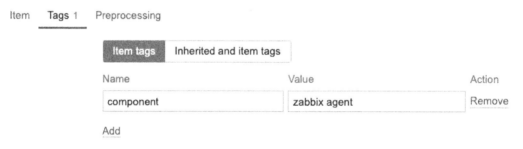

Figure 6.72 – Agent ping item

16. Then we will also go to the **Tags** page to add some tags to this item:

Figure 6.73 – HTTP service state item Tags tab

17. Now save the new item by clicking the blue **Add** button at the bottom of the page.

18. Now that we have two new items, let's navigate to the **Triggers** for this template.

19. Click the **Create trigger** button in the top-right corner and add the following trigger:

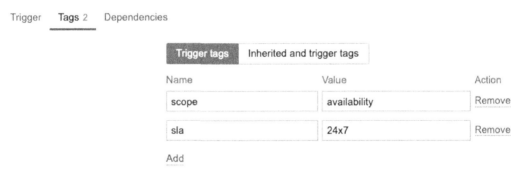

Figure 6.74 – ICMP down trigger configuration

20. On the **Tags** tab, let's also add a new tag, indicating that this trigger will be used in our SLA monitoring:

Trigger   **Tags** 2   Dependencies

Trigger tags	Inherited and trigger tags	
Name	Value	Action
scope	availability	Remove
sla	24x7	Remove

Add

Figure 6.75 – ICMP down trigger Tags tab

21. Now let's click the blue **Add** button to add this trigger. Then create another trigger using the **Create trigger** button in the top-right corner.

22. Let's add the following trigger:

Figure 6.76 – Agent unreachable trigger configuration

23. Make sure to add a tag for the SLA on this trigger as well on the **Tags** tab.

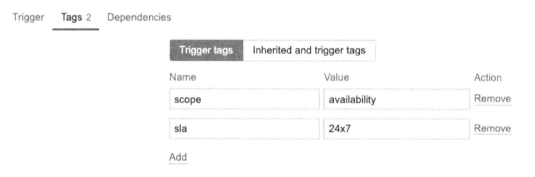

Figure 6.77 – Agent unreachable trigger Tags tab

24. Click the blue **Add** button to finish setting up this trigger.

Adding the business service monitoring configuration

That concludes our item and trigger configuration. We can now continue with actually setting up our business service monitoring:

1. First, let's define our SLA period by going to **Services | SLA** and clicking on the blue **Create SLA** button in the top-right corner. We'll define the following SLA:

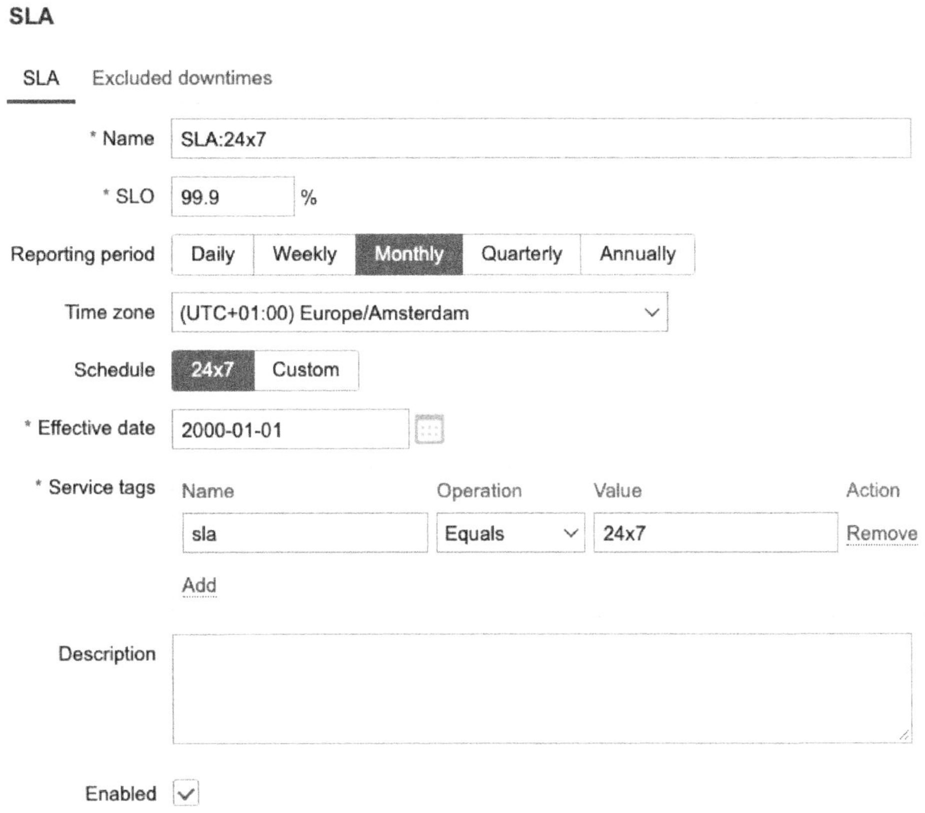

SLA

SLA   Excluded downtimes

* Name	SLA:24x7
* SLO	99.9 %
Reporting period	Daily Weekly **Monthly** Quarterly Annually
Time zone	(UTC+01:00) Europe/Amsterdam
Schedule	**24x7** Custom
* Effective date	2000-01-01

* Service tags

Name	Operation	Value	Action
sla	Equals	24x7	Remove

Add

Description

Enabled ✓

Figure 6 78 – Services | SLA, Zabbix SLA setup

2. Click on **Add** at the bottom of the window to save this SLA.

3. Next, go to **Services | Services** and select **Edit** using the slider in the top-right corner.

4. Now click **Create service** in the top-right corner to add a new service. We will add a new service for our Zabbix setup.

Figure 6.79 – Services | Services, Zabbix setup service

5. On the **Tags** tab, also make sure to add the following:

Figure 6.80 – Services | Services, Zabbix setup service, SLA

6. Click on the blue **Add** button at the bottom of the window to add this new service. Then click **Create service** in the top-right corner again to add the following:

Figure 6.81 – Services | Services, Zabbix server service

7. At the **Tags** tab also make sure to add the following:

Figure 6.82 – Services | Services, Zabbix server service, SLA

8. Click the blue **Add** button again and then **Create service** in the top-right corner again. We'll add another service on the same level as follows:

Figure 6.83 – Services | Services, Zabbix database service

9. On the **Tags** tab, also make sure to add the following:

Figure 6.84 – Services | Services, Zabbix database service, SLA

10. Let's click **Add** again to add this service.

11. Then we'll add the last child of the Zabbix setup by clicking the **Create service** button again.

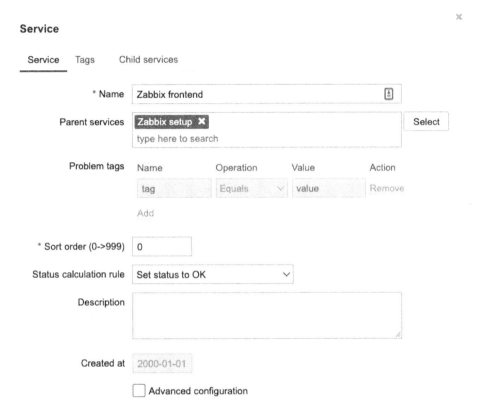

Figure 6.85 – Services | Services, Zabbix frontend service

12. Then select **Advanced configuration** and click on **Add** at **Additional rules**. We will add the following calculation here:

Figure 6.86 – Services | Services, Zabbix frontend service, additional rules

13. On the **Tags** tab, also make sure to add the following:

Figure 6.87 – Services | Services, Zabbix database service, SLA

14. Finish setting up this service by clicking the **Add** button at the bottom of the window.

15. Now, we'll have to add two more services, but this time under the Zabbix frontend. Click on **Zabbix frontend** and then **Create service** again and add the following:

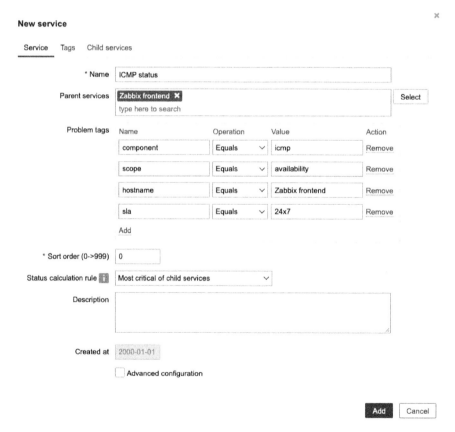

Figure 6.88 – Services | Services, Zabbix frontend, ICMP status child service

16. Click the blue **Add** button and then **Create service** again to add the last service.

17. Let's also add the following service:

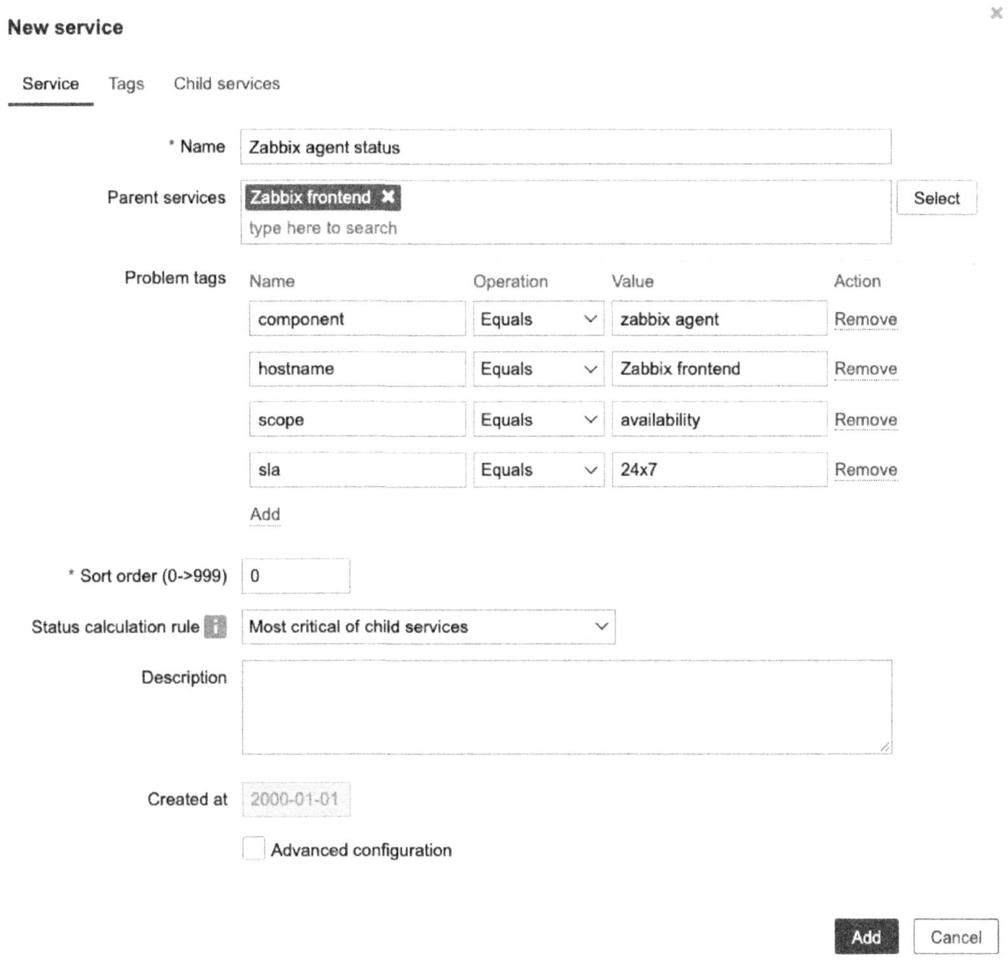

New service   ✕

Service   Tags   Child services

* Name	Zabbix agent status

Parent services	Zabbix frontend ✖			Select
	type here to search			

Problem tags

Name	Operation	Value	Action
component	Equals ⌄	zabbix agent	Remove
hostname	Equals ⌄	Zabbix frontend	Remove
scope	Equals ⌄	availability	Remove
sla	Equals ⌄	24x7	Remove

Add

* Sort order (0->999)	0

Status calculation rule ⓘ	Most critical of child services ⌄

Description

Created at	2000-01-01

☐ Advanced configuration

Add   Cancel

Figure 6.89 – Services | Services, Zabbix frontend, Zabbix agent status child service

18. Click the blue **Add** button to add this service and let's see if it works as expected.

How it works...

Let's take a look at what we have set up in our current configuration. We've used business service monitoring to monitor part of our Zabbix stack. Look at business service monitoring as a tree, where we just created two levels. Our initial level is the Zabbix setup, which consists of our Zabbix frontend, Zabbix server, and Zabbix database.

Beneath the Zabbix frontend level, we have one more level where we have defined two more services that represent the status of ICMP and the Zabbix agent. We only want to calculate the SLA if both ICMP and Zabbix agent are in a problem state.

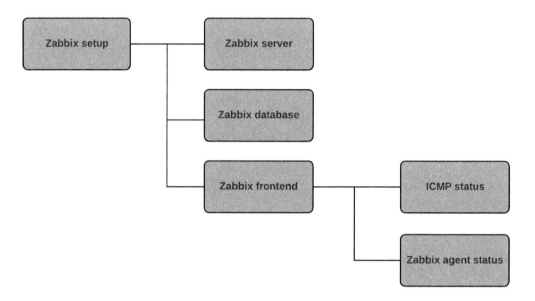

Figure 6.90 – Business service monitoring tree structure example

As you can see, we have a distinct tree structure forming once we start to visualize this in a drawing. The part where the magic happens in this case is the Zabbix frontend service, though, because this is where we defined what should happen to our SLA once something goes wrong with services.

Let's take another look at that level:

Service

Service   Tags 1   Child services 2

* Name	Zabbix frontend
Parent services	Zabbix setup ✖
	type here to search

Problem tags

Name	Operation	Value	Action
tag	Equals ∨	value	Remove

Add

* Sort order (0->999)	0
Status calculation rule	Set status to OK ∨
Description	
Created at	2000-01-01
	✓ Advanced configuration

Additional rules

Name	Action
High - If at least 2 child services have *High* status or above	Edit Remove

Add

Status propagation rule	As is ∨
Weight	0

Figure 6.91 – Zabbix frontend service completed

Because we defined that the service should always **Set status to OK**, it will only use what we defined in our **Additional rules** section. This is where we specified that we only want to affect our SLA calculation: **If at least 2 child services have High status or above**. Effectively, this means that our SLA is only going down if both the Zabbix agent is not reachable and ICMP is down.

We've built in a security measure for ourselves here, making sure that if someone stops the Zabbix agent but the server is still reachable by ICMP, the SLA won't be affected.

Now let's take a look at the end result that we can use to monitor these SLAs. Over at **Services | SLA report**, we can find all we need to know about if our SLA is being met. We can set the filter to a time period we want to find the SLA for and it will result in something like the following screenshot:

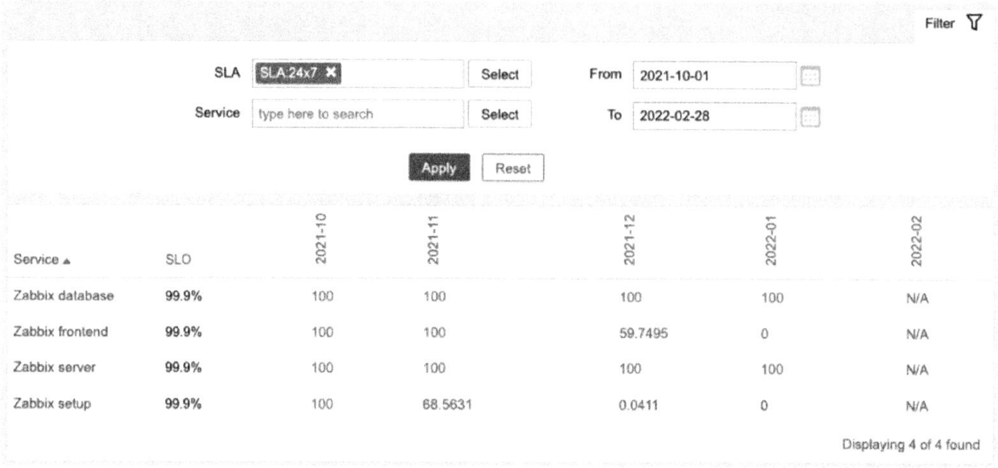
Filter
SLA
SLA:24x7
Select
From
2021-10-01
Service
type here to search
Select
To
2022-02-28
Apply
Reset
Service
SLO
2021-10
2021-11
2021-12
2022-01
2022-02
Zabbix database 99.9% 100 100 100 100 N/A
Zabbix frontend 99.9% 100 100 59.7495 0 N/A
Zabbix server 99.9% 100 100 100 100 N/A
Zabbix setup 99.9% 100 68.5631 0.0411 0 N/A
Displaying 4 of 4 found

Figure 6.92 – Services | SLA report, all services with our SLA:24x7 tag

We can see now see our monthly 24x7 SLA where an SLA of 99.9% is being expected. For our Zabbix set up back in October 2021 the SLA was 100, so we met our required SLA. Then in November 2021, we notice that the SLA dropped below 100, clearly indicating in red that our SLA was not met.

Drilling down even further and selecting our specific service Zabbix setup, we can create a more detailed overview:

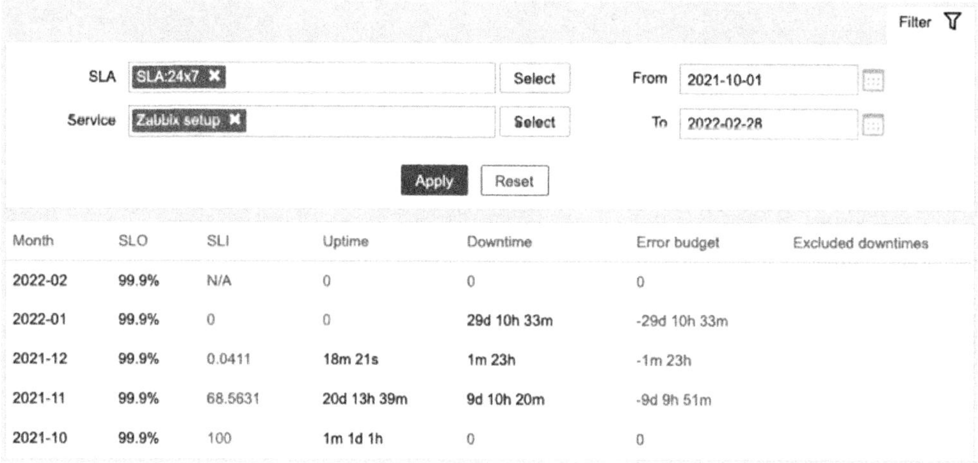
Filter
SLA
SLA:24x7
Select
From
2021-10-01
Service
Zabbix setup
Select
To
2022-02-28
Apply
Reset
Month
SLO
SLI
Uptime
Downtime
Error budget
Excluded downtimes
2022-02 99.9% N/A 0 0 0
2022-01 99.9% 0 0 29d 10h 33m -29d 10h 33m
2021-12 99.9% 0.0411 18m 21s 1m 23h -1m 23h
2021-11 99.9% 68.5631 20d 13h 39m 9d 10h 20m -9d 9h 51m
2021-10 99.9% 100 1m 1d 1h 0 0

Figure 6.93 – Services | SLA report, Zabbix setup services with our SLA:24x7 tag

Over here, we can see all the details regarding the up and downtime of our service and what our leftover error budget is like.

Using business service monitoring calculations like this, we can narrow down our services and how well they are calculated. In this case, we used a simple example with ICMP and the Zabbix agent trigger we know well by now, but the possibilities are endless using services in combination with tags.

There's more...

One of the main concerns with the old way of monitoring services through business service monitoring was the inability to automate and customize it. The automation has been mostly resolved through the use of tags, as we can now define tags on the host, template, or trigger level to define what's used in the business service monitoring configuration.

In terms of customization, Zabbix has given us a lot more options to do calculations.

Figure 6.94 – Zabbix service, additional rule options

Looking at the numerous options here, we can see that we have a lot more to play around with. Not only can we specify the exact number of child services we'd like to use in our calculations, but we can also even work with weights and percentages, giving us the options we might need to build more complex setups.

7
Using Discovery for Automatic Creation

This chapter is going to be all about making sure that you as a Zabbix administrator are doing as little work as possible on host and item creation. We are going to learn how to perform (or perfect, maybe) automatic host creation. Check out the recipes featured here to see just what we are going to discover.

In this chapter, we will first learn how to set up Zabbix discovery with Zabbix agent and **Simple Network Management Protocol** (**SNMP**). We will then set up active agent autoregistration. Later, we will also cover the automatic creation of Windows performance counters and **Java Managements Extension** (**JMX**) items.

In this chapter, we will cover the following recipes:

- Setting up Zabbix agent discovery
- Setting up Zabbix SNMP discovery
- Working with active agent autoregistration
- Using the new Windows performance counter discovery
- Discovering JMX objects

Technical requirements

As this chapter is all about host and item discovery, besides our Zabbix server we will need one new Linux host and a Windows host. Both these hosts will need Zabbix agent 2 installed, but not configured just yet.

Furthermore, we are going to need our JMX host, as configured in *Chapter 3, Setting Up Zabbix Monitoring*, and a new host with SNMP set up. To learn more about setting up an SNMP-monitored host, check out the *Working with SNMP monitoring* recipe in *Chapter 3, Setting Up Zabbix Monitoring*.

Setting up Zabbix agent discovery

A lot of Zabbix administrators use Zabbix agent extensively and thus spend a lot of time creating Zabbix agent hosts by hand. Maybe they don't know how to set up Zabbix agent discovery, maybe they didn't have time to set it up yet, or maybe they just prefer it this way. If you are ready to get started with Zabbix agent discovery, in this recipe we will learn just how easy it is to set it up.

Getting ready

Besides our Zabbix server, in this chapter's introduction I mentioned that we will need two (empty) hosts with Zabbix agent 2 installed: one Windows host and one Linux host. If you don't know how to install Zabbix agent 2, check out *Chapter 3, Setting Up Zabbix Monitoring*, or see the Zabbix documentation at `https://www.zabbix.com/documentation/current/en/manual/concepts/agent2`.

Let's give the servers the following hostnames:

- `lar-book-disc-lnx`: For the Linux host (use Zabbix agent 2)
- `lar-book-disc-win`: For the Windows host (use Zabbix agent 2)

How to do it...

1. Let's get started by logging in to our `lar-book-disc-lnx` Linux host and editing the following file:

   ```
   vim /etc/zabbix/zabbix_agent2.conf
   ```

2. Now, make sure your Zabbix agent 2 configuration file contains at least the following line:

   ```
   Hostname=lar-book-disc-lnx
   ```

3. For your Windows Zabbix agent, it's important to do the same. Edit the following file:

```
C:\Program Files\Zabbix Agent 2\zabbix_agent2.conf
```

4. Now, change the hostname by editing the following line:

```
Hostname=lar-book-disc-win
```

5. Next up, in our Zabbix frontend, navigate to **Configuration | Discovery**, and on this page, we are going to create a rule with the following settings:

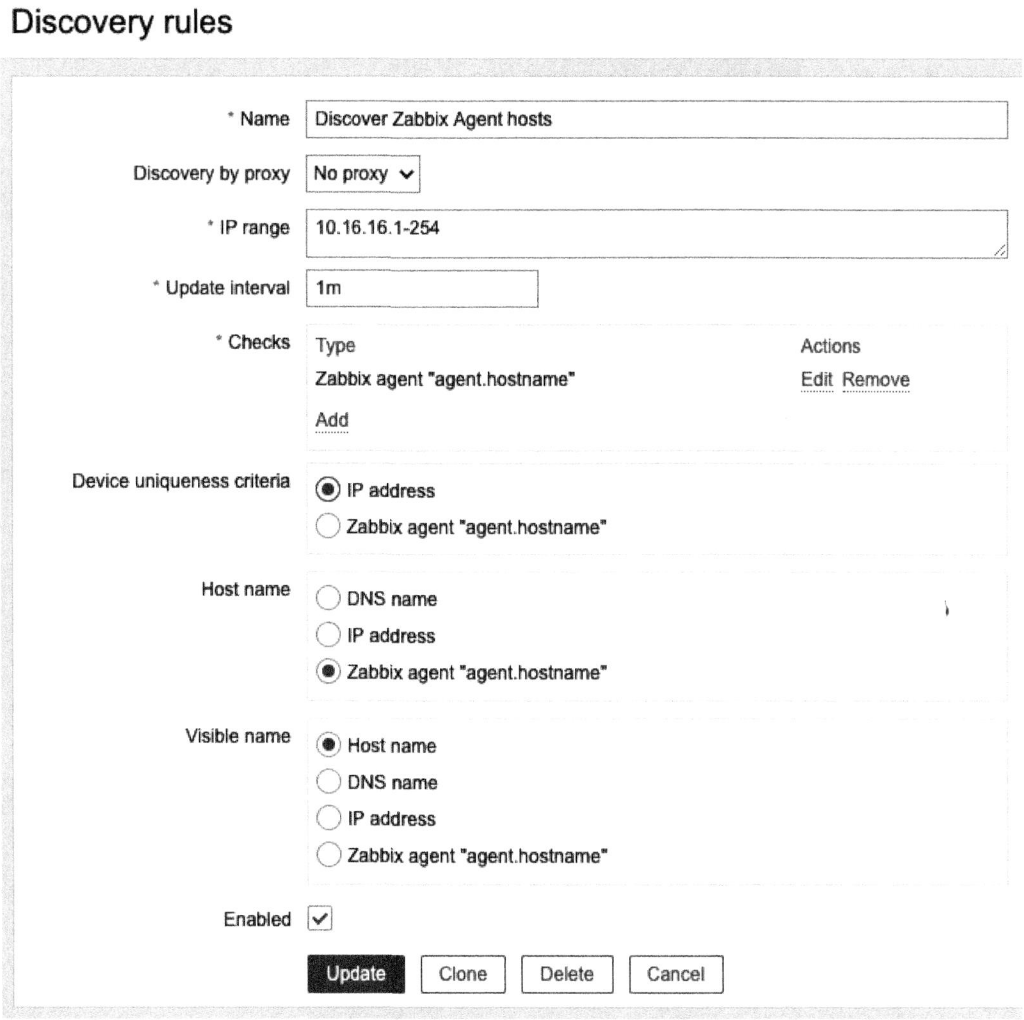

Discovery rules

* Name	Discover Zabbix Agent hosts
Discovery by proxy	No proxy ▾
* IP range	10.16.16.1-254
* Update interval	1m

* Checks	Type	Actions
	Zabbix agent "agent.hostname"	Edit Remove
	Add	

Device uniqueness criteria
- ◉ IP address
- ○ Zabbix agent "agent.hostname"

Host name
- ○ DNS name
- ○ IP address
- ◉ Zabbix agent "agent.hostname"

Visible name
- ◉ Host name
- ○ DNS name
- ○ IP address
- ○ Zabbix agent "agent.hostname"

Enabled ☑

[Update] [Clone] [Delete] [Cancel]

Figure 7.1 – Discovery rules page for Zabbix agent hosts

> **Important note**
> We are using an **Update interval** of 1 minute in this example. As this might take up a lot of resources on your server, make sure to adjust this value for your production environment. For example, 1 hour is a much better production value.

6. Click the blue **Add** button to move on.

7. After setting up the discovery rule, we will also need to set up an action to actually create the host with the right template. Navigate to **Configuration | Actions | Discovery actions**:

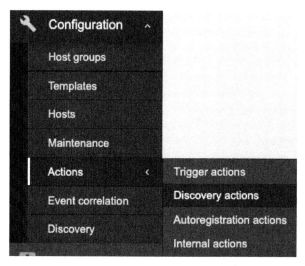

Figure 7.2 – Main-menu at Configuration | Actions

8. Here, we will click the **Create action** button in the top-right corner and fill out the next page with the following information:

Action   Operations

* Name | Auto discover Linux Zabbix Agent hosts

Type of calculation | And/Or ⌄ | A and B and C

Conditions

Label	Name	Action
A	Received value contains *lnx*	Remove
B	Discovery status equals *Up*	Remove
C	Service type equals *Zabbix agent*	Remove
Add		

Enabled ✓

* At least one operation must exist.

Figure 7.3 – Create Discovery action page for Zabbix agent hosts

> **Tip**
> When creating Zabbix actions, it's important to keep the order of creation for
> **Conditions** in mind. The labels seen in the preceding screenshot will be added
> in order of creation. This means that it's easier to keep track of your Zabbix
> actions if you keep the order of creation the same for all actions.

9. Next up, click the **Operations** tab. This is where we will add the following:

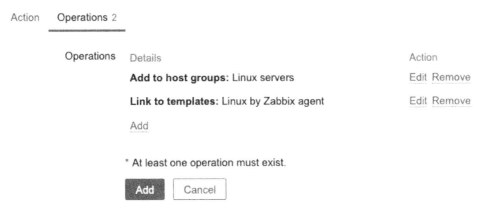

Action   Operations 2

Operations

Details	Action
Add to host groups: Linux servers	Edit Remove
Link to templates: Linux by Zabbix agent	Edit Remove
Add	

* At least one operation must exist.

Add   Cancel

Figure 7.4 – Create Discovery action | Operations page for Zabbix agent hosts

10. That's it for the Linux agent. Click the blue **Add** button, and let's continue to our Windows discovery rule.

11. Navigate to **Configuration | Host groups**. Create a host group for our Windows hosts by clicking **Create host group** in the top-right corner and filling out the group name:

Figure 7.5 – Create host group page for Windows server hosts

12. Click the blue **Add** button and navigate to **Configuration | Actions**.

13. Go to **Discovery actions** again and click **Create action**. We will fill out the same thing but for our Windows hosts this time:

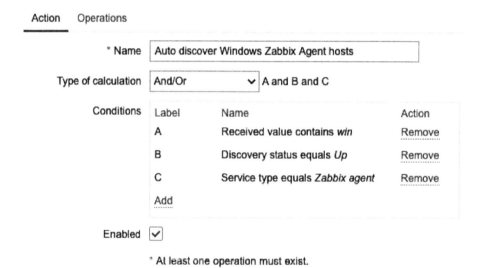

Figure 7.6 – Create Discovery action page for Windows Zabbix agents

14. Before clicking **Add**, let's also fill out the **Operations** page with the **Operations** shown in the following screenshot:

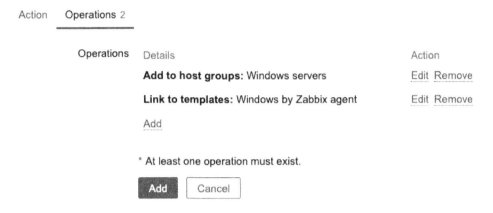

Figure 7.7 – Create Discovery action Operations page for Windows Zabbix agents

15. Now, we can click the blue **Add** button, and our second discovery action is present.

16. Move on to **Monitoring | Discovery**. This is where we can see if and when our hosts are discovered:

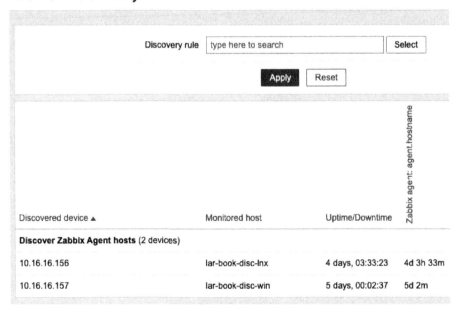

Figure 7.8 – Monitoring | Discovery page

> **Tip**
> Use the **Monitoring | Discovery** page to keep a close eye on the hosts you expect to show up in your Zabbix setup. It's very useful to track new hosts coming in and see which Zabbix discovery rule was used to create the host.

How it works...

Network discovery might not be very hard to set up initially, but there are loads of options to configure. For this example, we made the choice to use the `agent.hostname` key as our check. We create the Zabbix hostname based on what's configured in the Zabbix agent config file.

What happens is that Zabbix network discovery finds our hosts and performs our check. In this case, the check is: *What is the hostname used by the Zabbix agent?* This information, plus our IP address, is then triggering the action. Our action then performs our configured checks:

- Does the hostname contain `lnx` or `win`?

- Is the discovery status `UP`?

- Is the service type `Zabbix Agent`?

If all of those checks are true, our action will then create our newly discovered host with the following:

- Our configured host group plus the default `Discovered hosts` host group

- Our template as configured in our action

We will end up with two newly created hosts, with all the right settings:

Figure 7.9 – Configuration | Hosts page with our new hosts, Windows and Linux

There's more...

Creating the host by using the configuration file settings isn't always the right way to go, but it's a solid start to working with network discovery.

If you want a more flexible environment where you don't have to even touch the Zabbix agent configuration file, then you might want to use different checks on the discovery rule. Check out which keys we can use to build different discovery rules in the Zabbix documentation at `https://www.zabbix.com/documentation/current/en/ manual/config/items/itemtypes/zabbix_agent`.

Setting up Zabbix SNMP discovery

If you work with a lot of SNMP devices but don't always want to set up monitoring manually, network discovery is the way to go. Zabbix network discovery uses the same functionality as Zabbix agent discovery, but with a different configuration approach.

Getting ready

To get started with network discovery, we are going to need a host that we can monitor with SNMP. If you don't know how to set up a host such as this, check out the *Working with SNMP monitoring* recipe in *Chapter 3*, *Setting Up Zabbix Monitoring*. We'll also need our Zabbix server.

How to do it...

1. First, log in to your new SNMP-monitored host and change the hostname to the following:

    ```
    hostnamectl set-hostname lar-book-disc-snmp
    ```

2. Then, restart the SNMP daemon using the following command:

    ```
    exec bash
    systemctl restart snmpd
    ```

3. Now, navigate to **Configuration | Discovery** and click on **Create discovery rule** in the top-right corner.

4. We are going to create a new SNMP discovery rule, with an SNMP **Object Identifier (OID)** check type. Fill out the **Name** and **IP range** fields first, like this:

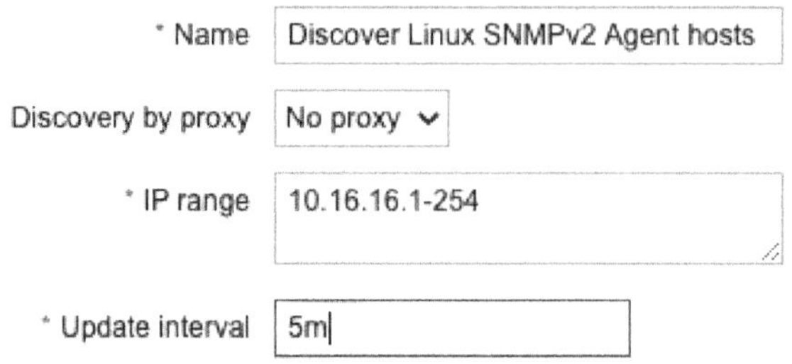

Figure 7.10 – Configuration | Discovery, discovery rule creation page for SNMPv2 agents

5. Make sure to fill out your own IP range in the **IP range** field.

6. Now, we are going to create our SNMP check. Click on **Add** next to **Checks**, and you'll see the following pop-up screen:

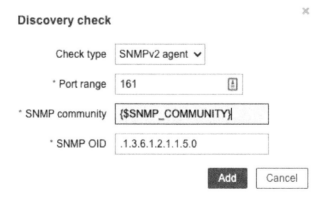

Figure 7.11 – Configuration | Discovery, discovery check creation pop-up window

7. We want our **Check type** to be **SNMPv2 agent** and we want to fill it with our community and a useful OID, which in this case will be the OID for the system name. Fill it out like this:

Figure 7.12 – Configuration | Discovery, discovery check creation pop-up window filled for SNMPv2 agents

> **Important note**
> Please note that our check type is *not* SNMP version-independent. We have
> three SNMP versions and thus three different check types to choose from,
> unlike with our new SNMP interface selection on the Zabbix 6 host screen.

8. After clicking **Add** again, fill out the rest of the page, as follows:

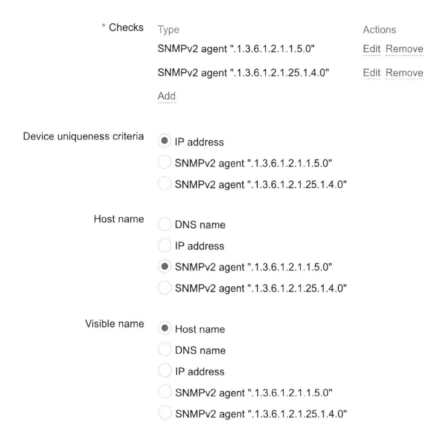

Figure 7.13 – Configuration | Discovery page for SNMPv2 agents

9. Last, but not least, click the **Add** button at the bottom of the page. This concludes
    creating our Zabbix discovery rule.

10. We will also need an action for creating our hosts from the discovery rule. Navigate
    to **Configuration | Actions**, and after using the dropdown to select **Discovery
    actions**, click on **Create action**.

11. We will fill out the page with the following information:

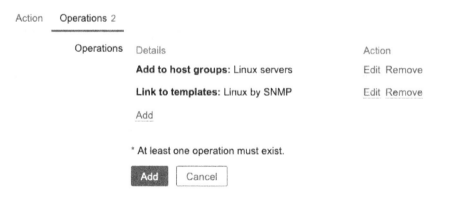

Action   Operations

* Name	Auto discover Linux SNMPv2 Agent hosts
Type of calculation	And/Or ∨ A and B and C

Conditions

Label	Name	Action
A	Received value contains *vmlinux*	Remove
B	Discovery status equals *Up*	Remove
C	Service type equals *SNMPv2 agent*	Remove
Add		

Enabled ☑

* At least one operation must exist.

Add   Cancel

Figure 7.14 – Configuration | Actions, action creation page for SNMPv2 agents

12. Before clicking **Add**, navigate to **Operations** and fill out this page with the following details:

Action   Operations 2

Operations

Details	Action
Add to host groups: Linux servers	Edit Remove
Link to templates: Linux by SNMP	Edit Remove
Add	

* At least one operation must exist.

Add   Cancel

Figure 7.15 – Configuration | Actions, action creation Operations tab for SNMPv2 agents

13. Now, click **Add** and navigate to **Monitoring | Discovery** to see if our host gets created:

Discovered device ▲	Monitored host	Uptime/Downtime	SNMPv2 agent: .1.3.6.1.2.1.1.5.0	SNMPv2 agent: .1.3.6.1.2.1.25.1.4.0
Discover Linux SNMPv2 Agent hosts (3 devices)				
10.16.16.152 (lar-book-centos)	lar-book-centos_2	5 days, 18:25:21	5d 18h 25m	
10.16.16.153	lar-book-agent_passive	5 days, 18:25:19	5d 18h 25m	5d 18h 25m
10.16.16.158	lar-book-disc-snmp	23:48:48	23h 48m 48s	3m 28s

Figure 7.16 – Monitoring | Discovery page for SNMPv2 agents

How it works...

In this recipe, we've created another discovery rule, but this time for SNMP. As you've noticed, the principle remains the same, but the application is a bit different.

When we created this Zabbix discovery rule, we gave it two checks instead of the one check we did in the previous recipe. We created one check on SNMP OID .1.3.6.1.2.1.1.5.0 to retrieve the hostname of the device through SNMP. We then put the hostname retrieved from the system into Zabbix as the Zabbix hostname of the system.

We also created a check on SNMP OID .1.3.6.1.2.1.25.1.4.0. This check will retrieve the following string, if present:

```
"BOOT_IMAGE=(hd0,gpt2)/vmlinuz 4.18.0-193.6.3.el8_2.x86_64
root=/dev/mapper/cl-root ro crashkernel=auto resume=/dev/
mapper/cl-swa"
```

If the string is present, it means that the boot image is Linux on this host. This is a perfect example of how we can retrieve multiple OIDs to do multiple checks in our Zabbix discovery rules. If we'd been monitoring a networking device, for instance, we could have picked an OID to see if it was a Cisco or a Juniper device. We would replace .1.3.6.1.2.1.25.1.4.0 with any OID and poll it. Then, we would create our action based on what we received (Juniper or Cisco) and add our templates accordingly.

> **Important note**
>
> General knowledge of SNMP structure is very important when creating Zabbix discovery rules. We want to make sure we use the right SNMP OIDs as checks. Make sure to do your research well, utilize SNMP walks, and plan out what OIDs you want to use to discover SNMP agents. This way, you'll end up with a solid monitoring infrastructure.

Working with active agent autoregistration

Using discovery to set up your Zabbix agents is a very useful method to automate your host creation. But what if we want to be even more upfront with our environment and automate further? That's when we use a Zabbix feature called **active agent autoregistration**.

Getting ready

For this recipe, we will need a new Linux host. We will call this host `lar-book-lnx-agent-auto`. Make sure to install the Zabbix agent 2 to this host. Besides this new host, we'll also need our Zabbix server.

How to do it...

1. Let's start by logging in to our new `lar-book-lnx-agent-auto` host and change the following file:

   ```
   vim /etc/zabbix/zabbix_agent2.conf
   ```

2. We will then edit the following line in the file. Make sure to enter your Zabbix server IP on this line:

   ```
   ServerActive=10.16.16.152
   ```

3. We can also change the following line in the file if we want to set our hostname in the file manually:

   ```
   Hostname=lar-book—lnx-agent-auto
   ```

   This is not a requirement though, as Zabbix agent will use the system hostname if it is not filled out.

4. Next up, we will navigate to our Zabbix frontend, where we'll go to **Configuration |
    Actions**.

5. Use the drop-down menu to go to **Autoregistration actions,** as in the following
    screenshot:

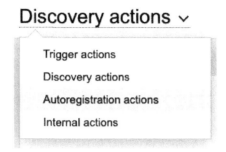

Figure 7.17 – Configuration | Actions page drop-down menu

6. Now, we will click the blue **Create action** button in the top-right corner to create a
    new action.

7. Fill out **Name** and then click on the **Add** text link:

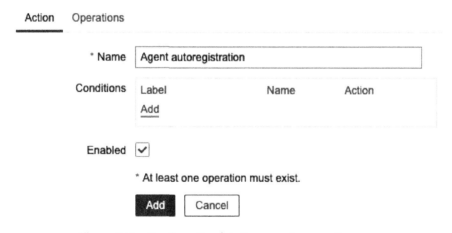

Figure 7.18 – Configuration | Actions, create new action page

8. We can set up a condition here to only register hosts with a certain hostname. Let's do this by filling out the window like this:

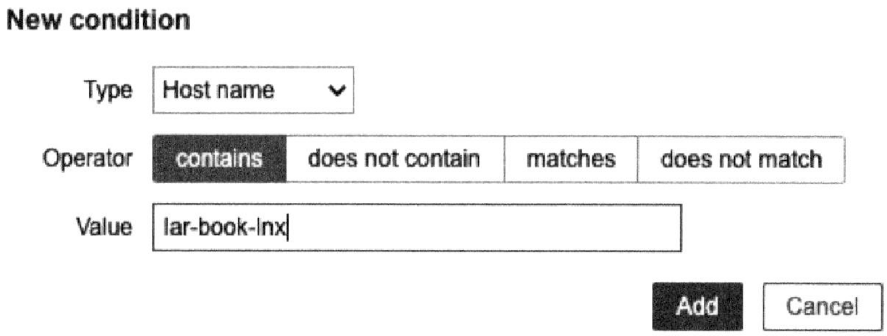

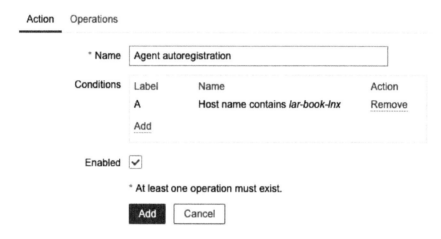

Figure 7.19 – Create action page, New condition window for host lar-book-lnx

Your page should now look like this:

Figure 7.20 – Create action page, filled with our information for host lar-book-lnx

> **Tip**
>
> We can set up conditions for different types of hosts. For instance, if we want to add Windows hosts, we set up a new action with a different hostname filter. This way, it is easy to maintain the right groups and templates, even with autoregistration.

9. Before clicking the blue **Add** button, let's go to the **Operations** tab.

10. Click on the **Add** text link, and you will see the following window:

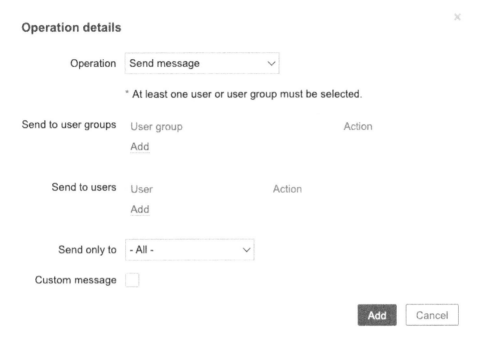

Figure 7.21 – Create action operations page, new operation window, Send message for host lar-book-lnx

11. Create an action to add the host to the **Linux servers** host group:

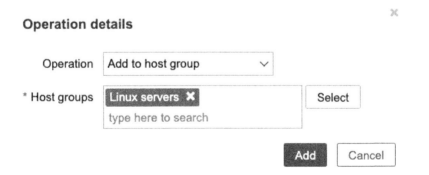

Figure 7.22 – Create action operations page, new operation window, Add to host group, lar-book-lnx

12. Create an action to add the host to the `Template OS Linux by Zabbix agent active` template:

Operation details
Operation
Link to template
* Templates
Linux by Zabbix agent active
type here to search
Select
Add
Cancel

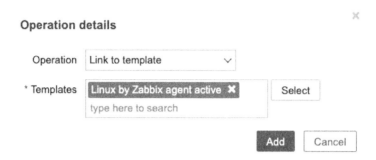

Figure 7.23 – Create action operations page, new operation window, Link to template, lar-book-lnx

13. Your finalized **Operations** page should now look like this, and we can click the blue **Add** button:

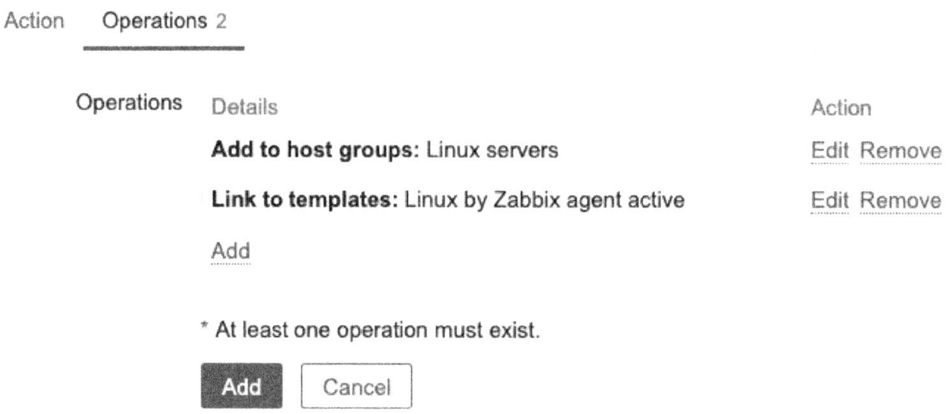

Action
Operations 2
Operations
Details
Action
Add to host groups: Linux servers
Edit Remove
Link to templates: Linux by Zabbix agent active
Edit Remove
Add
* At least one operation must exist.
Add
Cancel

Figure 7.24 – Create action operations page, filled with our information, lar-book-lnx

14. Navigate to **Configuration | Hosts**, and we can see our new active autoregistered host:

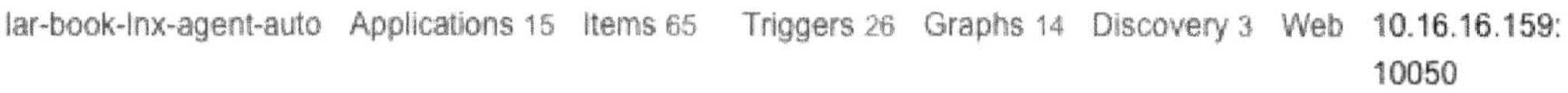

lar-book-lnx-agent-auto
Applications 15
Items 65
Triggers 26
Graphs 14
Discovery 3
Web
10.16.16.159:10050

Figure 7.25 – Configuration | Hosts page with host lar-book-lnx-agent-auto

How it works...

Active agent autoregistration is a solid method to let a host register itself. Once the `ServerActive=` line is set up with the Zabbix server IP, the host agent will start requesting configuration data from the Zabbix server. The Zabbix server will receive these requests, and if there is an action set up in Zabbix (as we just did in this recipe), the host autoregisters to Zabbix:

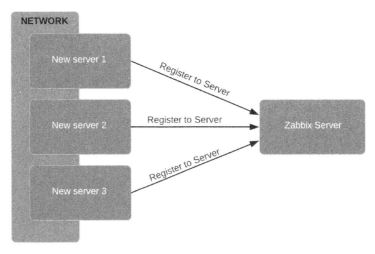

Figure 7.26 – Host autoregistration process

We can do a bunch of cool automations with this functionality. We could create a script to fill up our Zabbix agent configuration file with the right `ServerActive=` line on our hosts in a certain IP pool.

It would also be super-easy to set up new hosts with Ansible. We can automate the Zabbix agent installation with Ansible and we can add the `ServerActive=` line in the `/etc/zabbix/zabbix_agent2.conf` file using Ansible as well. Our Zabbix server autoregistration action will take care of the rest from here.

Zabbix agent autoregistration is a perfect way to get a zero-touch monitoring environment that's always up to date with our latest new hosts.

There's more...

Not every company uses hostnames that reflect the machine's OS or other attributes. This is when Zabbix `HostMetadata` can come in very useful. We can add this field to the active Zabbix agent configuration to reflect the attributes of the machine.

Afterward, we can use this `HostMetadata` in our Zabbix discovery action to do the same kind of filtering we did on the hostname.

We also have the **HostInterface** and **HostInterfaceItem** parameters in the Zabbix agent configuration file, which are used for autoregistration. The host will use the specified IP or DNS name as its Zabbix agent interface IP or DNS, as seen in the Zabbix frontend. We can also use this functionality to enable passive agent monitoring while using autoregistration to create the host.

Check out this link for more information:

```
https://www.zabbix.com/documentation/current/manual/discovery/
auto_registration#using_host_metadata
```

Using the new Windows performance counter discovery

In Zabbix 6, it is possible to discover Windows performance counters. In this recipe, we will go over the process of discovering Windows performance counters to use in our environments.

Discovering Windows performance counters might seem to be a little tricky at first, as it uses both Windows- and Zabbix-specific concepts. But once we finish this recipe you'll know exactly how to set it up.

Getting ready

In this chapter, we added the `lar-book-disc-win` host to our setup, which is the host used in our Zabbix agent discovery process. We can reuse this host to discover Windows performance counters easily.

Of course, we'll also need our Zabbix server.

How to do it...

1. Let's start by navigating to **Configuration | Templates** and creating a new template by clicking **Create template** in the top-right corner.
2. Create the following template:

Templates   Tags   Macros   Value mapping

* Template name	Windows performance by Zabbix agent
Visible name	Windows performance by Zabbix agent
Templates	type here to search [Select]
* Groups	Templates/Operating systems ✖ [Select] type here to search
Description	

[Add] [Cancel]

Figure 7.27 – Configuration | Templates, Create template page, Windows performance by Zabbix agent

3. Click on the blue **Add** button, which will bring you back to **Configuration |
    Templates**. Select the new template.

4. Now, before continuing with our template, navigate to your Windows frontend and
    open perfmon.exe:

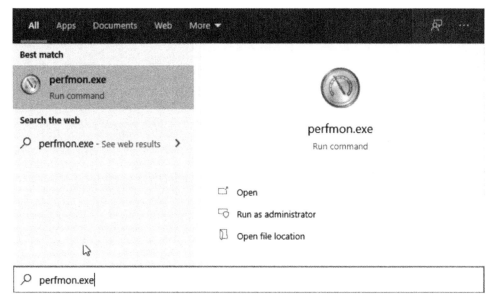

Figure 7.28 – Windows search bar, perfmon.exe

5.   This will open the following window:

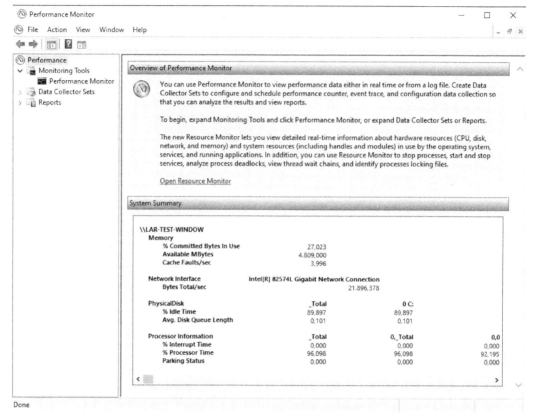

Figure 7.29 – Windows perfmon.exe

6.   Let's click on **Performance Monitor** and then on the green + icon. This will show you all the available Windows performance counters.

7.   Let's start by using the **Processor** counter.

8.   Go back to the **Configuration | Template** page in Zabbix and edit our new **Template Module Windows performance by Zabbix agent** template.

9.   When you are at the **Edit template** page, click on **Discovery rules** in the bar next to your template name.

10. Click on **Create new discovery rule** in the top-right corner and add the following rule:

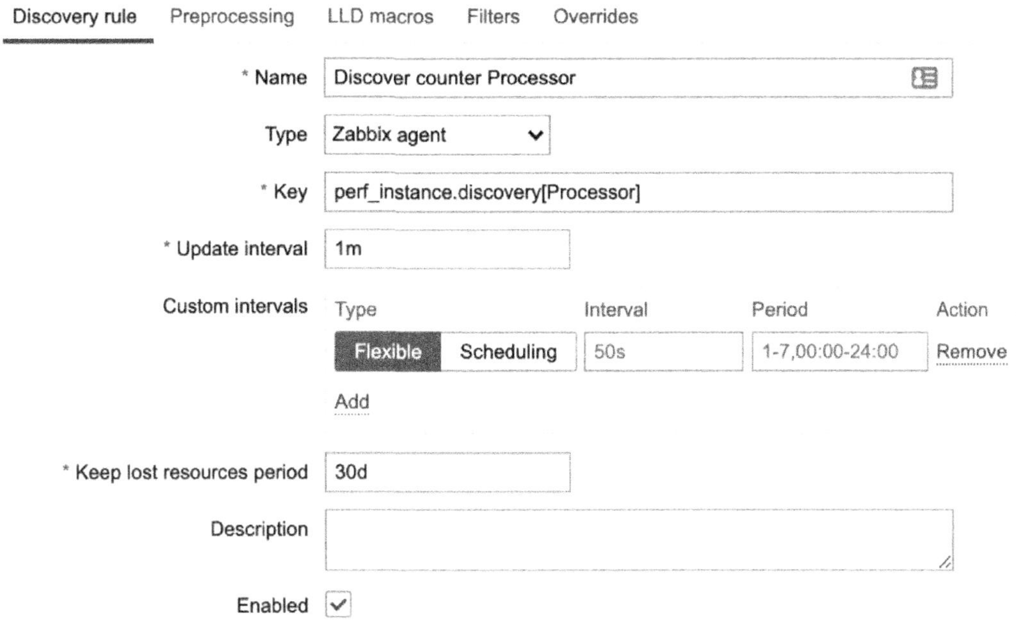

Discovery rule	Preprocessing	LLD macros	Filters	Overrides

* Name	Discover counter Processor	
Type	Zabbix agent	
* Key	perf_instance.discovery[Processor]	
* Update interval	1m	

Custom intervals

Type	Interval	Period	Action
Flexible Scheduling	50s	1-7,00:00-24:00	Remove

Add

* Keep lost resources period	30d
Description	
Enabled	✔

Figure 7.30 – Create Low-Level Discovery (LLD) rule page, Discover counter Processor

> **Important note**
> We are using an **Update interval** of 1 minute in this example. As this might take up a lot of resources on your server, make sure to adjust this value to your production environment. For example, 1 hour is a much better production value.

11. Click the blue **Add** button at the bottom and click our new `Discover counter Processor` discovery rule.

12. Click on **Item prototypes**, and in the top-right corner click on **Create item prototype**. We will then create the following item prototype:

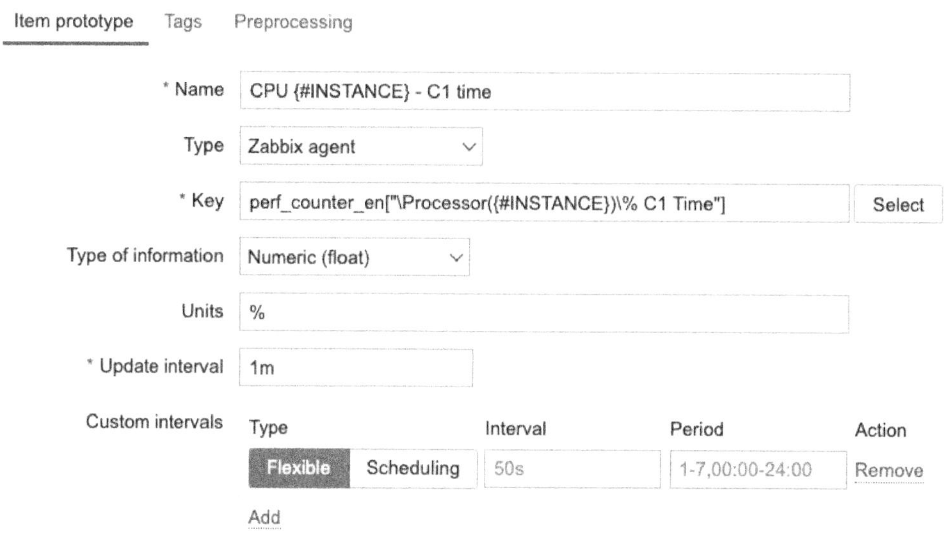

Item prototype	Tags	Preprocessing

* Name	CPU {#INSTANCE} - C1 time	
Type	Zabbix agent ⌄	
* Key	perf_counter_en["\Processor({#INSTANCE})\% C1 Time"]	Select
Type of information	Numeric (float) ⌄	
Units	%	
* Update interval	1m	

Custom intervals	Type	Interval	Period	Action
	Flexible Scheduling	50s	1-7,00:00-24:00	Remove
	Add			

Figure 7.31 – Create LLD item prototype page, CPU instance C1 time

13. On the **Tags** tab, do not forget to add some new tags as follows:

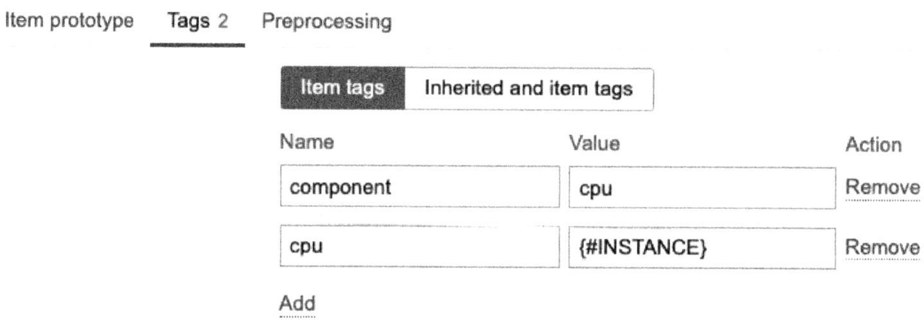

Item prototype	Tags 2	Preprocessing

Item tags	Inherited and item tags

Name	Value	Action
component	cpu	Remove
cpu	{#INSTANCE}	Remove
Add		

Figure 7.32 – Create LLD item prototype page tag tab, CPU instance C1 time

14. Save the new **Item prototype**, go to **Configuration | Hosts**, and click on `lar-book-disc-win`.

15. Add our **Windows performance by Zabbix agent** template:

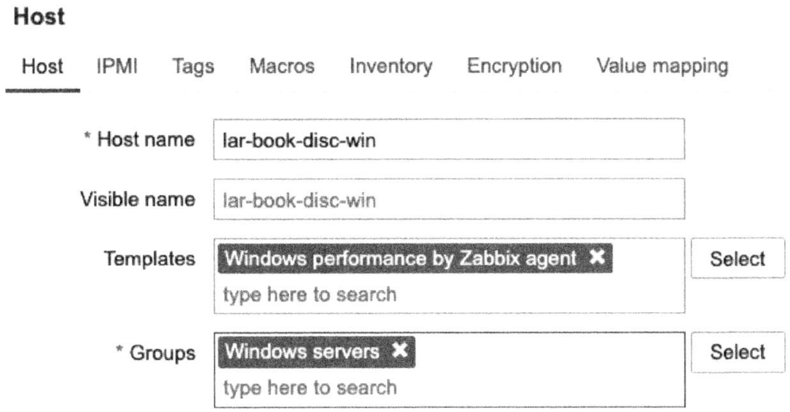

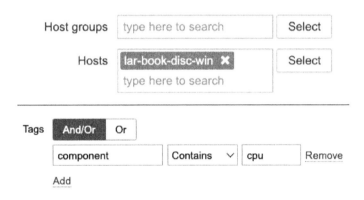

Figure 7.33 – Create LLD item prototype page, add Templates for lar-book-disc-win

16. After clicking on the blue **Update** button, we can navigate to **Monitoring | Latest data**. Add the following filters:

Figure 7.34 – Latest data filter on host lar-book-disc-win

17. We can now see our three newly created items:

	Host	Name ▲	Last check	Last value	Change
☐	lar-book-disc-win	CPU 0 - C1 time	35s	10.2439 %	-17.1768 %
☐	lar-book-disc-win	CPU 1 - C1 time	34s	38.0343 %	+11.4413 %
☐	lar-book-disc-win	CPU _Total - C1 time	33s	22.3135 %	-4.6934 %

Figure 7.35 – Monitoring | Latest data page for our host lar-book-disc-win

How it works...

Windows performance counters have been around for a long time and they are very important to anyone who wants to monitor Windows machines with Zabbix. Using **Low-Level Discovery (LLD)** in combination with Windows performance counters makes it a lot easier and more flexible to build solid Windows monitoring.

In this recipe, we created a very simple but effective Windows performance counter discovery rule by adding the discovery rule with the perf_instance. discovery[Processor] item key. The [Processor] part of this item key directly correlates to the perfmon.exe window we saw. If we look at the following screenshot, we already see **Processor** listed:

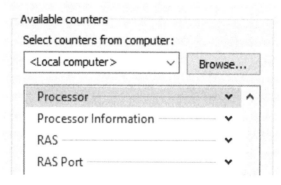

Figure 7.36 – perfmon.exe | Add Counters, Processor

When our discovery rule polls this item key, Zabbix agent will return the following value for our host:

```
[{"{#INSTANCE}":"0"},{"{#INSTANCE}":"1"},{"{#INSTANCE}":"_
Total"}]
```

This value means that Zabbix will fill the `{#INSTANCE}` macro with three values:

- `0`
- `1`
- `_Total`

We can then use these three values by using the `{#INSTANCE}` macro in our **Item prototype**, like we did here:

Name ▲
Key
CPU {#INSTANCE} - C1 time
perf_counter_en["\Processor({#INSTANCE})\% C1 Time"]

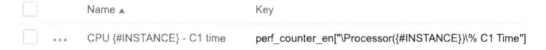

Figure 7.37 – Our created Item prototype, CPU C1 time

It will then create three items with our macro values, with the right keys to monitor the second part of our counter—`% C1 time`. If you expand the window in your `perfmon.exe` file, you can see all the different counters we could add to our item prototypes to monitor more Windows performance counters:

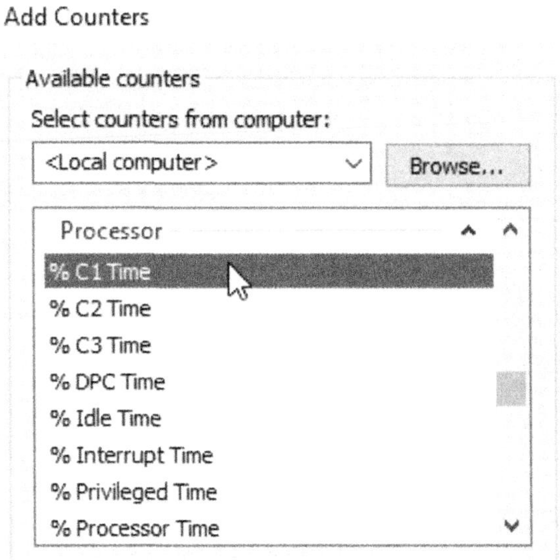
Add Counters
Available counters
Select counters from computer:
<Local computer>
Browse...
Processor
% C1 Time
% C2 Time
% C3 Time
% DPC Time
% Idle Time
% Interrupt Time
% Privileged Time
% Processor Time

Figure 7.38 – Perfmon.exe | Add Counters, Processor expanded

Discovering JMX objects

In *Chapter 3*, *Setting Up Zabbix Monitoring*, we went over setting up JMX monitoring in the recipe titled *Setting up JMX monitoring*. What we didn't cover yet though was discovering JMX objects.

In this recipe, we will go over how to set up JMX objects with LLD, and after you've finished this recipe, you'll know just how to set it up.

Getting ready

For this recipe, we will need the JMX host that you set up for the *Setting up JMX monitoring* recipe in *Chapter 3*, *Setting Up Zabbix Monitoring*. Make sure to finish that recipe before working on this one.

We will also need our Zabbix server with our Zabbix JMX host titled `lar-book-jmx`.

How to do it...

1. Let's start this recipe off by logging in to our Zabbix frontend and navigating to **Configuration | Templates**.

2. Create a new template by clicking on **Create template** in the top-right corner. Fill in the following fields:

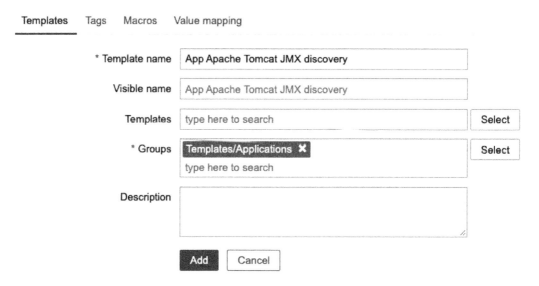

Figure 7.39 – Configuration | Templates, Create new template page, Apache Tomcat JMX discovery

3. After clicking the blue **Add** button, you will be taken back to **Configuration |**
Templates. Click on your new **Template App Apache Tomcat JMX discovery**
template.

4. We will now add our JMX discovery rule. Click on **Discovery rules** next to our
template name.

5. Now, click on **Create discovery rule** and fill in the following fields:

Discovery rule	Preprocessing	LLD macros	Filters	Overrides

* Name	Discover JMX object MemoryPool
Type	JMX agent
* Key	jmx.discovery[beans,"*":type=MemoryPool,name=*"]
* JMX endpoint	service:jmx:rmi:///jndi/rmi://{HOST.CONN}:{HOST.PORT}/jmxrmi
User name	
Password	
* Update interval	1m

Custom intervals	Type		Interval	Period	Action
	Flexible	Scheduling	50s	1-7,00:00-24:00	Remove
	Add				

* Keep lost resources period	0d

Figure 7.40 – Configuration | Templates, create new template page, Discover JMX object MemoryPool

6. Click on the blue **Add** button at the bottom of the page. Then, click on **Item**
prototypes next to your newly created **Discover JMX object MemoryPool**
discovery rule.

7.   We will now click on the **Create item prototype** button in the top-right corner and create the following item prototype:

Figure 7.41 – Item prototype creation page, MemoryPool Memory type

8.   Also make sure that on the **Tags** tab you add a new tag as component | memory pool:

Figure 7.42 – Item prototype creation page tag tab, MemoryPool Memory type

9.   Let's click on the blue **Add** button and move on.

10. Go to **Configuration | Hosts** and click on `lar-book-jmx`. We will add our template to this host.

11. Click on **Templates** and add the template, like this:

Figure 7.43 – Configuration | Hosts, add template to host lar-book-jmx

12. Click on the blue **Update** button.

13. When we navigate to **Monitoring | Latest data** now, we will filter on **Hosts |** `lar-book-jmx` and **Tag |** `component` with **Value |** `memory pool`, like this:

Figure 7.44 – Monitoring | Latest data page filters, host lar-book-jmx

14. We will then see the following results:

Host	Name ▲	Last check	Last value	Change	Tags
lar-book-jmx	MemoryPool: Code Cache - Memory type	13s	NON_HEAP		component: memory p...
lar-book-jmx	MemoryPool: Compressed Class Space - Memory type	13s	NON_HEAP		component: memory p...
lar-book-jmx	MemoryPool: Eden Space - Memory type	13s	HEAP		component: memory p...
lar-book-jmx	MemoryPool: Metaspace - Memory type	13s	NON_HEAP		component: memory p...
lar-book-jmx	MemoryPool: Survivor Space - Memory type	13s	HEAP		component: memory p...
lar-book-jmx	MemoryPool: Tenured Gen - Memory type	13s	HEAP		component: memory p...

Figure 7.45 – Monitoring | Latest data page for host lar-book-jmx with our results

How it works...

Monitoring JMX applications can be quite daunting at first, as there is a lot of work to figure out while building your own LLD rules. But now that you've built your first LLD rule for JMX, there is a clear structure in it.

First, for our discovery rule, we've picked the item key:

```
jmx.discovery[beans,"*:type=MemoryPool,name=*"]
```

MemoryPool is what we call an **MBean object** in Java. We poll this MBean object for several JMX objects and fill the macros accordingly.

We picked the name=* object to fill the {#JMXNAME} macro in this discovery rule. Our macro is then used in our item prototype to create our items.

Our items are then created, like this:

Name	Triggers	Key
Discover JMX object MemoryPool: MemoryPool Metaspace - Memory type		jmx["java.lang:type=MemoryPool,name=Metaspace",Type]
Discover JMX object MemoryPool: MemoryPool Tenured Gen - Memory type		jmx["java.lang:type=MemoryPool,name=Tenured Gen",Type]
Discover JMX object MemoryPool: MemoryPool Eden Space - Memory type		jmx["java.lang:type=MemoryPool,name=Eden Space",Type]
Discover JMX object MemoryPool: MemoryPool Survivor Space - Memory type		jmx["java.lang:type=MemoryPool,name=Survivor Space",Type]
Discover JMX object MemoryPool: MemoryPool Compressed Class Space - Memory type		jmx["java.lang:type=MemoryPool,name=Compressed Class Space",Type]
Discover JMX object MemoryPool: MemoryPool Code Cache - Memory type		jmx["java.lang:type=MemoryPool,name=Code Cache",Type]

Figure 7.46 – Items on our JMX-monitored host

If we look at the keys of the items, we can see that we poll the **Type** JMX attribute on every MemoryPool with different names.

That's how we create JMX LLD rules with ease.

There's more...

If you are not familiar with MBeans objects, then make sure to check out the Java documentation. This will explain to you a lot about what MBeans are and how they can be used for monitoring JMX attributes: https://docs.oracle.com/javase/tutorial/jmx/mbeans/index.html

> **Tip**
> Before diving deeper into using JMX object discovery, dive deeper into the preceding JMX object documentation. There's a lot of information in it and it will greatly improve your skills in creating these LLD rules.

8
Setting Up Zabbix Proxies

You can't preach about Zabbix without actually preaching about the use of Zabbix proxies—a nice addition at first, but a no-brainer by now. Anyone that's expecting to set up a Zabbix environment of a medium/larger size will need proxies. The main reason to use proxies is scalability, as Zabbix proxies offload the data collection and preprocessing load from the Zabbix server. This way we can scale up our Zabbix environment further and with greater ease.

In this chapter, we will first learn how to set up a Zabbix proxy. We will then learn how to work with passive and active Zabbix proxies, and also how to monitor hosts with either form of the Zabbix proxy. We will also cover some Zabbix network discovery using the proxies, and we'll learn how to monitor Zabbix proxies to keep them healthy. After these recipes, you'll have no more excuses for not setting up the proxies, as we'll cover most of the possible forms of proxy use in this chapter.

So, let's go through the following recipes and check out how to work with Zabbix proxies:

- Setting up a Zabbix proxy
- Working with passive Zabbix proxies
- Working with active Zabbix proxies

- Monitoring hosts with a Zabbix proxy
- Using discovery with Zabbix proxies
- Monitoring your Zabbix proxies

Technical requirements

We are going to need several new Linux hosts for this chapter, as we'll be building them as Zabbix proxies.

Set up two proxies by installing CentOS (or your preferred Linux distribution) on the following two new hosts:

- `lar-book-proxy-passive`
- `lar-book-proxy-active`

You'll also need the Zabbix server, with at least one monitored host. We'll be using the following new host with a Zabbix agent installed:

- `lar-book-agent-by-proxy`

Setting up a Zabbix proxy

Setting up a Zabbix proxy can be quite daunting if you don't have a lot of experience with Linux, but the task is quite simple once you get the hang of it. We will install a Zabbix proxy on our `lar-book-proxy-passive` server; you can repeat the task on `lar-book-proxy-active`.

Getting ready

Make sure to have your new Linux host ready and installed. We won't need our Zabbix server in this recipe yet.

You'll need a Zabbix repository for this recipe as well. Check out the following link to find the latest version: `https://www.zabbix.com/download`.

How to do it...

1. Let's start by logging in to the **command-line interface (CLI)** of our new `lar-book-proxy-passive` host.

2. Now, execute the following command to add the Zabbix repository for CentOS 8:

```
rpm -Uvh https://repo.zabbix.com/zabbix/6.0/rhel/8/
x86_64/zabbix-release-6.0-1.el8.noarch.rpm
dnf clean all
```

For Ubuntu, execute this command:

```
wget https://repo.zabbix.com/zabbix/6.0/ubuntu/pool/
main/z/zabbix-release/zabbix-release_6.0-1+ubuntu20.04_
all.deb
dpkg -i zabbix-release_6.0-1+ubuntu20.04_all.deb
apt update
```

3. Now, install Zabbix proxy by executing the following command.

RHEL-based systems:

```
dnf install zabbix-proxy-sqlite3
```

Ubuntu systems:

```
apt install zabbix-proxy-sqlite3
```

> **Tip**
> On RHEL-based servers, don't forget to set **Security-Enhanced Linux** (**SELinux**) to permissive or allow Zabbix proxy in SELinux for production. For lab environments it is fine to set SELinux to permissive, but in production I would recommend leaving it enabled. For Ubuntu systems, in a lab environment, we can disable AppArmor.

4. Now, edit the Zabbix proxy configuration by executing the following command:

```
vim /etc/zabbix/zabbix_proxy.conf
```

5. Let's start by setting the proxy mode on the `passive` proxy. The mode will be 1 on this proxy. On the `active` proxy, this will be 0:

```
ProxyMode=1
```

6. Change the following line to your Zabbix server address:

```
Server=10.16.16.152
```

> **Important note**
>
> When working with a Zabbix server in **High Availability** (**HA**), make sure to add the Zabbix server IP addresses here for every single node in your cluster. The proxy will only be sending data to the active node. Keep in mind that HA nodes are delimited by a semi-colon (;) instead of a comma (,).

7. Change the following line to your proxy hostname:

```
Hostname=1ar-book-proxy-passive
```

8. As we'll be using the `sqlite` version of the proxy for the example, change the `DBName` parameter to the following:

```
DBName=/tmp/zabbix_proxy.db
```

9. You can now enable Zabbix proxy and start it with the following two commands:

```
systemctl enable zabbix-proxy
systemctl start zabbix-proxy
```

10. You might want to check that the Zabbix proxy logs will restart, with the following command:

```
tail -f /var/log/zabbix/zabbix_proxy.log
```

How it works...

There are three versions of Zabbix proxy to work with:

- `zabbix-proxy-mysql`
- `zabbix-proxy-pgsql`
- `zabbix-proxy-sqlite3`

We've just done the setup for the `zabbix-proxy-sqlite3` package, which is the easiest method, if you ask me. The `sqlite3` version of Zabbix proxy makes it possible for us to set up a Zabbix proxy with great ease as we don't actually need to worry too much about database setup.

Please do note that the `sqlite3` versions might not be suited to Zabbix proxies with a lot of hosts and items. You get more options to scale a `mysql` or `pgsql` version of Zabbix proxy by the fine-tuning mechanisms installed with those database types.

> **Tip**
> Always pick the right type of Zabbix proxy for what you expect to need in the future. Although it is easy to switch proxies later, don't go too easy on this choice as you might save yourself hours in the future.

The amazing part about the `sqlite3` version is that if we run into database issues, it's very easy to just run the following:

rm -rf /tmp/zabbix_proxy.db

Zabbix proxy then creates a new database on startup, and we're all ready to start collecting again. Do note that we might lose some information that is in the proxy database and that has not yet been sent to the Zabbix server.

There's more...

More information about installing Zabbix proxies can be found here:

`https://www.zabbix.com/documentation/current/manual/`
`installation/install_from_packages`

Choose the distribution you are using, and you can find the guides for all the different variants of proxy installations.

Working with passive Zabbix proxies

Now that we have installed our Zabbix proxy in the previous recipe, we can start working with it. Let's start by setting up our passive Zabbix proxy in the frontend and see what we can do with it from the start.

Getting ready

You will need the `lar-book-proxy-passive` host for this recipe ready and installed with Zabbix proxy. We will also be using our Zabbix server in this recipe again.

How to do it...

1. Let's start by logging in to our Zabbix frontend and navigating to **Administration | Proxies**:

Figure 8.1 – Administration | Proxies page, no passive proxies

Our **Proxies** page is where we do all proxy-related configuration.

2. Let's add a new proxy with the blue **Create proxy** button in the top-right corner.

3. This will take us to the **Create proxy** page, where we will fill out the following information:

Figure 8.2 – Administration | Proxies, Create proxy page, lar-book-proxy-passive

4. Before clicking the blue **Add** button, let's take a look at the **Encryption** tab:

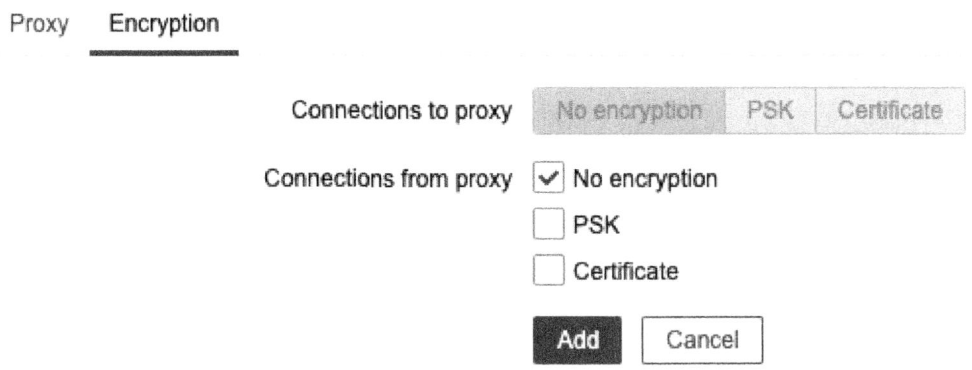

Proxy   Encryption

Connections to proxy   No encryption   PSK   Certificate

Connections from proxy   ☑ No encryption

☐ PSK

☐ Certificate

Add   Cancel

Figure 8.3 – Administration | Proxies, Create proxy Encryption page, lar-book-proxy-passive

5. By default, **No encryption** is checked here, which we'll leave be for this recipe.

> **Important note**
> A lot of valuable information is exchanged between Zabbix servers and
> Zabbix proxies. If you are working with insecure networks or just need an
> extra layer of security, use Zabbix proxy encryption. You can find more
> information on Zabbix encryption here: `https://www.zabbix.com/`
> `documentation/current/en/manual/encryption`

6. Now, click the blue **Add** button, which will take us back to our proxy overview page.

7. The **Last seen (age)** part of your newly added proxy should now show a time value,
   instead of **Never**:

	Name ▼	Mode	Encryption	Compression	Last seen (age)
☐	lar-book-proxy-passive	Passive	NONE	ON	28s

Figure 8.4 – Administration | Proxies page, Last seen (age)

How it works...

Adding proxies isn't the hardest task after we've already done the installation part. After
the steps we took in this recipe, we are ready to start monitoring with this proxy.

The proxy we just added is a passive proxy. These proxies work by receiving configuration from the Zabbix server, which the Zabbix server sends to the Zabbix proxy on port `10051`:

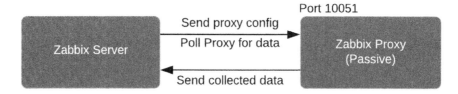

Figure 8.5 – Diagram showing active proxy connection

Once the passive proxy knows what to monitor, every time the Zabbix server polls for data, data is sent back in the same TCP stream. This means that the connection is always initiated from the Zabbix server side. Once it's set up, the Zabbix server will keep sending configuration changes and it will keep polling for new data.

Working with active Zabbix proxies

We now know how to install and add proxies. Let's set up our active proxy, like we did with the passive proxy in the previous recipe, and see how it works.

Getting ready

You will need the `lar-book-proxy-active` host for this recipe, ready and installed with Zabbix proxy. We will also be using our Zabbix server in this recipe.

How to do it...

1. Let's start by logging in to our Zabbix frontend and navigating to **Administration | Proxies**:

Figure 8.6 – Administration | Proxies page, no active proxies

2. Our **Proxies** page is where we do all configuration that's proxy-related.

3. Let's add a new proxy by clicking the blue **Create proxy** button in the top-right corner.

4. This will take us to the **Create proxy** page, where we will fill out the following information:

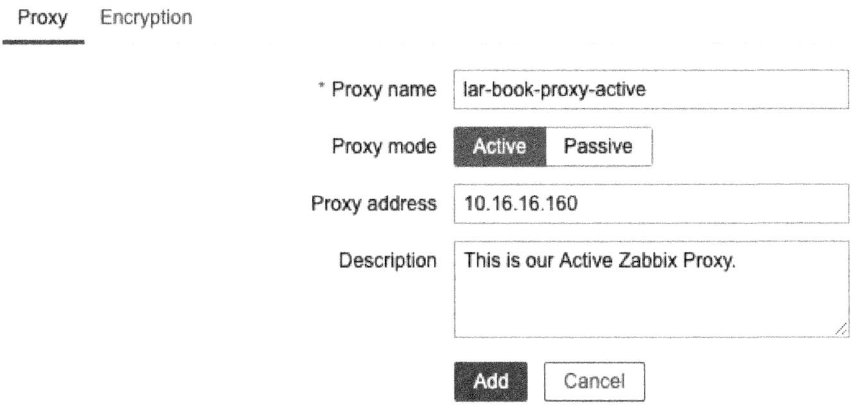

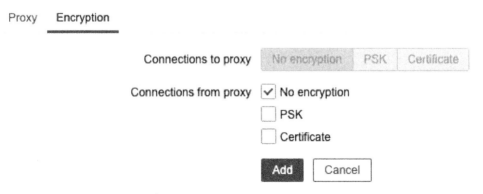

Figure 8.7 – Administration | Proxies, Create proxy page, lar-book-proxy-active

> **Tip**
> The **Proxy address** is actually optional for our active proxy. You do not have to add this for the Zabbix proxy to function, but it is recommended to keep things clear. Adding the Proxy address also functions as a sort of whitelist in this case, as only the IP address listed will be allowed to connect.

5. Before clicking the blue **Add** button, let's take a look at the **Encryption** tab:

Figure 8.8 – Administration | Proxies, Create proxy Encryption page, lar-book-proxy-active

6. By default, **No encryption** is checked here, which we'll leave be for this recipe.

7. Now, click the blue **Add** button, which will take us back to the proxy overview page.

8. Log in to the CLI and check the configuration with the following command:

```
vim /etc/zabbix/zabbix_proxy.conf
```

9. By default, the frequency at which the proxy requests configuration changes is 3,600 seconds (that is, 1 hour):

```
### Option: ConfigFrequency
#        How often proxy retrieves configuration data from Zabbix Server in seconds.
#        For a proxy in the passive mode this parameter will be ignored.
#
# Mandatory: no
# Range: 1-3600*24*7
# Default:
# ConfigFrequency=3600
```

Figure 8.9 – Zabbix proxy configuration file, ConfigFrequency

> **Tip**
> For active Zabbix proxies, it is also possible to force the Zabbix proxy to request configuration data from the Zabbix server with `zabbix_proxy -R config_cache_reload`. Keep in mind that this will not work on a passive Zabbix proxy!

10. The **Last seen (age)** part of your newly added proxy should now show a time value, instead of **Never**.

Name ▲	Mode	Encryption	Compression	Last seen (age)
lar-book-proxy-active	Active	NONE	ON	1s

Figure 8.10 – Administration | proxies page, Last seen (age)

Depending on your setting in the proxy configuration file, the **Last seen (age)** part may take a while to change.

> **Important note**
> Polling the Zabbix server for configuration too often might increase load but polling too infrequently will leave your Zabbix proxy waiting for a new configuration. Choose a frequency that is best suited to your environment.

How it works...

If you followed the *Working with passive Zabbix proxies* recipe from this chapter, the steps are about the same, except for the part where we add the proxy mode and the part where we checked the `ConfigFrequency` value.

The proxy we just added is an active proxy that works by requesting a configuration from the Zabbix server on port `10051`.

Port: 10051

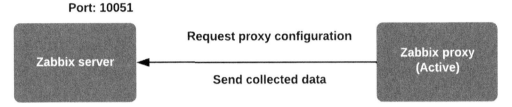

Figure 8.11 – Diagram showing active proxy connection

The Zabbix proxy keeps requesting configuration changes, and it keeps sending any new collected data to the Zabbix server every second or it sends out a heartbeat if no data is available.

Important note

It is recommended to use active Zabbix proxies, as we can use them to reduce the load on our Zabbix server. Use the passive proxy only when you have a good reason to do so.

Monitoring hosts with Zabbix proxy

We have our `active` and `passive` Zabbix proxies ready to use, so it's now time to add some hosts to them. Setting up the Zabbix frontend to monitor hosts with Zabbix proxies works in about the same way as monitoring directly from the Zabbix server. The backend and design change completely though, which I'll explain in the *How it works...* section of this recipe.

Getting ready

Make sure you have your `lar-book-proxy-passive` passive proxy and your `lar-book-proxy-active` active proxy ready by following all of the previous recipes in this chapter.

You will also need your Zabbix server and at least two hosts to monitor. We will be using `lar-book-agent_snmp` and `lar-book-agent` in the example, but any host with an active and passive Zabbix agent will work.

How to do it...

We'll configure a host on both our active and our passive proxies to show you what the difference is between these two. Let's start with the passive proxy.

Passive proxy

1. Let's start off this recipe by logging in to our Zabbix frontend and navigating to **Configuration | Hosts**.

2. Let's add the host with the passive agent to our passive proxy. In my case, this is the `lar-book-agent_snmp` host.

3. Click on the `lar-book-agent_snmp` host and change the **Monitored by proxy** field to `lar-book-proxy-passive`, as in the following screenshot:

Figure 8.12– Configuration | Hosts, Edit host page for host lar-book-agent_snmp

4. Now, click on the blue **Update** button. Our host will now be monitored by the Zabbix proxy.

> **Important note**
> Due to the configuration update interval of 1 hour, we can see the SNMP icon turn gray temporarily, and it may take up to 1 hour before monitoring continues. Be patient or force a configuration cache reload on both the Zabbix server and Zabbix proxy.

Active proxy

1. Let's do the same for our other `lar-book-agent` host by navigating back to **Configuration | Hosts**.

2. Click on the `lar-book-agent` host and edit the **Monitored by proxy** field to `lar-book-proxy-active`, as in the following screenshot:

Description	
Monitored by proxy	lar-book-proxy-active ▾
Enabled	✔

Update   Clone   Full clone   Delete   Cancel

Figure 8.13 – Configuration | Hosts, Edit host page for host lar-book-agent

3. Now, click on the blue **Update** button.

4. On the CLI of our monitored Linux host `lar-book-agent` host, execute the following command:

```
vim /etc/zabbix/zabbix_agent2.conf
```

5. When working with an active Zabbix agent we need to make sure to add the proxy IP address to the following line:

```
ServerActive=
```

Our host will now be monitored by the Zabbix proxy. Once again, this might take up to an hour.

How it works...

Monitoring hosts with a Zabbix proxy in passive or active mode works in the same way from the frontend. We merely configure which host is monitored by which proxy in our Zabbix frontend, and it will be done.

Let's take a look at how our **Simple Network Management Protocol (SNMP)** agent is now monitored by the passive proxy:

Figure 8.14 – A completely passive Zabbix setup with proxy

Our passive Zabbix proxy now collects data from our SNMP agent, and after this is collected, Zabbix server collects this data from our Zabbix proxy. Sounds like a whole process already, right?

Let's look at our active Zabbix proxy setup:

Figure 8.15 – A completely active Zabbix setup with proxy

Our active Zabbix proxy receives data from our active Zabbix agent and then sends this data to our Zabbix server. We've eliminated all the timers in this proxy setup altogether and are now receiving all of our data in the Zabbix server as soon as it's available.

This is why I would always recommend working with active proxies—and even active agents—as much as possible. If we look at the following screenshot, we can see a setup that you might see at a company:

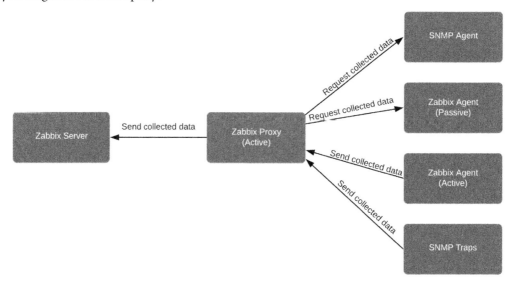

Figure 8.16 – An active Zabbix proxy setup with different monitored types

Fortunately, we have the option of using a lot of different combinations of setups. It is perfectly possible—and even logical—to combine your checks from a proxy, just as much as it would be with a Zabbix server. We can monitor all types from our proxy, whether it's a Zabbix agent, SNMP, or even **Java Management Extensions** (**JMX**) and the **Intelligent Platform Management Interface** (**IPMI**).

> Tip
>
> When designing a new Zabbix hosting infrastructure, start with adding proxies if possible. This way, you don't have to change a lot later. It's easy to add and change proxies, but it's harder to go from just using Zabbix server to using Zabbix proxies in your design.

There's more...

We now have a solid setup with some proxies up and running. We've figured out the difference between active and passive proxies and how they affect monitoring. But why would we build a setup like this? Well, Zabbix proxies are great for many environments—not just the big ones, but even sometimes in the smallest ones.

We can use Zabbix proxies to offload polling and preprocessing from our main Zabbix server, thus keeping the server clear for handling data like when writing to the Zabbix database.

We can use Zabbix proxies to monitor offsite locations, such as when you're a **Managed Service Provider** (**MSP**) and want to monitor a big customer network. We simply place a proxy on-site and monitor it. We can use industry-standard techniques like monitoring through a **virtual private network** (**VPN**) or simply set up a connection using built-in Zabbix proxy encryption.

When the VPN goes down, our proxy will keep collecting data on-site and send this to our Zabbix server when the VPN comes back up.

We can also use the Zabbix proxy to bypass firewall complications. When we place a proxy behind a firewall in a monitored network, we only need one firewall rule between the Zabbix server and the Zabbix proxy. Our Zabbix proxy then monitors the different hosts and sends the collected data in one stream to the Zabbix server.

With this, you have loads of options to use Zabbix proxies already.

See also

Check out this interesting blog post by Dmitry Lambert about some more cool hidden benefits of Zabbix proxies: `https://blog.zabbix.com/hidden-benefits-of-zabbix-proxy/9359/`.

Dmitry is an experienced Zabbix engineer and head of Zabbix Customer Support. His blog posts are easy to understand and provide some new angles to look at Zabbix from.

Using discovery with Zabbix proxies

In *Chapter 7, Using Discovery for Automatic Creation*, we talked about Zabbix and discovery. It is a very good idea to edit your discovery rules if you followed along with that chapter. Let's see how this would work in this recipe.

Getting ready

You'll need to have finished *Chapter 7, Using Discovery for Automatic Creation*, or have some discovery rules and active agent autoregistration set up.

I'll be using `lar-book-lnx-agent-auto`, `lar-book-disc-lnx`, and `lar-book-disc-win` hosts in this example. We will also need our Zabbix server.

How to do it...

Let's start with editing our discovery rule and then move on to editing our active agent to autoregister to the proxy.

Discovery rules

Starting with Zabbix discovery rules, let's look at how to make sure we do this from the Zabbix proxy:

1. Log in to the CLI of `lar-book-disc-lnx` and edit the `/etc/zabbix/zabbix_agent2.conf` file. Edit the following lines to include our Zabbix proxy address:

    ```
    Server=127.0.0.1,10.16.16.152,10.16.16.160,10.16.16.161
    ServerActive=10.16.16.160
    ```

2. Restart your Zabbix agent by executing the following command:

    ```
    systemctl restart zabbix-agent2
    ```

3. Now, make sure to log in to `lar-book-disc-win` and edit the `C:\Program Files\Zabbix agent\zabbix_agent2` file. Edit the following lines to include our Zabbix proxy address:

```
Server=127.0.0.1,10.16.16.152,10.16.16.160,10.16.16.161
ServerActive=10.16.16.160
```

> **Important note**
>
> On the `ServerActive` lines in our configuration files, make sure to only include the Zabbix proxy we want to send data to. The Zabbix agent will actively try to send data to all our Zabbix proxies or Zabbix servers listed here, so we should only list the one we want to use.

4. Restart your Zabbix agent by executing the following commands in the Windows command line:

```
zabbix_agent2.exe --stop
zabbix_agent2.exe --start
```

5. Next, navigate to **Configuration | Hosts** and delete the discovered hosts:

```
lar-book-disc-lnx
lar-book-disc-win
```

We do this to prevent duplicate hosts.

6. Now, navigate to **Configuration | Discovery**.

7. Click on **Discover Zabbix Agent hosts** and change the **Discovered by proxy** field, as shown in the following screenshot:

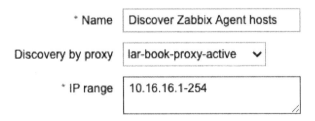

Figure 8.17 – Configuration | Actions, drop-down menu for discovery by proxy lar-book-proxy-active

8. Click on the blue **Update** button, and that's all there is to editing your discovery rule to be monitored by a proxy.

9.   You can now check out your newly discovered hosts under **Configuration | Hosts** and see that they are monitored by the proxy:

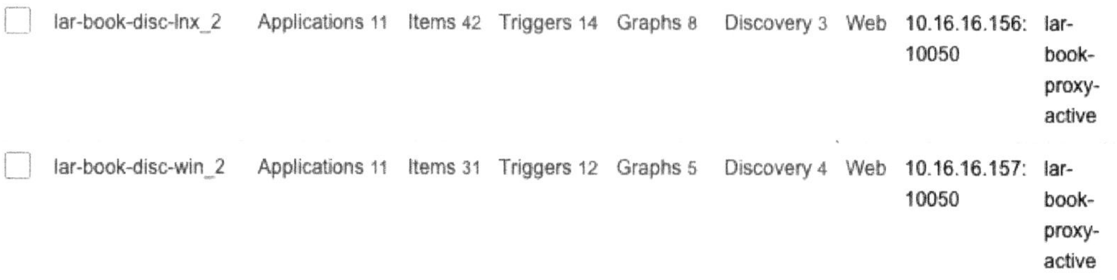

☐	lar-book-disc-lnx_2	Applications 11	Items 42	Triggers 14	Graphs 8	Discovery 3	Web	10.16.16.156: lar- 10050 book- proxy- active
☐	lar-book-disc-win_2	Applications 11	Items 31	Triggers 12	Graphs 5	Discovery 4	Web	10.16.16.157: lar- 10050 book- proxy- active

Figure 8.18 – Configuration | Hosts screen for discovered hosts

Active agent autoregistration

Moving on to active agent autoregistration, let's see how we can do this from our Zabbix proxy:

1.   Start by navigating to **Configuration | Hosts** and deleting `lar-book-lnx-agent-auto`.

2.   To do active agent autoregistration to a proxy, we have to log in to our `lar-book-lnx-agent-auto` host CLI.

3.   Edit the Zabbix agent configuration file with the following command:

```
vim /etc/zabbix/zabbix_agent2.conf
```

4.   Make sure to edit the following line to the Zabbix proxy address instead of the Zabbix server address:

```
ServerActive=10.16.16.160
```

5.   Restart the Zabbix agent:

```
systemctl restart zabbix-agent2
```

6. We can now see our host autoregister to the Zabbix proxy instead of the Zabbix server:

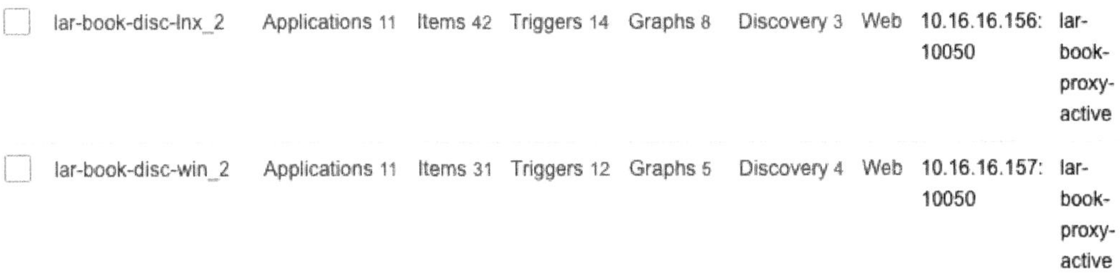

		Applications	Items	Triggers	Graphs	Discovery	Web		
☐	lar-book-disc-lnx_2	Applications 11	Items 42	Triggers 14	Graphs 8	Discovery 3	Web	10.16.16.156: 10050	lar-book-proxy-active
☐	lar-book-disc-win_2	Applications 11	Items 31	Triggers 12	Graphs 5	Discovery 4	Web	10.16.16.157: 10050	lar-book-proxy-active

Figure 8.19 – Configuration | Hosts screen for our two auto registered hosts

How it works...

Discovery with a Zabbix proxy works exactly the same as discovery with a Zabbix server. The only thing that changes is the location of where we are registering to or discovering from.

If you want to learn more about the process of discovery and auto registration, check out *Chapter 7, Using Discovery for Automatic Creation*, if you haven't already.

Monitoring your Zabbix proxies

A lot of Zabbix users—or even monitoring users in general—forget a very important part of their monitoring. They forget to monitor the monitoring infrastructure. I want to make sure that when you set up Zabbix proxies, you also know how to monitor the health of these proxies.

Let's check out how to do so in this recipe.

Getting ready

For this recipe, we will need our new `lar-book-proxy-active` Zabbix proxy. We will also need our Zabbix server to monitor the Zabbix proxy.

How to do it...

We are going to build some monitoring in our Zabbix frontend, but we'll also check the integrated monitoring options for Zabbix proxies. Let's start by building our own.

Monitoring the proxy with Zabbix

We can monitor our Zabbix proxy with Zabbix proxy itself to make sure we know exactly what's going on:

1. Let's start by logging in to our `lar-book-proxy-active` Zabbix proxy CLI.

2. Issue the following command to install Zabbix agent 2 for RHEL-based systems:

   ```
   dnf install zabbix-agent2
   ```

   For Ubuntu, issue this command:

   ```
   apt install zabbix-agent2
   ```

3. Edit the Zabbix agent configuration file by issuing the following command:

   ```
   vim /etc/zabbix/zabbix_agent2.conf
   ```

4. Edit the following lines to point toward `localhost`:

   ```
   Server=127.0.0.1
   ServerActive=127.0.0.1
   ```

5. Also, make sure to add the hostname to the Zabbix agent file:

   ```
   Hostname=lar-book-proxy-active
   ```

6. Now, log in to the Zabbix frontend and navigate to **Configuration | Hosts**.

7. Click on the blue **Create host** button in the top-right corner and add the following host:

Host

| Host | IPMI | Tags | Macros | Inventory | Encryption | Value mapping |

* Host name   lar-book-proxy-active

Visible name   lar-book-proxy-active

Templates   type here to search   Select

* Groups   Zabbix proxies ✕   Select
             type here to search

Interfaces   Type   IP address   DNS name   Connect to   Port   Default

Agent   127.0.0.1   IP   DNS   10050   ● Remove

Add

Description

Monitored by proxy   lar-book-proxy-active   ∨

Enabled ✓

Figure 8.20 – Configuration | Hosts, Create host page, lar-book-proxy-active

8. Take extra care at the **Monitored by proxy** field—we want to monitor from the proxy because we are doing Zabbix internal checks, which need to be handled by the Zabbix daemon that received this configuration.

9. Before clicking the blue **Add** button, make sure to add the **Templates**. Add the following templates to the host:

* Host name | lar-book-proxy-active

Visible name | lar-book-proxy-active

Templates | Zabbix proxy health ✕ | Linux by Zabbix agent active ✕ | Select
              | type here to search

Figure 8.21 – Configuration | Hosts, Create host page Templates tab for host lar-book-proxy-active

10. We can now click the blue **Add** button to create the host.

11. Now, navigate to **Monitoring | Latest data** and add the following filters:

Figure 8.22 – Monitoring | Latest data page with filters, host lar-book-proxy-active

12. We can now see our Zabbix proxy statistics, such as **Number of processed values per second** and **Utilization of configuration syncer internal processes**:

	Host	Name ▼	Last check	Last value	Change
☐	lar-book-proxy-active	Zabbix vmware cache, % used	59s	7.3369 %	-0.0005723 %
☐	lar-book-proxy-active	Zabbix queue over 10 minutes	3m 2s	0	
☐	lar-book-proxy-active	Zabbix queue	1m 1s	0	
☐	lar-book-proxy-active	Zabbix preprocessing queue ⁇	25s	0	
☐	lar-book-proxy-active	Zabbix history write cache, % used	58s	0 %	
☐	lar-book-proxy-active	Zabbix history index cache, % used	57s	0.4334 %	
☐	lar-book-proxy-active	Zabbix configuration cache, % used	1m	33.6491 %	
☐	lar-book-proxy-active	Zabbix agent ping ⁇	48s	Up (1)	
☐	lar-book-proxy-active	Zabbix agent availability ⁇	10s	available (1)	
☐	lar-book-proxy-active	Version of Zabbix agent running	2m 47s	6.0.0	
☐	lar-book-proxy-active	Host name of Zabbix agent running	2m 49s	Zabbix server	

Figure 8.23 – Monitoring | Latest data page with data from our Zabbix proxy

Monitoring the proxy remotely from our Zabbix server

We can also monitor our Zabbix proxy remotely from our Zabbix server, so let's see how that works:

1. Let's start by logging in to our `lar-book-proxy-active` host CLI and editing the following file:

```
vim /etc/zabbix/zabbix_agent2.conf
```

2. Edit the following lines to match your Zabbix server address (every node in an HA cluster):

```
Server=127.0.0.1,10.16.16.152
ServerActive=127.0.0.1,10.16.16.152
```

3. Also, edit the following file:

```
vim /etc/zabbix/zabbix_proxy.conf
```

4. Edit the following line to match your Zabbix server address:

```
StatsAllowedIP=127.0.0.1,10.16.16.152
```

5. Now, navigate to the Zabbix frontend and go to **Configuration | Hosts**.

6. Click on the blue **Create host** button in the top-right corner and add the following host:

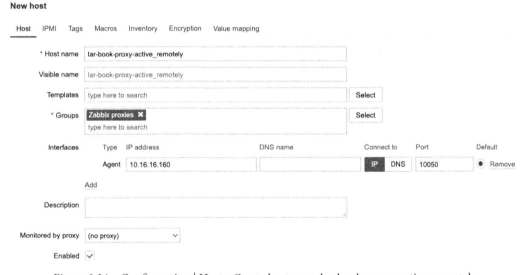

Figure 8.24 – Configuration | Hosts, Create host page, lar-book-proxy-active_remotely

7. Before clicking the blue **Add** button, make sure to add the right **Templates**. Add the following templates to the host:

Figure 8.25 – Configuration | Hosts, create new host page, Templates tab, lar-book-proxy-active_remotely

8. We can now click the blue **Add** button to create the host.

9. Back at **Configuration | Hosts**, click on your new `lar-book-proxy-active_remotely` host.

10. Go to **Macros** and add the following two macros:

Figure 8.26 – Configuration | Hosts, Edit host page, Macros tab, lar-book-proxy-active_remotely

11. Now, click on the blue **Update** button, and that's it for this host.

12. If we navigate to **Monitoring | Latest data** and check the items for this host, we can see data coming in:

Figure 8.27 – Monitoring | Latest data page for host lar-book-proxy-active_remotely

Monitoring the proxy from the Zabbix frontend

1. Let's start this off by navigating to **Administration | Queue**.

2. Use the drop-down menu to go to **Queue overview by proxy**:

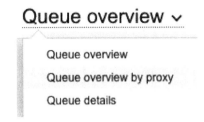

Figure 8.28 – Administration | Queue page drop-down menu

This will bring us to the page shown in the following screenshot:

Proxy	5 seconds	10 seconds	30 seconds
lar-book-proxy-active	0	0	0
lar-book-proxy-passive	0	0	0

Figure 8.29 – Administration | Queue page

How it works...

Monitoring your Zabbix proxies is an important task, thus we need to make sure that whenever we add a new Zabbix proxy, we are taking care of it like we would any other host.

Monitoring the proxy with Zabbix

By adding the Zabbix proxy as a host, we can make sure the Linux system that is running our Zabbix proxy is healthy. We also make sure that the Zabbix proxy applications running on this server are in good health.

Besides having the right triggers in these templates, we also get a load of options to troubleshoot issues with Zabbix proxy.

Zabbix proxy works just like Zabbix server when it comes to monitoring. This means that just as with Zabbix server, we need to keep the proxies in great health by tweaking the Zabbix proxy configuration file to our needs.

Scaling your proxies becomes a lot easier once you figure out what's going on with them. So, this is why we make sure to always monitor them. We monitor them from the proxy itself to make sure that we get the right information with the Zabbix internal checks.

Monitoring the proxy remotely from our Zabbix server

Now, when we monitor with the **Remote Zabbix proxy health**, things go a little differently. Instead of doing our checks from the Zabbix proxy itself, we do them remotely from the Zabbix server by defining the Zabbix proxy address and port in the macros. The Zabbix internal check type will still be used for this, executing the checks from the Zabbix server to the Zabbix proxy remotely in this case.

On top of that, it is of course still recommended that we also keep our Zabbix agent running in either passive or active mode.

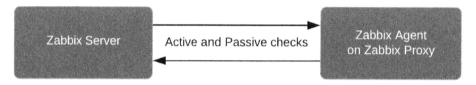

Figure 8.30 – Zabbix agent running on Zabbix proxy monitored by Zabbix server

This way, our Zabbix server is the one requesting and receiving information. Even when the proxy is having issues, the checks will still be done by Zabbix server.

We can use this template as a way to keep a closer eye on our proxy if we suspect issues with internal checks being performed locally, or we can use this template to bypass certain firewall setups. Both are valid reasons.

Monitoring the proxy from the Zabbix frontend

From the frontend, we can use the **Administration | Queue** page to monitor our proxies. The Zabbix **Queue** page is an important page, but a lot of new users neither know nor fully utilize this page.

When a part of Zabbix starts performing poorly, such as our example Zabbix proxy here, that's when we can see stuff happening in the queue. There are six options in the Zabbix **Queue**:

- **5 seconds**
- **10 seconds**
- **30 seconds**

- **1 minute**

- **5 minutes**

- **More than 10 minutes**

What the options in the **Queue** mean is that the Zabbix proxy has been waiting on receiving a value that's configured more than expected. I would state that anything up to 1 minute doesn't necessarily have to be an issue, but this depends on the type of check. The **5 minutes** or **More than 10 minutes** options can mean serious performance issues with your Zabbix proxy, and you would have to troubleshoot this issue. Make sure to keep a good eye on the Zabbix queue when you suspect issues, which are also included as triggers in the templates we added to monitor our Zabbix proxies.

9
Integrating Zabbix with External Services

In this chapter, we are going to set up some of the useful external service integrations that Zabbix has to offer. We can use these external services to notify our Zabbix users of ongoing problems.

We will start by learning how to set up in-company chat applications such as Slack and Microsoft Teams. Then, we will learn how to use a personal chat application such as Telegram before learning how to integrate Atlassian Opsgenie for even more extensive alerting.

Once you've completed these recipes, you will be able to effectively integrate certain services with Zabbix. This is a good starting point for working with external services in general and the easiest way to set up Slack, Teams, Opsgenie, and Telegram.

In this chapter, we will cover the following recipes:

- Setting up Slack alerting with Zabbix

- Setting up Microsoft Teams alerting with Zabbix

- Using Telegram bots with Zabbix

- Integrating Atlassian Opsgenie with Zabbix

Let's get started!

Technical requirements

For this chapter, we are going to need our Zabbix server, preferably how we set it up throughout this book, though any Zabbix 6 server with some alerts on it will do.

We will also need access to a few external services, as follows:

- Slack (free, to an extent)

  `https://slack.com/`
- Microsoft Teams (free, to an extent)

  `https://www.microsoft.com/microsoft-teams`
- Opsgenie (free, to an extent)

  `https://www.atlassian.com/software/opsgenie/`
- Telegram (free)

  `https://telegram.org/`

We will not cover how to set up the services themselves, but how to integrate them with Zabbix. Make sure you have set up the required service by following a guide and that you have some knowledge of the services in general.

Setting up Slack alerting with Zabbix

Slack is a widely used tool for easy text messaging, voice/video chat, and collaboration. In this recipe, we will learn how to use Zabbix Slack integration to send our Zabbix problem information to Slack so that we can gain a good overview of issues.

Getting ready

Make sure you have Slack set up. You can go to `https://slack.com/intl/en-in/` and set it up for free there. We will also need a Zabbix server with some active problems.

How to do it...

Follow these steps to complete this recipe:

1. Once you have set up and opened Slack, you should see the following page:

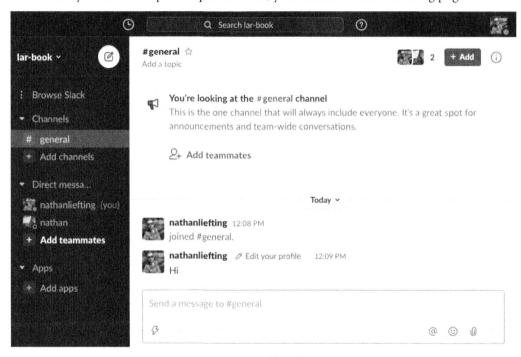

Figure 9.1 – Slack's default page

2. Let's create a new channel for our Zabbix notifications by clicking the **+Add channels** button. Then, from the dropdown that appears, click **Create a new channel**:

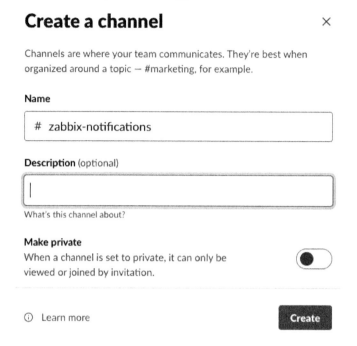

Figure 9.2 – Slack – Create a channel window

3. Click the green **Create** button. Then, on the next window, click the green **Done** button to add all members:

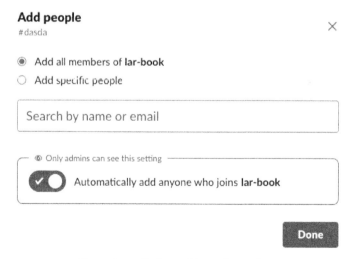

Figure 9.3 – Slack – Add people window

4. Now, navigate to the following link to create a Slack bot for working with Zabbix: `https://api.slack.com/apps`.

5. You will see the option **Create New App** on this page. Click the **Create New App** button, which brings us here:

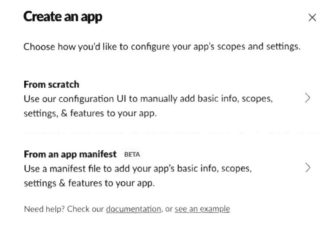

Figure 9.4 – Slack API – Create an app page

6. After clicking the **Create New App** button, we have to click on **From scratch**.

7. Then we'll see a pop-up window where we can set up our new Slack bot:

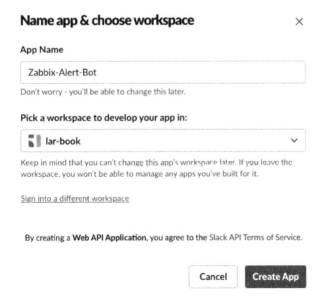

Figure 9.5 – Slack API – Name app & choose workspace window

8. Click on **Create App**. This will take you to the **Add features and functionality** page. On this page, click on **Bots**, as highlighted in the following screenshot:

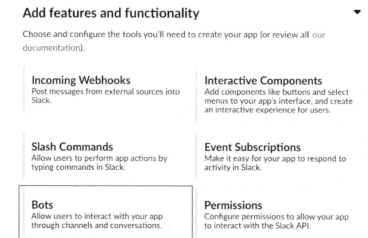

Figure 9.6 – Slack API – Add features and functionality page

9. This will take you to the new app's **Home** page. On the left-hand side of the page, click the **OAuth & Permissions** option.

10. Scroll down to **Scopes** and click on **Add an OAuth Scope**:

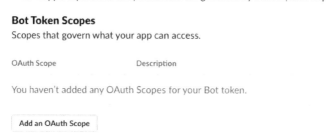

Figure 9.7 – Slack API – Scopes

11. From the drop-down menu, click on `chat:write` to allow our bot to write to a channel:

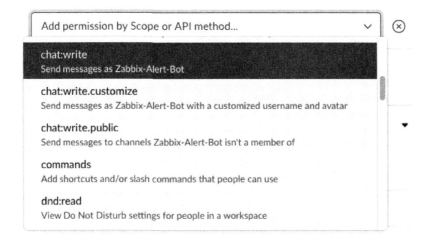

Figure 9.8 – Slack API – Add an OAuth Scope dropdown

12. Do the same for `im:write` and `groups:write`.

13. Scroll back up and click on the **Install to Workspace** button to finish setting up this app:

OAuth Tokens for Your Workspace

These OAuth Tokens will be automatically generated when you finish connecting the app to your workspace. You'll use these tokens to authenticate your app.

Figure 9.9 – Slack API – Install to Workspace button

14. Next, you will see a pop-up message. Click the green **Allow** button that appears.

15. After clicking **Allow**, you will see your new token. Copy the token by clicking the **Copy** button:

OAuth Tokens for Your Workspace

These tokens were automatically generated when you installed the app to your team. You can use these to authenticate your app. Learn more.

Bot User OAuth Token

xoxb-1412888539396-   Copy

Access Level: Workspace

Reinstall to Workspace

Figure 9.10 – Slack API – Our new Bot User OAuth Token

16. Lastly, add your bot to the **#zabbix-notifications** channel by going back to your Slack channel, clicking on the members in the top-right corner, and selecting **Integrations**:

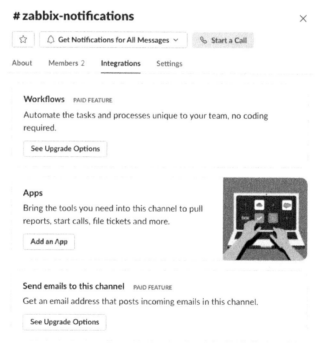

zabbix-notifications   ✕

☆   △ Get Notifications for All Messages ⌄   ✆ Start a Call

About   Members 2   **Integrations**   Settings

Workflows   PAID FEATURE

Automate the tasks and processes unique to your team, no coding required.

See Upgrade Options

Apps

Bring the tools you need into this channel to pull reports, start calls, file tickets and more.

Add an App

Send emails to this channel   PAID FEATURE

Get an email address that posts incoming emails in this channel.

See Upgrade Options

Figure 9.11 – Slack – Connect an app to a channel

17. Click on **Add an App**.

18. Simply add **Zabbix-Alert-Bot** by clicking the white **Add** button:

Figure 9.12 – Slack – Connect an app with a bot

19. Now, navigate to your Zabbix frontend and go to **Administration | Media types**.

20. Click on **Slack** to edit the Slack media type. You will see a whole list of preconfigured parameters. We need to paste our OAuth token into the bot_token parameter, like this:

Figure 9.13 – Zabbix Slack media type – Edit page

21. At the **Message templates** tab, we already have five message types configured. We can edit these to our liking if we would like to do so.

Figure 9.14 – Zabbix media type Slack – Edit page for message types

22. Now, let's create a new user group for our media types by navigating to **Administration | User groups** and clicking the **Create user group** button in the top-right corner. Add the following user group:

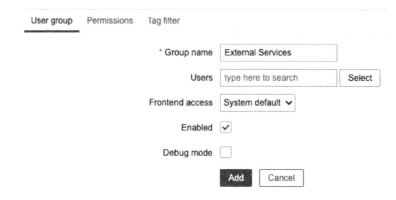

Figure 9.15 – Zabbix – Create user group page for the External Services group

23. Click on the **Permissions** tab and then click on **Select**. Make sure that you select all the groups and subgroups with at least **Read** permissions, like so:

Figure 9.16 – Zabbix – Create user group permissions page for the External Services group

> **Important Note**
>
> When applying permissions to the user group, make sure that you only add the host groups you want to receive notifications from. In my lab and even some production environments, I add all groups, but sometimes, we want to filter the notifications down. A great way to do this is to use different user groups and users so that you only receive notifications from host groups in certain channels. For a more in-depth look into Zabbix user permissions and triggers, check out *Chapter 2, Getting Things Ready with Zabbix User Management,* and *Chapter 4, Working with Triggers and Alerts,* respectively.

24. Now, click on the blue **Add** button and finish creating this user group.

25. Next, navigate to **Administration | Users** to create a Slack user. Click on the blue **Create user** button in the top-right corner.

26. Add the following user to your Zabbix server:

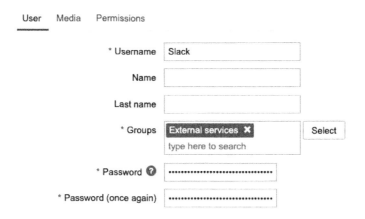

Figure 9.17 – Zabbix – Create user page for user Slack

27. Now, click on the **Media** tab and click on the underlined **Add** text. We will add the following media to this user:

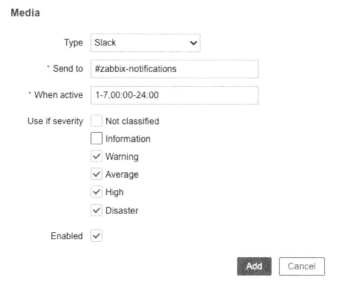

Figure 9.18 – Zabbix – Create user media page for user Slack

28. All users will also need a **User** role. To add it, go to **Permissions** and add the following:

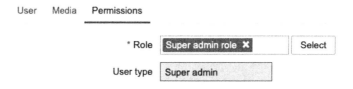

Figure 9.19 – Zabbix, Create user media page for user Slack, Permissions

> **Important Note**
>
> For convenience, we are adding the user in the **Super admin** user role in the example. This overrides the read-only permissions we assigned on the **External Services** user group. To limit the permissions, choose a **User** or **Admin** role for your user, which will adhere to the host group permissions we assigned earlier.

29. Click on the blue **Add** button at the bottom of the window and then on the blue **Add** button at the bottom of the page.

30. We will also need to add a macro to **Administration | General**. Use the drop-down menu to select **Macros** and add the following macro, which contains your Zabbix URL:

{$ZABBIX.URL}	http://10.16.16.152/zabbix/	T ˅

Add

Update

Figure 9.20 – Zabbix – Administration | General macros page with Zabbix URL

31. Click on the blue **Update** button.

32. Last but not least, go to **Administration | Actions** and on the **Trigger Actions** page, click on the blue **Create action** button.

33. Use `Notify external services` for the name of the action. We won't set up any conditions for this example, but it's recommended to do so in most cases.

34. Go to **Operations** and add the following operations:

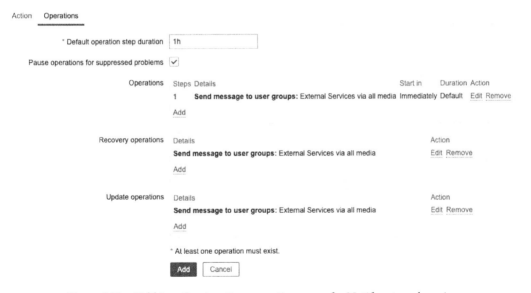

Figure 9.21 – Zabbix – Create action operations page for Notify external services

> **Tip**
> We could also use **Notify all involved** here to send a message to all the users involved in the **Operations** steps.

35. Now, click on the blue **Add** button. With that, you're done. You can now view any new problems (once they are generated by Zabbix) in your Slack channel:

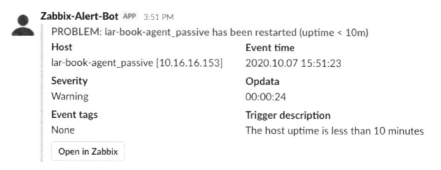

Figure 9.22 – Slack – Zabbix notification sent from our Zabbix server

How it works...

Working with media types might be something completely new to you, or you might have done it in the past. Regardless, starting from Zabbix 5, the process has changed a bit. In the days of Zabbix before Zabbix 5, we had to find the right media types online or make them ourselves.

Now, with Zabbix 6, we get a lot of preconfigured media types that are ready to be used. We just need to do the necessary setup and fill in the right information, just like we just did for Slack. We are then ready to send our problem-related information from Zabbix 6 to Slack every time a media type is created.

In this recipe, we told our Zabbix server to only send problem-related information with a severity of warning or higher to Slack, as shown in the following screenshot:

Figure 9.23 – Zabbix Media page for the Slack user

We can fully customize these severities, but we can also fully customize what severities we send to our Slack setup.

What we configured in this recipe is called a **Zabbix webhook**. A problem gets created in Zabbix and this problem matches our configured criteria, such as its severity. Our media type gets triggered and sends it to the configured links:

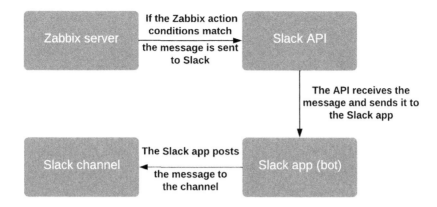

Figure 9.24 – Zabbix Slack integration diagram

Zabbix sends the problem to the Slack API, and then the API processes it has configured there. Then, the app we configured in Slack posts the problem to our channel.

Now that we've completed this recipe, we can view problems in Slack and keep an eye on our Zabbix alerts from there.

See also

If you want to do more with this integration, check out the Slack API documentation. There's a lot we can do with this API, and we can build a number of awesome apps/bots for our channels: `https://api.slack.com/`.

Setting up Microsoft Teams alerting with Zabbix

At the time of writing this book, I'm living in the Netherlands during the COVID-19 crisis. A lot of IT companies have been requested to make their employees work from home. Due to this, there's been a rise in the use of Microsoft Teams and applications like it. Suddenly, a lot of companies have started using Microsoft Teams and others to make working from home and collaboration easier.

Let's learn how we can make working with Microsoft Teams even better by integrating our Zabbix alerting into it.

Getting ready

We will need our Zabbix server to be able to create some problems for us. For this, you can use `lar-book-centos` from our previous chapters or any Zabbix server that you prefer.

We will also need general Microsoft Teams knowledge and, of course, Microsoft Teams itself set up and ready to go.

How to do it...

Follow these steps to complete this recipe:

1. Let's start by opening our Microsoft Teams application on either Windows, macOS, or Linux and creating a new channel. Go to **Teams** and click on the three dots (**...**) next to your team name, as shown in the following screenshot:

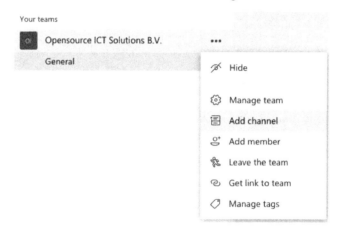

Figure 9.25 – MS Teams, Add channel option

2. In the **Add channel** window, fill in the following information to create our new channel:

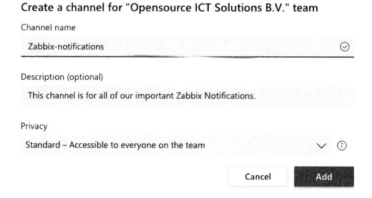

Figure 9.26 – MS Teams, Add channel window

3. Now, click the purple **Add** button to add the channel. Upon doing this, we will be able to see our new channel in the list.

4. Click on the three dots (**…**) next to your channel, as shown in the following screenshot:

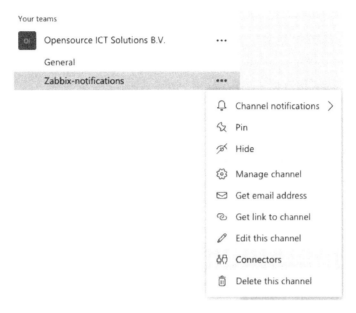

Figure 9.27 – MS Teams, Connectors option

5. We want to select the **Connectors** option from this drop-down menu. This allows us to add our Microsoft Teams connector to this channel.

6. We are using the search field here to find the official **Zabbix Webhook** connector:

Connectors for "Zabbix-notifications" channel in "Opensource ICT Solutions B.V." team   ✕

Keep your group current with content and updates from other services.

| zabbix ✕ | Search Results | Sort by: Popularity ⌄ |

MANAGE

Configured

My Accounts

Zabbix Webhook
Integrate Zabbix with Microsoft Teams by using this connector   **Add**

Figure 9.28 – MS Teams, Add connectors window

7. Click on the purple **Add** button next to the **Zabbix Webhook** connector to add this connector to our channel. This will open another pop-up window, where we must click the purple **Add** button again.

8. You will get another pop-up window, where you need to copy the webhook URL. Do this by clicking the white **Copy** button:

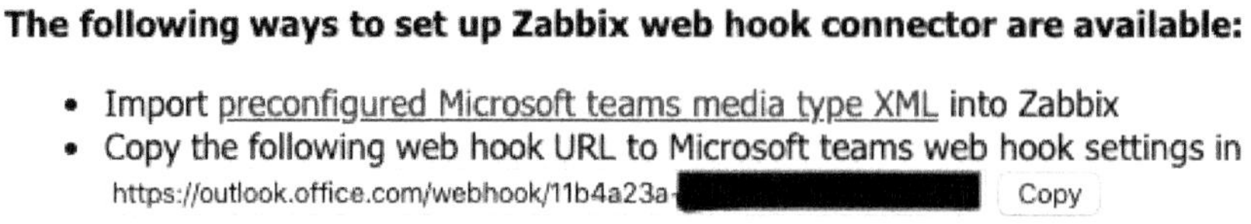

The following ways to set up Zabbix web hook connector are available:

- Import preconfigured Microsoft teams media type XML into Zabbix
- Copy the following web hook URL to Microsoft teams web hook settings in Zabbix:

  https://outlook.office.com/webhook/11b4a23a-▮▮▮▮▮▮▮▮▮   Copy

Figure 9.29 – MS Teams – Webhook URL

9. Now, click the purple **Save** button. Upon doing this, you can close the pop-up window.

10. Go to the Zabbix frontend and navigate to **Administration | Media types**. Click on the **MS Teams** media type here.

11. Scroll down until you see **teams_endpoint**. Paste the URL you copied previously here, as shown in the following screenshot:

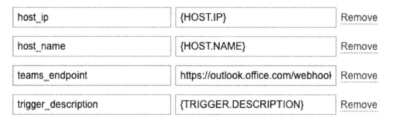

Figure 9.30 – Zabbix Administration | Media types, edit MS Teams page

12. Now, click the blue **Update** button at the bottom of the page.

13. If you didn't follow the previous recipe, then create a new user group for our media types by navigating to **Administration | User groups** and clicking the **Create user group** button in the top-right corner. Add the following user group:

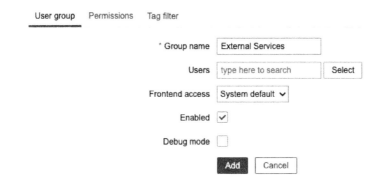

Figure 9.31 – Zabbix, Create user group page, the External Services group

14. Click on the **Permissions** tab and click on **Select**. Make sure that you select all the groups and subgroups with **Read** permissions. The **Permissions** tab will look like this:

Figure 9.32 – Zabbix – Create user group permissions page, the External Services group

15. Now, click on the blue **Add** button and finish creating this user group.

16. Navigate to **Administration | Users** and click on the blue **Create user** button in the top-right corner. Add the following user:

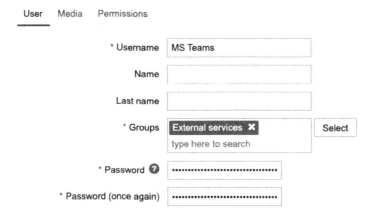

Figure 9.33 – Zabbix Administration | Media types – Create new user page, MS Teams

17. Next, go to the **Media** tab of the **Create user** page. Click the underlined **Add** text here to create the following media:

Figure 9.34 – Zabbix Administration | Media types – Create new user page, MS Teams

18. All users will also need a **User role**. To add it, go to **Permissions** and add the following:

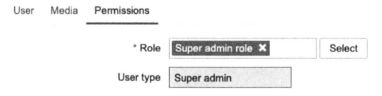

Figure 9.35 – Zabbix – Create user media page, user Slack, Permissions

> **Important Note**
>
> For convenience, we are adding the user in the **Super admin** user role in the example. This overrides the read-only permissions we assigned on the **External Services** user group. To limit the permissions, choose a **User** or **Admin** role for your user, which will adhere to the host group permissions we assigned earlier.

19. Once you've filled in this information, click the blue **Add** button at the bottom of the window and then the blue **Add** button at the bottom of the page.

20. If you didn't follow the previous recipe, then you will also need to add a macro to **Administration | General**. Use the drop-down menu on this page to select **Macros** and add the following macro, which contains your Zabbix URL:

Figure 9.36 – Zabbix Administration | General macros page, Zabbix URL for use with MS Teams

21. Click on the blue **Update** button. You will also need to go to **Administration |
    Actions** if you didn't follow the previous recipe and, on the **Trigger Actions** page,
    click on the blue **Create action** button.

22. Use `Notify external services` for the name of the action. We won't set up
    any conditions for this example, but it's recommended to do so in most cases.

23. Go to **Operations** and add the following operations:

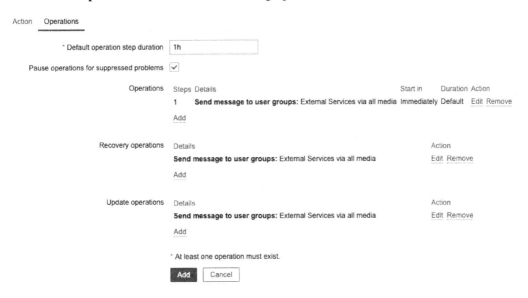

Figure 9.37 – Zabbix – Create action Operations page, Notify external services for use with MS Teams

> **Tip**
> We could also use **Notify all involved** here to send a message to all the users
> involved in the **Operations** steps.

24. Now, click on the blue **Add** button and you'll be done. You can now view new problems as they occur in your MS Teams channel:

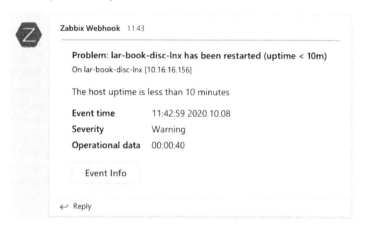

Figure 9.38 – A Zabbix problem in an MS Teams channel

How it works...

Microsoft Teams works in about the same way as our Slack setup. A problem is created in the Zabbix server and if that problem matches our configured conditions in Zabbix, we send that problem to our Microsoft Teams connector.

For instance, we configured Zabbix so that it only sends problems with a severity of warning or higher to Microsoft Teams, as shown here:

Figure 9.39 – Zabbix Media page for MS Teams users

Our Microsoft Teams connector catches our problem and since this connector is configured directly on our channel, it posts a notification to the channel:

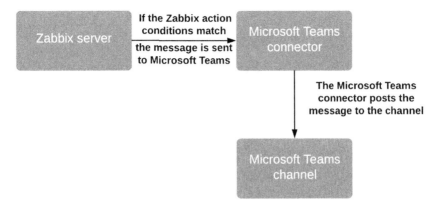

Figure 9.40 – Zabbix Microsoft Teams integration diagram

Now, we can see our Teams notifications in our channel and keep up to date with all our Zabbix issues directly via Microsoft Teams.

See also

For more information about the Zabbix webhook connector, check out this page: `https://appsource.microsoft.com/en-us/product/office/WA200001837?tab=Overview`.

Using Telegram bots with Zabbix

If you love automation in chat applications, you might have heard of or used Telegram messenger. Telegram has an extensive API and amazing bot features.

In this recipe, we are going to use a Telegram bot to create a Telegram group for Zabbix alerts. Let's get started.

Getting ready

Make sure you have your Zabbix server ready. You can use `lar-book-centos` or any Zabbix server capable of sending some alerts.

It would be useful if you have some knowledge of Telegram, but I'll be describing how to set it up step by step, even for those of you who have never used Telegram bots. Just make sure that you have the Telegram app on your computer and that your account is set up.

How to do it...

Follow these steps to complete this recipe:

1. First, let's create a new channel in Telegram. Click on the create icon next to the search box and select **New Group**:

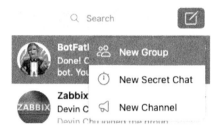

Figure 9.41 – Telegram – New Group button

2. Add another user – someone in your team that needs to get notifications as well. Fill in a group name and add a picture if you want:

Figure 9.42 – Telegram – New Group page

3. Now, click on the **Create** button in the top-right corner. This will take you to the **New Group** page.

4. Working with Telegram bots is made easy with the @BotFather user on Telegram. We can start creating our bot by searching for botfather and clicking the specified contact:

Figure 9.43 – Telegram – BotFather user

5. Let's start by issuing the /start command in the chat. This will provide you with a list of commands you can use:

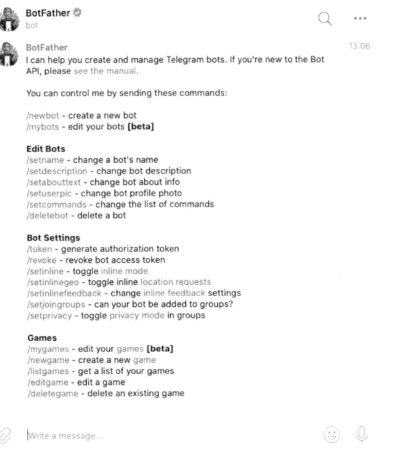

Figure 9.44 – Telegram – BotFather user help list

6. Now, let's immediately create a new bot by typing /newbot into the **BotFather** chat. Press *Enter* to send your message. This will give us the following result:

Figure 9.45 – Telegram – BotFather /newbot command

7. Type in the new name of the bot; we will call it zabbix-notfication-bot. Press *Enter* to send your name:

Figure 9.46 – Telegram – BotFather bot username

8. You will then be asked what username you want to give the bot. I will use lar_zbx_notfication_bot:

Figure 9.47 – Telegram – BotFather bot token

> **Important Note**
>
> Your bot username must be unique, so you can't use `lar_zbx_notification_bot` here. Pick a unique bot name that suits you and use that name throughout this recipe.

9.   Make sure that you save the **HTTP API** key somewhere safe.

10. Let's go back to our **Zabbix Notifications** group and add our bot. Click on the group in your list of chats and click on the group's name.

11. Now, click on **Add** to add the bot, as follows:

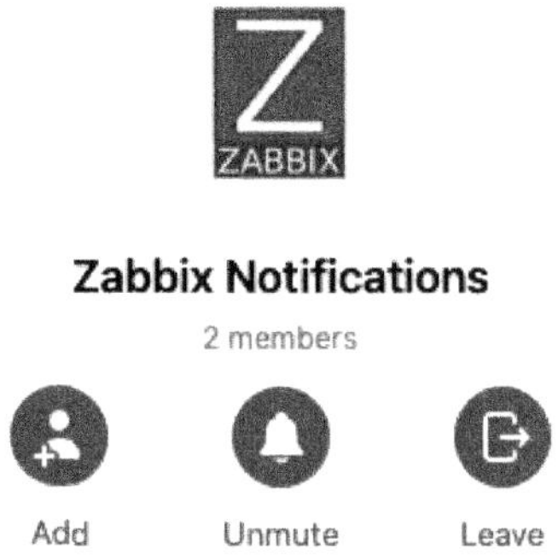

Zabbix Notifications

2 members

Add   Unmute   Leave

Figure 9.48 – Telegram – Add user to group button

12. Next, you will need to search for your bot using its username, as shown in the following screenshot:

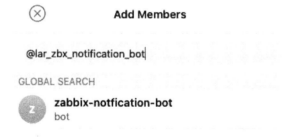

Figure 9.49 – Telegram – Add user to group page

13. Click on the bot and click on the **Add** button. With that, your bot has been added to the channel.

14. Let's navigate to the Zabbix frontend and go to **Administration | Media types**. Click on the media type titled **Telegram**.

15. Here, you must add the **HTTP API** key you generated earlier to the **Token** field of our media type:

Parameters	Name	Value	Action
	Message	{ALERT.MESSAGE}	Remove
	ParseMode		Remove
	Subject	{ALERT.SUBJECT}	Remove
	To	{ALERT.SENDTO}	Remove
	Token	128■■■AG■	Remove
	Add		

Figure 9.50 – Zabbix Administration | Media types – Edit Telegram Media type page

16. Click on the blue **Update** button at the bottom of the page to finish editing the **Telegram** media type.

17. Now, let's go back to Telegram and add another bot to our group. Go to our new group and click on the group's name. Click on **Add** to add the following user:

Figure 9.51 – Add user page for a Telegram group

18. Click on the user and click on **Add**. Then, navigate back to the Zabbix frontend.

19. If you haven't followed any of the preceding recipes, create a new user group for our media types by navigating to **Administration | User groups** and clicking the **Create user group** button in the top-right corner. Add the following user group:

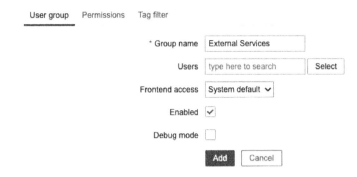

Figure 9.52 – Zabbix – Create user group page, External Services for use with Telegram

20. Click on the **Permissions** tab and click on **Select**. Make sure that you select all the groups and subgroups with **Read** permissions, as follows:

Figure 9.53 – Zabbix – Create user group permissions page, External Services for use with Telegram

21. Now, click on the blue **Add** button and finish creating this user group.

22. At this point, you must create a new user in Zabbix. However, to create this user, you are going to need our new group ID. Go back to Telegram and issue /getgroupid@myidbot in the group chat. You will receive a value that you will need to copy:

Figure 9.54 – Telegram user group ID

23. Let's navigate to **Administration | Users** and click the blue **Create user** button. Add the following user:

Figure 9.55 – Zabbix – Create user page, user Telegram

24. Now, select the **Media** tab and click on the underlined **Add** text. Add the following media:

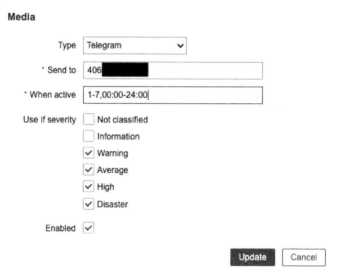

Figure 9.56 – Zabbix – Create user media page, user Telegram

25. All users will also need a **User role**. To add it, go to **Permissions** and add the following:

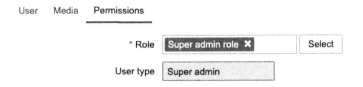

Figure 9.57 – Zabbix – Create user media page, user Slack, Permissions

> **Important Note**
>
> For convenience, we are adding the user in the **Super admin** user role in the example. This overrides the read-only permissions we assigned on the **External Services** user group. To limit the permissions, choose a **User** or **Admin** role for your user, which will adhere to the host group permissions we assigned earlier.

26. Make sure that you add the group ID to the **Send to** field without the – text and click on the blue **Add** button.

27. If you haven't followed the previous recipes, you will also need to go to **Administration | Actions**. Then, on the **Trigger Actions** page, click on the blue **Create action** button.

28. Use `Notify external services` for the name of the action. We won't set up any conditions for this example, but it's recommended to do so in most cases.

29. Go to **Operations** and add the following operations:

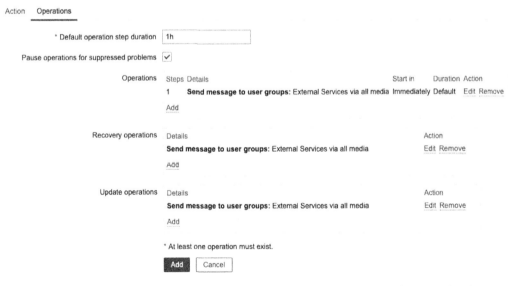

Figure 9.58 – Zabbix – Create action operations page, Notify external services for use with Telegram

> **Tip**
> We could also use **Notify all involved** here to send a message to all the users involved in the **Operations** steps.

30. Now, click on the blue **Add** button. With that, you're done. You can now view new problems in your Telegram group:

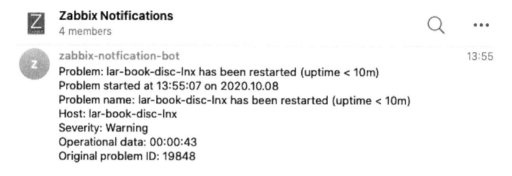

Figure 9.59 – Zabbix notifications in Telegram chat

How it works...

Slack apps, Microsoft connectors, and Telegram bots – they all work the same in the end. There's just another backend provided by the respective companies, but the Zabbix webhook remains.

Now that we've added our Zabbix Telegram integration, we are receiving notifications in our Telegram group via the Zabbix webhook:

Figure 9.60 – Zabbix Administration | Users – Edit user media page

However, we will only receive these notifications if they match our configured settings. For instance, we've added our media type so that it only sends problems with a severity of warning or higher to our Telegram bot:

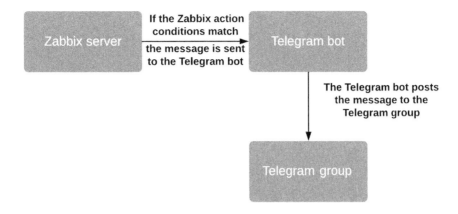

Figure 9.61 – Zabbix Telegram integration diagram

Our Zabbix server is now sending our problems that match the **Action** conditions to our Telegram bot. The bot catches these problems successfully. Because our bot is in our Telegram group, the problems are posted in our Telegram group.

There's more...

There's a very cool Zabbix community group on Telegram. Now that you have Telegram, do not forget to join using the following invite link: `https://t.me/ZabbixTech`.

See also

Make sure that you check out all the awesome features Telegram bots have to offer. There's a lot of information available directly from Telegram, and you can build amazing integrations by using them: `https://core.telegram.org/bots`.

Integrating Atlassian Opsgenie with Zabbix

Atlassian Opsgenie is so much more than just another integration service for receiving notifications. Opsgenie offers us a call system, an SMS system, iOS and Android apps, two-way acknowledgments, and even an on-call schedule.

I think Opsgenie is the best tool for replacing old-school call and SMS systems and fully integrating them with Zabbix. So, let's get started with Opsgenie and see how we can get this amazing tool set up.

Getting ready

Ensure that your Zabbix server is ready. I'll be using the `lar-book-centos` server, but any Zabbix server ready to send problems should work.

You are also going to need an Atlassian Opsgenie account with Opsgenie ready to go.

I won't show you how to create accounts, but we'll start this recipe with Opsgenie ready to go.

How to do it...

Follow these steps to complete this recipe:

1. Let's start by logging into our Atlassian Opsgenie setup and going to **Settings** on the home page. From the left sidebar, click on **Notifications**.

2. Make sure that you add your email and phone number here by using the + **Add email** and + **Add phone number** buttons. We need these in order to receive notifications:

Figure 9.62 – Opsgenie profile – Contact methods

3. Your settings will be automatically saved once you've added them, which means we can navigate away from **Settings** to **Teams** using the top bar.

4. From the **Teams** tab, click on the blue **Add team** button in the top-right corner. Then, add the following information:

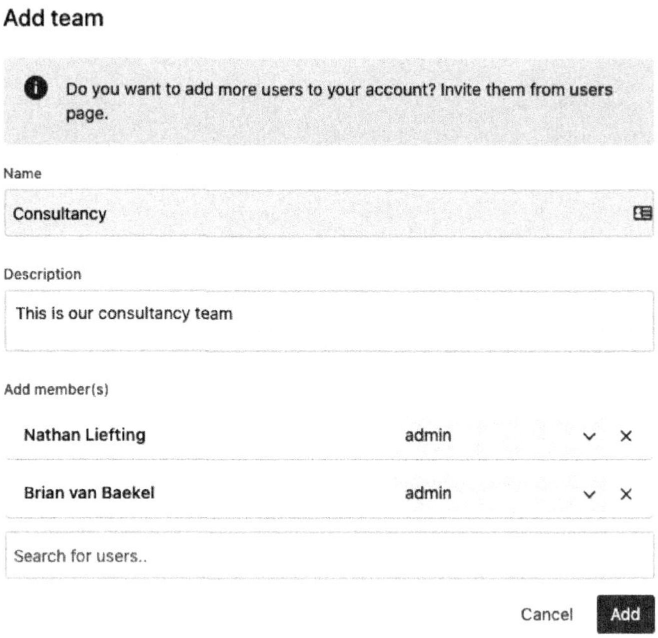

Add team

> ℹ️ Do you want to add more users to your account? Invite them from **users page**.

Name

Consultancy

Description

This is our consultancy team

Add member(s)

Nathan Liefting	admin	⌄ ✕
Brian van Baekel	admin	⌄ ✕

Search for users..

Cancel   **Add**

Figure 9.63 – Opsgenie – Add team window

5. I've set up our **Consultancy** team with two users that are part of this team. Click on the blue **Add** button at the bottom of the window to add the new team.

6. This will take you to the new **Consultancy team** page. Click on **Integrations** and click on the blue **Add integration** button in the top-right corner.

7. When we use the search field to search for the Zabbix integration, we can see it immediately, as shown in the following screenshot:

Integration list

zabbix   🔍   Group list by ⌄

⇄

ZABBIX

Zabbix

Figure 9.64 – Opsgenie – Add integration page

8. Hover over the Zabbix integration and click the blue **Add** button. This will take you to the next page, where a **Name** and **API Key** will be generated:

Figure 9.65 – Opsgenie – Add Zabbix integration page

9. Copy the **API Key** information and scroll to the bottom of the page. Here, click on the blue **Save integration** button.

10. Now, navigate to your Zabbix server CLI and execute the following code:

    For RHEL-based systems:

    ```
    wget https://github.com/opsgenie/oec-scripts/releases/
    download/Zabbix-1.1.6_oec-1.1.3/opsgenie-zabbix-
    1.1.6.x86_64.rpm
    ```

    For Ubuntu systems:

    ```
    wget https://github.com/opsgenie/oec-scripts/releases/
    download/Zabbix-1.1.6_oec-1.1.3/opsgenie-zabbix_1.1.6_
    amd64.deb
    ```

11. We can now install the downloaded Zabbix Opsgenie plugin by issuing the following command(s):

    For RHEL-based systems:

    ```
    rpm -i opsgenie-zabbix-1.1.6.x86_64.rpm
    ```

    For Ubuntu systems:

    ```
    dpkg -i opsgenie-zabbix_1.1.6_amd64.deb
    ```

12. Once you've installed the plugin, go to the Zabbix frontend. If you haven't followed any of the previous recipes, create a new user group for our media types by navigating to **Administration | User groups** and clicking the **Create user group** button in the top-right corner. Add the following user group:

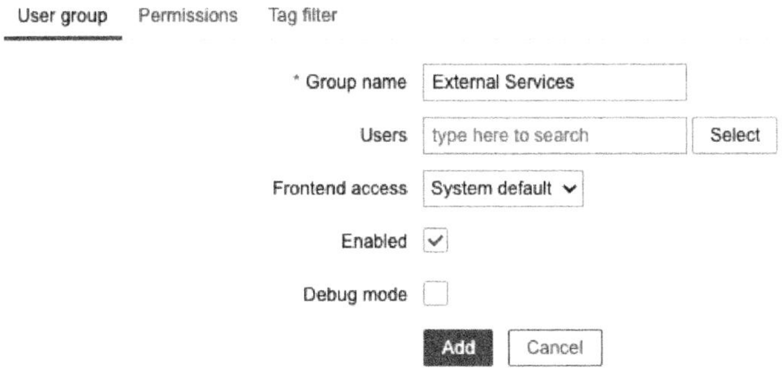

Figure 9.66 – Zabbix – Create user group page, the External Services group for use with Opsgenie

13. Click on the **Permissions** tab and click on **Select**. Make sure that you select all the groups and subgroups with **Read** permissions, as follows:

Figure 9.67 – Zabbix – Create user group permissions page, the External Services group for use with Opsgenie

14. Now, click on the blue **Add** button and finish creating this user group.

15. Next, navigate to **Administration | Actions**. On the **Trigger actions** page, click on the blue **Create** action button in the top-right corner.

16. In the **Name** field, type `Opsgenie action` and add the following items to **Conditions**:

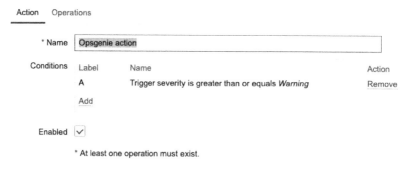

Figure 9.68 – Zabbix – Create new action page, Opsgenie action

17. Now, click on the **Operations** tab.

18. Click the underlined **Add** text option next to **Operations** to add your first operation. Set **Operation type** to **Remote command** and paste in the contents of the `/home/opsgenie/oec/opsgenie-zabbix/actionCommand.txt` file, as shown in the following screenshot:

Figure 9.69 – Zabbix – Create action operations window, Opsgenie action

19. Repeat *step 17* for **Recovery operations** and **Update operations**. It should look like this:

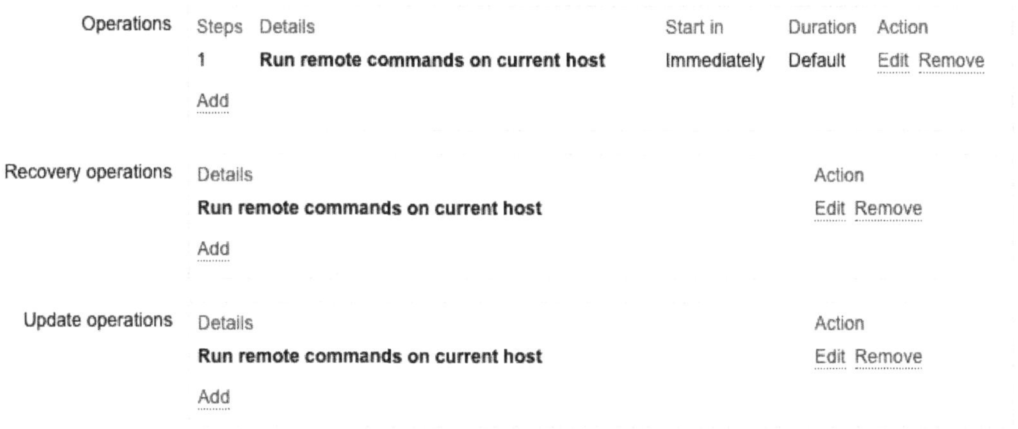

Operations	Steps	Details	Start in	Duration	Action
	1	**Run remote commands on current host**	Immediately	Default	Edit Remove
	Add				

Recovery operations	Details	Action
	Run remote commands on current host	Edit Remove
	Add	

Update operations	Details	Action
	Run remote commands on current host	Edit Remove
	Add	

Figure 9.70 – Zabbix – Create action operations page, Opsgenie action

20. Click on the blue **Add** button at the bottom of the page to finish setting up the action.

21. Now, you must configure the Opsgenie-to-Zabbix integration. Edit the config file with the following command:

```
vim /home/opsgenie/oec/conf/config.json
```

22. Make sure that you edit the apiKey, command_url, user, and password lines, as shown in the following screenshot:

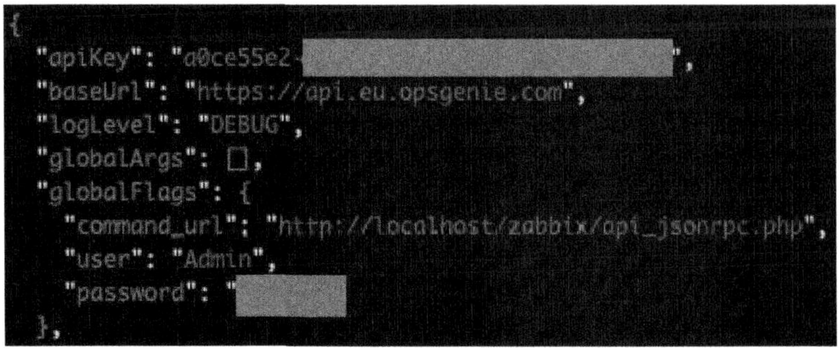

Figure 9.71 – Opsgenie config.json file

> **Important Note**
>
> You will need to edit `baseUrl` if you are not located in the United States. I am in Europe, so I changed it to `https://api.eu.opsgenie.com`.

23. That's it! You can now see your alerts coming in and acknowledge them from Opsgenie:

Figure 9.72 – Opsgenie alert from Zabbix

How it works...

When an alert is created in Zabbix, it is sent to Opsgenie via the Zabbix integration. This integration utilizes the Opsgenie API to catch our Zabbix information and send back a reply if required. This way, we have two-way communication between the two applications:

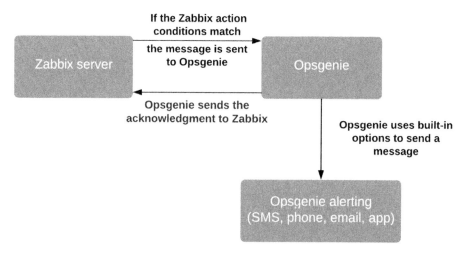

Figure 9.73 – Opsgenie setup diagram

Opsgenie is an amazing tool that can take several tasks away from your Zabbix server. I've used it in the past to migrate away from another monitoring tool to Zabbix. Opsgenie makes it easy to receive alerts from our products and centralize notifications:

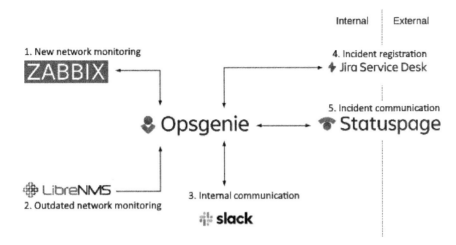

Figure 9.74 – Opsgenie setup example, inspired by Wadie

Another great feature of Atlassian Opsgenie is the integration it offers with other Atlassian products. We can build a setup like the one shown in the preceding diagram to integrate all the products used in our company.

There's more...

If you are interested in more information about Opsgenie, check out the following blog post:

```
https://blog.zabbix.com/scheduling-and-escalation-made-easy-
zabbix-and-opsgenie-integration/10005/
```

10
Extending Zabbix Functionality with Custom Scripts and the Zabbix API

Zabbix offers a lot of functionality out of the box. But where Zabbix really shines is customization, not only through the default frontend but especially with scripts and the Zabbix API.

In this chapter, I will go over the basics of using the Zabbix API. We will then see how a Python script can utilize the API to build something cool, such as a jumphost. After that, we'll use some scripts written by *Brian van Baekel* to schedule maintenance periods as a Zabbix user and to enable and disable hosts with limited permissions from a Zabbix map.

After following these recipes, you'll be more than ready to tackle the Zabbix API and you'll know how to use scripts to extend Zabbix functionality. This chapter will expand your possibilities with Zabbix to almost endless proportions and you'll be ready to become a professional Zabbix user yourself.

In this chapter, we will cover the following topics:

- Setting up and managing API tokens

- Using the Zabbix API for extending functionality

- Building a jumphost using the Zabbix API and Python

- Creating maintenance periods as a Zabbix user

- Enabling and disabling a host from Zabbix maps

Technical requirements

We are going to need a Zabbix server as well as some new Linux hosts. We will also need to have general knowledge of scripting and programming. We are going to use Python to extend some functionality of Zabbix, which we'll provide scripts for.

The code required for the chapter can be found at the following link:

```
https://github.com/PacktPublishing/Zabbix-6-IT-Infrastructure-
Monitoring-Cookbook/tree/main/chapter10
```

Make sure to keep all of this ready and you'll be sure to nail these recipes.

Setting up and managing API tokens

Let's start off our chapter by doing some pre-configuration for working with APIs in Zabbix. If you've worked with the Zabbix API before you might know it can be quite a hassle to use API calls to authenticate and get an API token for using it in your scripts. This is no longer the case, as we can generate API tokens using the Zabbix frontend.

Getting ready

For this recipe, all we'll need is the Zabbix setup running. We'll be using the frontend to generate the API token. From here we can use the API token in any of our integrations further on in this chapter.

How to do it...

1. First, let's log in to the Zabbix frontend as a Super admin user.

2. Navigate to **Administration | User groups** and click the blue **Create user group** button in the top-right corner.

3. Here we'll create a new user group. Fill in the **Group name** field as API users.

4. Switch to the **Permissions** tab and give your API user group permission to every user group by clicking the **Select** button and selecting every host group.

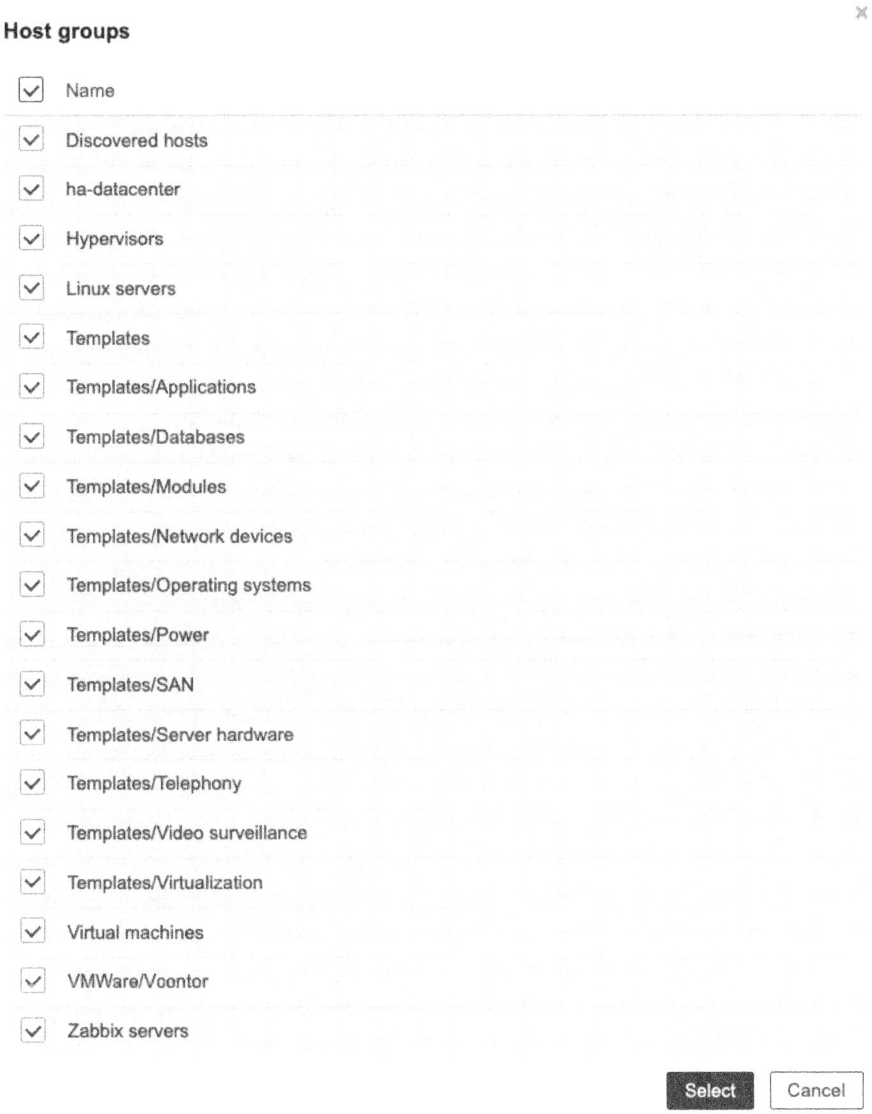

Host groups   ✕

☑	Name
☑	Discovered hosts
☑	ha-datacenter
☑	Hypervisors
☑	Linux servers
☑	Templates
☑	Templates/Applications
☑	Templates/Databases
☑	Templates/Modules
☑	Templates/Network devices
☑	Templates/Operating systems
☑	Templates/Power
☑	Templates/SAN
☑	Templates/Server hardware
☑	Templates/Telephony
☑	Templates/Video surveillance
☑	Templates/Virtualization
☑	Virtual machines
☑	VMWare/Voontor
☑	Zabbix servers

Select   Cancel

Figure 10.1 – Zabbix Administration | User groups, create user group page, API Users

5. Click the blue **Select** button at the bottom of this popup and click on **Read-write** then the small dotted **Add** button. It should now look like this:

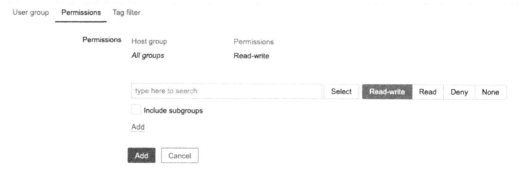

Figure 10.2 – Zabbix Administration | User groups, user group permissions page, API Users

> **Tip**
>
> Instead of creating the API user as Super admin, we can also limit the permissions by limiting the host group access on the **API Users** user group. This could be preferred in your environment, as you might want to limit API access. Use whatever fits your preference.

6. Click the blue **Add** button at the bottom of the page to add this new user group.

7. Now let's go to **Administration | Users** and click the blue **Create user** button in the top-right corner.

8. Here we will create a new user called the API user. Create the user as follows:

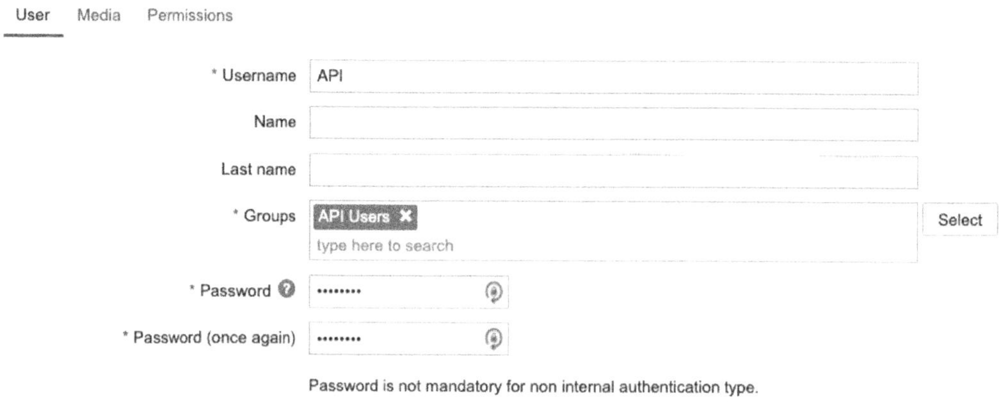

Figure 10.3 – Zabbix Administration | Users, user creation page, API user

9. Before adding the user, switch to the **Permissions** tab and add the **Super admin role**.

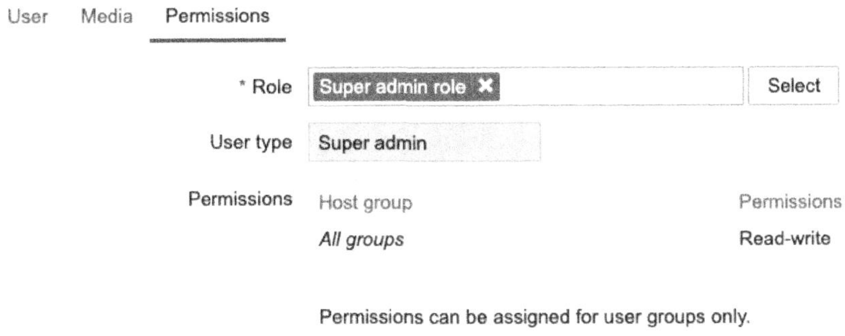

User   Media   Permissions

* Role   [Super admin role ✕]   [Select]

User type   Super admin

Permissions   Host group   Permissions

              All groups   Read-write

Permissions can be assigned for user groups only.

Figure 10.4 – Zabbix Administration | Users, user permissions page, API user

10. We can now add the user by clicking the blue **Add** button at the bottom of the page.

11. Next up we need to create some API tokens for this user. Navigate to **Administration | General | API tokens**.

12. Let's click the blue **Create API token** button in the top-right corner and fill in our **User** as API and our **Name** field as API book key. Set **Expires at** to somewhere far in the future or whatever you think might be secure. It will look like this:

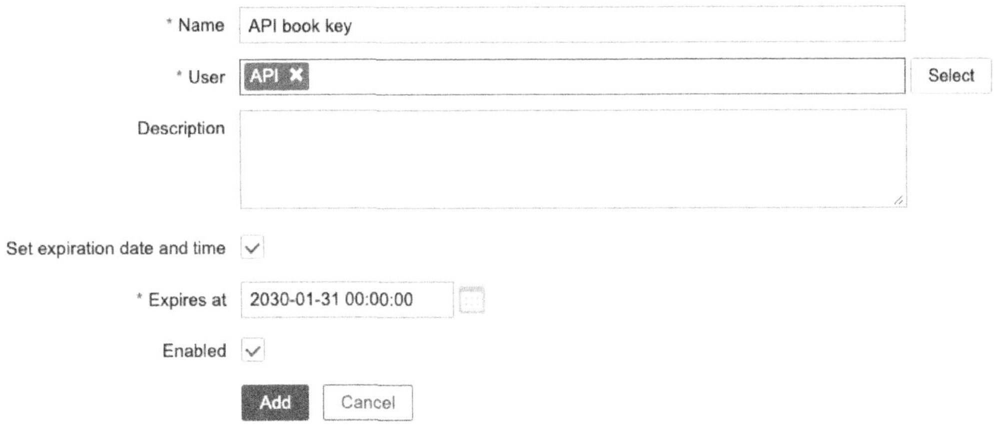

* Name   [API book key   ]

* User   [API ✕   ]   [Select]

Description   [   ]

Set expiration date and time   [✓]

* Expires at   [2030-01-31 00:00:00]   [▦]

Enabled   [✓]

        [Add]   [Cancel]

Figure 10.5 – Administration | General | API token, API token creation page

13. Click the blue **Add** button at the bottom of the page to generate the new API token. This will bring us to the next page:

Figure 10.6 – Zabbix API user API token generated page

14. Make sure to save the **Auth token** to a secure location, like a password vault. It will be important later in the labs.

15. We can click the **Close** button at the bottom of this page now. This will bring us back to the **API tokens** page where we can manage all of our created API tokens.

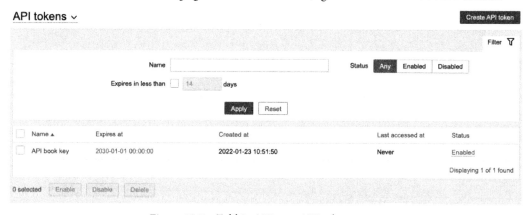

Figure 10.7 – Zabbix API user API tokens page

How it works...

Because Zabbix now comes with built-in API token management, it has become a lot easier to work with the Zabbix API. Using a dedicated API user, we can manage all of our tokens in a single location or we can set up private API tokens under our own user account.

In this case, we created a new API Users group. This is important because our API tokens still respect user permissions. If we create an API user under any other role than Super admin we can restrict our API access using the API Users group.

Make sure that you apply the role to the user and the permissions to the user group as you see fit in your environment. Also, make sure to set a reasonable expiration date for your API tokens, so we can make sure to regenerate them from time to time.

There's not much else to say about setting up and managing your API tokens, but let's see how we can apply what we have learned in this recipe in the next recipes.

Using the Zabbix API for extending functionality

An API is your gateway to getting started with extending the functionality of any piece of software. Luckily, Zabbix offers a solid working API that we can use to extend our functionality with ease.

In this recipe, we'll explore the use of the Zabbix API to do some tasks, creating a good basis to start working with the Zabbix API in your actual production environments.

Getting ready

We are going to need a Zabbix server with some hosts. I'll be using our host `lar-book-centos` from the previous chapters, but feel free to use any Zabbix server. I will also use another Linux host to do the API calls from, but this can be done from any Linux host.

We will need to install Python 3 on the Linux host, though, as we'll be using this to create our API calls.

Also, make sure you have an API user with an API token. It is recommended to use the one we created in the first recipe.

How to do it...

1. First, on our Linux CLI let's move to a new directory:

    ```
    cd /home/
    ```

2. Install Python 3 on the host with the following command:

    For RHEL-based systems:

    ```
    dnf install python3
    ```

For Ubuntu systems:

```
apt install python3
```

3. Python `pip` should've been installed with this package by default as well. If not, issue the following command:

For RHEL-based systems:

```
dnf install python3-pip
```

For Ubuntu systems:

```
apt install python3-pip
```

4. Now let's install our dependencies using Python `pip`. We'll need these dependencies as they'll be used in the script:

```
pip3 install requests
```

5. Download the start of our script from the Packt GitHub repo by issuing the following command:

```
wget https://raw.githubusercontent.com/PacktPublishing/
Zabbix-6-IT-Infrastructure-Monitoring-Cookbook/main/
chapter10/api_test.py
```

6. If you can't use `wget` from your host, you can download the script at the following URL: `https://github.com/PacktPublishing/Zabbix-6-IT-Infrastructure-Monitoring-Cookbook/tree/main/chapter10/api_test.py`.

7. Next up, we are going to edit our newly downloaded script by executing the following command:

```
vim api_test.py
```

8. First, let's change the IP address `10.16.16.152` in the `url` variable to the IP or DNS of your Zabbix server. Then make sure to edit the `api_token` variable by replacing `PUT_YOUR_TOKEN_HERE` with the API token we generated in the first recipe of this chapter:

```
url = "http://10.16.16.152/zabbix/api_jsonrpc.php"
api_token = "c01ce8726bfdbce02664ec8750f99
da1bbbcb3cb295d924932e2f2808846273"
```

9. We will also add some lines of code to our script to retrieve our host ID, hostname, and the interfaces of all our Zabbix hosts. Make sure to add your new code between the comments shown in the following screenshot:

```
#Add new code below here
```

```
#Add new code above here
```

Figure 10.8 – Comments showing where to put code

10. Now add the following lines of code:

```python
#Function to retrieve the hosts and interfaces
def get_hosts(api_token, url):

    payload = {
    "jsonrpc": "2.0",
    "method": "host.get",
    "params": {
        "output": [
            "hostid",
            "host"
        ],
        "selectInterfaces": [
            "interfaceid",
            "ip",
            "main"
        ]
    },
    "id": 2,
    "auth": api_token
    }
    resp = requests.post(url=url, json=payload )
    out = resp.json()
    return out['result']
```

11. Then, we'll also add lines to write the requested information to a file so we can see what happens after execution:

```
#Write the results to a file
def generate_host_file(hosts,host_file):


    hostname = None
    f = open(host_file, "w")
    #Write the host entries retrieved from Zabbix
    for host in hosts:
        hostname = host['host']
        for interface in host["interfaces"]:
            if interface["main"] == "1":
                f.write(hostname + " " + interface["ip"]
+ "\n")


    f.close()
    return
```

12. You should be able to execute this now by executing the following:

```
python3 api_test.py
```

13. This should run but it won't give you any output. If this doesn't work, make sure to retrace your steps.

14. Let's check out the file to see what happened by executing the following:

```
cat /home/results
```

15. The output of the preceding command should look like this:

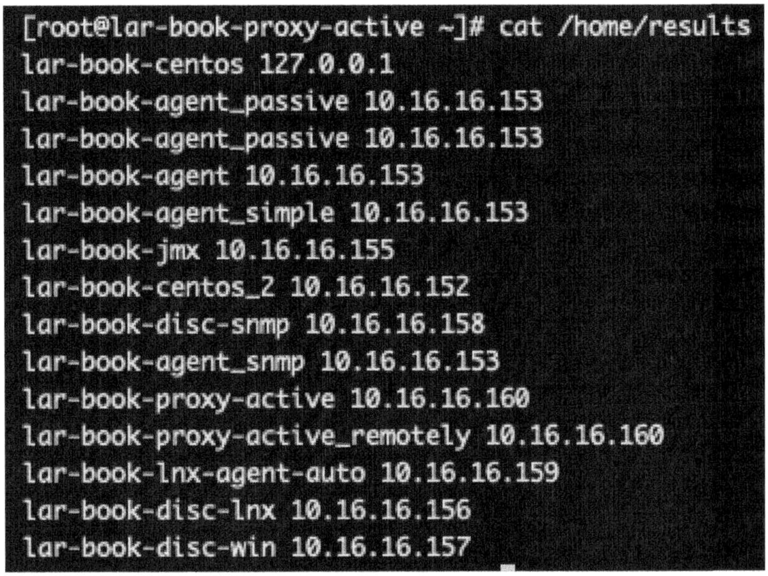

```
[root@lar-book-proxy-active ~]# cat /home/results
lar-book-centos 127.0.0.1
lar-book-agent_passive 10.16.16.153
lar-book-agent_passive 10.16.16.153
lar-book-agent 10.16.16.153
lar-book-agent_simple 10.16.16.153
lar-book-jmx 10.16.16.155
lar-book-centos_2 10.16.16.152
lar-book-disc-snmp 10.16.16.158
lar-book-agent_snmp 10.16.16.153
lar-book-proxy-active 10.16.16.160
lar-book-proxy-active_remotely 10.16.16.160
lar-book-lnx-agent-auto 10.16.16.159
lar-book-disc-lnx 10.16.16.156
lar-book-disc-win 10.16.16.157
```

Figure 10.9 – The cat command with our results showing in the file

We've now written a short script in Python to use the Zabbix API.

How it works...

Coding with the Zabbix API can be done with Python, but it's definitely not our only option. We can use a wide variety of coding languages, including Perl, Go, C#, and Java.

In our example though, we've used Python, so let's see what we do here. If we look at the script, we have two main functions:

- get_hosts
- generate_host_file

First, we filled in our `api_token` and `url` variables, which are used to authenticate against the Zabbix API. We then use these to call on the `get_hosts` function to retrieve information from the Zabbix API:

```
payload = {
  "jsonrpc": "2.0",
  "method": "host.get",
  "params": {
      "output": [
          "hostid",
          "host"
      ],
      "selectInterfaces": [
          "interfaceid",
          "ip",
          "main"
      ]
  },
  "id": 2,
  "auth": api_token
}
```

Figure 10.10 – Python function Zabbix API payload

Looking at the code, we use a JSON payload to request information such as `host` for the hostname, `hostid` for the host ID, and `ip` for the interface's IP address.

Now, if we look at our last function, `generate_host_file`, we can see that we write the host with an interface IP to the `/home/results` file. This way we have a solid script for writing host information to a file.

If you're not familiar with Python or coding in general, working with the Zabbix API might be a big step to take. Let's take a look at how the API actually works:

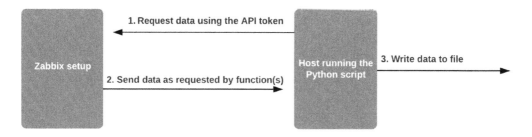

Figure 10.11 – Python script Zabbix API functionality diagram

In *step 1*, we make an API call, using our target URL and API token as specified in our variables for authentication. Next, in *step 2*, we receive the data as requested in our Python function from Zabbix to further use in our Python script.

Step 3 is our data processing step. We can do anything we want with the data received from the Zabbix API, but in our case, we format the data and write it to a file. That's how we use the Zabbix API for extending functionality. This is the step where our file gets filled with hostnames and IP information.

See also

If you are interested in learning more about the Zabbix API, check out the Zabbix documentation at `https://www.zabbix.com/documentation/current/en/manual/api`.

Building a jumphost using the Zabbix API and Python

A lot of organizations have a jumphost (sometimes referred to as a bastion host) to access servers, switches, and their other equipment from a host. A jumphost generally has all the firewall rules needed to access everything important. Now if we keep our monitoring up to date, we should have every single host in there as well.

My friend, ex-colleague, and fellow Zabbix geek, *Yadvir Singh*, had the amazing idea to create a Python script to export all Zabbix hosts with their IPs to the `/etc/hosts` file on another Linux host. Let's see how we can build a jumphost just like his.

Getting ready

We are going to need a new host for this recipe with Linux installed and ready. We'll call this host `lar-book-jump`. We will also need our Zabbix server, for which I'll use `lar-book-centos`.

Also, it is important to navigate to *Yadvir's* GitHub account, drop him a follow, and star his repository if you think this is a cool script: `https://github.com/cheatas/zabbix_scripts`.

> **Important Note**
>
> Setting up this script will override your `/etc/hosts` file every time the script is executed. Only use this script when you understand what it's doing, make sure you use an empty host for this lab, and check the default `/etc/hosts` settings.

How to do it...

1. If you haven't already created an API user with an API token, make sure to check out the first recipe of this chapter first.

2. Install Python 3 on the host CLI with the following command:

   For RHEL-based systems:

   ```
   dnf install python3
   ```

   For Ubuntu systems:

   ```
   apt-get install python3
   ```

3. Python pip should've been installed with this package by default as well. If not, issue the following command:

   For RHEL-based systems:

   ```
   dnf install python3-pip
   ```

   For Ubuntu systems:

   ```
   apt-get install python3-pip
   ```

4. Now let's install our dependencies using Python `pip`. We'll need these dependencies as they'll be used in the script:

   ```
   pip3 install requests
   ```

5. First things first, log in to our new Linux host, `lar-book-jump`, and download Yadvir's script to your Linux host with the following command:

   ```
   wget https://raw.githubusercontent.com/cheatas/zabbix_
   scripts/main/host_pull_zabbix.py
   ```

6. If you can't use `wget` from your host, you can download the script at the following URL: `https://github.com/cheatas/zabbix_scripts/blob/main/host_pull_zabbix.py`.

7. As a backup, we also provide this script in the Packt repository. You may download this version at `https://github.com/PacktPublishing/Zabbix-6-IT-Infrastructure-Monitoring-Cookbook/tree/main/chapter10/host_pull_zabbix.py`.

8. Now let's edit the script by executing the following command:

```
vim host_pull_zabbix.py
```

9. First, let's edit the `zabbix_url` variable by replacing `https://myzabbix.com/api_jsonrpc.php` with the IP address or DNS name of our Zabbix frontend:

```
zabbix_url = "http://10.16.16.152/zabbix/api_jsonrpc.php"
```

10. We do not need to fill out our username and password as that was only required on older Zabbix versions. Instead, we will need an API token, as generated in the first recipe in this chapter. Fill in the `api_token` variable in the script as follows:

```
api_token = "c01ce8726bfdbce02664ec8750f99da1bbbcb3cb295
d924932e2f2808846273"
```

11. We also need to uncomment the following lines:

```
zabbix_hosts = get_hosts(api_token,zabbix_url)
generate_host_file(zabbix_hosts,"/etc/hosts")
```

12. The end of the script should now look like this:

```
#If you do not have a API token yet, use the following line to aquire it.
#Once printed, copy the token and paste it in the variable below.

#print(get_api_token(zabbix_url))

api_token = "c01ce8726bfdbce02664ec8750f99da1bbbcb3cb295d924932e2f2808846273"

#once the API token has been set, comment the print line again and uncomment the follwoing lines.

zabbix_hosts = get_hosts(api_token,zabbix_url)
generate_host_file(zabbix_hosts,"/etc/hosts")
```

Figure 10.12 – End of the script after receiving the API token and with commenting removed

13. Last but not least, make sure to comment and uncomment the right lines for your
Linux distro. It will look like this:

Ubuntu:

```
    #For Debian based hosts
    f.write('''127.0.0.1 localhost\n\n''')

    #For RHEL based hosts
#    f.write('''127.0.0.1    localhost localhost.localdomain localhost4 localhost4.localdomain4
#::1          localhost localhost.localdomain localhost6 localhost6.localdomain6\n\n''')

# The following lines are desirable for IPv6 capable hosts
    f.write('''::1 localhost ip6-localhost ip6-loopback
fe00::0 ip6-localnet
ff00::0 ip6-mcastprefix
ff02::1 ip6-allnodes
ff02::2 ip6-allrouters\n\n\n''')
```

Figure 10.13 – Print to file for Ubuntu systems

For RHEL-based systems:

```
    #For Debian based hosts
    #f.write('''127.0.0.1 localhost\n\n''')

    #For RHEL based hosts
    f.write('''127.0.0.1    localhost localhost.localdomain localhost4 localhost4.localdomain4
::1          localhost localhost.localdomain localhost6 localhost6.localdomain6\n\n''')

# The following lines are desirable for IPv6 capable hosts
    f.write('''::1 localhost ip6-localhost ip6-loopback
fe00::0 ip6-localnet
ff00::0 ip6-mcastprefix
ff02::1 ip6-allnodes
ff02::2 ip6-allrouters\n\n\n''')
```

Figure 10.14 – Print to file for RHEL-based systems

14. That's all there is to do, so we can now execute the script again and start using it.
Let's execute the script as follows:

```
python3 host_pull_zabbix.py
```

15. Test whether it worked by looking at the host file with the following command:

```
cat /etc/hosts
```

This should give us an output like that in the following screenshot:

```
[root@lar-book-jump ~]# cat /etc/hosts
127.0.0.1    localhost localhost.localdomain localhost4 localhost4.localdomain4
::1          localhost localhost.localdomain localhost6 localhost6.localdomain6

::1 localhost ip6-localhost ip6-loopback
fe00::0 ip6-localnet
ff00::0 ip6-mcastprefix
ff02::1 ip6-allnodes
ff02::2 ip6-allrouters


lar-book-centos 127.0.0.1
lar-book-agent_passive 10.16.16.153
lar-book-agent_passive 10.16.16.153
lar-book-agent 10.16.16.153
```

Figure 10.15 – /etc/hosts filled with our script information

16. We can now try to SSH directly to the name of a host, instead of having to use the IP, by issuing the following command:

```
ssh lar-book-agent_passive
```

17. We can also use it to find hosts from the file with the following command:

```
cat /etc/hosts | grep agent
```

18. Let's do one more thing. We want this script to be as up to date as possible. So, let's add a cronjob. Issue the following command to add a cronjob:

```
crontab -e
```

19. Then add the following line, making sure to fill in the right script location for your setup:

```
*/15 * * * * $(which python3) /home/host_pull_zabbix.py
>> ~/cron.log 2>&1
```

That's it – we will now have an up-to-date /etc/hosts file all the time with our new Python script and Zabbix.

How it works...

If your organization uses Zabbix as the main monitoring system, you now have the skills and knowledge to create an organized, reliably up-to-date, and easy-to-use jumphost.

Jumphosts are super useful when set up correctly, but it's important to keep them clean so that they are easy to update.

By using this script, we only add Python 3 and a simple script as a requirement to the server, but the end result is a jumphost that knows about all hosts in the environment.

If you've followed along with the previous *Using the Zabbix API for extending functionality* recipe, then you might notice that it works in roughly the same way. We can see in the following diagram how we utilize the script:

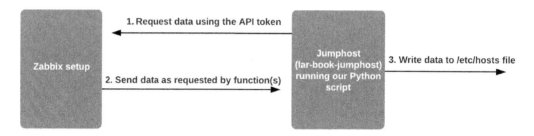

Figure 10.16 – Jumphost using script functionality diagram

After editing, our script will start at *step 1* of the diagram to request data with an API call, where we use the API token to authenticate. We receive this data in *step 2*. In the script, we add our default values and then write all the hostnames and IP addresses to the /etc/ hosts file.

Now, because a Linux host uses the /etc/hosts file for hostname-to-IP translation, we can use the real names of servers in Zabbix to SSH to the hosts. This makes it easier for us to use the jumphost, as we can use the same name as the hostname we know from the Zabbix frontend.

See also

Yadvir will keep updating the script after writing this recipe (we've been using version 1.0 so far). Make sure to follow his GitHub account and star his repository to get the updates. Also, if you have some cool ideas for additions, you can always open a pull request.

The Zabbix community is all about sharing cool ideas and useful scripts like this one. As *Yadvir* has shown, we can get very valuable stuff from each other. Be like *Yadvir* – use the Zabbix community GitHub and support other Zabbix users by adding to their GitHub repositories. We can find the Zabbix community GitHub using the link here:

```
https://github.com/zabbix/community-templates
```

Creating maintenance periods as a Zabbix user

It used to not be possible to schedule maintenance periods as a Zabbix user, which is why we created these scripts. In Zabbix 6, we can actually make it possible by using user roles, but these scripts are still relevant to provide quick access to maintenance creation. For some companies, this may be very useful, to limit the number of navigation actions required to do things using the frontend. In this recipe, I will show you just how to work with this Python script.

Getting ready

For this recipe, all we are going to need is our Zabbix server, some knowledge of Python, and some knowledge of the Zabbix API.

How to do it...

1. First, let's log in to our Zabbix server CLI and create a new directory:

    ```
    mkdir /etc/zabbix/frontendscripts
    ```

2. Change to the new directory:

    ```
    cd /etc/zabbix/frontendscripts
    ```

3. Now download the `Public` script from the *Opensource ICT Solutions* GitHub:

    ```
    wget https://github.com/OpensourceICTSolutions/zabbix-
    maintenance-from-frontend/archive/v2.0.tar.gz
    ```

4. If you can't use `wget` from your host, check out the script here: `https://github.com/OpensourceICTSolutions/zabbix-maintenance-from-frontend/releases/tag/v2.0`.

5. Unzip the file with the following command:

    ```
    tar -xvzf v2.0.tar.gz
    ```

6. Remove the `tar` file using the following command:

```
rm v2.0.tar.gz
```

7. Move the script over from the newly created folder with the following command:

```
mv zabbix-maintenance-from-frontend-2.0/maintenance.py ./
```

8. We are going to need Python to use this script so let's install it as follows:

    For RHEL-based systems:

```
dnf install python3 python3-pip
```

    For Ubuntu systems:

```
apt-get install python python-pip
```

9. We will also need the `requests` module from `pip`, so let's install it with the following command:

```
pip3 install requests
```

10. Now let's edit the script with the following command:

```
vim maintenance.py
```

11. In this file, we will change the `url` and `token` variables. Change the `url` variable to match your own Zabbix frontend IP or DNS name. Then replace PUT_YOUR_TOKEN_HERE with your Zabbix API token. I will fill in the following, but be sure to enter your own information:

```
url = 'http://10.16.16.152/zabbix/api_jsonrpc.php?'
token = "
c01ce8726bfdbce02664ec8750f99da1bbbcb3cb295d924932
e2f2808846273 "
```

12. Now we can move on to our Zabbix frontend to add a frontend script. Navigate to **Administration | Scripts**, then click the blue **Create script** button in the top-right corner.

13. Now add the following script:

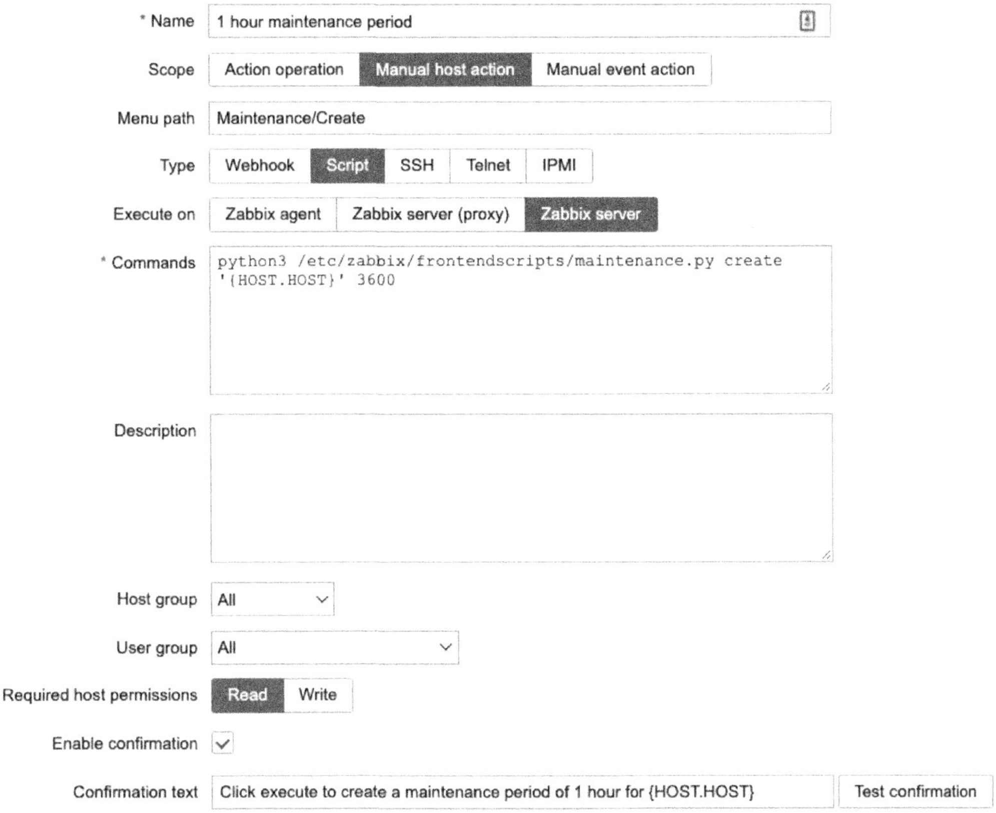

* Name	1 hour maintenance period		
Scope	Action operation	**Manual host action**	Manual event action
Menu path	Maintenance/Create		
Type	Webhook	**Script**	SSH Telnet IPMI
Execute on	Zabbix agent	Zabbix server (proxy)	**Zabbix server**
* Commands	python3 /etc/zabbix/frontendscripts/maintenance.py create '{HOST.HOST}' 3600		
Description			
Host group	All		
User group	All		
Required host permissions	**Read** Write		
Enable confirmation	✓		
Confirmation text	Click execute to create a maintenance period of 1 hour for {HOST.HOST}		Test confirmation

Figure 10.17 – Zabbix Administration | Scripts, create script page, 1 hour maintenance period

14. Click on the blue **Add** button and then, on the next page, click the blue **Create script** button in the top-right corner again.

15. Add the second script as follows:

Figure 10.18 – Zabbix Administration | Scripts, Create script page, 24 hour maintenance period

16. Click on the blue **Add** button and then, on the next page, click the blue **Create script** button in the top-right corner again.

17. Add the third and final script as follows:

Figure 10.19 – Zabbix Administration | Scripts, Create script page, delete maintenance period

18. Now click the blue **Add** button to finish adding the final script.

19. Let's test the script by navigating to **Monitoring | Hosts**. Here we can click on any hostname available.

20. This will then open a drop-down menu where we can select to schedule maintenance for this host:

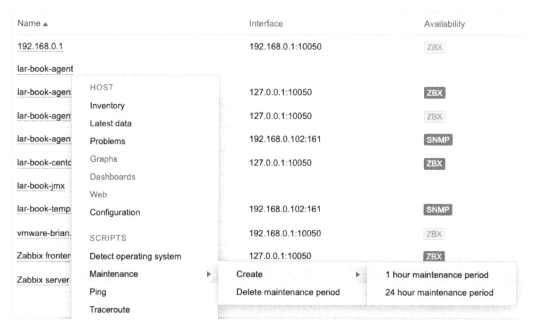

Figure 10.20 – Zabbix Monitoring | Hosts page with dropdown from underlined hostname

21. If we click on **1 hour maintenance period**, we get a confirmation window to execute the scheduling of our maintenance period:

Figure 10.21 – Zabbix confirmation window before execution

22. Click on **Execute** and then navigate to **Configuration | Maintenance**. We can now see our new maintenance period:

Name ▲	Type	Active since	Active till	State	Description
Maintenance period for: lar-book-agent	With data collection	2020-10-28 16:21	2020-10-28 17:21	Active	This maintenance period is created by a script.

Figure 10.22 – Zabbix Configuration | Maintenance page showing host lar-book-agent

How it works...

The script we just used was built in Python utilizing the Zabbix API. With this script, we can now schedule maintenance periods from the Zabbix frontend as a Zabbix user.

This works because the **Monitoring | Hosts** option is available even to Zabbix users. Instead of using the user's frontend permissions, our script uses the API user for execution. Because our Zabbix API user has more user permissions, it can execute the script that gets host information from a Zabbix database and creates a maintenance period using the information. Looking at the following diagram, we can see the process of this script:

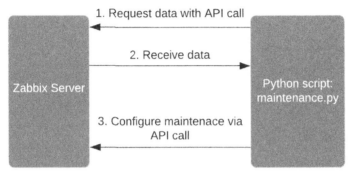

Figure 10.23 – Python script maintenance.py execution diagram

As we can see in the preceding diagram, our script follows roughly the same steps as other Zabbix API utilities. Since the Zabbix API is very flexible, we can pull data and write data to do almost anything we could do from the frontend.

We can now use this new function from anywhere in the Zabbix frontend where we see a dotted line with the hostname, even from Zabbix maps. We can see an example of when we clicked on such a dotted line in *Figure 10.20*.

See also

Brian van Baekel created the script used in this recipe for a customer at *Opensource ICT Solutions* and then open sourced it. Because Zabbix has a very cool community working to extend the possibilities of Zabbix even further, we too upload some of our scripts. Sharing is caring, so check out the other open-sourced scripts on the GitHub repo at `https://github.com/OpensourceICTSolutions`.

Enabling and disabling a host from Zabbix maps

We've noticed that it is not possible to enable and disable hosts as a Zabbix user. For some companies, this may be a requirement, so we've created an extension for it. In this recipe, I will show you just how to work with this Python script and execute it from a map.

Getting ready

For this recipe, all we are going to need is our Zabbix server, some knowledge of Python, and some knowledge of the Zabbix API.

How to do it...

1. First, let's log in to our Zabbix server CLI and create a new directory:

    ```
    mkdir /etc/zabbix/frontendscripts
    ```

2. Change to the new directory:

    ```
    cd /etc/zabbix/frontendscripts
    ```

3. Now download the public script from the *Opensource ICT Solutions* GitHub:

    ```
    wget https://github.com/OpensourceICTSolutions/zabbix-
    toggle-hosts-from-frontend/archive/v2.0.tar.gz
    ```

4. If you can't use wget from your host, you can check out the script here: https://github.com/OpensourceICTSolutions/zabbix-toggle-hosts-from-frontend/releases/tag/v2.0.

5. Unzip the file with the following command:

    ```
    tar -xvzf v2.0.tar.gz
    ```

6. Remove the tar file using the following command:

    ```
    rm v2.0.tar.gz
    ```

7. Move the script over from the newly created folder with the following command:

```
mv zabbix-toggle-hosts-from-frontend-2.0/enable_disable-host.py ./
```

8. We are going to need Python to use this script, so let's install it as follows:

For RHEL-based systems:

```
dnf install python3 python3-pip
```

For Ubuntu systems:

```
apt-get install python python-pip
```

9. We will also need the `requests` module from pip. Install it as follows:

```
pip3 install requests
```

10. Now let's edit the script with the following command:

```
vim enable_disable-host.py
```

11. In this file, we will change the `url` and `token` variables. Change the `url` variable to match your own Zabbix frontend IP or DNS name. Then replace PUT_YOUR_TOKEN_HERE with your Zabbix API token. I will fill in the following, but be sure to enter your own information:

```
url = 'http://10.16.16.152/zabbix/api_jsonrpc.php?'
token = " c01ce8726bfdbce02664ec8750f99da1bbbcb3cb295d
924932e2f2808846273 "
```

12. Now, we can move on to our Zabbix frontend to add a frontend script. Navigate to **Administration | Scripts**, then click the blue **Create script** button at the top right.

13. Add the following script:

Figure 10.24 – Zabbix Administration | Scripts, Create script page, Enable

14. Click on the blue **Add** button and then, on the next page, click the blue **Create script** button in the top-right corner again.

15. Now add the second and final script as follows:

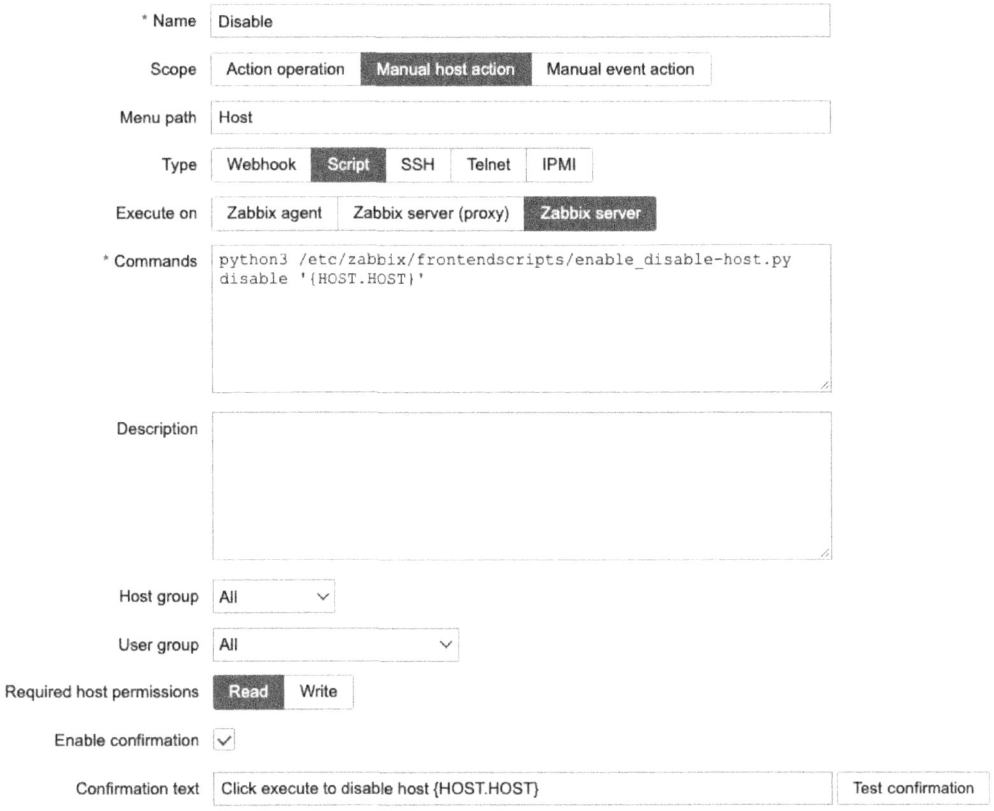

* Name	Disable
Scope	Action operation **Manual host action** Manual event action
Menu path	Host
Type	Webhook **Script** SSH Telnet IPMI
Execute on	Zabbix agent Zabbix server (proxy) **Zabbix server**
* Commands	`python3 /etc/zabbix/frontendscripts/enable_disable-host.py disable '{HOST.HOST}'`
Description	
Host group	All
User group	All
Required host permissions	**Read** Write
Enable confirmation	✓
Confirmation text	Click execute to disable host {HOST.HOST} Test confirmation

Figure 10.25 – Zabbix Administration | Scripts, Create script page, Disable

16. Now navigate to **Monitoring | Maps**, and you should see a map called **Local network** here, as it's included with Zabbix by default. Click this map (or any other map with hosts in it).

17. Now, if you click on a host on the map, you will see a drop-down menu like this:

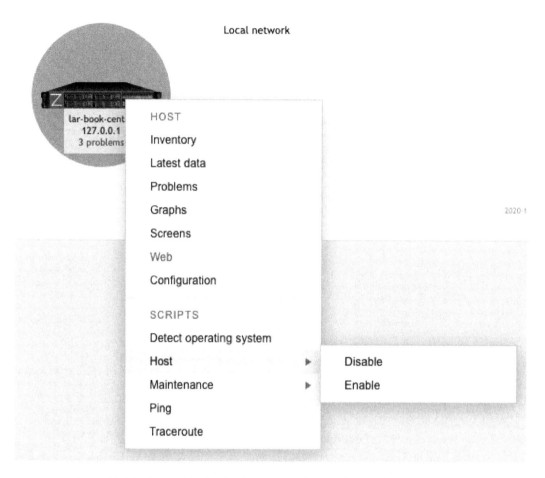

Figure 10.26 – Zabbix Monitoring | Maps, Local network map drop-down menu

18. If we click on **Disable** here, we will get a pop-up message as follows:

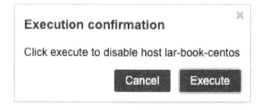

Figure 10.27 – Zabbix script confirmation window

19. Click on the blue **Execute** button and this host will be disabled. Navigate to **Monitoring | Hosts** to confirm if this worked. You should see that the host is **Disabled**.

20. Back at **Monitoring | Maps**, you can enable the host again with the same drop-down menu. This time, select **Enable**.

How it works...

The script we just used was built in Python utilizing the Zabbix API. With this script, we can now enable and disable hosts from the Zabbix frontend as a Zabbix user.

This works because the **Monitoring | Maps** option is available even to Zabbix users. This script uses the API user for execution though. Since our Zabbix API user has more user permissions, it can execute the script that gets host information from a Zabbix database and creates a maintenance period using the information. As we can see in the following diagram, our script follows roughly the same steps as the other Zabbix API utilities:

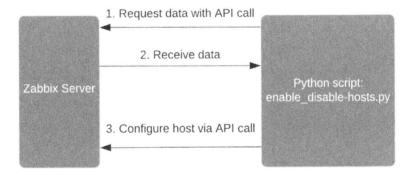

Figure 10.28 – Python script maintenance.py execution diagram

Because the Zabbix API is very flexible, we can pull data and write data to do almost anything we could do from the frontend.

We can now use this cool function from anywhere in the Zabbix frontend where we see a dotted line with the hostname, even from **Monitoring | Hosts**.

See also

Brian van Baekel created this script for a customer at *Opensource ICT Solutions* and then open sourced it. Because Zabbix has a very cool community that continues to extend the possibilities of Zabbix even further, we too upload some of our scripts. Sharing is caring, so check out the other open-sourced scripts at `https://github.com/OpensourceICTSolutions`.

11
Maintaining Your Zabbix Setup

Like any good piece of software, Zabbix needs to be maintained in order to keep working over the years. A lot of users have been running their setups since the days of Zabbix 2.0. It's perfectly viable to do this if you bring the right knowledge of Zabbix to the equation.

In this chapter, I am going to show you how to do some of the most important parts of Zabbix maintenance to make sure you can keep your setup available and running smoothly. We are going to cover creating maintenance periods, how to make backups, how to upgrade Zabbix and various Zabbix components, and how to do some performance maintenance.

We'll cover these in the following recipes:

- Setting Zabbix maintenance periods
- Backing up your Zabbix setup
- Upgrading the Zabbix backend from older PHP versions to PHP 7.2 or higher
- Upgrading a Zabbix database from older MariaDB versions to MariaDB 10.5
- Upgrading your Zabbix setup
- Maintaining Zabbix performance over time

Technical requirements

We are going to need several important servers for these recipes. First of all, we are going to need a running Zabbix 6 server for which to set up maintenance periods and do performance tuning.

We will need one of the following servers:

- A CentOS 8 server running Zabbix server 5, a PHP version before 7.4, and a MariaDB version before 10.6

- An Ubuntu 18.04 or 20.04 server running Zabbix server 5.0, a PHP version before 7.4, and a MariaDB version before 10.6

I will call this server `lar-book-zbx5`, which you can run with a distribution of your choice.

If you do not have any prior experience with Zabbix, this chapter may prove a good challenge, as we are going to go into the more advanced Zabbix processes in depth.

Setting Zabbix maintenance periods

When we are working on our Zabbix server or on other hosts, it's super useful to set up maintenance periods in the Zabbix frontend. With maintenance periods we can make sure that our Zabbix users don't get alerts going off because of our maintenance. Let's see how we can schedule maintenance periods in this recipe.

Getting ready

All we are going to need in this recipe is our Zabbix server, for which I'll use `lar-book-centos`. The server will need at least some hosts and host groups to create maintenance periods for. Furthermore, we'll need to know how to navigate the Zabbix frontend.

How to do it...

1. Let's get started with this recipe by logging in to our frontend and navigating to **Configuration | Maintenance**.

2. We are going to click on the blue **Create maintenance period** button in the top-right corner.

3. This will bring us to the next page, where we can set up our maintenance period. On the first tab, **Maintenance**, fill in the following:

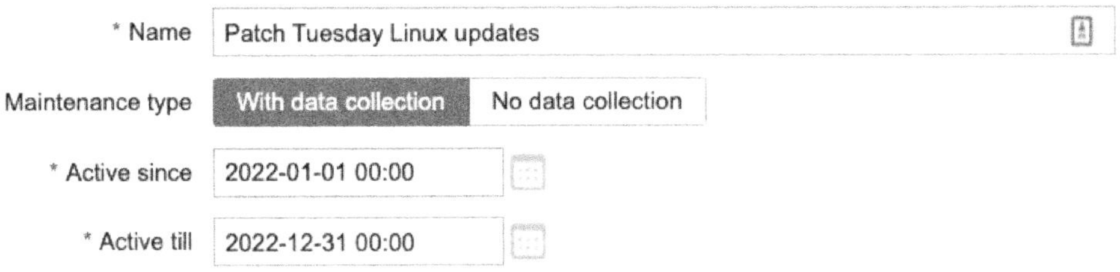

* Name	Patch Tuesday Linux updates	🖹
Maintenance type	With data collection No data collection	
* Active since	2022-01-01 00:00	
* Active till	2022-12-31 00:00	

Figure 11.1 – Zabbix Configuration | Maintenance, create maintenance page, Patch Tuesday

4. Now, at the **Periods** part, we'll create a new maintenance period. We need to click on the underlined **Add** text.

5. This will bring us to a pop-up window where we can set the maintenance period. We need to fill in the following information:

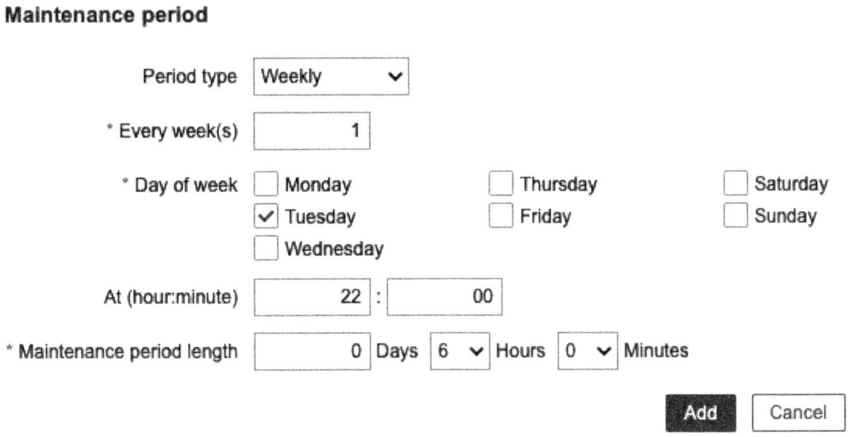

Maintenance period

Period type	Weekly
* Every week(s)	1
* Day of week	☐ Monday ☐ Thursday ☐ Saturday ✔ Tuesday ☐ Friday ☐ Sunday ☐ Wednesday
At (hour:minute)	22 : 00
* Maintenance period length	0 Days 6 ∨ Hours 0 ∨ Minutes

Add   Cancel

Figure 11.2 – Zabbix Configuration | Maintenance, create maintenance period window, Patch Tuesday

6. Now click the blue **Add** button to continue. You should now see that our maintenance period is filled in:

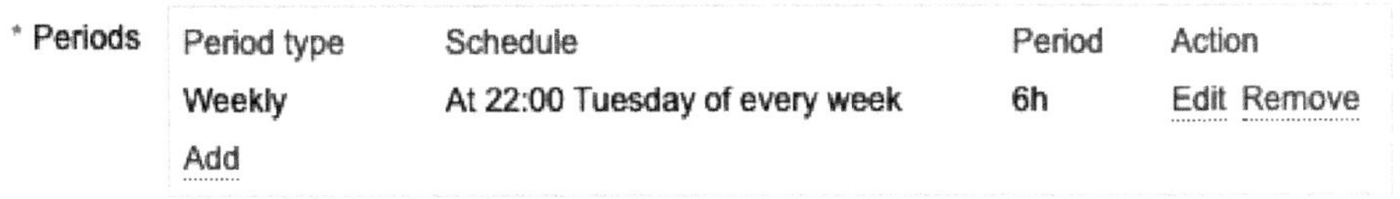

* Periods	Period type	Schedule	Period	Action
	Weekly	At 22:00 Tuesday of every week	6h	Edit Remove
	Add			

Figure 11.3 – Zabbix Configuration | Maintenance, create maintenance period page, Patch Tuesday

7. Now click on the **Hosts and groups** tab to fill out what hosts will be affected by the maintenance.

8. Next to **Host groups**, click on the **Select** button and select the host group Linux servers. Our page should look like this:

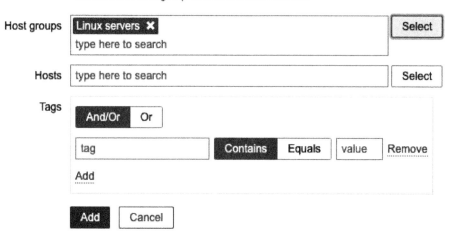

Figure 11.4 – Zabbix Configuration | Maintenance, add hosts to maintenance page, Patch Tuesday

9. Now click on the blue **Add** button at the bottom of the page to finish creating the maintenance period. This will bring us back to our **Maintenance periods** page, where we should see that our maintenance window has been created.

How it works...

When configuring actions in Zabbix, we tell Zabbix to do a certain defined operation when a trigger is fired. Maintenance periods work by suppressing these Zabbix operations for the time period defined in the maintenance period. We do this to make sure that no Zabbix users are notified of any problems going on as maintenance is being done on a host. Of course, it's a good idea to only use this during the time that we are actually working on the hosts in question.

In the case of this recipe, we've created a recurring maintenance period for the entire year, 2022. Let's say the organization we're working for has a lot of Linux hosts that need to be patched weekly. We set up the maintenance period to recur weekly every Tuesday between 22:00 and 04:00.

Now keep in mind that after December 31, 2022, Zabbix will stop this maintenance period as it won't be active any longer. We have two time/date values to bear in mind when setting up scheduled maintenance. The **Active since/Active till** time/date value of the maintenance period and the period's time/date value of the maintenance period. This allows us to create more flexible periods and recurring ones like we just did.

Also, take note that this maintenance period is **With data collection**. We can also create a maintenance period with the option of **No data collection**. When we use the **With data collection** option, we will keep collecting data but won't send any problems to Zabbix Users. If we want to stop collecting the data, simply select the **No data collection** option.

Lastly, keep in mind that Zabbix calculates a new maintenance period every minute on 0 seconds. If you create a maintenance period in the very near future or on the exact minute, you might have to wait a bit for it to take effect.

Backing up your Zabbix setup

Before working on any Zabbix setup, it is vital to make a backup of everything important. In this recipe, I will take you through some of the most important steps you should always take before doing maintenance on your Zabbix setup.

Getting ready

We are going to need our Zabbix server, for which I'll use `lar-book-centos`. Make sure to get the CLI to the server ready, as this whole recipe will use the Linux CLI.

How to do it...

1. Let's start by logging in to our Zabbix server via the Linux CLI and create some new directories that we are going to use for our Zabbix backups. Preferably, this directory would be on another partition:

```
mkdir /opt/zbx-backup/
mkdir /opt/zbx-backup/database/
mkdir /opt/zbx-backup/zbx-config/
mkdir /opt/zbx-backup/web-config/
mkdir /opt/zbx-backup/shared/
mkdir /opt/zbx-backup/shared/zabbix/
mkdir /opt/zbx-backup/shared/doc/
```

2. It's important to back up all of our Zabbix configuration data, which is located at
/etc/zabbix/. We can manually copy the data from our current folder to our
new backup folder by issuing the following command:

```
cp -r /etc/zabbix/ /opt/zbx-backup/zbx-config/
```

3. Now, let's do the same for our httpd configuration:

```
cp /etc/httpd/conf.d/zabbix.conf /opt/zbx-backup/
web-config/
```

> **Important Note**
>
> Please note that if you are using NGINX or Apache2 on a Debian-based system,
> your web configuration location might be different. Adjust your command
> accordingly.

4. It's also important to keep our Zabbix PHP files and binaries backed up. We can do
that using the following commands:

```
cp -r /usr/share/zabbix/ /opt/zbx-backup/shared/zabbix/
cp -r /usr/share/doc/zabbix-* /opt/zbx-backup/shared/doc/
```

5. We could also create a cronjob to automatically compress and back up these files
for us every day at 00:00. Simply issue the following command:

```
crontab -e
```

6. And add the following information:

```
0 0 * * * tar -zcvf /opt/zbx-backup/zbx-config/zabbix.
tar.gz /etc/zabbix/ >/dev/null 2>&1
0 0 * * * tar -zcvf /opt/zbx-backup/web-config/zabbix-
web.tar.gz /etc/httpd/conf.d/zabbix.conf >/dev/null 2>&1
0 0 * * * tar -zcvf /opt/zbx-backup/shared/zabbix/zabbix_
usr_share.tar.gz /usr/share/zabbix/ >/dev/null 2>&1
0 0 * * * tar -zcvf /opt/zbx-backup/shared/doc/zabbix_
usr_share_doc.tar.gz /usr/share/doc/ >/dev/null 2>&1
```

7. These are all of the most important files we need to back up from our Zabbix
stack. Let's move on to our database. We could now additionally use a rotation
tool such as logrotate to manage our files.

8. Backing up our database is quite easy. We can simply use the built-in tools provided by MySQL and PostgreSQL. Issue the following command for your respective database:

For MySQL databases:

```
mysqldump --add-drop-table --add-locks --extended-insert
--single-transaction --quick -u zabbixuser -p zabbixdb >
/opt/zbx-backup/database/backup_zabbixDB_<DATE>.sql
```

For PostgreSQL databases:

```
pg_dump zabbixdb > /opt/zbx-backup/database/backup_
zabbixDB_<DATE>.bak
```

> **Important Note**
>
> For MySQL databases, there are also tools like ExtraBackup and for Postgres we could use PGBarman. It's never a bad idea to look into tools like this to create the backups for your system, but the built-in examples provided here can prove to be just as useful.

9. Make sure to add the right location, as the database dump will be quite large if the database itself is large. Preferably, dump to another disk/partition or even better, another machine.

10. We can also do this with a cronjob by issuing the following command:

```
crontab -e
```

11. Then for MySQL, add the following line where -u is the username, -p is the password, and the database name is zabbix. This is the command for MySQL:

```
* * * * 6 mysqldump -u'zabbixuser' -p'password' zabbixdb
> /opt/zbx-backup/database/backup_zabbixDB.sql
```

12. If you want to back up a PostgreSQL database with a cronjob, we will need to create a file in our user's home directory:

```
vim ~/.pgpass
```

13. We add the following to this file, where zabbixuser is the username and zabbixdb is the database name:

```
#hostname:port:database:username:password
localhost:5432:zabbixuser:zabbixdb:password
```

14. Then we can add a cronjob for PostgreSQL as follows:

```
* * * * 6 pg_dump --no-password -U zabbixuser zabbixdb >
/opt/zbx-backup/database/backup_zabbixDB_date.bak
```

15. We can also add a cronjob to only keep a certain number of days' worth of backups. Issue the following command:

```
crontab -e
```

16. Then add the following line, where +60 is the number of days you want to keep backups for:

```
* * * * 6 find /opt/zbx-backup/database/-mtime +60 -type
f -delete
```

17. That concludes our demonstration of backing up our Zabbix components the easy way.

How it works...

A Zabbix setup consists of several components. We have the Zabbix frontend, Zabbix server, and Zabbix database. These components in this setup require different pieces of software to run on, as shown in the following diagram:

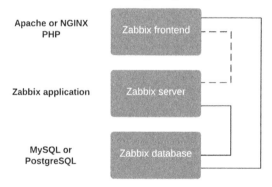

Figure 11.5 – Zabbix key components setup diagram

Looking at the preceding diagram, we can see that our Zabbix frontend runs on a web engine such as Apache or NGINX. We also need PHP to run our Zabbix web pages. This means that we have to back up two components:

- The web engine: Apache, NGINX, or another
- PHP

The Zabbix server is a proprietary application designed by Zabbix, so we only need to back up one thing here:

- The Zabbix server config files

Then last, but definitely not least, we need to make a backup of our database. The most common databases used are MySQL and PostgreSQL, so we only need to do one thing for this:

- Create a dump of the Zabbix database.

There's more...

Backing up your Zabbix setup like this is one thing, but of course, it's not everything. Make sure you have the correct backups of your Linux system, using snapshots and other technologies.

When you follow standard backup implementations, you should be prepared against any unforeseen circumstances with your Zabbix setup.

Optionally upgrading the Zabbix backend from PHP 7.2 to PHP 7.4

RHEL7, Ubuntu 16.04, and Debian 9 (Stretch) are no longer supported by Zabbix, thus our upgrade recipe no longer includes any information about the upgrade path from PHP versions before 7.2 to version 7.2 or higher. All the newer Linux versions already ship with PHP7.2 or higher, which means that when we are upgrading a Zabbix setup from Zabbix version 5 to Zabbix 6, we can upgrade immediately.

The PHP requirement for Zabbix 6 is the same as it was for Zabbix 5, meaning that as long as we are running PHP 7.2 or higher, we can run the latest Zabbix 6 release. Nevertheless, I like to work in a "future-proofing" kind of way, so in this recipe, we will go over how to upgrade PHP 7.2 to 7.4.

Getting ready

For this recipe, we will need our server installed with a RHEL8-based system, which will be running Zabbix server 5 with PHP version 7.2.

Another possibility is that you have a server running a Debian-based distribution like Ubuntu 18.04, Debian 10, or a newer version of those Linux distributions. These also include PHP version 7.2 or higher by default.

I will call either server `lar-book-zbx5` throughout this recipe.

Lastly, make sure to take backups of your system and read the release notes for the new version you're installing.

How to do it...

This recipe is split into two different sections, one for RHEL8-based systems and another for Ubuntu systems. We will start by going through the steps for RHEL8.

RHEL8-based systems

If you are already running PHP version 7.2 on a RHEL8-based system, the upgrade process is a bit simpler. Let's check out how we can upgrade our server `lar-book-zbx5` in this case.

1. First, always verify what PHP version we are running with the following command:

    ```
    php-fpm --version
    ```

2. If the version is older than 7.4, we can continue with the next step. We'll execute the following:

    ```
    dnf module list php
    ```

3. This will show us something like the following screenshot:

```
[root@lar-book-zbx6 ~]# dnf module list php
Last metadata expiration check: 1:05:12 ago on Sun 12 Dec 2021 10:49:23 AM CET.
CentOS Linux 8 - AppStream
Name          Stream            Profiles                      Summary
php           7.2 [d][e]        common [d], devel, minimal    PHP scripting language
php           7.3               common [d], devel, minimal    PHP scripting language
php           7.4               common [d], devel, minimal    PHP scripting language

Hint: [d]efault, [e]nabled, [x]disabled, [i]nstalled
```

Figure 11.6 – RHEL8 DNF Module list for PHP

4. If your screen looks about the same, with 7.2 or 7.3 being the default PHP module, reset your already available PHP modules:

    ```
    dnf module reset php
    ```

5. Make sure to answer with Y. Then we will enable the latest PHP version with the following command:

    ```
    dnf module enable php:7.4
    ```

6. Answer with Y again to enable PHP 7.4 and then we can upgrade our PHP version by using the `dnf update` command.

7. Answer Y again and your PHP version will now be running the latest PHP 7.4 version.

These steps have been tested on both a CentOS 8 and Rocky Linux RHEL system, so they should work with any RHEL8-based system either in Stream or when it's a full rebuilt.

Ubuntu systems

1. Let's start by adding the PPA repository to our host with the following command:

```
apt install software-properties-common
add-apt-repository ppa:ondrej/php
```

2. Now update the repositories with the following command:

```
apt update
```

3. On some installations, the key of the repository might not be available, so you might see an error reading `key is not available`. You can fix this with the following command, where `PUB_KEY_HERE` is the key shown in the error:

```
apt-key adv --keyserver keyserver.ubuntu.com --recv- keys
PUB_KEY_HERE
```

4. Now we can install PHP version 7.4 with the following command:

```
apt install -y php7.4 php7.4-fpm php7.4-mysql php7.4-
bcmath php-7.4-mbstring php-7.4-gd php-7.4-xml
```

5. That's it, the version of PHP should now be the one we want. Check the version of PHP with the following command:

```
php --version
```

How it works...

Because Zabbix server 6 requires us to install PHP version 7.2 or higher, we do not need to upgrade the PHP version first. It's the same requirement we already had for Zabbix 5. If you are still running RHEL7, Ubuntu 16.04, or Debian 9 (Stretch), then you will need to upgrade your Linux system first. Zabbix 6 has dropped support for these older Linux versions in favor of installation simplicity in terms of package management.

Now, it is still possible to run Zabbix on older Linux versions by building from packages, but it is not recommended.

In this recipe, we did do an upgrade from PHP 7.2 (or 7.3) to PHP 7.4, which is the latest supported stable version at the time of writing. Doing this upgrade will not break our current Zabbix server installation, as PHP is backward-compatible. As mentioned, this is an optional upgrade as PHP 7.2 is enough to run Zabbix 6, but it is always good to run the latest stable release of software to make sure that you are ready for the future.

Now that we have upgraded PHP, we are ready to move on to upgrading the Zabbix database engine.

Upgrading a Zabbix database from older MariaDB versions to MariaDB 10.6

For our Zabbix 6 installation, we are going to need MariaDB 10.5 or a newer supported version, so, it is a good idea to keep your database version up to date. MariaDB regularly makes improvements
to how MySQL handles certain aspects of performance.

This recipe details how to upgrade MariaDB to the latest stable version, which is MariaDB 10.6 at the time of writing.

Getting ready

For this recipe, we will need our server which we called `lar-book-zbx5`. At this point, the server is running a RHEL8-based distribution.

Another option is that you have a server running a Debian-based distribution like Ubuntu 18.04, Debian 10, or a newer version of those Linux distributions. We will be upgrading the MariaDB instance on this server to version 10.6.

If you've followed the *Optionally upgrading the Zabbix backend from PHP 7.2 to PHP 7.4* recipe, your server will now be running PHP version 7.4. If not, it's a good idea to follow that recipe first.

Also, make sure to take backups of your system and read the release notes for the new version you're installing.

How to do it...

1. First things first, let's log in to our Linux host CLI to check out our versions. Issue the following commands:

   For Zabbix server:

   ```
   zabbix_server --version
   ```

   For PHP:

   ```
   php-fpm --version
   ```

   For MariaDB:

   ```
   mysql --version
   ```

2. After verifying our versions match the versions mentioned in the *Getting ready* section of this recipe, let's move on to upgrade our version of MariaDB.

RHEL-based systems

1. On our RHEL-based server, the first thing we'll do after checking the versions is to stop our MariaDB server:

   ```
   systemctl stop mariadb
   ```

2. Now set up a repository file for MariaDB with the following command:

   ```
   vim /etc/yum.repos.d/MariaDB.repo
   ```

3. We will add the following code to this new file. Make sure to add the correct architecture after `baseurl` if using anything other than `amd64`:

   ```
   # MariaDB 10.6 CentOS repository list
   # http://downloads.mariadb.org/mariadb/repositories/
   [mariadb]
   name = MariaDB
   baseurl = http://yum.mariadb.org/10.6/rhel8-amd64
   gpgkey=https://yum.mariadb.org/RPM-GPG-KEY-MariaDB
   gpgcheck=1
   ```

4. Now upgrade your MariaDB server with the following command:

   ```
   dnf install MariaDB-client MariaDB-server
   ```

5. Restart the MariaDB service with the following command:

```
systemctl start mariadb
```

6. That's it, MariaDB should now be upgraded to the intended version. Check the version again with the following command to make sure:

```
mysql --version
```

Ubuntu systems

1. On our Ubuntu server, the first thing we'll do after checking the versions is to stop our MariaDB server:

```
systemctl stop mariadb
```

2. We can use the MariaDB repository setup script to update to the right repository. Execute the following command:

```
curl -sS https://downloads.mariadb.com/MariaDB/mariadb_
repo_setup | bash
```

3. This will add the latest MariaDB package to the /etc/apt/sources.list.d/ mariadb.list file. To see if it is on version 10.6, check it with the following command:

```
vim /etc/apt/sources.list.d/mariadb.list
```

4. The file should look like the following code block. If it doesn't look right, edit it to match. Make sure to add the correct architecture on the deb lines if using anything other than amd64:

```
# MariaDB Server
# To use a different major version of the server, or to
pin to a specific minor version, change URI below.
deb [arch=amd64] http://downloads.mariadb.com/MariaDB/
mariadb-10.6/repo/ubuntu focal main
# MariaDB MaxScale
# To use the latest stable release of MaxScale, use
"latest" as the version
# To use the latest beta (or stable if no current beta)
release of MaxScale, use "beta" as the version
```

```
deb [arch=amd64] http://downloads.mariadb.com/MaxScale/
latest/ubuntu focal main
# MariaDB Tools
deb [arch=amd64] http://downloads.mariadb.com/Tools/
ubuntu focal main
```

5. We need to remove our old MariaDB packages with the following command:

```
apt remove --purge mariadb-server mariadb-client zabbix-
server-mysql
```

6. Now upgrade the MariaDB server version with the following command:

```
apt install mariadb-server mariadb-client zabbix-server-
mysql
```

7. Restart MariaDB with the following command:

```
systemctl restart mariadb-server
```

8. Then issue the upgrade command:

```
mariadb-upgrade
```

9. That's it, MariaDB should now be upgraded to the correct version. Check the version again with the following command:

```
mysql --version
```

How it works...

Now, while it might not be a requirement, it is a smart idea to upgrade your database version regularly. New versions of your database engine might include improvements to stability and performance, both of which could improve your Zabbix server greatly.

Do keep the release notes and bug reports on your scope though. MariaDB 10.6 is, at the time of writing, the newest version on the market. You might want to stick back one or two releases as these are still in support and have been running in production for a while already. After all, nobody likes unforeseen issues such as bugs.

For Zabbix 6, we do need to install at least MariaDB 10.5 or a newer supported version though, so keep that in mind.

There's more...

If you really cannot upgrade to MariaDB version 10.5 or, if you are running another database, the supported version for that one, then there's a new Zabbix feature. Zabbix 6 now allows us to run unsupported database versions. When we edit the Zabbix server configuration files at `/etc/zabbix/zabbix_server.conf`, we can add the following parameter:

```
AllowUnsupportedDBVersions=1
```

This will allow you to run an older version of your database, but keep in mind that it is not recommended to do so. Check out the current Zabbix LTS installation requirements here:

```
https://www.zabbix.com/documentation/current/en/manual/
installation/requirements
```

Upgrading your Zabbix setup

As we've seen throughout the book already, Zabbix 6 offers a great deal of cool new features. Zabbix 6.0 is a **Long-Term Support** (**LTS**) release, so just like 4.0 and 5.0, you will receive long-term support for it. Let's see how we can upgrade a Zabbix server from version 5.0 to version 6.0.

Getting ready

For this recipe, we will need our server called `lar-book-zbx5`. At this point, your server will be running either a RHEL8-based Linux distribution or a Debian-based distribution like Ubuntu 18.04, Debian 10, or newer versions of those distributions.

If you've followed the *Optionally upgrading the Zabbix backend from PHP 7.2 to PHP 7.4* recipe, your server will now be running PHP version 7.4. If not, it's a good option to follow that recipe first.

If you've followed the *Upgrading a Zabbix database from older MariaDB versions to MariaDB 10.5* recipe, it will now be running MariaDB version 10.5. If not, it's wise to follow that recipe first.

Also, make sure to take backups of your system and read the release notes for the new version you're installing.

How to do it...

First things first, let's log in to our Linux host CLI to check out our software versions:

1. Issue the following commands to check the software versions respectively:

   For Zabbix server:

   ```
   zabbix_server --version
   ```

   For PHP:

   ```
   php-fpm --version
   ```

   For MariaDB:

   ```
   mysql --version
   ```

2. After verifying our versions match the versions mentioned in the *Getting ready* section of this recipe, let's move on to upgrade our Zabbix server.

RHEL-based systems

First, we will start with upgrading the Zabbix server on a RHEL-based system:

1. Let's stop our Zabbix server components with the following command:

   ```
   systemctl stop zabbix-server zabbix-agent2
   ```

2. On our server, let's issue the following command to add the new Zabbix 6.0 repository:

   ```
   rpm -Uvh https://repo.zabbix.com/zabbix/6.0/rhel/8/
   x86_64/zabbix-release-6.0-1.el8noarch.rpm
   ```

3. Run the following command to clean the repositories:

   ```
   dnf clean all
   ```

4. Now upgrade the Zabbix setup with the following command:

   ```
   dnf upgrade zabbix-server-mysql zabbix-web-mysql zabbix-
   agent2
   ```

5. Additionally, install the Zabbix Apache configuration:

   ```
   dnf install zabbix-apache-conf
   ```

6. Start the Zabbix components with the following command:

```
systemctl restart zabbix-server zabbix-agent
```

7. When we check if the server is running, it should say Active (running) when we issue the following command:

```
systemctl status zabbix-server
```

8. If not, we check the logs with the following command, so we can see what is happening:

```
tail -f /var/log/zabbix/zabbix_server.log
```

9. Check the log file for any notable errors and if you find any, fix them before continuing.

10. If we start the server again, this error should be gone and the Zabbix server should keep running:

```
systemctl restart zabbix-server
```

11. Then, upgrade the Apache frontend configuration with the following commands:

```
dnf clean all
dnf install zabbix-apache-conf
```

12. Do not forget to update the time zone of the php-fpm module with the following command:

```
vim /etc/php-fpm.d/zabbix.conf
```

13. Now restart the Zabbix components with the following command:

```
systemctl restart httpd php-fpm zabbix-server mariadb
```

14. Now everything should be working as expected and we should see the new Zabbix 6 frontend, as shown in the following screenshot:

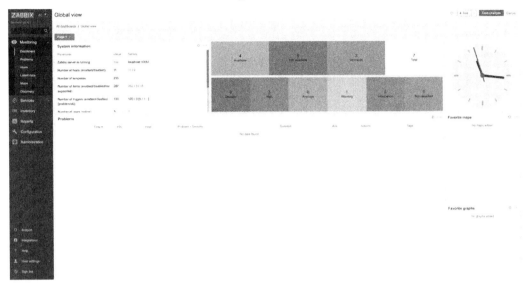

Figure 11.7 – Zabbix 6 frontend after the CentOS upgrade

Ubuntu systems

1. First, let's stop our Zabbix server components with the following command:

```
systemctl stop zabbix-server zabbix-agent2
```

2. Now add the new repository for Zabbix 6 on Ubuntu with the following commands:

```
wget https://repo.zabbix.com/zabbix/6.0/ubuntu/pool/
main/z/zabbix-release/zabbix-release_6.0-1+ubuntu20.04_
all.deb
```
```
dpkg -i zabbix-release_6.0-1+ubuntu20.04_all.deb
```

> **Important Note**
>
> Always check zabbix.com/download to get the right repository for your systems. In the example, I used the Ubuntu repository. Switch this out for the right repository for your system.

3. Update the repository information with the following command:

```
apt update
```

4. Now upgrade the Zabbix server components with the following command:

```
apt install -only-upgrade zabbix-server-mysql zabbix-
frontend-php zabbix-agent2
```

5. Make sure to not overwrite your Zabbix server configuration. If you do overwrite your configuration file, you can restore it from the backup taken in the *Backup up your Zabbix setup* recipe.

6. Then install the new Zabbix Apache configuration with the following command:

```
apt install zabbix-frontend-php
```

7. Restart the Zabbix server components with the following command and you should be done:

```
systemctl restart zabbix-server httpd zabbix-agent2
```

8. We check the logs with the following command so we can see what is happening:

```
tail -f /var/log/zabbix/zabbix_server.log
```

9. Check the log file for any notable errors and if you find any, fix them before continuing.

10. If we start the server again, this error should be gone and the Zabbix server should keep running:

```
systemctl restart zabbix-server
```

11. This should conclude the upgrade process, and if we go to the frontend, we should see the new Zabbix 6 frontend:

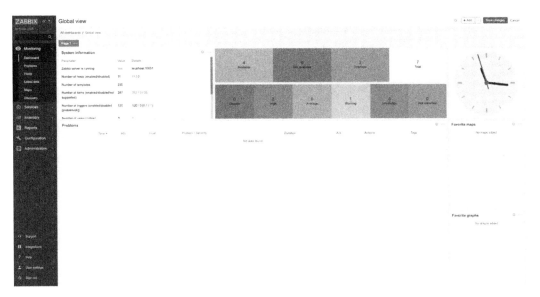

Figure 11.8 – Zabbix 6 frontend after the Ubuntu upgrade

How it works...

Upgrading Zabbix can be an easy task when we are running the latest version of Linux. When we are running older versions of software though, we might run into some issues.

The recipe we've just followed shows us the upgrade process for a Zabbix 5 instance resulting in a setup running Zabbix 6, along with the most common issues we might run into.

> **Important Note**
> While upgrading, make sure to keep an eye on your `zabbix_server.log` file, as this file will tell you if something is wrong during the upgrade process.

We already had a PHP version higher than 7.2 as this was the requirement for Zabbix 5, making the upgrade process to Zabbix 6 quite straightforward. For the database though, Zabbix introduced some new requirements, for example, requiring MariaDB 10.5 or a newer supported version for your Zabbix setup.

Now that you've upgraded all the components, you should be ready to work with Zabbix 6 and your setup will be future-proof for a while – of course, until Zabbix 7 comes out, when we might see some new requirements come along.

See also

Make sure to check out the Zabbix documentation for the versions you are upgrading from and to. Zabbix always includes detailed descriptions of the requirements and processes to make it as easy as possible for you to upgrade. Check out the right documentation for your version at:

```
https://www.zabbix.com/documentation/current/en/manual/
installation/upgrade
```

Maintaining Zabbix performance over time

It's important to make sure that your Zabbix setup keeps performing well over time. There are several key components that are important to keep your Zabbix setup performing optimally. Let's see how to work on some of these components and keep your Zabbix setup running smoothly.

Getting ready

All we are going to need for this recipe is a Zabbix 6 server configured with either a MySQL or PostgreSQL database backend.

How to do it...

We will go through three of the main problems people face whilst maintaining Zabbix server performance. First things first, let's look at the Zabbix processes and how to edit them.

Zabbix processes

A regular problem people face is a Zabbix process being too busy. Let's log in to our Zabbix frontend and check out how this problem might look.

First, let's start by logging in to our Zabbix server frontend and check out some messages:

1. When we navigate to **Monitoring | Dashboard** and then select the default dashboard **Global view**, we might see something like this:

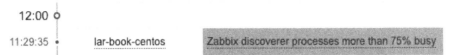

Figure 11.09 – Zabbix problem from our Zabbix server, discoverer processes 75% busy

2. Then we navigate to **Monitoring | Hosts** and click on **Latest data** for the Zabbix server host (in my case, called `lar-book-centos`). This will take us to the latest data for our host.

3. For the filters, type `discoverer` in the **Name** field, then click on **Graph**. This will show you the following graph:

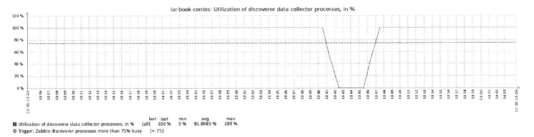

Figure 11.10 – Zabbix server discoverer graph, Utilization of discoverer data collector in %

This graph is at 100% almost all the time, which explains why we see the problem shown in *Figure 11.10* on our dashboard.

4. Let's log in to the Linux CLI of our Zabbix server to edit this process.

5. Edit the following file on your Zabbix server:

```
vim /etc/zabbix/zabbix_server.conf
```

6. Now, if we want to give our Zabbix server's `discoverer` process more room, we need to edit the correct parameter. Scroll down until you see the following:

```
### Option: StartDiscoverers
#          Number of pre-forked instances of discoverers.
#
# Mandatory: no
# Range: 0-250
# Default:
# StartDiscoverers=1
```

Figure 11.11 – Zabbix server configuration file, StartDiscoverers default

7. Now add a new line under this and add the following line:

```
StartDiscoverers=2
```

8. If your file now looks like the following screenshot, you can save and exit the file:

```
### Option: StartDiscoverers
#          Number of pre-forked instances of discoverers.
#
# Mandatory: no
# Range: 0-250
# Default:
# StartDiscoverers=1
StartDiscoverers=2
```

Figure 11.12 – Zabbix server configuration file, StartDiscoverers 2

9. For the changes to take effect, we will need to restart the Zabbix server with the following command:

```
systemctl restart zabbix-server
```

10. Now if we go back to our Zabbix frontend, we should still be at our graph so we can see the following:

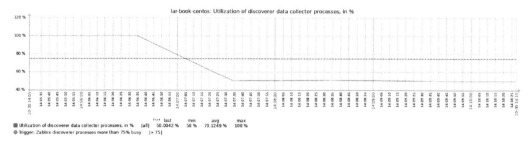

Figure 11.13 – Zabbix server discoverer graph

The utilization of our discoverer process has gone down, which means our problem won't show up anymore. That's how we edit Zabbix server processes.

Zabbix housekeeper

Another very common problem people face is the Zabbix housekeeper process being too busy. Let's log in to our Zabbix frontend and check out the problem:

1. When we navigate to **Monitoring | Dashboard** and then select the default dashboard **Global view**, we might see something like this:

Host	Problem • Severity
lar-book-centos	Zabbix housekeeper processes more than 75% busy

Figure 11.14 – Zabbix problem for Zabbix housekeeper

2. Similar to editing any Zabbix process, we can also edit the Zabbix housekeeper process. Let's log in to the Linux CLI of our Zabbix server to edit our process.

3. Edit the following file on your Zabbix server:

```
vim /etc/zabbix/zabbix_server.conf
```

4. Now, if we want to edit this process, we need to edit the correct parameters. Scroll down until you see the following:

```
### Option: HousekeepingFrequency
#       How often Zabbix will perform housekeeping procedure (in hours).
#       Housekeeping is removing outdated information from the database.
#       To prevent Housekeeper from being overloaded, no more than 4 times HousekeepingFrequency
#       hours of outdated information are deleted in one housekeeping cycle, for each item.
#       To lower load on server startup housekeeping is postponed for 30 minutes after server start.
#       With HousekeepingFrequency=0 the housekeeper can be only executed using the runtime control option.
#       In this case the period of outdated information deleted in one housekeeping cycle is 4 times the
#       period since the last housekeeping cycle, but not less than 4 hours and not greater than 4 days.
#
# Mandatory: no
# Range: 0-24
# Default:
# HousekeepingFrequency=1
```

Figure 11.15 – Zabbix configuration file, HousekeepingFrequency 1

5. This is our first housekeeper parameter. Let's edit this parameter by adding the following line under this block:

```
HousekeepingFrequency=2
```

> **Important Note**
>
> Making the interval longer is not going to solve your issue; at most, you are delaying the inevitable. It is only recommended to change this setting to make it till the next maintenance window and it should be avoided as much as possible.

6. Now scroll down until you see the following:

```
### Option: MaxHousekeeperDelete
#       The table "housekeeper" contains "tasks" for housekeeping procedure in the format:
#       [housekeeperid], [tablename], [field], [value].
#       No more than 'MaxHousekeeperDelete' rows (corresponding to [tablename], [field], [value])
#       will be deleted per one task in one housekeeping cycle.
#       If set to 0 then no limit is used at all. In this case you must know what you are doing!
#
# Mandatory: no
# Range: 0-1000000
# Default:
# MaxHousekeeperDelete=5000
```

Figure 11.16 – Zabbix configuration file, HousekeepingDelete 5000

7. The preceding screenshot shows our second housekeeper parameter. Let's edit this parameter by adding the following line under this code block:

```
MaxHousekeeperDelete=20000
```

8. For the changes to take effect, we will need to restart the Zabbix server with the following command:

```
systemctl restart zabbix-server
```

Tuning a MySQL database

1. Let's see how we can tune a MySQL database with ease. First off, let's go to the following link in our browser: https://github.com/major/MySQLTuner-perl.

2. This link brings us to an open source GitHub project started by *Major Hayden*. Be sure to follow the repository and do all you can to help out. Let's download the script from the GitHub repository or simply use the following command:

```
wget https://raw.githubusercontent.com/major/ MySQLTuner-perl/master/mysqltuner.pl
```

3. Now we can execute this script with the following command:

```
perl mysqltuner.pl
```

4. This will bring us to a prompt for our MySQL database credentials. Fill them out and continue:

```
[root@lar-book-centos ~]# perl mysqltuner.pl
 >>  MySQLTuner 1.7.19 - Major Hayden <major@mhtx.net>
 >>  Bug reports, feature requests, and downloads at http://mysqltuner.pl/
 >>  Run with '--help' for additional options and output filtering

[--] Skipped version check for MySQLTuner script
Please enter your MySQL administrative login: root
Please enter your MySQL administrative password: [OK] Currently running supported MySQL version 10.3.17-MariaDB
```

Figure 11.17 – MySQL tuner script execution

5. Now, the script will output a lot of information that you will need to read carefully, but the most important part is at the end – everything after Variables to adjust:

```
Variables to adjust:
  *** MySQL's maximum memory usage is dangerously high ***
  *** Add RAM before increasing MySQL buffer variables ***
    query_cache_size (=0)
    query_cache_type (=0)
    query_cache_limit (> 1M, or use smaller result sets)
    join_buffer_size (> 256.0K, or always use indexes with JOINs)
    performance_schema = ON enable PFS
    innodb_buffer_pool_size (>= 2.9G) if possible.
    innodb_log_file_size should be (=16M) if possible, so InnoDB total log files size equals to 25% of buffer pool size.
```

Figure 11.18 – MySQL tuner script output

> **Important Note**
>
> DO NOT simply copy over the output from this script. The script is simply giving us an indicator of what might be tuned in our MySQL settings. Always look up the settings suggested and read about the best practices for those settings.

6. We can edit these variables in the MySQL my.cnf file. In my case, I edit it with the following command:

```
vim /etc/my.cnf.d/server.cnf
```

7. Now, you simply edit or add the variables that are suggested in the script and then restart your MySQL server:

```
systemctl restart mariadb
```

How it works...

We've just done three of the main performance tweaks we can do for a Zabbix server, but there's a lot more to do. Let's take a look at what we've just edited, consider why we've edited it, and find out whether it's really that simple.

Zabbix processes

Zabbix processes are a big part of your Zabbix server setup and must be edited with care. In this recipe, we've only just edited the discoverer process on a small installation. This problem was easy as the server had more than enough resources to account for another process running.

Now if we look at the following diagram, we can see the situation as it was before we added a new discoverer process:

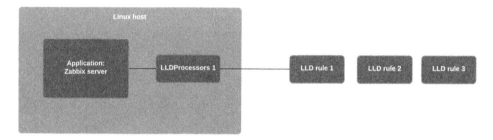

Figure 11.19 – Zabbix server single-process setup diagram

We can see our **Linux host** running our **Zabbix server** application and we can see our **LLDProcessors 1** process discovering **LLD rule 1**. **LLD rule 2** and **LLD rule 3** are queueing up as one LLDProcessor subprocess can only handle one rule at a time.

As we've seen that this is apparently too heavy for our system, we have added another LLDProcessor:

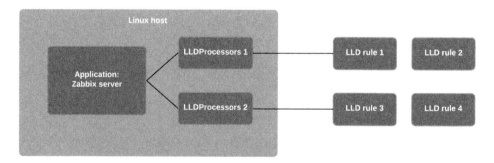

Figure 11.20 – Zabbix server multiple-process setup diagram

Our new setup will balance the load to a certain extent. It's only possible for a discovery rule to be handled by a single discoverer process. This means that if we have multiple discovery rules, we can add discoverers like this to make sure there are enough resources available per discovery rule. It works the same for the other processes – more processes mean better distributions of tasks.

However, there are several things to be careful of here. First of all, not all issues can be solved by simply throwing more resources at them. Some Zabbix setups are configured poorly, where there's something in the configuration making our processes unnecessarily busy. If we deal with the poor configuration aspect, we can take away the high load, thus we need fewer processes.

The second thing I'd like to stress is that we can keep adding processes to our Zabbix server configuration – within limits. Before we reach those limits though, you are definitely going to reach the roof of what our Linux host hardware is capable of. Make sure you have enough RAM and CPU power to actually run all these processes or use Zabbix proxies for offloading.

Zabbix housekeeper

Now for the housekeeper, a very important process for Zabbix administrators that haven't set up MySQL partitioning or PostgreSQL TimescaleDB partitioning yet. The Zabbix housekeeper process is a process that connects to our database and then drops information line by line that has *expired*. You might think, how do you mean expired? Well, we can set limits in the Zabbix server for how long an item should be kept in the database.

If we look at **Administration | General** and then use the drop-down menu to go to **Housekeeping**, part of what we will see is shown in the following screenshot:

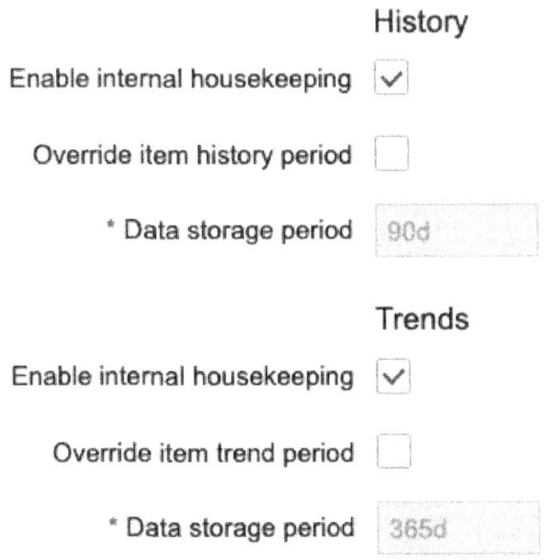

Figure 11.21 – Zabbix server history and trends housekeeping setup

These are our global **History** and **Trends** housekeeping parameters. This defines how long an item's data should be kept in our database. If we look at an item on a template or host, we can also see these parameters:

Figure 11.22 – Zabbix item history and trends housekeeping parameters

These settings override the global settings so you can tweak the housekeeper further. That's how the housekeeper keeps your database in check.

But now, let's look at the tweaks we made in our Zabbix server configuration file, the first of which is `HousekeepingFrequency`. Housekeeping frequency is how often the housekeeper process is started. We've lowered this from every hour to every two hours. Now you might think that's worse, but it doesn't have to be. A lot of the time, we see that housekeeping is not done after one hour and then it just keeps going on and on.

We also changed the `MaxHousekeeperDelete` parameter, which is something completely different. This determines how many database rows our Zabbix housekeeper is allowed to delete in each run. The default settings determined that every hour, we can delete 5,000 database rows. With our new settings, we can now delete 20,000 database rows every two hours.

How does this change anything at all? Well, it might not. It completely depends on your setup. Tweaking the Zabbix housekeeper is different for every setup, and you will have to determine your optimum settings for yourself. Try to balance what you see in your graphs with the two settings we've discussed here to see how well you can optimize it.

However, at one point, your Zabbix setup might grow big enough and Zabbix housekeeping won't be able to keep up. This is when you'll need to look at MySQL partitioning or PostgreSQL TimescaleDB. There's no predefined point where the Zabbix housekeeper won't be able to keep up, so it is smarter to just start with MySQL partitioning or PostgreSQL TimescaleDB right from the start. After all, any setup might grow larger than expected, right?

Tuning a MySQL database

Now for tuning your MySQL database with the `mysqltuner.pl` script. This script does a lot in the background, but we can summarize it as follows: it looks at what the current utilization of your MySQL database is, and then outputs what it thinks the correct tuning variables would be.

Do not take the script output as a given, as with Zabbix housekeeping, there is no way to give you a definitive setup for your database. Databases are simply more complicated than just doing some tweaks and being done with it.

The script will definitely help you tweak your MySQL database to an extent, especially for smaller setups. But make sure to extend your knowledge by reading blogs, guides, and books about databases regularly.

There's more...

We went over how to tune a MySQL database, but we didn't go over how to tune a PostgreSQL instance. There's a wide variety of options out there to do this, so for more on that I recommend checking out the PostgreSQL wiki at `https://wiki.postgresql.org/wiki/Performance_Optimization`. There are different varieties and different preferences at play here. Make sure to check them all out well and pick the one that works the best for you.

12
Advanced Zabbix Database Management

Whether you've been using Zabbix for a while or you are looking toward setting up your first production instance, database management is important right from the start. A lot of the time, people set up their Zabbix database and don't know yet that it will be a big database. The Zabbix housekeeper just can't keep up when your database grows beyond a certain size and that's where we need to look toward different options.

In this chapter, we'll look into keeping our Zabbix database from using up 100% disk space when the Zabbix housekeeper is not keeping up. For MySQL users, we'll look into using database partitioning to keep our database in check. For PostgreSQL users, we'll look toward the brand-new TimescaleDB support. Last but not least, we'll also check out how to secure our connection between the Zabbix server and database.

We'll do all this in the following recipes:

- Setting up MySQL partitioning for your Zabbix database
- Using the PostgreSQL TimescaleDB functionality
- Securing your Zabbix MySQL database

Without further ado, let's get started on these recipes and learn all about managing our database.

Technical requirements

We are going to need some new servers for these recipes. One Linux server needs to run Zabbix server 6 with MySQL (MariaDB) set up; we'll call this host `lar-book-mysql-mgmt`. We will also need a Linux server running Zabbix server 6 with PostgreSQL, which we'll call `lar-book-postgresql-mgmt`.

We'll also need two servers for creating a secure Zabbix database setup. One server will be running the MySQL (MariaDB) database; let's call this server `lar-book-secure-db`. Then, connecting externally to a Zabbix database, we'll have our Zabbix server, which we'll call `lar-book-secure-zbx`.

The code files can also be accessed from the GitHub repository here:

`https://github.com/PacktPublishing/Zabbix-6-IT-Infrastructure-Monitoring-Cookbook/tree/main/chapter12`

Setting up MySQL partitioning for your Zabbix database

When working with a MySQL database, the biggest issue we face is how MySQL stores its data by default. There is no real order to the data that we can use if we want to drop large chunks of data. MySQL partitioning solves this issue; let's see how we can configure it to use for our Zabbix database.

> **Important Note**
> Here at Opensource ICT Solutions, we have fixed the script to work with MySQL 8. The script should work for *any* MySQL setup once more. Check out the link for more information: `https://github.com/OpensourceICTSolutions/zabbix-mysql-partitioning-perl`.

Getting ready

For this recipe, we are going to need a running Zabbix server with a MySQL database. I'll be using MariaDB in my example, but any MySQL flavor should be the same. The Linux host I'll be using is called `lar-book-mysql-mgmt`, which already meets the requirements.

If you are running these steps in a production environment, make sure to create your database backups first as things can always go wrong.

How to do it...

1. First things first, let's log in to our Linux CLI to execute our commands.

2. It's a good idea to use TMUX because partitioning can take several days for big databases. If TMUX is not installed, install it first before proceeding.

   The RHEL-based command is as follows:

   ```
   dnf install tmux
   ```

   The Ubuntu command is as follows:

   ```
   apt install tmux
   ```

3. Open a new tmux session by issuing the following command:

   ```
   tmux
   ```

   > **Important Note**
   > It's not required to run partitioning in a tmux window, but definitely smart. Partitioning a big database can take a long time. You could move your database to another machine with ample resources (CPU, memory, disk speed) to partition, or if that's not a possibility stop the Zabbix server process for the duration of the partitioning process.

4. Now, let's log in to the MySQL application as the root user with the following command:

   ```
   mysql -u root -p
   ```

5. Now, move to use the Zabbix database with the following command:

   ```
   USE zabbix;
   ```

6. We are going to need to partition some tables here, but to do this, we need to know the UNIX timestamp on our tables:

   ```
   SELECT FROM_UNIXTIME(MIN(clock)) FROM 'history';
   ```

You will receive an output like this:

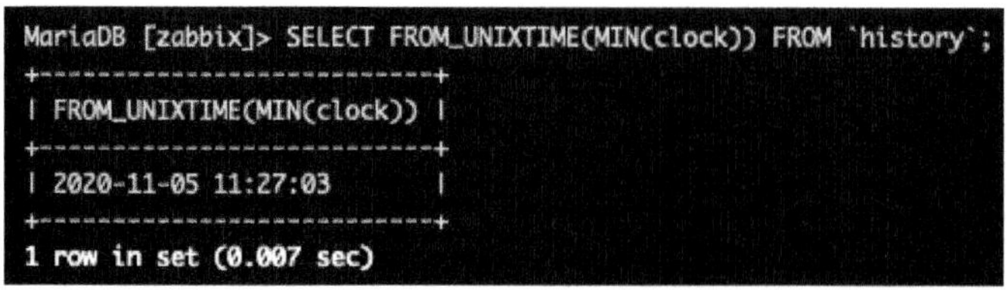

Figure 12.1 – MySQL returning a timestamp on the table history

7. This timestamp should be about the same for every single table we are going to partition. Verify this by running the same query for the remaining history tables:

```
SELECT FROM_UNIXTIME(MIN(clock)) FROM 'history';

SELECT FROM_UNIXTIME(MIN(clock)) FROM 'history_uint';

SELECT FROM_UNIXTIME(MIN(clock)) FROM 'history_str';

SELECT FROM_UNIXTIME(MIN(clock)) FROM 'history_text';

SELECT FROM_UNIXTIME(MIN(clock)) FROM 'history_log';
```

8. A table might return a different value or even no value at all. We need to take this into account when creating our partitions. A partition showing NULL has no data, but an earlier date means we need an earlier partition:

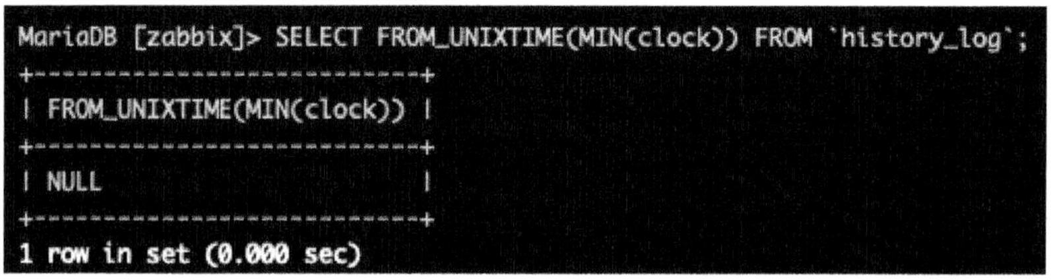

Figure 12.2 – MySQL returning a timestamp on the history_log table

9. Let's start with the history table. We are going to partition this table by day, and we are going to do this up until the date it is today; for me, it is 11-11-2020. Let's prepare the following MySQL query (for example, in a notepad):

```
ALTER TABLE 'history' PARTITION BY RANGE ( clock)
(PARTITION p2020_11_05 VALUES LESS THAN (UNIX_
TIMESTAMP("2020-11-06 00:00:00")) ENGINE = InnoDB,

 PARTITION p2020_11_06 VALUES LESS THAN (UNIX_
TIMESTAMP("2020-11-07 00:00:00")) ENGINE = InnoDB,

 PARTITION p2020_11_07 VALUES LESS THAN (UNIX_
TIMESTAMP("2020-11-08 00:00:00")) ENGINE = InnoDB,

 PARTITION p2020_11_08 VALUES LESS THAN (UNIX_
TIMESTAMP("2020-11-09 00:00:00")) ENGINE = InnoDB,
```

```
    PARTITION p2020_11_09 VALUES LESS THAN (UNIX_
TIMESTAMP("2020-11-10 00:00:00")) ENGINE = InnoDB,

    PARTITION p2020_11_10 VALUES LESS THAN (UNIX_
TIMESTAMP("2020-11-11 00:00:00")) ENGINE = InnoDB,

    PARTITION p2020_11_11 VALUES LESS THAN (UNIX_
TIMESTAMP("2020-11-12 00:00:00")) ENGINE = InnoDB);
```

> **Tip**
>
> If we only have 7 days of history data, creating this list by hand is not that hard.
> If we want to do it on a big existing database, it can be a big list to edit by hand.
> It's easy to create a big list using software like Excel or by creating a small script.

10. Make sure that the oldest partition here matches the timestamp we collected in *Step 9*. In my case, the oldest data was from November 5, so this is my oldest partition. Also, make sure that your newest partition matches the date you are partitioning on.

11. Copy and paste the prepared MySQL query from *Step 9* and press *Enter*. This might take a while, as your table might be quite large. After you're done, you will see the following:

```
MariaDB [zabbix]> ALTER TABLE `history` PARTITION BY RANGE ( clock)
    -> (PARTITION p2020_11_05 VALUES LESS THAN (UNIX_TIMESTAMP("2020-11-06 00:00:00")) ENGINE = InnoDB,
    ->  PARTITION p2020_11_06 VALUES LESS THAN (UNIX_TIMESTAMP("2020-11-07 00:00:00")) ENGINE = InnoDB,
    ->  PARTITION p2020_11_07 VALUES LESS THAN (UNIX_TIMESTAMP("2020-11-08 00:00:00")) ENGINE = InnoDB,
    ->  PARTITION p2020_11_08 VALUES LESS THAN (UNIX_TIMESTAMP("2020-11-09 00:00:00")) ENGINE = InnoDB,
    ->  PARTITION p2020_11_09 VALUES LESS THAN (UNIX_TIMESTAMP("2020-11-10 00:00:00")) ENGINE = InnoDB,
    ->  PARTITION p2020_11_10 VALUES LESS THAN (UNIX_TIMESTAMP("2020-11-11 00:00:00")) ENGINE = InnoDB,
    ->  PARTITION p2020_11_11 VALUES LESS THAN (UNIX_TIMESTAMP("2020-11-12 00:00:00")) ENGINE = InnoDB);
Stage: 1 of 2 'Copy to tmp table'   10.2% of stage done
Stage: 2 of 2 'Enabling keys'        0% of stage done
Query OK, 9853 rows affected (3.618 sec)
Records: 9853  Duplicates: 0  Warnings: 0
```

Figure 12.3 – MySQL returning a successful query result for the history table

12. Do the same partitioning for the remaining history tables; make sure to use the other UNIX timestamps for the earliest partition:

   - `history_uint`
   - `history_str`
   - `history_text`
   - `history_log`

13. Once you've partitioned all the history tables, let's partition the `trends` tables. We have two of these called `trends` and `trends_uint`.

14. We are going to check the timestamps again with the following:

```
SELECT FROM_UNIXTIME(MIN(clock)) FROM 'trends';
SELECT FROM_UNIXTIME(MIN(clock)) FROM 'trends_uint';
```

15. For these tables, it's important to focus on what the earliest month is. For my tables, this is month 11 of the year 2020.

16. Now, let's prepare and execute the partitioning for this table. Let's do three extra partitions starting from the earliest date seen in the timestamp at *Step 14*:

```
ALTER TABLE 'trends' PARTITION BY RANGE ( clock)
(PARTITION p2020_11 VALUES LESS THAN (UNIX_
TIMESTAMP("2020-12-01 00:00:00")) ENGINE = InnoDB,
 PARTITION p2020_12 VALUES LESS THAN (UNIX_
TIMESTAMP("2021-01-01 00:00:00")) ENGINE = InnoDB,
 PARTITION p2021_01 VALUES LESS THAN (UNIX_
TIMESTAMP("2021-02-01 00:00:00")) ENGINE = InnoDB);
```

17. Again, we partition from the earliest collected UNIX timestamp, up until the current month. But there's no harm in creating some new partitions for future data:

```
MariaDB [zabbix]> ALTER TABLE `trends` PARTITION BY RANGE ( clock)
    -> (PARTITION p2020_11 VALUES LESS THAN (UNIX_TIMESTAMP("2020-12-01 00:00:00")) ENGINE = InnoDB,
    ->  PARTITION p2020_12 VALUES LESS THAN (UNIX_TIMESTAMP("2021-01-01 00:00:00")) ENGINE = InnoDB,
    ->  PARTITION p2021_01 VALUES LESS THAN (UNIX_TIMESTAMP("2021-02-01 00:00:00")) ENGINE = InnoDB);
Stage: 2 of 2 'Enabling keys'     0% of stage done
Query OK, 194 rows affected (1.398 sec)
Records: 194  Duplicates: 0  Warnings: 0
```

Figure 12.4 – MySQL returning a successful query result for the trends table

18. Do the same thing for the `trends_uint` table.

19. That concludes the actual partitioning of the database. Let's make sure our partitions remain managed. On your Linux host, download the partitioning script with the following command:

```
wget https://raw.githubusercontent.com/
OpensourceICTSolutions/zabbix-mysql-partitioning-perl/
main/mysql_zbx_part.pl
```

20. If you can't use wget, simply download the script from the following link: https://github.com/OpensourceICTSolutions/zabbix-mysql-partitioning-perl/blob/main/mysql_zbx_part.pl.

Alternatively, you can download the partitioning script using the Packt GitHub here:

```
https://github.com/PacktPublishing/Zabbix-6-IT-
Infrastructure-Monitoring-Cookbook/tree/main/chapter12/
mysql_zbx_part.pl
```

21. Now, create the directory and move the script to the `/usr/lib/zabbix/` folder with the following command:

```
mkdir /usr/lib/zabbix/
mv mysql_zbx_part.pl /usr/lib/zabbix/
```

22. We are going to customize some details in the script. Edit the script with the following:

```
vim /usr/lib/zabbix/mysql_zbx_part.pl
```

We need to edit some text at the following part:

```perl
my $db_schema = 'zabbix';
my $dsn = 'DBI:mysql:'.$db_schema.':mysql_socket=/var/lib/mysql/mysql.sock';
my $db_user_name = 'zabbix';
my $db_password = 'password';
my $tables = {  'history' => { 'period' => 'day', 'keep_history' => '30'},
                'history_log' => { 'period' => 'day', 'keep_history' => '30'},
                'history_str' => { 'period' => 'day', 'keep_history' => '30'},
                'history_text' => { 'period' => 'day', 'keep_history' => '30'},
                'history_uint' => { 'period' => 'day', 'keep_history' => '30'},
                'trends' => { 'period' => 'month', 'keep_history' => '12'},
                'trends_uint' => { 'period' => 'month', 'keep_history' => '12'},
```

Figure 12.5 – MySQL Zabbix partitioning script user parameters

23. Edit `$db_schema` to match your Zabbix database name.

24. Edit `$db_user_name` to match your Zabbix database username.

25. Edit `$db_password` to match your Zabbix database password.

26. Now, at the `$tables` variable, we are going to add some of the most important details. This is where we'll add how many days of history data we want to keep and how many months of trends data. Add your values; the default settings keep 30 days of history data and 12 months of trends data.

27. Also, make sure to edit the `my $curr_tz = 'Europe/Amsterdam';` line to match your own time zone.

> **Tip**
>
> If you are using a version of Zabbix before 2.2 or a MySQL version before 5.6 or if you are running MySQL 8, then there are some extra lines of configuration that need to be commented and uncommented in the script. If this applies to you, read the comments in the `mysql_zbx_part.pl` script file and edit it. Additionally, check out the GitHub repo mentioned in the introduction of this recipe.

28. Before executing the script, we are going to need to install some Perl dependencies. On RHEL 8, we will need the `PowerTools` repo. Install the dependencies with the following.

    The RHEL-based commands are as follows:

    ```
    dnf config-manager --set-enabled PowerTools
    dnf update
    dnf install perl-Sys-Syslog
    dnf install perl-DateTime
    ```

    The Ubuntu commands are as follows:

    ```
    apt install liblogger-syslog-perl
    apt install libdatetime-perl
    ```

29. Make the script executable with the following command:

    ```
    chmod +x /usr/lib/zabbix/mysql_zbx_part.pl
    ```

30. Then, this is the moment where we should be ready to execute the script to see whether it is working. Let's execute it:

    ```
    /usr/lib/zabbix/mysql_zbx_part.pl
    ```

31. Once your script has finished running, let's see whether it was successful with the following command:

    ```
    journalctl -t mysql_zbx_part
    ```

32. You should see an output like this:

```
Nov 05 15:29:12 lar-book-mysql-mgmt mysql_zbx_part[9027]: Creating a partition for trends_uint table (p2021_02)
Nov 05 15:29:12 lar-book-mysql-mgmt mysql_zbx_part[9027]: ALTER TABLE zabbix.trends_uint ADD PARTITION (PARTITION p2021_02 VALUES le
Nov 05 15:29:13 lar-book-mysql-mgmt mysql_zbx_part[9027]: Creating a partition for trends_uint table (p2021_03)
Nov 05 15:29:13 lar-book-mysql-mgmt mysql_zbx_part[9027]: ALTER TABLE zabbix.trends_uint ADD PARTITION (PARTITION p2021_03 VALUES le
Nov 05 15:29:13 lar-book-mysql-mgmt mysql_zbx_part[9027]: Creating a partition for trends_uint table (p2021_04)
Nov 05 15:29:13 lar-book-mysql-mgmt mysql_zbx_part[9027]: ALTER TABLE zabbix.trends_uint ADD PARTITION (PARTITION p2021_04 VALUES le
Nov 05 15:29:13 lar-book-mysql-mgmt mysql_zbx_part[9027]: Creating a partition for trends_uint table (p2021_05)
Nov 05 15:29:13 lar-book-mysql-mgmt mysql_zbx_part[9027]: ALTER TABLE zabbix.trends_uint ADD PARTITION (PARTITION p2021_05 VALUES le
Nov 05 15:29:13 lar-book-mysql-mgmt mysql_zbx_part[9027]: Creating a partition for trends_uint table (p2021_06)
Nov 05 15:29:13 lar-book-mysql-mgmt mysql_zbx_part[9027]: ALTER TABLE zabbix.trends_uint ADD PARTITION (PARTITION p2021_06 VALUES le
Nov 05 15:29:14 lar-book-mysql-mgmt mysql_zbx_part[9027]: Creating a partition for trends_uint table (p2021_07)
Nov 05 15:29:14 lar-book-mysql-mgmt mysql_zbx_part[9027]: ALTER TABLE zabbix.trends_uint ADD PARTITION (PARTITION p2021_07 VALUES le
Nov 05 15:29:14 lar-book-mysql-mgmt mysql_zbx_part[9027]: Creating a partition for trends_uint table (p2021_08)
Nov 05 15:29:14 lar-book-mysql-mgmt mysql_zbx_part[9027]: ALTER TABLE zabbix.trends_uint ADD PARTITION (PARTITION p2021_08 VALUES le
Nov 05 15:29:14 lar-book-mysql-mgmt mysql_zbx_part[9027]: Creating a partition for trends_uint table (p2021_09)
Nov 05 15:29:14 lar-book-mysql-mgmt mysql_zbx_part[9027]: ALTER TABLE zabbix.trends_uint ADD PARTITION (PARTITION p2021_09 VALUES le
[root@lar-book-mysql-mgmt ~]#
```

Figure 12.6 – MySQL Zabbix partitioning script results

33. Now, execute the following command:

```
crontab -e
```

34. To automate the execution of the script, add the following line to the file:

```
0 0 * * * /usr/lib/zabbix/mysql_zbx_part.pl
```

35. The last thing we are going to need to do is to go to the Zabbix frontend. Navigate to **Administration | General**.

36. Now, use the drop-down menu to go to **Housekeeping**:

Figure 12.7 – Zabbix Administration | General drop-down menu, Housekeeping option

37. As the script will take over database **History** and **Trend** deletion, the housekeeping for the **History** and **Trends** tables must be disabled. It will look like the following:

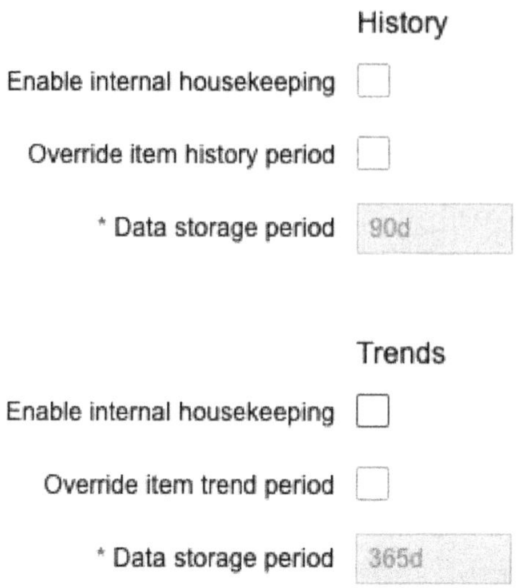

History

Enable internal housekeeping ☐

Override item history period ☐

* Data storage period   90d

Trends

Enable internal housekeeping ☐

Override item trend period ☐

* Data storage period   365d

Figure 12.8 – Zabbix Administration | General | Housekeeping disabled for History and Trends

That concludes our Zabbix database partitioning setup.

How it works...

Database partitioning seems like a daring task at first, but once you break it down into chunks, it is not that hard to do. It is simply the process of breaking down our most important Zabbix database tables into time-based partitions. Once these partitions are set up, we simply need to manage these tables with a script and we're ready.

Look at the following figure and let's say today is **07-11-2020**. We have a lot of partitions managed by the script. All of our **History** data today is going to be written to the partition for this day and all of our **Trends** data is going to be written into the partition for this month:

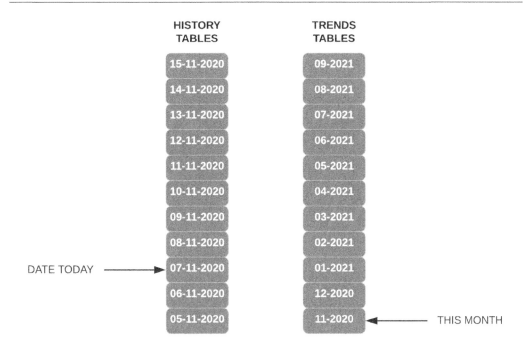

Figure 12.9 – Zabbix partitioning illustration

The actual script does only two things. It creates new partitions and it deletes old partitions.

For deleting partitions, once a partition reaches an age older than specified in the $tables variable, it drops the entire partition.

For creating partitions, every time the script is run, it creates 10 partitions in the future starting from today. Except of course when a partition already exists.

This is better than using the housekeeper for one clear reason. It's simply faster! The Zabbix housekeeper goes through our database data line by line to check the UNIX timestamp and then it deletes that line when it reaches data older than specified. This takes time and resources. Dropping a partition, though, is almost instant.

One downside of partitioning a Zabbix database, though, is that we can no longer use the frontend item history and trend configuration. This means we can't specify different history and trends for different items; it's all global now.

See also

When I first started using Zabbix, I did not have a book like this one. Instead, I relied heavily on the resources available online and my own skillset. There are loads of great guides for partitioning and other stuff available on the internet. If something isn't mentioned in this book, make sure to Google it and see if there's something available online. You might also want to check out some amazing books written by our Zabbix peers, and of course, if you've figured out something by yourself, sharing is caring!

Using the PostgreSQL TimescaleDB functionality

TimescaleDB is an open source relational PostgreSQL database extension for time-based series data. Using PostgreSQL TimescaleDB is a solid way to work around using the Zabbix housekeeper to manage your PostgreSQL database. In this recipe, we will go over the installation of PostgreSQL TimescaleDB on a new server and how to set it up with Zabbix.

Getting ready

We will need an empty Linux server. I'll be using my server called `lar-book-postgresql-mgmt`.

How to do it...

We have a bit of a different process for RHEL-based and Ubuntu systems, which is why we have split this *How to do it...* section in two. We will start with Ubuntu systems.

Ubuntu installation

1. Let's log in to our Linux CLI and add the PostgreSQL repo with the following commands:

```
echo "deb http://apt.postgresql.org/pub/repos/apt/ $(lsb_
release -c -s)-pgdg main" | tee /etc/apt/sources.list.d/
pgdg.list
```
```
wget --quiet -O -https://www.postgresql.org/media/keys/
ACCC4CF8.asc | apt-key add -
```
```
apt update
```

2. Now, add the TimescaleDB repository:

```
add-apt-repository ppa:timescale/timescaledb-ppa
apt update
```

3. Now, install TimescaleDB with the installation command:

```
apt install timescaledb-postgresql
```

4. Start and enable PostgreSQL 12:

```
systemctl enable postgresql
systemctl start postgresql
```

5. Now, continue with the *TimescaleDB configuration* section of this recipe.

RHEL-based installation

1. Let's start by logging in to our Linux CLI. We will need PostgreSQL version 11 or higher. Let's install version 12; first, disable AppStream:

```
dnf -qy module disable postgresql
```

2. Add the correct repository:

```
dnf install https://download.postgresql.org/pub/repos/
yum/reporpms/EL-8-x86_64/pgdg-redhat-repo-latest.noarch.
rpm
```

3. Then, install PostgreSQL:

```
dnf install postgresql13 postgresql13-server
```

4. Make sure to initialize the database:

```
/usr/pgsql-13/bin/postgresql-13-setup initdb
```

5. Now, edit the following file:

```
vim /etc/yum.repos.d/timescale_timescaledb.repo
```

6. Add the repo information to the file and save it:

```
[timescale_timescaledb]
name=timescale_timescaledb
baseurl=https://packagecloud.io/timescale/timescaledb/
el/7/$basearch
repo_gpgcheck=1
gpgcheck=0
   enabled=1
gpgkey=https://packagecloud.io/timescale/timescaledb/
gpgkey
sslverify=1
sslcacert=/etc/pki/tls/certs/ca-bundle.crt
metadata_expire=300
```

7. Install TimescaleDB with the installation command:

```
dnf install timescaledb-postgresql-12
```

8. Now, continue with the *TimescaleDB configuration* section of this recipe.

TimescaleDB configuration

In this section, we'll go over how to set up TimescaleDB after finishing the installation process. There's a lot more to configure, so let's check it out:

1. Let's start by running the following command:

```
timescaledb-tune
```

2. Sometimes this does not work, and you want to specify the PostgreSQL location like this:

```
timescaledb-tune --pg-config=/usr/pgsql-12/bin/pg_config
```

3. Go through the steps and answer the questions with yes or no accordingly. For a first-time setup, yes on everything is good.

4. Now, restart PostgreSQL:

```
systemctl restart postgresql
```

5. If you haven't already, download and install Zabbix with the following. The RHEL-based commands are as follows:

```
rpm -Uvh https://repo.zabbix.com/zabbix/6.0/rhel/8/
x86_64/zabbix-release-6.0-1.el8.noarch.rpm
```
```
dnf clean all
```
```
dnf install zabbix-server-pgsql zabbix-web-pgsql zabbix-
apache-conf zabbix-agent2
```

The Ubuntu commands are as follows:

```
wget https://repo.zabbix.com/zabbix/6.0/ubuntu/pool/
main/z/zabbix-release/zabbix-release_6.0-1+ubuntu20.04_
all.deb
```
```
dpkg -i zabbix-release_6.0-1+ubuntu20.04_all.deb
```
```
apt update
```
```
apt install zabbix-server-pgsql zabbix-frontend-phpphp-
pgsql zabbix-apache-conf zabbix-agent
```

6. Create the initial database with the following:

```
sudo -u postgres createuser --pwprompt zabbix
```
```
sudo -u postgres createdb -O zabbix zabbix
```

7. Import the database schema for PostgreSQL:

```
zcat /usr/share/doc/zabbix-server-pgsql*/create.sql.gz |
sudo -u zabbix psql zabbix
```

8. Add the database password to the Zabbix configuration file by editing it:

```
vim /etc/zabbix/zabbix_server.conf
```

9. Add the following lines, where password is your password as set in *Step 6* and DBHost is empty:

```
DBHost=
```
```
DBPassword=password
```

10. Now, enable the TimescaleDB extension with the following command:

```
echo "CREATE EXTENSION IF NOT EXISTS timescaledb
CASCADE;" | sudo -u postgres psql zabbix
```

11. Unpack the `timescale.sql` script located in your Zabbix share folder:

```
gunzip /usr/share/doc/zabbix-sql-scripts/postgresql/
timescaledb.sql.gz
```

12. Now, let's run `timescale.sql`:

```
cat /usr/share/doc/zabbix-sql-scripts/postgresql/
timescaledb.sql| sudo -u zabbix psql zabbix
```

13. One more thing before moving to the frontend. We need to edit the `pg_hba.conf` file to allow our Zabbix frontend to connect. Edit the following file:

```
vim /var/lib/pgsql/12/data/pg_hba.conf
```

14. Make sure the following lines match in your file; they need to end with md5:

```
# "local" is for Unix domain socket connections only
local all all
md5
# IPv4 local connections:
host all   all   127.0.0.1/32
md5
# IPv6 local connections:
host all   all   ::1/128
md5
```

15. Now, start Zabbix and finish the frontend setup using the following commands:

On RHEL-based systems:

```
systemctl restart zabbix-server zabbix-agent2 httpd
php-fpm
systemctl enable zabbix-server zabbix-agent2 httpd
php-fpm
```

On Ubuntu systems:

```
systemctl restart zabbix-server zabbix-agent2 apache2
php-fpm
systemctl enable zabbix-server zabbix-agent2 apache2
php-fpm
```

16. Once we navigate to the frontend and we've logged in to our setup, navigate to **Administration | General**. Use the drop-down menu to select **Housekeeping**.

17. We can now edit the following parameters to match our preferences and TimescaleDB will take care of maintaining the data retention period:

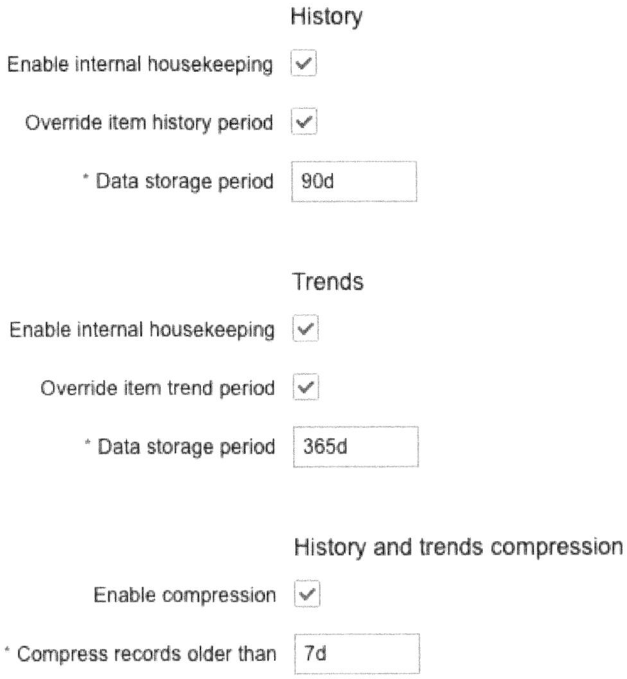

History

Enable internal housekeeping ✓

Override item history period ✓

* Data storage period | 90d |

Trends

Enable internal housekeeping ✓

Override item trend period ✓

* Data storage period | 365d |

History and trends compression

Enable compression ✓

* Compress records older than | 7d |

Figure 12.10 – Zabbix Administration | General | Housekeeping, TimescaleDB-specific options

How it works...

Using the TimescaleDB functionality with your Zabbix setup is a solid integration with your PostgreSQL database. The extension is supported by Zabbix and you can expect it to only get better in the near future.

Now, how TimescaleDB works is by dividing up your PostgreSQL hypertable into time-based chunks. If we look at the following figure, we can see how that looks:

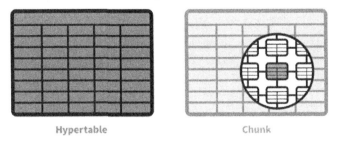

Hypertable   Chunk

Figure 12.11 – TimescaleDB hypertable chunks diagram

These time-based chunks are a lot faster to drop from the database than using the Zabbix housekeeper. The Zabbix housekeeper goes through our database data line by line to check the UNIX timestamp and then it drops the line when it reaches data older than specified. This takes time and resources. Dropping a chunk though is almost instant.

Another great thing about using TimescaleDB with a Zabbix database is that we can still use the frontend item history and trend configuration. On top of that, TimescaleDB can compress our data, to keep databases smaller.

The downside is that we can't specify different history and trends for different items; it's all global now.

See also

This recipe details the installation of PostgreSQL TimescaleDB. As this process is constantly changing, you might need to include some new information from the official TimescaleDB documentation. Check out their documentation here:

```
https://docs.timescale.com/latest/getting-started/
installation/rhel-centos/installation-yum
```

Securing your Zabbix MySQL database

Another great added feature for the Zabbix server is the ability to encrypt data between the database and Zabbix components. This is particularly useful when you are running a split database and the Zabbix server over the network. A **Man in the Middle** (**MITM**) or other attacks can be executed on the network to gain access to your monitoring data.

In this recipe, we'll set up MySQL encryption between Zabbix components and the database to add another layer of security.

Getting ready

We are going to need a Zabbix setup that uses an external database. I'll be using the Linux `lar-book-secure-db` and `lar-book-secure-zbx` hosts.

The new server called `lar-book-secure-zbx` will be used to connect externally to the `lar-book-secure-db` database server. The database servers won't run our Zabbix server; this process will run on `lar-book-secure-zbx`.

Make sure that MariaDB is already installed on the `lar-book-secure-db` host and that you are running a recent supported version that is able to use encryption. If you don't know how to upgrade your database, check out, in *Chapter 11*, *Maintaining Your Zabbix Setup*, the recipe named *Upgrading Zabbix database from older MariaDB versions to MariaDB 10.5*, or check the documentation online.

How to do it...

1. Make sure your host files on both hosts from the *Getting ready* section contain the hostname and IP for your Linux hosts and edit the file with the following:

   ```
   vim /etc/hosts
   ```

2. Then, fill in the file with your hostnames and IPs. It will look like this:

   ```
   10.16.16.170 lar-book-secure-db
   10.16.16.171 lar-book-secure-zbx
   ```

3. On the `lar-book-secure-db` MySQL server, if you haven't already, create the Zabbix database by logging in to MySQL:

   ```
   mysql -u root -p
   ```

4. Then, issue the following command to create the database:

   ```
   create database zabbix character set utf8mb4 collate
   utf8mb4_ bin;
   ```

5. Also, make sure to create a user that will be able to access the database securely. Make sure the IP matches the IP from the Zabbix server (and one for the Zabbix frontend if separated):

   ```
   create user 'zabbix'@'10.16.16.171' identified BY
   'password';
   grant all privileges on zabbix.* to
   'zabbix'@'10.16.16.171';
   flush privileges;
   ```

6. Quit MySQL and then make sure to run the secure `mysql` script with the following:

   ```
   mariadb_secure_installation
   ```

7. Log in to `lar-book-secure-zbx` and install the Zabbix server repo with the following command:

```
rpm -Uvh https://repo.zabbix.com/zabbix/6.0/rhel/8/
x86_64/zabbix-release-6.0-1.el8.noarch.rpm
dnf clean all
```

8. Let's add the MariaDB repository on our server:

```
wget https://downloads.mariadb.com/MariaDB/mariadb_repo_
setup
chmod +x mariadb_repo_setup
./mariadb_repo_setup
```

9. Then, install the Zabbix server and its required components. Use the following RHEL-based command:

```
dnf install zabbix-server-mysql zabbix-web-mysql zabbix-
apache-conf zabbix-agent2 zabbix-sql-scripts mariadb-
client
```

Use the following Ubuntu command:

```
apt install zabbix-server-mysql zabbix-frontend-php
zabbix-apache-conf zabbix-agent2 mariadb-client
```

10. From the Zabbix server, connect to the remote database server and import the database schema and default data with the following command:

```
zcat /usr/share/doc/zabbix-sql-scripts/mysql/server.sql.
gz | mysql -h 10.16.16.170 -uzabbix -p zabbix
```

11. Now we are going to open the file called `openssl.cnf` and edit it by issuing the following command:

```
vim /etc/pki/tls/openssl.cnf
```

12. In this file, we need to edit the following lines:

```
countryName_default = XX
stateOrProvinceName_default = Default Province
localityName_default = Default City
0.organizationName_default = Default Company Ltd
organizationalUnitName_default.=
```

13. It will look like this filled out completely:

```
[ req_distinguished_name ]
countryName                          = Country Name (2 letter code)
countryName_default                  = NL
countryName_min                      = 2
countryName_max                      = 2

stateOrProvinceName                  = State or Province Name (full name)
stateOrProvinceName_default          = Noord-Holland

localityName                         = Locality Name (eg, city)
localityName_default                 = Amsterdam

0.organizationName                   = Organization Name (eg, company)
0.organizationName_default           = Opensource ICT Solutions

# we can do this but it is not needed normally :-)
#1.organizationName                  = Second Organization Name (eg, company)
#1.organizationName_default          = World Wide Web Pty Ltd

organizationalUnitName               = Organizational Unit Name (eg, section)
organizationalUnitName_default       = Opensource ICT Solutions

commonName                           = Common Name (eg, your name or your server\'s hostname)
commonName_max                       = 64

emailAddress                         = Email Address
emailAddress_max                     = 64
```

Figure 12.12 – OpenSSL config file with our personal defaults

14. We can also see this line:

```
dir = /etc/pki/CA     # Where everything is kept
```

15. This means the default directory is /etc/pki/CA; if yours is different, act accordingly. Close the file by saving and continue.

16. Let's create a new folder for our private certificates using the following command:

```
mkdir -p /etc/pki/CA/private
```

17. Now, let's create our key pair in the new folder. Issue the following command:

```
openssl req -new -x509 -keyout /etc/pki/CA/private/
cakey.pem -out /etc/pki/CA/cacert.pem -days 3650 -newkey
rsa:4096
```

18. You will be prompted for a password now:

```
Generating a RSA private key
...........................................++++
............................................................................................++++
writing new private key to '/etc/pki/CA/private/cakey.pem'
Enter PEM pass phrase:
```

Figure 12.13 – Certificate generation response asking for a password

19. You might also be promoted to enter some information about your company. It will use the default we filled in earlier, so you can just press *Enter* up until Common Name.

20. Fill in Root CA for Common Name and add your email address like this:

```
Country Name (2 letter code) [NL]:
State or Province Name (full name) [Noord-Holland]:
Locality Name (eg, city) [Amsterdam]:
Organization Name (eg, company) [Opensource ICT Solutions]:
Organizational Unit Name (eg, section) [Opensource ICT Solutions]:
Common Name (eg, your name or your server's hostname) []:Root CA
Email Address []:nathan@oicts.nl
```

Figure 12.14 – Certificate generation response asking for information, Root CA

21. Next up is creating the actual signed certificates that our Zabbix server will use. Let's make sure that OpenSSL has the right files to keep track of signed certificates:

```
touch /etc/pki/CA/index.txt
echo 01 > /etc/pki/CA/serial
```

22. Then, create the folders to keep our certificates in:

```
mkdir /etc/pki/CA/unsigned
mkdir /etc/pki/CA/newcerts
mkdir /etc/pki/CA/certs
```

23. Now, let's create our certificate signing request for the lar-book-secure-zbx Zabbix server with the following command:

```
openssl req -nodes -new -keyout /etc/pki/CA/private/
zbx-srv_key.pem -out /etc/pki/CA/unsigned/zbx-srv_req.pem
-newkey rsa:2048
```

24. You will be prompted to add a password and your company information again. Use the default up until Common Name. We will fill out our Common Name, which will be the server hostname, and we'll add our email address like this:

```
Country Name (2 letter code) [NL]:
State or Province Name (full name) [Noord-Holland]:
Locality Name (eg, city) [Amsterdam]:
Organization Name (eg, company) [Opensource ICT Solutions]:
Organizational Unit Name (eg, section) [Opensource ICT Solutions]:
Common Name (eg, your name or your server's hostname) []:lar-book-secure-zbx
Email Address []:nathan@oicts.nl
```

Figure 12.15 – Certificate generation response asking for information, lar-book-secure-zbx

25. Let's do the same for our lar-book-secure-db server:

```
openssl req -nodes -new -keyout /etc/pki/CA/private/
mysql-srv_key.pem -out /etc/pki/CA/unsigned/mysql-srv_
req.pem -newkey rsa:2048
```

The response will look like this:

```
Country Name (2 letter code) [NL]:
State or Province Name (full name) [Noord-Holland]:
Locality Name (eg, city) [Amsterdam]:
Organization Name (eg, company) [Opensource ICT Solutions]:
Organizational Unit Name (eg, section) [Opensource ICT Solutions]:
Common Name (eg, your name or your server's hostname) []:lar-book-secure-db
Email Address []:nathan@oicts.nl
```

Figure 12.16 – Certificate generation response asking for information, lar-book-secure-db

> **Important Note**
> Our certificates need to be created without a password; otherwise, our MariaDB and Zabbix applications won't be able to use them. Make sure to specify the -nodes option.

26. Now, sign the certificate for lar-book-secure-zbx with the following command:

```
openssl ca -policy policy_anything -days 365 -out /
etc/pki/CA/certs/zbx-srv_crt.pcm -infiles /etc/pki/CA/
unsigned/zbx-srv_req.pem
```

27. You will be prompted with the question Sign the certificate? [y/n]. Answer this and all the following questions with Y.

28. Now, let's do the same thing for the lar-book-secure-db certificate:

```
openssl ca -policy policy_anything -days 365 -out/etc/
pki/CA/certs/mysql-srv_crt.pem -infiles/etc/pki/CA/
unsigned/mysql-srv_req.pem
```

29. Let's log in to the `lar-book-secure-db` MySQL server and create a directory for our newly created certificates:

```
mkdir /etc/my.cnf.d/certificates/
```

30. Add the right permissions to the folder:

```
chown -R mysql. /etc/my.cnf.d/certificates/
```

31. Now, back at the new `lar-book-secure-zbx` Zabbix server, copy over the files to the database server with the following commands:

```
scp /etc/pki/CA/private/mysql-srv_key.pem
root@10.16.16.170:/etc/my.cnf.d/certificates/mysql-srv.
key
scp /etc/pki/CA/certs/mysql-srv_crt.pem
root@10.16.16.170:/etc/my.cnf.d/certificates/mysql-srv.
crt
scp /etc/pki/CA/cacert.pem root@10.16.16.170:/etc/
my.cnf.d/certificates/cacert.crt
```

32. Now, back at the `lar-book-secure-db` MySQL server, add the right permissions to the files:

```
chown -R mysql:mysql /etc/my.cnf.d/certificates/
chmod 400 /etc/my.cnf.d/certificates/mysql-srv.key
chmod 444 /etc/my.cnf.d/certificates/mysql-srv.crt
chmod 444 /etc/my.cnf.d/certificates/cacert.crt
```

33. Edit the MariaDB configuration file with the following command:

```
vim /etc/my.cnf.d/server.cnf
```

34. Add the following lines to the configuration file under the `[mysqld]` block:

```
bind-address=lar-book-secure-db
ssl-ca=/etc/my.cnf.d/certificates/cacert.crt
ssl-cert=/etc/my.cnf.d/certificates/mysql-srv.crt
ssl-key=/etc/my.cnf.d/certificates/mysql-srv.key
```

35. Log in to MySQL with the following command:

```
mysql -u root -p
```

36. Make sure our Zabbix MySQL user requires SSL encryption with the following:

```
alter user 'zabbix'@'10.16.16.152' require ssl;
flush privileges;
```

Make sure the IP matches the IP from the Zabbix server (and one for the Zabbix frontend, if separated), just like we did in *Step 2*.

37. Quit out of the MariaDB CLI and then restart MariaDB with the following command:

```
systemctl restart mariadb
```

38. Now, back on the `lar-book-secure-zbx` Zabbix server, create a new folder for our certificates:

```
mkdir -p /var/lib/zabbix/ssl/
```

39. Copy the certificates over to this folder with the following:

```
cp /etc/pki/CA/cacert.pem /var/lib/zabbix/ssl/
cp /etc/pki/CA/certs/zbx-srv_crt.pem/var/lib/zabbix/ssl/
zbx-srv.crt
cp /etc/pki/CA/private/zbx-srv_key.pem/var/lib/zabbix/
ssl/zbx-srv.key
```

40. Edit the Zabbix server configuration file to use these certificates:

```
vim /etc/zabbix/zabbix_server.conf
```

41. Make sure the following lines match our `lar-book-secure-db` database server's setup:

```
DBHost=lar-book-secure-db
DBName=zabbix
DBUser=zabbix
DBPassword=password
```

42. Now, make sure our SSL-related configuration matches our new files:

```
DBTLSConnect=verify_full
DBTLSCAFile=/var/lib/zabbix/ssl/cacert.pem
DBTLSCertFile=/var/lib/zabbix/ssl/zbx-srv.crt
DBTLSKeyFile=/var/lib/zabbix/ssl/zbx-srv.key
```

43. Also, make sure to add the right permissions to the SSL-related files:

```
chown -R zabbix:zabbix /var/lib/zabbix/ssl/
chmod 400 /var/lib/zabbix/ssl/zbx-srv.key
chmod 444 /var/lib/zabbix/ssl/zbx-srv.crt
chmod 444 /var/lib/zabbix/ssl/cacert.pem
```

44. Start and enable the Zabbix server with the following:

RHEL-based systems:

```
systemctl restart zabbix-server zabbix-agent2 httpd
php-fpm
systemctl enable zabbix-server zabbix-agent2 httpd
php-fpm
```

Ubuntu systems:

```
systemctl restart zabbix-server zabbix-agent2 apache2
php-fpm
systemctl enable zabbix-server zabbix-agent2 apache2
php-fpm
```

45. Then, navigate to the Zabbix frontend and fill in the right information as shown in the following screenshot:

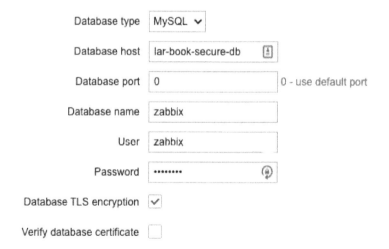

Figure 12.17 – Zabbix frontend configuration, database step

46. When we click **Next step**, we need to fill out some more information:

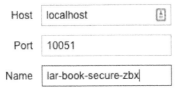

Zabbix server details

Please enter the host name or host IP address and port number of the Zabbix server, as well as the name of the installation (optional).

Host	localhost
Port	10051
Name	lar-book-secure-zbx

Figure 12.18 – Zabbix frontend configuration, server details step

47. Then, after clicking **Next step**, **Next step**, and **Finish**, the frontend should now be configured and working.

How it works...

This was quite a long recipe, so let's break it down quickly:

- In *Steps 1* through *9*, we prepared our servers

- In *Steps 10* through *37*, we executed everything needed to create our certificates

- In *Steps 38* through *47*, we set up our Zabbix frontend for encryption

Going through all these steps, setting up your Zabbix database securely can seem like quite a daunting task, and it can be. Certificates, login procedures, loads of settings, and more can all add up to become very complicated, which is why I'd always recommend diving deeper into encryption methods before trying to set this up yourself.

If your setup requires encryption, though, this recipe is a solid starting point for your first-time setup. It works very well in an internal setting, as we are using private certificates.

Make sure to renew them yearly, as they are only valid for 365 days.

All Zabbix components, except for communication between the Zabbix server and Zabbix frontend, can be encrypted as shown in the following diagram:

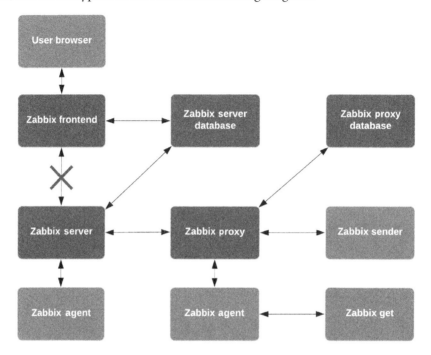

Figure 12.19 – Zabbix encryption scheme possibilities

We've set up encryption between the following:

- The Zabbix server and MariaDB
- The Zabbix frontend and MariaDB

This means that when our Zabbix server or frontend requests or writes data to our database, it will be encrypted. Because our Zabbix applications are running on a different server than our Zabbix database, this might be important. For example, our setup might look like this:

Figure 12.20 – Zabbix setup with an external network diagram

Let's say the cloud is called **Some company** in a network that isn't managed by us. There are several switches and routers in this network that are used for numerous clients with their own VLANs. If one of these devices gets compromised somehow, all of our Zabbix data could be seen by others.

Even if the network equipment is ours, there might still be a compromised device in the network and our data can be seen. This is why you might want to add encryption, to add that extra layer of security. Whether it's breaches in other companies and their network that you want to secure against or whether it's against your own breaches, securing your database as we did in this recipe might just save you from leaking all that data.

13
Bringing Zabbix to the Cloud with Zabbix Cloud Integration

For the last chapter, we have prepared something special. As a long-time Zabbix user, the importance of cloud integration for tools such as Zabbix has not gone unnoticed. For some people, the cloud can be daunting, and thus with this chapter, I want to show you just how easy it can be to start working with the most popular cloud providers and Zabbix.

We are going to start by talking about monitoring the **Amazon Web Services** (**AWS**) cloud with Zabbix. Then we will also see how the same things are done using Microsoft Azure so we can clearly see the differences.

After going through these cloud products, we'll also check out container monitoring with Docker, a very popular product that can also benefit greatly from setting up Zabbix monitoring. Follow these recipes closely and you will be able to monitor all of these products easily and work to extend the products using Zabbix. This chapter comprises the following recipes:

- Setting up AWS monitoring
- Setting up Microsoft Azure monitoring
- Building your Zabbix Docker monitoring

Technical requirements

As this chapter focuses on AWS, Microsoft Azure, and Docker monitoring, we are going to need a working AWS, Microsoft Azure, or Docker setup. The recipe does not cover how to set these up, so make sure to have your own infrastructure at the ready.

Furthermore, we are going to need our Zabbix server running Zabbix 6. We will call this server zbx-home in this chapter.

You can download the code files for this chapter from the following GitHub link: https://github.com/PacktPublishing/Zabbix-6-IT-Infrastructure-Monitoring-Cookbook/tree/main/chapter13.

Setting up AWS monitoring

A lot of infrastructure is moving toward the cloud these days and it's important to keep an eye on this infrastructure as much as you would if it were your own hardware. In this recipe, we are going to discover how to monitor **Relational Database Service** (**RDS**) instances and S3 buckets with our Zabbix setup.

Getting ready

For this recipe, we are going to need our AWS cloud with some S3 buckets and/or RDS instances in it already. Of course, we will also need our Zabbix server, which we'll call zbx-home in this recipe.

Then, last but not least, we will require some templates and hosts, which we can import. We can download the XML files here: `https://github.com/PacktPublishing/Zabbix-6-IT-Infrastructure-Monitoring-Cookbook/tree/main/chapter13`.

> **Important Note**
>
> Using Amazon CloudWatch is not free, so you will incur costs. Make sure you check out the Amazon pricing for AWS CloudWatch before proceeding: `https://aws.amazon.com/cloudwatch/pricing/`.

How to do it...

Setting up AWS monitoring might seem like a daunting task at first, but once we get the hang of the technique it's not that difficult. Let's waste no more time and check out one of the methods we could use:

1. Let's start by logging in to our Zabbix server with the hostname `zbx-home`.

2. On the Zabbix server, download the AWS CLI installation package with the following command:

```
curl https://awscli.amazonaws.com/awscli-exe-
linux-x86_64.zip -o "awscliv2.zip"
```

The result will look like this:

```
[root@zbx-home ~]# curl "https://awscli.amazonaws.com/awscli-exe-linux-x86_64.zip" -o "awscliv2.zip"
  % Total    % Received % Xferd  Average Speed   Time    Time     Time  Current
                                 Dload  Upload   Total   Spent    Left  Speed
100 33.5M  100 33.5M    0     0  9061k      0  0:00:03  0:00:03 --:--:-- 9059k
[root@zbx-home ~]#
```

Figure 13.1 – curl command execution for AWS CLI

3. If you haven't already done so, install `unzip` with the following command.

For RHEL-based systems:

```
dnf install unzip
```

For Ubuntu systems:

```
apt install unzip
```

4. After installing the `unzip` application, we can use it to unzip our AWS CLI installation package with the following command:

```
unzip -q awscliv2.zip
```

5. We are now ready to install our AWS CLI with the following command:

```
./aws/install
```

The output will look like this:

```
[root@zbx-home ~]# ./aws/install
You can now run: /usr/local/bin/aws --version
```

Figure 13.2 – AWS CLI install command execution

6. Next up, log in to your AWS account by navigating to the following URL in your browser: `https://signin.aws.amazon.com/`.

7. Once logged in, we can navigate to **My Security Credentials** listed in your user profile in the top-right corner:

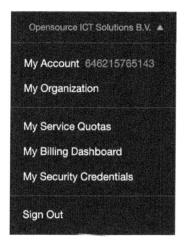

Figure 12.3 – AWS web frontend user profile

8. On the next page, click on **Access keys (access key ID and secret access key)**. This will open up the following screen:

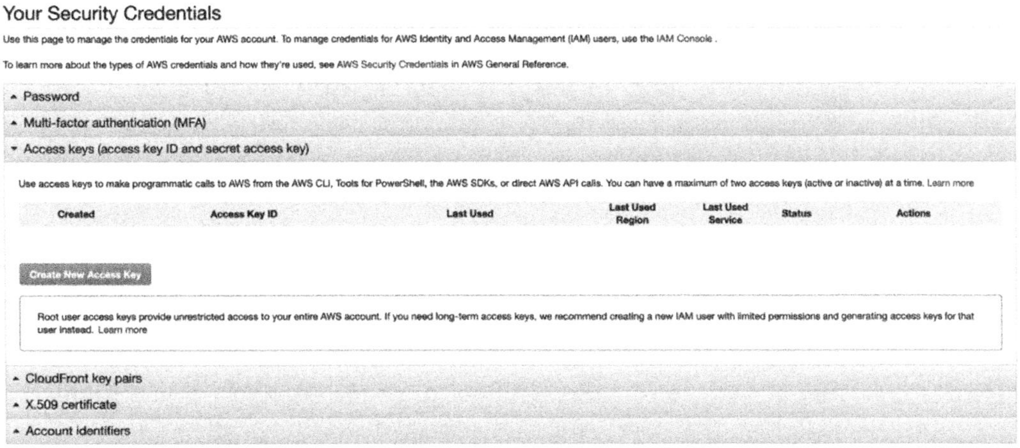

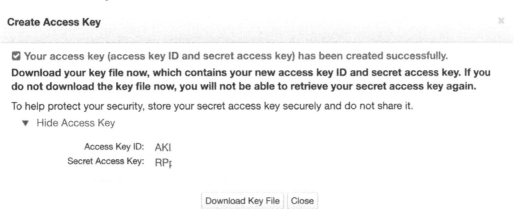

Figure 13.4 – AWS access keys page

9. Click on **Create New Access Key** to create a new access key. You should see the following:

Create Access Key

✅ Your access key (access key ID and secret access key) has been created successfully.

Download your key file now, which contains your new access key ID and secret access key. If you do not download the key file now, you will not be able to retrieve your secret access key again.

To help protect your security, store your secret access key securely and do not share it.

▼ Hide Access Key

Access Key ID: AKI
Secret Access Key: RPf

Download Key File   Close

Figure 13.5 – AWS access key details

10. Make sure to note down the access key ID and the secret access key as we will need them later.

11. Back in the Linux CLI, let's create some folders:

```
mkdir /var/lib/zabbix
chown zabbix:zabbix /var/lib/zabbix/
```

12. Then, let's log in to our zabbix user. It is important to execute the following commands on the correct Linux users, so switch to the zabbix user with the help of the following command:

```
su -s /bin/bash zabbix
```

13. Under the zabbix user, enter the following command:

```
aws configure
```

14. Fill in the AWS Access Key ID and AWS Secret Access Key fields we noted down earlier. Also, make sure to change your default region to your preferred region and set the output format to json. It will look like this:

```
[zabbix@zbx-home ~]$ aws configure
AWS Access Key ID [****************TPOA]: AK
AWS Secret Access Key [****************5EoP]
Default region name [eu-central-1]:
Default output format [json]:
[zabbix@zbx-home ~]$
```

Figure 13.6 – AWS configure command on the Linux CLI

15. Configuration under the zabbix user is now complete and you can switch back with the following command:

```
exit
```

16. Now, switch directories with the help of the following command:

```
cd /usr/lib/zabbix/externalscripts
```

17. Then, create a new script file called aws_script.sh in this directory with the help of the following command:

```
vim aws_script.sh
```

18. Add the following lines to the script and save the file:

```
#!/bin/bash
instance=$1
metric=$2
now=$(date +%s)
aws cloudwatch get-metric-statistics --metric-name
$metric --start-time "$(echo "$now - 300" | bc)"
--end-time "$now" --period 300 --namespace AWS/RDS
--dimensions Name=DBInstanceIdentifier,Value="$instance"
--statistics Average—dimension
Name=DBInstanceIdentifier,Value="$instance" --statistics
Average
```

19. Make sure the zabbix Linux user can execute this script by setting the permissions with the following command:

```
chown zabbix:zabbix aws_script.sh
chmod 700 aws_script.sh
```

20. We also need to add functionality to the Zabbix agent. Do this by adding user parameters. On the Zabbix server Linux CLI, switch directory with the help of the following command.

For the Zabbix agent:

```
cd /etc/zabbix/zabbix_agentd.d/
```

For the Zabbix agent 2:

```
cd /etc/zabbix/zabbix_agent2.d/
```

21. Now, create a new file with the following command:

```
vim userparameter_aws.conf
```

22. Then, insert the following lines:

```
#Buckets
UserParameter=bucket.discovery,aws s3api list-buckets
--query "Buckets[]"

UserParameter=bucket.get[*], aws s3api list-objects
--bucket "$1" --output json --query "[sum(Contents[].
Size), length(Contents[])]"
```

```
#RDS
UserParameter=rds.discovery,aws rds describe-db-instances
--output json --query "DBInstances"
UserParameter=rds.metrics.discovery[*],aws cloudwatch
list-metrics --namespace AWS/RDS --dimensions
Name=DBInstanceIdentifier,Value="$1" --output json
--query "Metrics"
```

23. Reload your Zabbix agent user parameters as follows:

```
zabbix_agentd -R userparameter_reload
```

> **Tip**
> Using user parameters will work with both the Zabbix agent and Zabbix agent
> 2. This means that irrespective of whether you are required to run the old or
> new agent, you can set up AWS monitoring without any issues.

24. Let's now confirm whether it is working. Navigate to your Zabbix frontend and go to **Configuration | Templates**.

25. Click on the blue **Import** button and add the template_aws.xml file, which we can download from Packt's GitHub repository at the following link: https://github.com/PacktPublishing/Zabbix-6-IT-Infrastructure-Monitoring-Cookbook/tree/main/chapter13/template_aws.xml.

26. Then, navigate to **Configuration | Hosts**, click on the blue **Import** button, and import the aws_hosts.xml file, which we can download from Packt's GitHub repository at the following link: https://github.com/PacktPublishing/Zabbix-6-IT-Infrastructure-Monitoring-Cookbook/tree/main/chapter13/aws_hosts.xml.

27. This will import an AWS template called **Template AWS discovery** and add two AWS hosts – **Bucket discovery** and **RDS discovery**.

That's the final step for this recipe. Check out the new templates, hosts, and how it all fits together in the *How it works…* section.

How it works...

Now that we've done all the setup at the Linux CLI level and have imported the templates and hosts, let's see what they do. Under **Configuration | Hosts**, we can now see two new hosts.

First, let's look at the **AWS Bucket discovery** host. This host will discover our AWS buckets, such as the S3 bucket. We can see that the host only has one configuration, which is a discovery rule. If we go to this discovery rule, called **Bucket discovery**, we can see that it uses the item key bucket.discovery. This item key is defined by us in the user parameters and executes the following command:

```
aws s3api list-buckets --query "Buckets[]"
```

We do this to get every single AWS bucket and put it in the {#NAME} LLD macro.

Furthermore, there are three item prototypes on the discovery rule. The most important item prototype is the one called {#NAME}, which will use the Zabbix agent to execute the user parameter with the bucket.get item key for every bucket found for the {#NAME} LLD macro we just discovered in the discovery rule.

The bucket.get item key then executes the command we defined, which is the following:

```
aws s3api list-objects --bucket "$1" --output json --query
"[sum(Contents[].Size), length(Contents[])]"
```

This command gets all of our information from the AWS buckets found and adds them to an item on our **AWS Bucket discovery** host. We can then use dependent items as in the two examples cited to extract the information from the item and put them in different items. Check out *Chapter 3, Setting Up Zabbix Monitoring*, for more information on dependent items.

We also have our **AWS RDS discovery** host, which will discover AWS RDS instances. If we check out the host, we can see only one configuration, which is the discovery rule **Instance discovery**. This discovery rule has one host prototype on it to create new hosts from every RDS found in our AWS setup. It uses the rds.discovery item key, which executes the following command:

```
aws rds describe-db-instances --output json --query
"DBInstances"
```

This puts every RDS instance in the {#NAME} LLD macro and creates a new Zabbix host for it. After creating the host, it will also make sure that the AWS RDS discovery template is linked to the new host. The template has a discovery rule to get some RDS metrics from the RDS instance using the item key rds.metrics.discovery, which executes the following command:

```
aws cloudwatch list-metrics --namespace AWS/RDS --dimensions
Name=DBInstanceIdentifier,Value="$1" --output json --query
"Metrics"
```

What we are doing here is using the AWS CLI to execute commands on our Zabbix server through the Zabbix agent user parameters. The Zabbix agent runs the AWS CLI command and retrieves data from AWS CloudWatch. These metrics are stored in the database and then used in our items.

Now that we've seen how to use AWS CloudWatch, we can extend the Zabbix agent further by adding extra user parameters or by creating more dependent items and using this information.

There's more...

It takes time to start monitoring with AWS CloudWatch as we need a good understanding of the AWS CLI commands with the use of CloudWatch. When you use the templates provided in this recipe as a basis, you have a solid foundation on which to build.

Make sure to check out the AWS documentation for more information on the commands that we can use at the following link:

```
https://docs.aws.amazon.com/cli/latest/reference/#available-
services
```

Setting up Microsoft Azure monitoring

The Microsoft Azure cloud is a big player in the cloud market these days and it's important to keep an eye on this infrastructure as much as you would your own hardware. In this recipe, we are going to discover how to monitor Azure instances with our Zabbix setup.

Getting ready

For this recipe, we are going to need our Azure cloud with an Azure DB instance in it already. The recipe does not cover how to set up an Azure DB instance, so make sure to have this in advance. We will also need our Zabbix server, which we'll call zbx-home in this recipe.

We have split up the Azure CLI installation aspect into RHEL-based and Ubuntu systems. Make sure to use the guide that is appropriate for you.

Then, last but not least, we will require some templates and hosts, which we can import. We can download the XML files here: `https://github.com/PacktPublishing/Zabbix-6-IT-Infrastructure-Monitoring-Cookbook/tree/main/chapter13.`

How to do it...

For Azure monitoring, we face some of the same techniques as we do for AWS monitoring. It is a bit daunting, but easier than it looks. Let's check out one of the techniques we can use for Azure monitoring:

1. First things first, log in to the Zabbix server Linux CLI.

2. We are going to install the Azure CLI on our Zabbix server.

Let's cover RHEL-based systems first.

RHEL-based Azure CLI installation

First things first, let's check out the installation process on a RHEL-based host:

1. Let's import the Azure repository key:

   ```
   rpm --import https://packages.microsoft.com/keys/
   microsoft.asc
   ```

2. Then, create the repository file with the following command:

   ```
   echo -e "[azure-cli]
   name=Azure CLI
   baseurl=https://packages.microsoft.com/yumrepos/azure-cli
   enabled=1
   gpgcheck=1
   gpgkey=https://packages.microsoft.com/keys/microsoft.
   asc"| tee /etc/yum.repos.d/azure-cli.repo
   ```

3. Now, run the installation command to install the Azure CLI with the following command:

   ```
   dnf -y install azure-cli
   ```

Ubuntu Azure CLI installation

Now, let's check out the installation process on a Ubuntu host:

1. Install the required dependent packages with the following command:

   ```
   apt install ca-certificates curl apt-transport-https
   lsb-release gnupg
   ```

2. Now, download and install the Microsoft signing key with the help of the following command:

```
curl -sL https://packages.microsoft.com/keys/microsoft.
asc |gpg --dearmor | tee /etc/apt/trusted.gpg.d/
microsoft.gpg > /dev/null
```

3. Then, add the Azure CLI repository with the following command:

```
AZ_REPO=$(lsb_release -cs)
```
```
echo "deb [arch=amd64] https://packages.microsoft.com/
repos/azure-cli/ $AZ_REPO main" | tee /etc/apt/sources.
list.d/azure-cli.list
```

4. Then, update the repository information and install the Azure CLI with the following command:

```
apt update
```
```
apt install azure-cli
```

Setting up Azure monitoring

Now that we've installed the Azure CLI we can start setting up the Azure monitoring:

1. We will need to log in as the zabbix user. Make sure to use a Bash terminal with the zabbix user. Use the following command:

```
su -s /bin/bash zabbix
```

2. As the zabbix user, we can now use the following command to log in to the Azure CLI:

```
az login
```

3. You will be asked to provide Azure with the key and a token shown in the Azure CLI. Use the **Key** and **Token** options on the following web page: https://aka.ms/devicelogin.

4. Once you've logged in successfully, log out from the zabbix user with the help of the following command:

```
exit
```

5. Now, let's add some functionality to the Zabbix agent on our Zabbix server by using user parameters.

6. Still on the Zabbix server CLI, switch to the Zabbix agent directory with the help of the following command.

   For the Zabbix agent:

   ```
   cd /etc/zabbix/zabbix_agentd.d/
   ```

   For the Zabbix agent 2:

   ```
   cd /etc/zabbix/zabbix_agent2.d/
   ```

7. Create a new file with the following command:

   ```
   vim userparameter_azure.conf
   ```

8. In this file, insert the following lines:

   ```
   UserParameter=azure.db.discovery,az resource list
   --resource-type "Microsoft.DBforMySQL/servers"
   ```

9. We will also require a Zabbix externalscript. Let's switch directory with the following command:

   ```
   cd /usr/lib/zabbix/externalscripts/
   ```

10. Then, create an azure_script.sh script by executing the following command:

    ```
    vim azure_script.sh
    ```

11. We then need to add the following lines:

    ```
    #!/bin/bash
    id=$1
    metric=$2
    curr=$(date --utc +%Y-%m-%dT%H:%M:%SZ)
    new=$(date --utc -d "($curr) -5minutes" +%Y-%m-%dT%H:%M:%SZ)


    az monitor metrics list --resource $id --metric "$metric"
    --start-time "$new" --end-time "$curr" --interval PT5M
    ```

12. Save the file and make sure to set the correct permissions with the help of the following command:

    ```
    chown zabbix:zabbix azure_script.sh
    chmod 700 azure_script.sh
    ```

13. We can now restart our Zabbix agent with the following command.

    For the Zabbix agent:

    ```
    systemctl restart zabbix-agent
    ```

    For the Zabbix agent 2:

    ```
    systemctl restart zabbix-agent2
    ```

14. We can now configure our Zabbix frontend by importing a template and a host.

15. Open your Zabbix frontend and navigate to **Configuration | Templates**. Here, we need to click on the blue **Import** button and import the `template_azure.xml` file, which we can download at `https://github.com/PacktPublishing/Zabbix-6-IT-Infrastructure-Monitoring-Cookbook/tree/main/chapter13/template_azure.xml`.

16. We will also need to import a host. Go to **Configuration | Hosts** and click on the blue **Import** button to import the `azure_host.xml` file, which can be downloaded here: `https://github.com/PacktPublishing/Zabbix-6-IT-Infrastructure-Monitoring-Cookbook/blob/main/chapter13/azure_host.xml`.

That's the final step for this recipe. Let's stay with the frontend and check out the new templates, hosts, and how it all fits together in the *How it works...* section.

How it works...

If you've followed the recipe regarding AWS monitoring, you might think that Azure monitoring works the same. In fact, we employ a different Zabbix monitoring technique here, so let's check it out.

After adding the template and the host to our Zabbix server, we can go to **Configuration | Hosts** and check out our new host. We can see one new host here called **Discover Azure DBs**. When we examine this host, we can see that it only has one configuration, which is a discovery rule called **Discover Azure DBs**, like the host.

Under this discovery rule, we find a single host prototype called `{#NAME}`. This host prototype uses the discovery rule's `azure.db.discovery` item key to execute the following command:

```
az resource list --resource-type "Microsoft.DBforMySQL/servers"
```

With this command, the {#NAME} LLD macro is filled with our Azure DB instances, and we create a new host for every single Azure DB instance found. The new hosts then get the `Azure DB` template added to it.

When we check out the template under **Configuration | Templates**, we can see that it has 12 items. Let's check out the item **CPU Load**. This item is of the **External check** type, which uses its `azure_script.sh[{$ID},cpu_percent]` item key to execute the external script `azure_script.sh` and feed it the parameters {$ID} and `cpu_percent`. The script that is executed uses the Azure CLI to retrieve the values and we put this value in the Zabbix database.

There's more...

We can discover way more from Azure using the method applied in this recipe. The script we employed is used to get metrics from Azure, which we can put in items by feeding them the correct parameters.

Check out the Azure CLI documentation for more information on the metrics retrieved using the script at the following link:

```
https://docs.microsoft.com/en-us/cli/azure/monitor/
metrics?view=azure-cli-latest
```

Building your Zabbix Docker monitoring

Ever since the release of Zabbix 5, monitoring your Docker containers became a lot easier with the introduction of Zabbix agent 2 and plugins. Using the Zabbix agent 2 and Zabbix 6, we are able to monitor our Docker containers out of the box.

In this recipe, we are going to see how to set this up and how it works.

Getting ready

For this recipe, we require some Docker containers. We won't go over the setup of Docker containers, so make sure to do this yourself. Furthermore, we are going to need Zabbix agent 2 installed on those Docker containers. Zabbix agent does not work in relation to this recipe; Zabbix agent 2 is required.

We also need our Zabbix server to actually monitor the Docker containers. We will call our Zabbix server `zbx-home`.

How to do it...

Let's waste no more time and dive right into the process of monitoring your Docker setup with Zabbix:

1. First things first, log in to the Linux CLI of your Docker container.

2. Add the repository for installing Zabbix components.

   For RHEL-based systems:

   ```
   rpm -Uvh https://repo.zabbix.com/zabbix/6.0/rhel/8x86_64/
   zabbix-release-6.0-1.el8.noarch.rpm
   dnf clean all
   ```

   For Ubuntu systems:

   ```
   wget https://repo.zabbix.com/zabbix/6.0/ubuntu/pool/
   main/z/zabbix-release/zabbix-release_6.0-1+ubuntu20.04_
   all.deb
   dpkg -i zabbix-release_6.0-1+ubuntu20.04_all.deb
   apt update
   ```

3. Now, install Zabbix agent 2 with the following command.

   For RHEL-based systems:

   ```
   dnf install zabbix-agent2
   ```

   For Ubuntu systems:

   ```
   apt install zabbix-agent2
   ```

4. Following installation, make sure to edit the configuration file of the newly installed Zabbix agent 2 with the help of the following command:

   ```
   vim /etc/zabbix/zabbix_agent2.conf
   ```

5. Find the line that says Server and add your Zabbix server IP address to the file as follows:

   ```
   Server=10.16.16.102
   ```

6. Make sure to save the file and then restart Zabbix agent 2 with the following command:

   ```
   systemctl restart zabbix-agent2
   ```

7. Now, we need to add the `zabbix` user to the Docker group by executing the following command:

```
gpasswd -a zabbix docker
```

8. Now, navigate to your Zabbix server frontend. Go to **Configuration** | **Hosts** and click on the blue **Create host** button.

9. Let's create a new host called `Docker containers` and make sure to link the `Docker by Zabbix agent 2` template to the host.

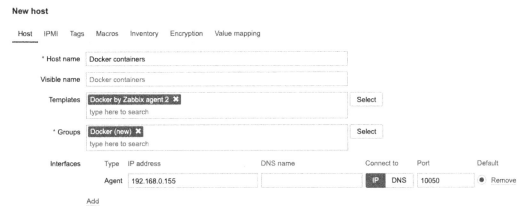

Figure 13.7 – New Docker host configuration

That's all there is to monitoring Docker containers with Zabbix server. Let's now see how it works.

How it works...

Docker monitoring in Zabbix these days is easy, due to the new Zabbix agent 2 support and default templates. On occasion though, a default template does not cut it, so let's break down the items used.

Almost all the items we can see on our host are dependent items, most of which are dependent on the master item, `Docker: Get info`. This master item is the most important item on our Docker template. It executes the `docker.info` item key, which is built into the new Zabbix agent 2. This item retrieves a list with all kinds of information from our Docker setup. We use the dependent items and preprocessing to get the values we want from this master item.

The Docker template also contains two Zabbix discovery rules, one to discover Docker images and one to discover Docker containers. If we check out the discovery rule for Docker containers called `Containers discovery`, we can see what happens. Our Zabbix Docker host will use the `docker.containers.discovery` item key to find every container and put this in the {#NAME} LLD macro. In the item prototypes, we then use this {#NAME} LLD macro to discover statistics with another master item, such as `docker.container_info`. From this master item, we then use the dependent items and preprocessing again to include this information in other item prototypes as well. We are now monitoring a bunch of statistics straight from our Docker setup.

If you want to get values from Docker that aren't in the default template, check out the information collected with the master items on the template. Use a new dependent item (prototype) and then use preprocessing to get the correct data from the master item.

There's more...

If you want to learn more about the Zabbix agent 2 Docker item keys, check out the supported item key list for Zabbix agent 2 under the Zabbix documentation:

```
https://www.zabbix.com/documentation/current/en/manual/config/
items/itemtypes/zabbix_agent/zabbix_agent2?s[]=docker.s
```

Index

`Packt.com`

Subscribe to our online digital library for full access to over 7,000 books and videos, as well as industry leading tools to help you plan your personal development and advance your career. For more information, please visit our website.

Why subscribe?

- Spend less time learning and more time coding with practical eBooks and Videos from over 4,000 industry professionals

- Improve your learning with Skill Plans built especially for you

- Get a free eBook or video every month

- Fully searchable for easy access to vital information

- Copy and paste, print, and bookmark content

Did you know that Packt offers eBook versions of every book published, with PDF and ePub files available? You can upgrade to the eBook version at `packt.com` and as a print book customer, you are entitled to a discount on the eBook copy. Get in touch with us at `customercare@packtpub.com` for more details.

At `www.packt.com`, you can also read a collection of free technical articles, sign up for a range of free newsletters, and receive exclusive discounts and offers on Packt books and eBooks.

Other Books You May Enjoy

If you enjoyed this book, you may be interested in these other books by Packt:

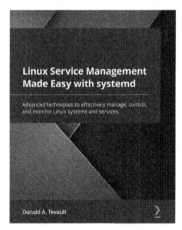

Linux Service Management Made Easy with systemd

Donald A. Tevault

ISBN: 9781801811644

- Use basic systemd utilities to manage a system
- Create and edit your own systemd units
- Create services for Podman-Docker containers
- Enhance system security by adding security-related parameters
- Find important information with journald
- Analyze boot-up problems
- Configure system settings with systemd utilities

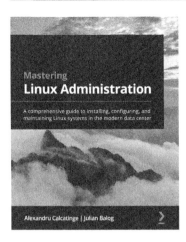

Mastering Linux Administration

Alexandru Calcatinge, Julian Balog

ISBN: 9781789954272

- Understand how Linux works and learn basic to advanced Linux administration skills
- Explore the most widely used commands for managing the Linux filesystem, network, security, and more
- Get to grips with different networking and messaging protocols
- Find out how Linux security works and how to configure SELinux, AppArmor, and Linux iptables
- Work with virtual machines and containers and understand container orchestration with Kubernetes
- Work with containerized workflows using Docker and Kubernetes
- Automate your configuration management workloads with Ansible

Packt is searching for authors like you

If you're interested in becoming an author for Packt, please visit `authors.packtpub.com` and apply today. We have worked with thousands of developers and tech professionals, just like you, to help them share their insight with the global tech community. You can make a general application, apply for a specific hot topic that we are recruiting an author for, or submit your own idea.

Share Your Thoughts

Now you've finished *Zabbix 6 IT Infrastructure Monitoring Cookbook - Second Edition*, we'd love to hear your thoughts! Scan the QR code below to go straight to the Amazon review page for this book and share your feedback or leave a review on the site that you purchased it from.

`https://packt.link/r/180324691X`

Your review is important to us and the tech community and will help us make sure we're delivering excellent quality content.

Printed in Great Britain
by Amazon

84616426R00289